GARNE]
SEWERS

"The truth is that the whole of our sanitary legislation is in a state which I hardly like to characterise in the language that naturally suggests itself; and the attempt to extract from the various details of the legislation a set of harmonious principles, always underlying the specific provisions, is, I am afraid, futile."

— *the late Mr. Justice Wills, in 1896.*

GARNER'S LAW OF SEWERS AND DRAINS

TENTH EDITION

S. H. Bailey
Professor of Public Law,
University of Nottingham

Published in 2010 by
Thomson Reuters (Legal) Limited (Registered in England & Wales,
Company No 1679046. Registered Office and address for service:
100 Avenue Road, Swiss Cottage,
London NW3 3PF) trading as Sweet & Maxwell.

For further information on our products and services, visit
www.sweetandmaxwell.com

Typeset by LBJ Typesetting Ltd of Kingsclere
Printed and bound in Great Britain by CPI Anthony Rowe,
Chippenham and Eastbourne

ISBN: 978-0-41404-495-1

No natural forests were destroyed to make this product;
only farmed timber was used and replanted.

A CIP catalogue record of this book is available
for the British Library.

Previously published by Shaw & Sons Limited

First Edition	*Published*	June 1950
	Reprinted	March 1954
Second Edition	*Published*	March 1960
Third Edition	*Published*	November 1962
	Reprinted	November 1965
Fourth Edition	*Published*	January 1969
	Reprinted	November 1971
Fifth Edition	*Published*	January 1975
	Reprinted	September 1976
Sixth Edition	*Published*	March 1981
Seventh Edition	*Published*	June 1991
Eighth Edition	*Published*	November 1995
Ninth Edition	*Published*	June 2004

CONTENTS

Chapter 3—CONSTRUCTION OF PUBLIC SEWERS

Chapter 4—CONSTRUCTION OF SEWERS BY PRIVATE INDIVIDUALS

Chapter 9—DRAINAGE OF PREMISES

PREFACE TO THE TENTH EDITION

In the six years since the last edition there has been a steady stream of relevant new cases and legislative developments. Full account of these has been taken in preparing this new edition although the basic structure of the book remains the same. The Director General of Water Services and Ofwat have been succeeded by the Water Services Regulation Authority (also known as Ofwat). Work has continued on the policy under which sewerage undertakers are to assume responsibility for private sewers and lateral drains. Further steps have been taken to reduce the adverse environmental effects that can and do arise from the sewerage infrastructure. It remains to be seen whether the change of government will bring further policy changes in this area.

This edition sees a change of publisher from Shaw & Sons to Sweet & Maxwell. Sweet & Maxwell has had, and continues to have, a particular strength as publishers in the area of local government law and provides an eminently suitable new home for the book. The change has taken place (certainly from my perspective) seamlessly, and I am very grateful to the new team for their support in the preparation of the new edition, including the preparation of the tables and index.

I have retained from the last edition a tribute to the original author of this book, my late colleague and friend Jack Garner.

S.H Bailey
Nottingham
24 9 10

J. F. GARNER
1914–1997

It is a matter of great sadness to record the death of John Francis ("Jack") Garner, the author of this Encyclopædia. Jack Garner was a pioneer and long advocate of environmental law. His large contribution to the development of environmental law as a separate legal specialism is recognised nationally by the United Kingdom Environmental Law Association's annual Garner Lecture.

Jack graduated from King's College, London, with a First Class Honours degree in law in 1936. After serving as a major in the army in India during the war, Jack entered local government and became the town clerk of Andover. While town clerk, he began his career as the author of the many highly successful books for legal practitioners for which he remains well known. Jack's own favourite – not just because of the title – was his standard work on The Law of Sewers and Drains. During the same period, he also undertook some part-time law teaching at the University of Southampton. Finding that he enjoyed teaching, Jack abandoned local government for academic life. He was first appointed a Senior Lecturer in Law at the University of Birmingham and, in 1964, became the Professor of Public Law at the University of Nottingham, a post that he held until his retirement in 1980.

Jack was a warm sociable human being, who will be greatly missed by his many friends. His last years were tinged with sadness with the death of his wife and made arduous by the eventual total loss of his sight. He bore this last affliction with remarkable fortitude and remained to the very end the cheerful and engaging man of whom so many people were so very fond.

(Printed in *Garner's Environmental Law*, Issue 57, November 1997.)

PREFACE TO THE FIRST EDITION

It is the purpose of this work to endeavour to bring some degree of order into chaos, and to attempt to achieve what was described by Mr. Justice Wills, over 50 years ago,[1] as "futile", namely to extract from our sanitary legislation a set of harmonious principles. The writer is not rash enough to suggest that such principles have in fact been extracted in the pages that follow, but if this book results in illuminating to any extent what is one of the darkest patches of our statute law, it is considered that the main object of the book will have been achieved. In endeavouring to attain this objective, the author has been greatly assisted by that indispensable friend, "Lumley's Public Health". Unfortunately the assistance of the Legislature, who had the opportunity of abolishing such oddities as "single private drains" in 1936, has not been so extensive. The law relating to future sewers and drains was considerably simplified by the Public Health Act 1936, but the status of pre-1937 sewers and drains was left to be determined in accordance with the earlier, unsatisfactory, legislation.

The law relating to sewers and drains is commonly regarded as referring to the relevant provisions of the Public Health Acts, and it is so understood in the present work. For this reason therefore, incidental discussion only is included on the allied subject of land drainage, but some comment has been included on the topic of the prevention of river pollution.

The law relating to the Metropolis, being of very specialised nature, is not here dealt with, nor is there any discussion of the law of Scotland or of Northern Ireland.

References are included throughout to the copyright forms of Shaw and Sons Ltd. Specimen forms will gladly be supplied on request.

The law is stated in this book as it was on 1st June 1950.

J.F.G.
Bognor Regis

TABLE OF STATUTES

TABLE OF STATUTORY INSTRUMENTS

TABLE OF CASES

Chapter 1

INTRODUCTORY

BACKGROUND

The law of sewers and drains has been a neglected area. This is perhaps understandable for, as noted by the House of Lords Select Committee on the European Communities in its report in 1991 on Municipal Waste Water Treatment: **1–001**

> "Sewerage, more than any other form of waste, lends itself to an 'out of sight, out of mind' attitude. Most of us would rather forget that it exists, let alone discuss what to do with it, and we are able to do so since the means of collecting and treating sewage are buried under roads, or shut away on the edges of towns."[1]

However, as the Committee also affirmed:

> "The efficient control of sewage effluent has always been an index of the state of any civilised society, necessary for aesthetic and health reasons, and as a primary tool in the management of water systems."[2]

A number of factors have combined to give the subject greater prominence. These include the significant growth in domestic concern for environmental matters, graphically illustrated in the present context by objections to the presence of untreated sewage at bathing beaches; increased political and public interest in the provision of water and sewerage services arising from privatisation and from significant increases in the levels of charges; and the impact of European environmental law, most importantly the Bathing Water Directive of 1976 and the Urban Waste Water Treatment Directive of 1991.[3]

Historically, the prime concern lying behind the provision of sewerage systems has been the protection and promotion of public health. The key developments took place in the second half of the nineteenth century when the establishment of such systems was identified as a high priority by municipal sanitary authorities, under the influence of the Local Government Board, and significant developments in

---

[1] 10th Report, 1990–91 H.L. 50-I, p.7.

[2] 10th Report.

[3] Dir.76/160 and 91/271.

engineering enabled this to be done without (as many feared) posing additional threats to public health.[4] London's sewer system was begun in 1858 and finished in 1865 and there were significant advances in many towns between then and the end of the century.[5] By the 1880s, the major cities had built new sewage treatment plants.[6]

The position in the 1990s was that 96 per cent of the UK's population was connected to the sewerage system (the highest percentage in the EU) and 83 per cent of sewage was treated, including almost all that disposed to inland waters (comparable with the then FRG, Denmark and the Netherlands).[7]

A review of private sewers and drains in 2003 reproduced data from the English House Condition Survey estimating the proportion of households served by a completely private sewer system, i.e. a private system which did not eventually connect into a public sewer.[8] The majority of private systems were in rural settings.[9] The government has decided that existing private sewers and lateral drains[10] connected to the public sewerage network should be transferred into the ownership of the statutory water and sewerage companies.[11] The estimated length of public and private sewers and lateral drains are as follows:

Table 1: Quantities of Assets[12]

Asset Type	**Quantity or share**
Domestic drains—not transferring	207,000 km[13]
Public sewers—already with WASCs	323,000 km[14]
Private sewers	184,000 km[15]

---

[4] See A.S. Wohl, *Endangered Lives: Public Health in Victorian Britain* (Cambridge: Harvard University Press, 1983), Ch.4, "The Valleys of the Shadow of Death".
[5] Wohl, *Endangered Lives*, 1983, pp.107–108.
[6] Wohl, *Endangered Lives*, 1983, p.110.
[7] DoE Memorandum to the House of Lords Select Committee on the European Communities ("Report on Municipal Waste Water Treatment" (1990–91 H.L. 50), Vol.II, p.3). See also the Second Report of the Select Committee on Environment, Transport and Regional Affairs, "Sewage Treatment and Disposal", 1997–98 HC 266.
[8] DEFRA, Welsh Assembly Government, "Review of Existing Private Sewers and Drains in England and Wales", Consultation Paper, July 2003, para.5.5. See Table 2.
[9] DEFRA, Consultation Paper, July 2003, para.5.7.
[10] For the definition of "lateral drain", see p.67.
[11] See further pp.126–127.
[12] This table is taken from DEFRA, "Impact Assessment of transfer of private sewers to statutory water and sewerage companies", November 5, 2008. The information was provided by OFWAT to DEFRA in September 2008.
[13] See UKWIR 2007 report 07/RG/07/12 "Uncertainties within private sewers model".
[14] June Returns for 2007–08 from sewerage companies.
[15] June Returns for 2007–08 from sewerage companies.

Lateral drains	36,000 km[16]
Private sewers and laterals to transfer	220,000 km
Public sewerage network total after transfer	543,000 km
Public sewerage network uplift after transfer	68%
Combined private sewers, laterals and domestic drains before transfer	428,000 km
% of which transferring	52%

Table 2: Drainage Attributes by Construction Date

	Construction Date		
All EHCS Data	*Pre 1945*	*1945–1990*	*1991–2001*
Total households in category	7,830,661	11,298,453	1,351,142
1. Mains	95.9%	98.9%	97.8%
2. Septic tank	3.0%	0.8%	1.7%
3. Cesspool	0.7%	0.1%	0.0%
4. Private	0.3%	0.1%	0.3%
9. Unknown	0.1%	0.1%	0.2%
Percentage indicating faults with the drainage system	3.9%	2.8%	1.7%

The contribution that the sewerage system makes to the preservation of public health is now taken for granted. Concern instead has focused on the impact of the operation of the system on the environment, and on the need for significant attention to the ageing infrastructure, which together have given rise to a need for very substantial investment.

DEFINITION OF SEWERS AND DRAINS

The definition of the terms "sewer" and "drain" must seem a necessary preliminary to satisfactory discussion of the law which governs them. Upon examination, however, the matter presents some difficulty in view of the absence of comprehensive formal definition. An associated, and vitally important, question is the legal status of pipes and conduits recognised as "sewers"—in particular as between public and private ownership. **1–002**

[16] June Returns for 2007–08 from sewerage companies.

(a) Common law

1–003 At common law the terms "sewers" and "drains" had no specialised meaning[17] and were used in a non-technical sense to signify a conduit or channel for the carrying off of surface water, sewage or faecal matter. A "sewer" was understood to mean, in general, a large drain or a public drain.

(b) Public health legislation

1–004 Such precise definition of these terms as is available is derived not from common law but originally from nineteenth-century sanitary legislation. The earliest major English legislation in this area, the Public Health Act 1848, used the word "drain" to signify a passage for the outflow of sewage from a single building, the word "sewer" meaning any system of drainage which was not a "drain" so defined. Refinements of definition were added by the Public Health Act 1875. These earlier definitions are not now operative but retain some modern relevance in so far as reference to them may be necessary to establish the present status of particular conduits.[18] The current statutory definition is given by s.219(1) of the Water Industry Act 1991, which provides that:

> " 'drain' means (subject to subs.(2) below) a drain used for the drainage of one building or of any buildings or yards appurtenant to buildings within the same curtilage."

The term "sewer" is, unfortunately, not defined precisely, but s.219(1) does state that the term:

> " 'sewer' includes (without prejudice to subs.(2) below) all sewers and drains (not being drains within the meaning given by this subsection[19]) which are used for the drainage of buildings and yards appurtenant to buildings."

---

[17] In Tudor times the "Commissioners of Sewers" were established by statute to regulate land drainage, especially in the Fens. Here "sewers" were used to signify land drains rather than the modern conduits for sewage. In *Callis on Sewers* (1647), it was said (at p.57) that "a sewer is a fresh water trench compassed in on both sides with a bank, and is a small current or little river".

[18] See Ch.2.

[19] A connection leading from a public sewer to the curtilage of a single dwelling (sometimes described as a "lateral") is therefore a drain and not a public sewer, even if it was laid by the local authority prior to the coming into force of the Water Act 1973. See below, p.65.

Section 219(2)(a) provides that:

> "references to a pipe, including references to a main, a drain or a sewer, shall include references to a tunnel or conduit which serves or is to serve as the pipe in question and to any accessories for the pipe."[20]

Section 219(1) also defines the term "public sewer": **1–005**

> " 'public sewer' means a sewer for the time being vested in a sewerage undertaker[21] in its capacity as such, whether vested in that undertaker by virtue of a scheme under Schedule 2 to this Act or under section 179 above or otherwise;[22] and 'private sewer' shall be construed accordingly."

The distinction in detail between "public" and "private" sewers is of very considerable importance in this branch of the law and is considered in Ch.2, below.

It is therefore a basic principle that both sewers and drains, as understood in the Public Health Acts and later legislation, up to and including the Water Industry Act 1991, should be designed (or used) to drain buildings and constructed objects such as roads, as distinct from land itself. In the application and clarification of these definitions judicial interpretation has been of some importance. The key issue is what is the "essential character" of the channel or conduit in question?[23] This is a question of fact.[24] Particularly difficult issues can arise in determining whether a natural watercourse has become a sewer.

It will be noted that the starting point in analysing the statutory definition of "sewer" under section 219(1) is a core concept, not further

---

[20] These definitions are essentially the same as those found in s.343 of the Public Health Act 1936, which is still in force for the remaining purposes of that Act.

[21] i.e. a company so appointed under the Water Industry Act 1991 s.6.

[22] As to the vesting process, see Ch.2, below.

[23] Per Oliver L.J. in *British Railways Board v Tonbridge and Malling DC* (1981) 79 L.G.R. 565, 575. Where the question is whether a natural stream has become a sewer, "one has to ask whether the circumstances are such that the stream has substantially lost its original character and taken on the character of a sewer": per Oliver L.J. at p.572. This was agreed by the parties in *Raglan Housing Association Ltd v Southampton CC* [2007] EWCA Civ 785; [2008] 2 All E.R. 44 to be the appropriate test (see Sir Andrew Morritt C. at [80]), although members of the Court of Appeal seemed to have some doubts (see Toulson L.J. at [61] and Sir Andrew Morritt C. at [80]).

[24] *Falconar v Corp of South Shields* (1895) 11 T.L.R. 223, per Lord Halsbury.

defined in the statute,[25] of "all sewers and drains",[26] to which qualifications are then imposed by the statute.[27] Much of the case law addresses the meaning of the undefined core concept, and in particular the word "sewer" within it; some decisions focus on the meaning of the statutory qualifications. A number of points emerge from the decisions.

1–006 First, the channel of a sewer need not necessarily be an artificial construction.[28] In general, however, a natural stream which was not brought within the definition of "sewer" by the nineteenth-century sanitary legislation would generally not now be capable in law of becoming "a sewer". In *George Legge and Son v Wenlock Corp*[29] Lord Maugham remarked that:

> "generally speaking, the beds and banks of natural rivers and streams are not sewers within the term as used in the Act [of 1875] .... To prevent misconception I will add that no doubt there are circumstances in which the bed and banks of what was once a natural stream might, prior to the Act of 1875, have become substantially nothing but a channel for sewage."[30]

The House of Lords in this case held that it was not possible for the status of a natural stream to be changed to that of a sewer by the discharge of sewage into it where that constituted an offence against section 3 of the Rivers Pollution Prevention Act 1876.[31] Accordingly, it seems clear, in any event, that no natural streams can after 1876

---

[25] Or in the predecessor legislation, the Public Health Acts 1875 and 1936. It submitted, with respect, that Sir Andrew Morritt C. in *Raglan Housing Association Ltd v Southampton CC* [2007] EWCA Civ 785; [2008] 2 All E.R. 44 at [88] was wrong to regard the approach of Oliver L.J. in *British Railways Board v Tonbridge and Malling DC* (1981) 79 L.G.R. 565, 572 (above, n.23) as in some way different from or inconsistent with the statutory definition in what is now s.219(1); it sets out an approach to the determining the meaning of words *within* that statutory definition. Furthermore, the point is not that the word sewer has to be considered "divorced from a particular statutory context" (Sir Andrew Morritt C. at [84]); it is that that context itself provides no help in determining the natural and ordinary meaning of that particular word.

[26] "Included" in the meaning of "sewer" for the purpose of the 1991 Act.

[27] Excluding "drains" as defined by s.219(1); they must be "used for the drainage of buildings and yards appurtenant to buildings".

[28] *Falconar v Corp of South Shields*.

[29] [1938] A.C. 204.

[30] *George Legge and Son*, p.219. The *Falconar* case was distinguished on the ground that in that case the legality of the discharge of the sewage into the stream was not in question.

[31] This made it an offence for any person to cause or knowingly permit to fall or flow into any stream any solid or liquid sewage matter; in the case of a channel used, constructed or in the process of construction as at August 15, 1876, it was a defence to show that best practicable means had been used to render the sewage harmless. Section 17 of the 1875 Act had previously provided that local authorities were not authorised to convey unpurified sewage into any natural stream or watercourse.

have become sewers through the discharge of sewage into them. The discharge of raw sewage into natural watercourses clearly continues to be a serious breach of pollution control.[32]

Secondly, although it will normally be the case, it does not seem actually to be necessary that a "sewer" should carry sewage or foul matter. In *Ferrand v Hallas Land and Building Co*,[33] A.L. Smith L.J. said *obiter*[34]:

> "It will be noticed that a sewer need not necessarily convey sewage matter in order to constitute it as a sewer. It would be none the less a sewer within the Act of 1875 if it conveyed only rain or surface water. The draining off of rain or surface water, collected from different premises by different feeders into one main drain, would constitute that main drain a 'sewer' within the meaning of the Act."

Similarly, a pipe has been held to be a "drain" where it only carried off rain water from the roof of a house.[35]

Thirdly, a natural watercourse does not become a "sewer" simply by being piped or culverted. Thus, in *Shepherd v Croft*,[36] a natural underground watercourse was held not to have become a "sewer" by virtue of being piped by the owner of land through which it flowed. Similarly, in *British Railways Board v Tonbridge and Malling DC*,[37] three natural watercourses had in the nineteenth century been diverted into a culvert in which the flow passed under a railway embankment. As a result of subsequent residential development upstream the flow of water had markedly increased, albeit through run off from the buildings rather than with foul water. The British Railways Board, as successor to the original railway company, claimed that the culvert had become a sewer and was therefore the responsibility of the (then) water authority for the area. The Court of Appeal held that the disturbance of the natural flow by the embankment and the consequent direction into the culvert did not make the watercourses into "sewers." Per Oliver L.J.[38]: **1–007**

---

[32] See in particular the Water Resources Act 1991 ss.85–104, below, pp.167–202.

[33] [1893] 2 Q.B. 135.

[34] at p.144.

[35] *Holland v Lazarus* (1897) 66 L.J.Q.B. 285, approved by the Court of Appeal in *Silles v Fulham BC* [1903] 1 K.B. 829 (but note the comments of Channell J. in *Heaver v Fulham BC* [1904] 2 K.B. 383, 393–394).

[36] [1911] 1 Ch. 521. See also *Raglan Housing Association Ltd v Southampton CC* [2007] EWCA Civ 785; [2008] 2 AllE. R. 44.

[37] (1981) 79 L.G.R. 565, C.A.

[38] at p.575. His Lordship referred to and adopted the approach of Lord Maugham in the *Wenlock* case, above.

> "On the facts as found . . . it is . . . clear that there has been no alteration in the essential character of the three watercourses and the culvert since 1840 and the mere fact that the surface drainage of the built-up area has been collected and diverted into them through a number of outfalls so as to produce a significant increase in the volume of water carried off, cannot possibly constitute them, either individually or collectively, sewers or a sewer within the ordinary meaning of that term."

The Public Health Act 1936 distinguished between "sewers" and watercourses, e.g. in s.30, and one channel could clearly not be both. Consequently the culvert in the instant case was not a "sewer".

Fourthly, the major, albeit not the sole, factor relevant to determining whether a natural watercourse has become a "sewer" is the character of the flow. This emerges from the decision of the Court of Appeal in *Raglan Housing Association Ltd v Southampton CC*.[39] Here, the Court of Appeal[40] held that a particular stretch of channel had not changed status from natural watercourse to sewer. A number of factors taken into account by the judge in the county court in coming to the opposite conclusion were on the facts irrelevant: the fact that it had been culverted (it was not known by whom); the fact that it occasionally carried foul sewage[41]; and a change of course. It was to be assumed (and indeed probable) that the flow still included natural groundwater unless the person claiming a change of status established otherwise. That left for consideration the factor that the flow now included a great deal more surface water than it used to, including conduits that formed part of the surface water sewer network: the view here was "something very much more than that is needed".[42] The court also recognised that the nature of the flow is not necessarily the sole criterion. The position might have been different,

---

[39] [2007] EWCA Civ; [2008] 2 All E.R. 44.

[40] Sir Anthony May C. and Lloyd L.J., Toulson L.J., dissenting, reversing the decision of the judge in the county court.

[41] There were a number of CSOs upstream (the parties were not agreed if this term meant "combined sewage overflow" or "consented storm overflow"), but the terms and basis of the CSOs were not in evidence.

[42] Lloyd L.J. at [53]. Sir Andrew Morritt C. agreed: paras [87]–[89]; he also stated (para.[85]) that "the nature of the contents or flow of the culvert is the most significant factor in the determination of the question whether what was once a natural watercourse has become a sewer".

for example, if the stretch had been culverted by a sewerage authority or sewerage undertaker acting in that capacity.[43]

Fifthly, it has been said that a "sewer" must cause effluent to flow from one place to another and thus it:

> "must be in some form a line of flow by which sewage or water of some kind, such as would be conveyed by a sewer, should be taken from a point to a point and then discharged. It must have a *terminus a quo* and a *terminus ad quem*."[44]

It would therefore seem that a line of pipes terminating in a cesspool **1–008** would not be a "sewer",[45] nor would a line of pipes with no proper outfall[46] or a conduit linking two cesspools.[47] A cesspool or storage tank is not a part of the sewer, unless it is really a mere catchpit from which an outflow pipe runs to a sewer or other proper outfall.[48] It seems, therefore, that a drain serving any number of buildings, whether or not within the same curtilage, which discharges into a cesspool or cesspit (not being a mere catchpit), is not capable of being a public sewer.[49]

Sixthly, it does not follow that because one part of a channel is a sewer that another part of it is also a sewer. Where the question is whether part of a channel is a sewer, evidence as to what has happened to other parts is not irrelevant, but the issue should be addressed by reference to the specific stretch at issue.[50]

---

[43] See Lloyd L.J. at [19]–[20], Toulson L.J. at [20] and Sir Andrew Morritt C. at [86], referring to *United Water Utilities Water Ltd v Sefton Metropolitan BC* [2001] EWCA Civ 1284 (CA held that the culverting of a natural watercourse in the 1950s had been undertaken under Pt XI of the Public Health Act 1936 (general powers) and not Pt II (sewerage powers); reference to the culvert in contemporary council minutes as a "sewer" had been made in error).

[44] Per Buckley L.J. in *Pakenham v Ticehurst R.D.C.* (1903) 67 J.P. 448.

[45] *Meader v West Cowes Local Board* [1892] 3 Ch. 18 and *Butt v Snow* (1903) 67 J.P. 454. It is doubtful, however, whether the principle herein applied relates to a case where a drainage system terminating in private drainage "works" has been approved by the local authority as being initially satisfactory. Thus, a conduit ending in tanks from which the effluent was raised by mechanical means and then discharged, all of which had been constructed by a private individual and approved by the local authority, was held to be a sewer in *AG v Peacock* [1926] Ch. 241.

[46] Per Maugham J. (obiter) in *Clark v Epsom R.D.C.* [1929] 1 Ch. 287, 294. However, the mere fact that a particular outfall is not satisfactory or may cause a nuisance does not prevent the line of pipes draining into it from being a "sewer" in law and from having vested in a local authority under the 1875 Act.

[47] *Button v Tottenham U.D.C.* (1898) 62 J.P. 423.

[48] *Pakenham v Ticehurst R.D.C.* (1903) 67 J.P. 448.

[49] As to which see Ch.2.

[50] *Raglan Housing Association Ltd v Southampton CC* [2007] EWCA Civ 785, per Lloyd L.J. at [28] and [29]. However, the status of a stretch downstream is "unlikely" to be relevant: *ibid.*

Seventhly, where the facts are in dispute, the burden of proof lies on the party claiming that a natural watercourse has become a sewer.[51]

1–009 Eighthly, a distinct question may arise whether a sewer or drain is "used for drainage of buildings and yards appurtenant to buildings". At first instance in *British Railways Board v Tonbridge and Malling DC*,[52] Judge Finlay, sitting as a judge of the Chancery Division, held that the culvert was a sewer, but not "used for the drainage of buildings". The test for whether a sewer was so used was one of function.[53] His conclusions were summarised as follows by Oliver L.J. in the Court of Appeal[54]:

> "[the test] . . . was not whether the channel concerned in fact carried water or soil deriving from buildings, but what was the function for which the channel was constructed and existed. Here the function of the watercourses and the culvert was to carry away all the surface water from the catchment area as a whole regardless of its origin, and the fact that a part of the flow derived from the outfalls of surface drains associated with buildings and yards did not mean that the culvert was being 'used for the drainage of buildings etc.' "

In view of the decision of the Court of Appeal on the "logically anterior point"[55] of whether the channel constituted a "sewer",[56] this issue did not strictly arise for consideration by the Court of Appeal. Nevertheless, Oliver L.J. noted that the court rejected the submission of counsel for the Board that Judge Finlay had misunderstood or failed to apply the decision of the Court of Appeal in *Hutton v Esher U.D.C.*[57]:

> "That case merely established . . . that a purpose-built sewer for the drainage of buildings does not cease to be a statutory sewer simply because, in addition to drainage from buildings, it carried water also from other sources. [Counsel] seeks to derive from that case the precisely converse proposition that a natural stream does become a sewer if, in addition to other waters, it carries water

[51] *Raglan Housing Association*, per Lloyd L.J. at [42].
[52] Above.
[53] *Blackdown Properties Ltd v Ministry of Housing and Local Government* [1967] Ch. 115.
[54] at p.571.
[55] Per Oliver L.J. at p.571.
[56] Above.
[57] [1974] Ch. 167.

derived from the drainage of buildings. That is a simple *non sequitur* and we mention it only to emphasise that the decision at which we have arrived ought not to be taken as necessarily involving a dissent from the ground upon which the judge decided the case. On the view which we take of [the] first point, it becomes unnecessary to express any opinion as to that ground."[58]

It is clear that a sewer designed for the drainage of buildings does not cease to be a sewer for the purposes of the relevant legislation merely because, without reconstruction, it is not used at all.[59]

Finally, it should be noted that for the purposes of the provisions of the 1936 Act covering "sanitation and buildings"[60] it was stated that:

"any reference . . . to a drain or to a sewer shall be construed as including a reference to any manholes, ventilating shafts, pumps or other accessories belonging to that drain or sewer. . . ."[61]

The Water Industry Act 1991 provides that references to a drain or sewer include references to any "accessories for the pipe".[62]

On the other hand, a pumping main or trunk sewer is nonetheless a sewer, and in most circumstances will also clearly be a public sewer.

Subject to the above observations, the terms "sewer" and "drain" **1–010**
should be interpreted in accordance with normal practice in the light of their ordinary or "dictionary" meaning.[63] For example, gutters and

---

[58] Per Oliver L.J. at p.575.

[59] Per Stamp J. in *Blackdown Properties Ltd v Ministry of Housing and Local Government* [1967] Ch. 115 at p.123. Similarly, where a sewer is constructed for the purposes of draining a number of premises, it is a "sewer" notwithstanding that it is so far serving one building: *J. Pullan & Sons Ltd v Leeds CC* (1990) 7 Constr. L.J. 222, C.A. (accordingly, the authority was bound to declare the sewer vested in itself by virtue of an agreement with the developer); *Bromley LBC v Morritt (No.1)* (1999) 79 P.C.C.R. 536; *Ramdhun v Thames Water Utilities Ltd* [2010] EWHC 1014 (QB)

[60] ss.14–90.

[61] Public Health Act 1936 s.90(4); see also Building Act 1984 s.126.

[62] Water Industry Act 1991 s.219(2). "Accessories" in relation to a "water main, sewer or other pipe", includes any manholes, ventilating shafts, inspection chambers, settling tanks, wash-out pipes, pumps, ferrules or stopcocks for the main, sewer or other pipe, or any machinery or other apparatus which is designed or adapted for use in connection with the use or maintenance of the main, sewer or other pipe or of another accessory for it", but not any electronic communication apparatus unless it is or is to be in the close vicinity of the pipe or accessory and intended to be used only in connection with its use or maintenance: s.219(1), definition as amended by the Communications Act 2003, Sch.17, para.110.

[63] In the absence of judicial authority, dictionaries may be consulted in the interpretation of statutes, see Asquith J. in *Kerr v Kennedy* [1942] 1 K.B. 409. Also F.A.R. Bennion, *Bennion on Statutory Interpretation*, 5th edn, London: LexisNexis, 2008, pp.1222–1223.

fall pipes are probably not "drains" in law and are almost certainly not "sewers", even if they serve more than one set of premises. Such a usage would be highly artificial and would seem an unjustified imposition upon the statutory language.

Thus, in Diagram 1[64] in Appendix A, the surface water drain taking rain from houses 1, 2 and 3 to the soakway at point X on A's property is not sewer but a drain, whereas the foul drain leading to the stream at point Y, is a sewer *from* point B.

(c) Other legislation

1–011 The term "sewer" in other legislation is not necessarily to be given the same, limited interpretation as is found in public health legislation and its modern equivalent, the Water Industry Act 1991. For example, in *Doncaster BC v Secretary of State for the Environment*,[65] it was held that permitted development rights in respect of "any works for the purposes of inspection, repairing or renewing any sewer, main, pipe, cable or other apparatus" in Pt 10 of Sch.2 to the Town and Country Planning General Development Order 1988[66] applied to any "sewer" within the ordinary English meaning of that word, and so included any drain.

THE MODERN BACKGROUND TO SEWERAGE SERVICES

1–012 Until recent times, controls over the provision and maintenance of sewers and drains in England and Wales were almost exclusively the concern of local authorities, subject only to the minimum of supervision by central government. The law was principally to be found in the Public Health Acts 1848 and 1875, replaced by the Public Health Act 1936. Minor alterations followed, mainly in the Public Health Act 1961. The Water Act 1973 transferred many of the functions of local authorities in this field to 10 water authorities and the public sewers of local authorities were thereby vested in those water authorities.[67]

---

[64] See p.290.

[65] (1996) 74 P&CR 428.

[66] SI 1988/1813. See now the Town and Country Planning (General Permitted Development) Order 1995 (SI 1995/418) Sch.2 Pt 10.

[67] See A. Telling, *Water Authorities* (1974). The transfer was effected by the Local Authorities (England) (Property etc.) Order 1973 (SI 1973/1861) arts 7, 8, and the Local Authorities (Wales) (Property etc.) Order 1973 (SI 1973/1863) arts 7, 8. The whole of the local authorities' interests were transferred: see *Sheffield CC v Yorkshire Water Services* [1991] 1 W.L.R. 58, where Sir Nicolas Browne-Wilkinson V.C. rejected the argument that the transferor councils retained an interest in the proceeds of any sale of the assets for profit following privatisation.

More recently, the Water Act 1989 made revolutionary changes in law and administration. This Act was in turn consolidated with other legislation into the Water Industry Act 1991, the Water Resources Act 1991, the Land Drainage Act 1991 and the Water Consolidation (Consequential Provisions) Act 1991.[68] Further amendments were effected by the Competition and Service (Utilities) Act 1992 and the Water Act 2003.

Designed to privatise the water industry, the 1989 Act transferred the water and sewerage assets of the water authorities to limited liability companies operating under the regime of the Companies Acts. Individually, these successor companies, one for each of the former water authorities, were originally wholly owned by the central government. Then, as from November 1, 1989, the shares in holding companies for the successor companies were offered for sale on the private market. Each successor company was formally appointed by the Secretary of State to operate as a water undertaker and sewerage undertaker for the area of the former water authority, except in cases where before 1989 there was a statutory water company; in those instances the statutory company remained and the successor company was appointed only as a sewerage undertaker.

The Water Act 1989 repealed several key sections of the 1936 Act, in particular s.20 (definition of public sewer) and s.24 (maintenance of certain lengths of public sewer). The remaining provisions of the 1936 Act in relation to sewers were consolidated in the Water Industry Act 1991. Important changes have also been introduced by the Urban Waste Water Treatment (England and Wales) Regulations 1994[69] which implement the Urban Waste Water Treatment Directive.[70] These regulations affect both the collection and treatment of waste water.

The functions of local authorities relating to controls over the drainage of individual premises were left virtually unaltered by the 1989 and 1991 Acts, but the provisions relating to the prevention of river pollution contained in Pt 2 of the Control of Pollution Act 1974 were replaced by new and more stringent controls in the 1989 Act, subsequently found in Pt 3 of the Water Resources Act 1991.[71]

---

[68] See the Law Commission's "Report on the Consolidation of the Legislation relating to Water" (Law Com. No.198, Cm. 1483, 1991).

[69] SI 1994/2841.

[70] Dir.91/271.

[71] ss.82–104. See below, pp.167–202.

THE AUTHORITIES

1–013 The Act of 1989 introduced a plethora of authorities concerned with sewerage services at different levels. This made a striking change from the straightforward situation before 1973 when the only authorities concerned were the local authorities, subject in very minor respects to the general supervision of the Secretary of State, or formerly the Ministry of Health. These authorities will now be outlined *seriatim*.

(a) The Secretary of State

1–014 The Secretary of State[72] has very considerable duties under the Water Industry Act 1991. In the first place it is the duty of the Secretary of State to ensure that a sewerage undertaker is appointed for all areas of England and Wales.[73] Appointments may be made by the Secretary of State or, with the consent of or under a general authorisation given by the Secretary of State, by the Water Services Regulation Authority.[74] The Secretary of State (or WSRA) may by notice terminate an appointment or vary the area to which it relates. However, in the case of termination or a decrease in area this may only take effect if a replacement undertaker is appointed to ensure continuity. Furthermore, an appointment or variation replacing a company as undertaker may not be made unless the company consents, or the appointment or variation relates only to part of that area none of the premises in which is served by the company,[75] or is made in circumstances set out in the conditions of

---

[72] i.e. the Secretary of State for Environment, Food and Rural Affairs (for England). In relation to any water or sewerage undertaker whose area is wholly or mainly in Wales, most of the powers of the Secretary of State have been transferred to the National Assembly: National Assembly for Wales (Transfer of Functions) Order 1999 (SI 1999/672) Sch.1, as amended by SI 2000/253 Sch.3(e), the Water Act 2003 s.100, SI 2004/3044, Sch.2 and SI 2006/3334, Sch. para.(b). In some cases, the powers are exercisable concurrently with the Secretary of State.

[73] Water Industry Act 1991 s.7(1).

[74] Water Industry Act 1991 s.6, as amended by the Water Act 2003 s.36(2) and Sch.8 para.3 (the latter amendment providing that a company cannot be appointed as a sewerage or water undertaker if it is a licensed water supplier). The initial appointments were made by the Secretary of State.

[75] Premises in part of an area are served by an undertaker if they are "drained by means of a relevant sewer or drain" (1991 Act s.36(3), as amended by the 1992 Act s.40(5), and the Water Act 2003 s.97(2)(a)). A "relevant sewer or drain" means any of the following: (a) a public sewer or lateral drain vested in that company; (b) a sewer or lateral drain in relation to which that company has made a declaration of vesting under s.102 which has not yet taken effect; (c) a sewer or lateral drain in relation to which that company has entered into an agreement under s.104: s.36(4), as amended by the Water Act 2003 s.97(2)(b).

appointment.[76] The last of these points is dealt with in Condition O of the standard Conditions of Appointment,[77] which states that for the purposes of what is now s.7(1)(c) of the 1991 Act:

> "the only circumstances in which an appointment or variation to which section [7] applies may be made in relation to the area for which the Appointee holds the Appointment as . . . sewerage undertaker . . . are where the Secretary of State has given the Appointee at least 10 years' notice, expiring not earlier than 25 years after the transfer date, to terminate the relevant Appointment in relation to the whole of its area and the said period of notice has expired."

This is the only route by which an appointment may be terminated apart from the making of a special administration order by the High Court.[78] In addition, an "inset appointment" of another company as water retailer may be made for parts of an undertaker's area where each of the premises in those parts are or are likely to be supplied with not less than 50 megalitres of water in any period of 12 months (250 megalitres where the area of the undertaker is wholly or mainly in Wales) and the person who is the customer in relation to each of the premises consents in writing.[79]

An appointment of an undertaker may include:

---

[76] Water Industry Act 1991 s.7(1)–(4)(a), (b), (c). As to the procedure for appointments and variations, see ss.8–10 and Sch.2, ss.8 and 9, as amended by the Competition and Service (Utilities) Act 1992 s.40(3), (4) and Sch.2 para.17, and Sch.2 as amended by the Water Act 2003 Sch.8, para.51.

[77] *Instrument of Appointment of the Water and Sewerage Undertakers* (HMSO, 1989), p.99.

[78] See below, pp.27–29.

[79] 1991 Act s.7(4)(bb), (5) and (6), inserted by the Competition and Service (Utilities) Act 1992 s.40(1), (2), and amended by SI 2000/1842 reg.2(1), (2) and the Water and Sewerage Undertakers (Inset Appointments) Regulations 2005 (SI 2005/268), reg.2(2) (reducing the figure for England from 100 megalitres). See OFWAT, *Inset Appointments: Guidance for Applicants* (February 1999), varied by a Letter (January 23, 2009), "Policy on New Appointments and Variations" (OFWAT website). The policy states that a potential inset appointee must be able to finance the proper carrying out of its functions as undertaker and that the customers whose supplier is changed should be no worse off; in *R. (on the application of Welsh Water Ltd) v Water Services Regulation Authority (Ofwat)* [2009] EWHC 3493 (Admin), a challenge to the lawfulness and rationality of this policy was rejected; the policy was justified as promoting competition and the court held that there was no implied requirement that it be shown that the appointee would provide a service more beneficial for the consumers affected. "Inset appointments" are now termed "new appointments" and "variations". The Cave Review (see p.31) recommended that this regime should be extended to cover sewerage services for non-domestic customers, and this was accepted.

(a) such conditions (including conditions affecting non-core business activities) as appear to the Secretary of State (or WSRA) to be requisite or expedient having regard to his duties under Pt 1;

(b) conditions for the purposes of s.7(4)(c); and

(c) conditions requiring payment(s) to the Secretary of State on or during the appointment.

1–015 Conditions may make provision for their ending or modification.[80] Conditions are enforceable by orders under ss 18 and 24. Without prejudice to the generality of (a) above, conditions may require the undertaker to comply with any direction given by the WSRA as to such matters as are specified in the appointment or are of a description so specified; or not to do or to do specified things except in so far as the WSRA consents otherwise. The conditions may provide for the reference to and determination by the Secretary of State or the WSRA or, on a reference by the WSRA, the Competition Commission, of such questions arising under the appointment and such other matters, including (in the case of references to the Commission) disputes as to determinations by the WSRA, as are specified in the appointment. An undertaker can require a matter to be referred to the Commission. The Commission must determine any matter referred in accordance with the the principles which apply by virtue of Pt 1 of the 1991 Act in relation to determinations under Ch.1 of Pt 2 by the WSRA.[81] Where the question or matter referred to the Commission concerns the review of a price control imposed on the undertaker, and the Commission is to decide to what extent it is reasonable to take into account costs incurred by the undertaker in making the reference, the Commission must also have regard to the extent to which, in its view, its determination is likely to support the undertaker's (rather than the WSRA's) claims in relation to the question or matter referred.[82] A report of the Competition Commission under s.12 must be made to the WSRA and must include definite conclusions on the questions or matters referred, together with such

---

[80] 1991 Act s.11, as amended by the Water Act 2003, s.36(2).

[81] 1991 Act s.12 (1)–(3), as amended by SI 1999/506 art.30; the Competition Act 1998 Sch.10 para.13(2)(a), (b); the Enterprise Act 2002 Sch.25 para.25(3); and the Water Act 2003 ss 36(2) and 54 and Sch.9.

[82] 1991 Act s.12(3A), inserted by the Water Act 2003 s.54(1) and (2). Sections 14(4) and (5), 16A and 16B of the 1991 Act apply to references under s.12: s.12(3B), inserted by the 2003 Act s.54(1) and (2).

an account of their reasons as in the Commission's opinion, is expedient for facilitating a proper understanding of those questions or matters and of their conclusions.[83]

Once appointed, each sewerage undertaker must comply with a series of duties prescribed by the 1991 Act and Regulations, including a duty to provide adequate sewerage arrangements for its area.[84] These duties are enforceable by the Secretary of State or the WSRA by means of enforcement orders and special administration orders. These are considered below.[85] The Secretary of State may prescribe standards of performance in relation to sewerage services.[86]

The Secretary of State was formerly order a duty to make a "merger reference" to the Competition Commission in respect of any actual or prospective merger of two or more "water enterprises", i.e. an enterprise carried on by a water or sewerage undertaker.[87] Mergers were excluded where the assets of the target company did not exceed £30 million.[88] In determining whether any matter operated, or might be expected to operate, against the public interest, the Competition Commission was to have regard to the desirability of giving effect to the principle that the ability of the Director-General of Water Services in carrying out his functions to make comparisons between different water enterprises shall not be prejudiced.[89]

New ss.32 to 35 of the 1991 Act were substituted, from December **1–016**
29, 2004,[90] by s.70 of the Enterprise Act 2002. The duty to refer a merger of two or more water enterprises[91] falls on the Office of Fair Trading (OFT) rather than the Secretary of State. There is an exemption where the value of the turnover of the water enterprise being taken over does not exceed or would not exceed £10 million; or where the only water enterprises already belonging to the person making the takeover are enterprises each of which has a turnover the value of which does not exceed, or would not exceed £10 million. Regulations may be made as to the calculation of "turnover" for this

---

[83] 1991 Act s.12(3C), inserted by the 2003 Act s.54(1) and (2).

[84] 1991 Act s.94.

[85] See pp.24–29.

[86] See below, pp.38–40.

[87] 1991 Act s.32, as amended by SI 1999/506 art.30(b).

[88] 1991 Act s.33, and see the Water Enterprises (Merger) Modification Regulations 1994 (SI 1994/73).

[89] 1991 Act ss.34 and 35, as amended by the Competition and Service (Utilities) Act 1992 s.39 and SI 1999/506 art.30(b).

[90] See the Enterprise Act 2002 (Commencement No.7 and Transitional Provisions and Savings) Order 2004 (SI 2004/3233), Sch.

[91] "Water enterprise" is defined as an enterprise carried on by a relevant undertaker: substituted s.35(1), as amended by the Water Act 2003 Sch.7 para.27(2). The new heading to s.32 is "Duty to refer merger of water or sewerage undertaking".

purpose.[92] Provisions of the Enterprise Act 2000 are applied to such mergers by Sch.47A to the 1991 Act.[93]

The first questions to be determined by the Competition Commission are whether there will be or has been a water merger and, if so, whether that merger may be expected to, or has, prejudiced the ability of the WSRA, in carrying out its functions by virtue of this Act, to make comparisons between different water enterprises. Proposals for change to the merger regime are contained in the "Cave Review: Independent Review of Competition and Innovation in Water Markets".[94] These include that retail-only mergers should be removed from the regime and that for other mergers the threshold should be raised to £70 million.

The Secretary of State has numerous other detailed powers under the Act, which will be referred to in their appropriate context. He has a general power to publish information concerning the functions of water and sewerage undertakers.[95]

Section 2 of the Water Industry Act 1991 imposes a number of duties on the Secretary of State as to when and how he should exercise and perform his powers and duties relating to the regulation of sewerage undertakers.[96]

The Secretary of State is also subject to general environmental and recreational duties[97]; these are, however, subject to the overriding general duties set out in s.2.

The Secretary of State must also exercise his functions under (inter alia) Pt 4 of the Water Industry Act 1991 and the Urban Waste Water Treatment (England and Wales) Regulations 1994 so as to secure compliance with the requirements of the Water Framework Directive (Directive 2000/60).[98]

(b) The Director General of Water Services and OFWAT

1–017 The Water Act 1989 s.5 provided for the appointment by the Secretary of State of the Director General of Water Services as regulator. The

---

[92] See the Water Mergers (Determination of Turnover) Regulations 2004 (SI 2004/3206).

[93] Inserted by the 2002 Act s.70(2) and Sch.6. The detailed modifications are set out in the Water Mergers (Modification of Enactments) Regulations 2004 (SI 2004/3202).

[94] April 2009. See below, p.31. The government is consulting on these proposals.

[95] 1991 Act s.201, as amended by the Enterprise Act 2002 Sch.25 para.25(a). And the Water Act 2003 s.36(2) and Sch.8 para.43.

[96] These are set out in the section on the WSRA, below, pp.21–23.

[97] 1991 Act ss.3–5, discussed in relation to sewerage undertakers, below, pp.103–106.

[98] Water Environment (Water Framework Directive) (England and Wales) Regulations 2003 (SI 2003/3242) reg.3 and Sch.2.

Director was an independent officer and was supported by OFWAT, a non-ministerial government department. He was continued in office by s.1 of the Water Industry Act 1991. He was appointed initially for a five-year period but could be re-appointed.[99] From April 1, 2006, the Director was replaced by the Water Services Regulation Authority.[100]

(c) The Water Services Regulation Authority and the Consumer Council for Water

(i) Constitution of the new bodies

By virtue of Pt 2 of the Water Act 2003,[101] two new bodies were **1–018** established. The office of Director General of Water Services was abolished and replaced by the Water Services Regulation Authority (WSRA), with effect from April 1, 2006, after completion of the then current Periodic Review. The Authority consists of a chairman and at least two other members, appointed by the Secretary of State after consulting the National Assembly for Wales before appointing any member, and after consulting the chairman before appointing any other member. It is a body corporate and its functions are performed on behalf of the Crown. It may establish committees and regulate its own procedure and must prepare and revise a code of practice.[102] It has retained the name OFWAT.

There is in addition a Consumer Council for Water, also a body corporate, but not to be regarded as a servant or agent of the Crown or as enjoying any status, immunity or privilege of the Crown. It was established from October 1, 2005. The Council inherited the functions of Customer Service Committees.[103] The council is independent of the WSRA. The Council must establish such "Regional Committees" as the National Assembly may direct, for relevant undertakers whose areas are wholly or mainly in Wales, and as the Secretary of State may direct, for other relevant undertakers. A direction may provide for the allocation of each relevant undertaker to a specified Regional Committee. These powers of direction may only be exercised within

---

[99] The first Director, Ian Byatt, was succeeded by Philip Fletcher on August 1, 2000.

[100] Philip Fletcher, the former Director, became non-executive chair of the WSRA, working with a chief executive.

[101] ss.34–56; Sch.1.

[102] Water Industry Act 1991 s.1A, inserted by the 2003 Act s.34 and Sch.1. In Welsh, the Authority may be known as "Awdurdod Rheoleiddio Gwasanaethau Dŵr."

[103] These were established by the 1991 Act s.28. Ten were appointed from 2002, known as Water Voice Committees. The 10 chairmen comprised the Water Voice Council. The CSCs were under a duty to investigate complaints under the 1991 Act ss.29 and 30, as originally enacted.

six months of the commencement of s.35; thereafter, it falls to the Council to establish such committees as it thinks appropriate or alter the allocation of a relevant undertaker to a Committee, subject to the approval of the National Assembly or the Secretary of State. The purposes of a Committee are to provide advice and information to the Council on consumer matters[104] affecting the areas of the relevant undertakers allocated to that Committee and such other purposes as the Council may determine. The Council may appoint other committees. It must exercise and perform its powers and duties in the manner which it considers is best calculated to contribute to the achievement of sustainable development. The Council consists of a chairman appointed by the Secretary of State, one other member appointed by the National Assembly, and such other members as may be appointed by the Secretary of State. It must report annually on its activities.[105]

The Authority and the Council, the Council and the Secretary of State, and the Council and the National Assembly must respectively make arrangements to secure co-operation and the exchange of information and the consistent treatment of matters which affect both of them, and enshrine them in a memorandum of agreement.[106] The functions of the Director General of Water Services were transferred to the WSRA.[107] The expenses of the Council and of the WSRA, the Secretary of State and the National Assembly, in relation to the Council's establishment, may be required to be met by companies holding an appointment as an undertaker by payment conditions included in that appointment by virtue of s.11(1)(c) of the 1991 Act.[108]

The WSRA and the Council must, before each financial year, each publish a forward work programme containing a general description of the projects, other than those comprising routine activities in the exercise of its functions, which it plans to undertake during the year, and an estimate of overall expenditure for the year. It must first publish a draft for comment. The WSRA must also make an Annual Report.[109]

---

[104] i.e. any matter connected with the interests of consumers, both existing and future. "The interests of consumers" means the interests of consumers in relation to (a) the supply of water by means of a water undertaker's supply system to premises either by water undertakers or licensed water suppliers; and (b) the provision of sewerage services by sewerage undertakers: 1991 Act s.27A(13).

[105] 1991 Act s.27A and Sch.3A, inserted by the 2003 Act s.35 and Sch.2. In Welsh the Council may be known as "Cyngor Defnyddwyn Dŵr."

[106] 1991 Act s.27B, inserted by the 2003 Act s.35.

[107] 2003 Act s.36 and Sch.3. The Secretary of State could make one or more transfer schemes.

[108] 2003 Act s.37.

[109] 1991 Act ss.192A, 192B, inserted by the 2003 Act s.38.

(ii) General duties

The general duties with respect to the water industry under s.2 of the Water Industry Act 1991, that applied to the Secretary of State and the Director, were amended. Section 2 now has effect for imposing duties on the Secretary of State and on the WSRA as to when and how they should perform: (a) in the case of the Secretary of State, the powers and duties conferred or imposed on him by virtue of the provisions of the Act relating to the regulation of water and sewerage undertakers and of licensed water suppliers[110]; and (b) in the case of the WRSA, the powers and duties conferred by any of those provisions, or the provisions relating to the financial conditions of requisitions[111] or the movement of certain pipes.[112] These powers and duties must be exercised and performed in the manner which the Secretary of State or WSRA considers is best calculated: **1–019**

(a) to further the "consumer objective";

(b) to secure that the functions of a water or sewerage undertaker are properly carried out as respects every area of England and Wales;

(c) to secure that companies holding appointments as such undertakers are able (in particular, by securing reasonable returns on their capital) to finance the proper carrying out of those functions; and

(d) to secure that the activities authorised by the licence of a licensed water supplier and any statutory functions imposed on it in consequence of the licence are properly carried out.

The "consumer objective" is to protect the interests of consumers, wherever appropriate by promoting effective competition between persons engaged in, or in commercial activities connected with, the provision of water and sewerage services. For the purposes of (a) above, the Secretary of State or WSRA must have regard to the interests of individuals who are disabled or chronically sick, of pensionable age, with low incomes, residing in rural areas, and customers of companies appointed as water or sewerage undertakers, whose premises are not eligible to be supplied by a licensed water supplier. This

---

[110] i.e. the provisions in Pt 2 of the 1991 Act (except s.27A and Sch.3A), or in ss.37A to 38, 39, 39B, 39C, 66B, 66D, 66F to 66H, 66K, 66L, 95, 96, 153, 181, 182, 192A, 192B, 195, 195A and 201–203.

[111] i.e. ss.42, 43, 43A, 48, 51C, 99, 100 and 100A of the 1991 Act.

[112] i.e. s.185 of the 1991 Act.

is, however, not to be taken as implying that regard may not be had to the interests of other descriptions of consumer. The Secretary of State and WSRA may also have regard to the interests of consumers in relation to electricity, gas and communications.

1–020 Subject to the above requirements, the Secretary of State and WSRA must exercise and perform these powers and duties in the manner which he or it considers is best calculated:

(a) to promote economy and efficiency on the part of companies carrying out functions as relevant undertakers;

(b) to secure that no undue preference is shown, and no undue discrimination in the fixing by such companies of water and drainage charges;

(c) to secure that consumers are protected as regards benefits from the disposal of a company's protected land;

(d) to ensure that consumers are also protected as respects any activities of such companies or persons appearing to be connected with them not attributable to the exercise of functions of a relevant undertaker; and

(e) to contribute to the achievement of sustainable development.

The Secretary of State and WSRA must also have regard to the principles of best regulatory practice, including the principles under which regulatory activities should be transparent, accountable, proportionate, consistent and targeted only at cases in which action is needed.

These duties (and those under s.2A of the 1991 Act) do not apply in relation to anything done by the WSRA in the exercise of Competition Act functions conferred by s.31(3) of the 1991 Act (although regard can be had to these matters), and do not affect any obligation of the WSRA or the Secretary of State to perform or comply with any other duty or requirement arising under an enactment, by virtue of any Community obligation as otherwise.[113]

1–021 Guidance may be issued from time to time by the Secretary of State and by the Assembly, after consultation, about the making by the WSRA of a contribution towards the attainment of any social or environmental policies set out or referred to in the guidance. In formulating guidance, the Secretary of State and the Assembly must,

---

[113] 1991 Act s.2, as amended by the Competition Act 1998 Sch.10 para.5, the Enterprise Act 2002 Sch.25 para.25(2), and the Water Act 2003 ss.36(2) and 39.

where practicable, have regard to the costs and benefits which may be expected to result from the guidance. The WSRA must, in exercising and performing the powers and duties mentioned in s.2(1) of the 1991 Act, have regard to any such guidance.[114]

Section 72 of the Regulatory Enforcement and Sanctions Act 2008 applies to the exercise of regulatory functions[115] by the WSRA.[116] In exercising a regulatory function the WSRA must keep that function under review and secure that in exercising the function it does not (a) impose burdens which it considers to be unnecessary, or (b) maintain burdens which it considers to have become unnecessary. This does not require the removal of a burden which has become unnecessary where its removal would, having regard to all the circumstances, be impracticable or disproportionate. It must from time to time, in respect of successive 12-month periods, publish a statement setting out what it proposes to do and has done pursuant to these requirements in relation to the function.

(iii) Regulations concerning performance standards

The Secretary of State's power under s.95 of the 1991 Act to make **1–022** regulations relating to standards of performance in connection with sewerage services may be exercised on the application of the WSRA or otherwise; in the latter case, regulations can only be made if the Secretary of State considers that they will contribute towards the attainment of policies relating to public health or the environment, or that there are exceptional reasons why it is otherwise in the public interest that they should be made.[117]

(iv) Modification of conditions of appointment

The WSRA has power to modify the conditions of appointment of a **1–023** sewerage undertaker, with the undertaker's consent, although such action cannot relieve the undertaker of its statutory duties and may in

[114] 1991 Act s.2A, inserted by the 2003 Act s.40. See DEFRA, "Statutory Social and Environmental Guidance to the Water Services Regulation Authority (OFWAT)", August 2008, http://www.defra.gov.uk [Accessed July 29, 2010]; and Welsh Ministers, "Social and Environmental Guidance to Ofwat", December 2008, *http://wales.gov.uk/docs/desh/publications/090304watersegofwaten.doc* [Accessed July 29, 2010].

[115] i.e. (a) a function under any enactment of imposing requirements, restrictions or conditions, or setting standards or giving guidance, in relation to any activity; or (b) a function which relates to the securing of compliance with, or the enforcement of, requirements, restrictions, conditions, standards or guidance which under or by virtue of any enactment relate to any activity: definition in s.32(2) of the Legislative and Regulatory Reform Act 2006 applied by the 2008 Act s.74.

[116] See s.73(2)(e). This does not apply to any function exercised under competition law.

[117] 1991 Act s.96, as amended by the 2003 Act s.42.

certain cases be blocked by the Secretary of State.[118] Where consent cannot be obtained to a proposed modification, it has power to make a "modification reference" to the Competition Commission requiring it to investigate and report on whether specified matters relating to the carrying on of sewerage functions "operate, or may be expected to operate, against the public interest", and whether this could be remedied or prevented by modification of the Conditions of Appointment.[119] Copies of a report thereafter received must be sent by the WSRA to the Company concerned and to the Secretary of State and must also be published in such a fashion as may be appropriate to draw it to the attention of "persons likely to be affected by it."[120] The report may in due course lead to a modification of the conditions of appointment of the sewerage undertaker by the WSRA, subject to the Commission's power to veto modifications proposed by it and substitute others.[121]

(v) Enforcement orders

1–024 The WSRA or the Secretary of State[122] must make a provisional or final enforcement order under s.18 of the 1991 Act where it or he is satisfied that an undertaker is contravening[123] any of the Conditions of Appointment, or any other statutory or other requirement made so enforceable by an enactment or subordinate legislation. A number of provisions of the 1991 Act are expressly made enforceable under s.18.[124]

---

[118] Water Industry Act 1991 s.13, as amended by the Water Act 2003 s.13.

[119] Water Industry Act 1991 s.14, as amended by the Competition Act 1998 Sch.10 para.13(3); SI 1999/506 art.1; the Enterprise Act 2002 Sch.25 para.25(1), (4); and the Water Act 2003 ss.36(2) and 55. Time limits are set by s.14A and powers of investigation conferred by s.14B, inserted by the Enterprise Act 2002 Sch.25 para.25(1), (5), and amended by the 2003 Act s.36(2).

[120] Water Industry Act 1991 s.15, as amended by the Enterprise Act 2002 Sch.25 para.25(6) and the 2003 Act s.36(2).

[121] ss.16, 16A, 16B, as amended and inserted by the Water Act 2003, ss.36(2) and 55. And see also s.17 subss.(1), (2) and (4) as substituted by the Enterprise Act 2002, Sch. 9, para. 7, enabling the OFT, the Competition Commission or the Secretary of State to include in a relevant order (defined in subs.(2)) provisions modifying the conditions of appointment of an undertaker where requisite or expedient to give effect to any provision made by the order.

[122] Depending on who is the "enforcement authority". The WSRA is the enforcement authority in relation to the Conditions of Appointment; otherwise it is as specified in the particular statutory provision or provision of subordinate legislation that makes a requirement enforceable under s.18: s.18(6).

[123] Or has contravened and is likely to do so again.

[124] Including the general duties under s.94 of the 1991 Act and the Urban Waste Water Treatment (England and Wales) Regulations 1994 (SI 1994/2841). Others include ss.3, 4, 19, 37, 96A, 116A, 130, 143A, 181, 182, 185, 191, 196, 198, 199, 200, 202, 205, 208, Sch.11, paras 3, 5. See below, pp.70–71, 130–133. Section 18 also applies in respect of contraventions of conditions of water abstraction licences under Chapter 1A of Part 1 of the 1991 Act, inserted by the Water Act 2003 Pt 1: see the 2003 Act Sch.8 para.4.

An order must make "such provisions as is requisite for the purpose of securing compliance with that condition or requirement". The order must be a "final" order unless it appears to the WSRA (or Secretary of State) that it is requisite that a "provisional" order be made instead of taking steps towards a final order. In determining whether it is so requisite, it or he must have regard in particular to the extent to which any person is likely to sustain loss or damage in consequence of any contravention before a final order may be made. Where a provisional order is made, the WSRA (or Secretary of State) must confirm it, with or without modifications, if it or he is satisfied as set out above. If it is not confirmed, it lapses at the end of such period (not exceeding three months) as is determined by or under the order. An enforcement order must require the undertaker, according to the circumstances, to do or not to do specified things, takes effect at such time, being the earliest practicable time as is determined by or under the order, and may be revoked at any time by the enforcement authority who made it.

There are exceptions to the duty to make an order or confirm a provisional order, if the WSRA (or Secretary of State) is satisfied:

(a) that the contraventions or apprehended contraventions are trivial in nature[125];

(aa) that the extent to which the undertaker caused or contributed to, or was likely to cause or contribute to, a contravention was trivial[126];

(b) that the undertaker has given and is complying with an undertaking to take all such steps as appear to it or him for the time being to be appropriate to secure or facilitate compliance[127];

---

[125] In Standing Committee D, the Minister, Michael Howard M.P., stated that "It is very unlikely that circumstances giving rise to a danger to health could be properly regarded as trivial" (col.923, February 9, 1989). See *R. v Director General of Water Services, ex p. Lancashire CC* (1998) 96 L.G.R. 296 (contraventions of Condition of Appointment of water undertaker concerning the procedure for disconnections of water supply to domestic premises for non-payment of charges, arising out of the installation of prepayment water devices ("budget payment units"), held not to be trivial).

[126] Inserted by the Water Act 2003 Sch.8 para.5.

[127] A decision to accept an undertaking may be challenged on an application for judicial review: *R. v Secretary of State for the Environment, ex p. Friends of the Earth Ltd* [1994] 2 C.M.L.R. 760 (challenge to undertakings accepted from water undertakers following breaches of requirements as to water intended for human consumption rejected on the facts). See *ENDS Report* 231, April 1994, pp.46–47 (R. Macrory). An appeal to the Court of Appeal was dismissed: [1996] Env. L.R. 198. An undertaking is itself enforceable as a requirement under s.18: s.19(2).

(c) that the general duties under Pt 1 of the Act preclude the making or confirmation of the order.[128]

The WSRA is not required to make or confirm an order if it is satisfied that the most appropriate way of proceeding is under the Competition Act 1998.[129] If the WSRA or Secretary of State is so satisfied under ss.(1) or (1A) it or he must serve a notice on the undertaker, and publish it.[130]

The procedure for making an order is set out in s.20.[131] The WSRA (or Secretary of State) must generally give prior notice by publication and by serving a copy on the undertaker, and consider any representations or objections that are duly made.[132] The order itself must similarly be published and served. The undertaker has 42 days from service of the order to challenge its validity in the High Court on the ground that it is ultra vires s.18 or the requirements of s.20 have not been complied with. Otherwise, its validity may not be questioned in any legal proceedings whatsoever.[133]

Breach of an enforcement order may give rise to an action for damages,[134] and the enforcement authority may seek an injunction or other appropriate relief to secure compliance.[135]

---

[128] 1991 Act s.19(1), as amended by the 2003 Act s.36(2). This is subject to the Drinking Water (Undertakings) (England and Wales) Regulations 2000 (SI 2000/1297): subs.(1), as amended by SI 2000/1297 reg.8. The Minister (above n.124) also indicated that the circumstances in (c) would be unlikely to apply where there was any danger to public health (col.923–924, February 9, 1989). It was held that s.19(1)(c) only exempted the Director if he was precluded from acting by another duty; the general obligation of the Director under the 1991 Act s.2(3)(a) to exercise his powers and duties in the manner best calculated to ensure that every customer is protected as respects the fixing and recovery of water charges is not such a duty: *R. v Director General of Water Services, ex p. Lancashire CC* (1998) 96 L.G.R. 296 (holding that the Director did not have a discretion not to make an enforcement order in respect of the use of pre-payment devices which were contrary to the statutory code on the ground that he considered their use to be in the best interests of some customers).

[129] 1991 Act s.19(1A), inserted by the Competition Act Sch.10 para.13(6) and amended by the 2003 Act s.36(2).

[130] 1991 Act s.19(3), as amended by the Competition Act 1998 Sch.10 para.13(7) and the 2003 Act s.36(2). This does not apply if the Secretary of State so directs under s.208 in the interests of national security.

[131] As amended by the Water Act 2003 s.36(2) and Sch.8 para.6.

[132] Again, subject to exceptions for reasons of national security: s.20(9).

[133] 1991 Act s.21. This would exclude an application for judicial review on any ground before or after the 42-day period: *Smith v East Elloe R.D.C.* [1956] A.C. 736.

[134] See below, pp.72–73. Breach of an undertaking does not, however, give rise to a claim for damages.

[135] 1991 Act s.22, as amended by the Water Act 2003 s.36(2) and Sch.8 para.7.

(vi) Financial penalties

In addition to the powers under s.22 of the 1991 Act,[136] where the WSRA is satisfied that a company holding an appointment as an undertaker has contravened or is contravening any condition of appointment or has failed or is failing to achieve any standard of performance prescribed under s.38(2) or 95(2) of the 1991 Act, the WSRA may impose on the company a penalty of such amount as is reasonable in all the circumstances of the case. The WSRA, the Secretary of State and the Assembly have the same power in respect of contraventions of requirements enforceable under s.18 in relation to which he or it is the enforcement authority. The undertaker must be given at least 21 days' notice and an opportunity to make representations or objections. No penalty may exceed 10 per cent of the company's turnover.[137] An enforcement authority cannot impose a penalty where it is satisfied that the most appropriate way of proceeding is under the Competition Act 1998. Each enforcement authority must publish, and have regard to, a statement of policy with respect to the imposition of penalties and the determination of their amount. A company may appeal to the High Court against the imposition or amount of the penalty or the date by which it is to be paid, on the grounds that the enforcement authority had no power to impose it, or the interests of the company have been prejudiced by non-compliance with specified requirements, or the date(s) for payment specified is unreasonable.[138] **1–025**

(vii) Special administration orders

A more draconian procedure is available in the form of "special administration orders"[139] in respect of companies holding appointments as undertakers. Such an order may be made by the High Court on the application of the Secretary of State (or, with the Secretary of State's consent, the WSRA), if the court is satisfied: **1–026**

(a) that there has been or is likely to be such a contravention of any principal duty[140] as is serious enough to make it inappropriate for the company to continue to hold its appointment;

---

[136] Above, p.26.

[137] Turnover is determined in accordance with the Water Industry (Determination of Turnover for Penalties) Order 2005 (SI 2005/477).

[138] 1991 Act ss.22A–22F, inserted by the 2003 Act s.48(1).

[139] 1991 Act ss.23–26, as amended by the Water Act 2003 s.36(2) and Sch.8 paras 8–11 (to apply in respect of licensed water suppliers), and the Flood and Water Management Act 2010 Sch.5 paras 3.5 and 6.

[140] i.e. in relation to sewerage undertakers, a requirement imposed by s.94: see below, pp.70–71, 130–133; no exemption notice must have been served under s.19(3): see above, p.26.

(b) that there has been or is likely to be such a contravention of a final or confirmed provisional enforcement order as is similarly serious;

(c) that the company is or is likely to be unable to pay its debts;

(d) that the circumstances would justify presentation of a petition for winding-up under s.440 of the Companies Act 1985[141]; or

(e) that the company is unable or unwilling adequately to participate in arrangements certified by the Secretary of State or the WSRA to be necessary in relation to a proposal for termination of appointment under Condition O of the Conditions of Appointment.[142]

A special administration order directs that the company's affairs, business and property are to be managed by a person appointed by the High Court to achieve the purposes of the order in a manner which protects the respective interests of the company's members and creditors. The purposes of such an order are to transfer so much of the undertaking as is necessary to ensure that the functions as undertaker may be properly carried out and to continue carrying out those functions pending the transfer.[143] Where an order is made on the grounds that the company is or is likely to be unable to pay its debts, the purpose of the order is to rescue the company as a going concern and the transfer purpose applies only if the special administrator thinks that it is not likely to be possible to achieve that or transfer is likely to secure more effective performance of functions or activities.[144] Where an order is made the Secretary of State may provide financial assistance.[145] Where a transfer purpose is pursued, the special administrator

---

[141] The making of a winding-up order is itself barred by s.25 of the 1991 Act in respect of any company holding an appointment as undertaker. Similarly, voluntary winding-up and insolvency proceedings are barred by s.26.

[142] 1991 Act s.24.

[143] 1991 Act s.23(1), (2). Provisions of the Insolvency Act 1986 are applied by Sch.3, as amended by the 2003 Act s.36(2) and Sch.8 para.52. Section 23(3) and Sch.3 are to be replaced (from a day to be appointed) by new s.23(3)–(3D), inserted by the 2010 Act Sch.5 para.6. These apply Sch.B1 to the Insolvency Act 1986, subject to regulations made by the Secretary of State. Transfer schemes are governed by Sch.2, as amended by the 2003 Act s.36(2) and Sch.8 para.51, and the 2010 Act Sch.5 para.1.

[144] 1991 Act s.23(2B)–(2G), inserted (from a day to be appointed) by the 2010 Act Sch.5 para.3. For the purposes of rescuing the company as a going concern, a special administrator may propose a company voluntary arrangement under Pt 1 of the Insolvency Act 1986 or a compromise or arrangement under Pt 26 of the Companies Act 2006: s.23(2D). The Secretary of State may make regulations: s.23(2E)–(2G).

[145] 1991 Act ss.153 and 154, to be amended by the Flood and Water Management Act 2010 Sch.5 para.4.

may "hive down" or transfer the whole or part of a company's business to a wholly-owned subsidiary in advance of a transfer of securities to one or more new owners.[146]

(viii) The Authority's register

The WSRA must maintain a public register of such matters as the appointments of undertakers, enforcement orders, undertakings, special administration orders, financial penalties and guidance concerning charges schemes given by the Secretary of State.[147] **1–027**

(ix) Review and information functions

The WSRA is under a duty to keep under review the carrying on both in England and Wales and elsewhere of activities connected with the matters in relation to which sewerage undertakers carry out functions; and to collect information with respect to the carrying out by the appointed companies of their functions as sewerage undertakers, and information with respect to the companies themselves, with a view to informing itself of matters with respect to which powers and duties are conferred on it.[148] The Secretary of State may give directions to the WSRA indicating considerations it should take into account in determining the order of priority in which matters are to be brought under review and in determining whether to exercise its powers under Pts 2 to 5 and 7 of the 1991 Act.[149] **1–028**

It must also collect information with respect to the compensation paid by sewerage undertakers under the Customer Service Standards specified in the regulations made by the Secretary of State[150] and the levels of overall performance achieved by sewerage undertakers in connection with the provision of sewerage services.[151] It has power to direct the undertakers to give him relevant information for this purpose.[152] Furthermore, it must arrange for the publication, at least annually, of such of the information collected by it or given to it as

---

[146] 1991 Act Sch.5 para.5.

[147] 1991 Act s.195, as amended by the Water Industry Act 1999 Sch.3 para.4 and SI 1999/506 art.30, the Water Act 2003 ss.36(2), 48, Sch.3 para.4, Sch.8 para.42, Sch.9 Pt 2 and SI 2005/3076 reg.5(2). See the Director General of Water Services Register (Inspection and Charges) Order 1989 (SI 1989/1154), which has effect under this section.

[148] 1991 Act s.27(1), (2), as amended by the Water Act 2003 s.36(2), Sch.8, para.12(1)–(3).

[149] 1991 Act s.27(3), as amended by the 2003 Act s.36(2).

[150] See below, pp.38–40.

[151] 1991 Act s.95A(1), inserted by the Competition and Service (Utilities) Act 1992 s.31 and amended by the 2003 Act s.36(2).

[152] 1991 Act s.95A(2), (3).

appears expedient to give to customers or potential customers[153]; and it may direct the undertakers to inform their customers, at least annually, about their overall performance against the specified standards.[154]

(x) Competition

1–029 It is also the WSRA's duty to provide information, advice and assistance to the Secretary of State or the OFT relating to the functions of a sewerage undertaker or the carrying out of such functions by an appointed company; this information is to be provided on request or when it considers it expedient to do so.[155] The functions of the OFT under Pt 4 of the Enterprise Act 2002 (other than ss.166 and 171) are concurrent functions of the WSRA and the OFT so far as they relate to commercial activities connected with the supply of water or the provision of sewerage services.[156] The WSRA is also entitled to exercise, concurrently with the OFT, the functions of the OFT under the Competition Act 1998, Pt 1 (other than ss.31D (1)–(6), 38(1) to (6) and 51) so far as relating to (a) agreements, decisions or concerted practices of the kind mentioned in s.2(1) of the 1998 Act[157]; or (b) conduct of the kind mentioned in section 18(1) of that Act,[158], agreements, decisions or concerted practices or abuses of the kind mentioned in Art.81(1) or 82 of the EC Treaty, which relate to commercial activities connected with the supply of water or securing a supply of water or with the provision or securing of sewerage services.[159] The OFT and

---

[153] 1991 Act s.95A(4), (5) as amended by the 2003 Act s.36(2).

[154] 1991 Act s.96A, inserted by the Competition and Service (Utilities) Act 1992 s.32 and amended by the 2003 Act s.36(2). This duty is enforceable under s.18, see above, pp.24–26.

[155] 1991 Act s.27(4), as amended by the Enterprise Act 2002 Sch.25 para.25(1), (7), and the Water Act 2003 s.36(2), Sch.8 para.12(4).

[156] 1991 Act s.31(2), (2A), substituted by the Enterprise Act 2002 Sch.9 Pt 2 para.19(1), (2) and amended by the 2003 Act s.36(2).

[157] i.e. which (a) may affect trade within the UK, and (b) have as their objects or effect the prevention, restriction or distortion of competition within the UK.

[158] i.e. any conduct on the part of one or more undertakings which amounts to the abuse of a dominant position in a market which may affect trade within the UK.

[159] 1991 Act s.31(3), substituted by SI 2004/1261 Sch.2 para.4(2)(a), and amended by the 2003 Act s.36(2). The WSRA normally handles potential breaches of the Competition Act 1998 in the water and sewerage sectors in England and Wales, but always consults the OFT: OFWAT, "A Guide to complaining to OFWAT under the Competition Act 1998", April 2, 2006, *http://www.ofwat.gov.uk/consumerissues/prs_lft_gudtocompca98.pdf* [Accessed July 29, 2010]. See also Information Note 45, "Competition Law in the Water and Sewerage Industry", April 28, 2006; and OFT, "Guidance on the Application of the Competition Act 1998 in the Water and Sewerage Sectors", March 2010, *http://www.oft.gov.uk* [Accessed July 29, 2010]. For cases arising out of the application of competition law to water and sewerage undertakers, see *Independent Water Co Ltd v WSRA* [2007] C.A.T. 6; *Albion Water Ltd v Dwr Cymru Cyf* [2008] EWCA Civ 536; [2009] 2 All E.R. 279; and *Albion Water Ltd v WSRA* [2009] C.A.T. 12.

the WSRA must consult each other before exercising the powers under s.31(2). In 2009, the "Cave Review: Independent Review of Competition and Innovation in Water Markets"[160] made a series of recommendations for change which the government decided to take forward.[161] These include the legal separation of large companies' retail operations and reforms to the mergers regime and the regime for inset appointments.

(xi) Disputes

Finally, the WSRA has powers to consider complaints[162] and to determine disputes. A number of powers to determine disputes were added by the Competition and Service (Utilities) Act 1992.[163] In determining disputes referred to him under the 1991 Act, it must follow such practice and procedure as it considers appropriate, it must give reasons and may order the payment of his costs and expenses.[164] A determination by it is final.[165] However, it is not to determine any such dispute which is the subject of proceedings before a court, or with respect to which judgment has been given by a court.[166] **1–030**

(xii) Overriding duties

The WSRA is also subject to the general environmental and recreational duties in sections 3 to 5 of the Act.[167] **1–031**

---

[160] April 2009, Defra website.

[161] "Budget 2009", para.4.28; Defra, "Consultation on the Cave Review of competition and innovation in water markets" (September 2009); OFWAT website ("Market reform").

[162] See below, pp.32–33.

[163] s.35, introducing powers to determine disputes, under, inter alia, ss.105 (adoption of sewers), 106 (right to communicate with public sewers), 107 (right of sewerage undertakers to undertake the making of communications with public sewers), 112 (requirement that proposed drain or sewer be constructed so as to form part of a general system), 113 (power to alter drainage system of premises), 116 (power to close or restrict use of public sewers); see below, pp.116, 121, 125, 141–142, 214–220, 220–22, 237.

[164] Any provision as to costs and expenses is enforceable as if it were a County Court judgment: s.30A(5)(b); in deciding to make any such provision, the WSRA is to have regard to the conduct and means of the parties and any other relevant circumstances: s.30A(7). The WSRA's procedures for determining disputes are subject to "informal supervision" by the Council on Tribunals (*Annual Report of the Council on Tribunals 1991–92* (1992–93 H.C. 316), pp.22–23).

[165] This term does not exclude judicial review: *R. v Medical Appeal Tribunal, ex p. Gilmore* [1957] 1 Q.B. 574.

[166] 1991 Act s.30A, inserted by the Competition and Service (Utilities) Act 1992 s.34, and amended by the 2003 Act s.36(2).

[167] See below, pp.103–106.

(xiii) General functions of the Consumer Council for Water

1–032 The Council must have regard to the interests of consumers.[168] It has the functions of obtaining and keeping under review information about consumer matters and the views of consumers; the provision of advice and information to public authorities, undertakers and other persons whose activities may affect the interest of consumers; the provision of information to consumers; and power to publish information and advice about consumer matters.[169] The WSRA must consult the Council in relation to the exercise of each of its functions, except where the Council has indicated that it does not wish to be consulted or the WSRA considers that it would be clearly inappropriate to consult the Council. Where the WSRA is required by any provision of the 1991 Act to publish a notice or any other document, it must send a copy to the Council.[170] The Council may direct the WSRA and any company holding an appointment as an undertaker or a licensed water supplier to provide it with specified information; if they fail to comply, they may be required to give a notice of reasons, which the Council may, subject to certain restrictions, publish. Conversely, the WSRA, the Secretary of State or the National Assembly may require the Council to provide information to it or him, or, if it fails to comply, a notice of reasons. The Secretary of State may make regulations prescribing descriptions of information that the person to whom a direction is given may refuse to supply, or the circumstances in which such a person may refuse to comply with a direction.[171] The Council must publish statistical information about complaints made by consumers about any matter relating to the activities of sewerage undertakers.[172]

(xiv) Complaints

1–033 Where a complaint which any person has against a relevant undertaker in relation to any matter connected with its functions is referred to the Council by or on behalf of the complainant, the Council must investigate the complaint to determine whether it should make representations to the undertaker. This does not apply to any complaint appearing to the Council to be frivolous or vexatious. If it appears to the Council that the complaint is one the WSRA would be required to

---

[168] 1991 Act s.27C, inserted by the 2003 Act s.43(1). These are defined in the same terms as for the WSRA; above.

[169] 1991 Act ss.27D–27G, inserted by the 2003 Act s.43(1).

[170] 1991 Act ss.30ZA, 30ZB, inserted by the 2003 Act s.43(2).

[171] 1991 Act ss.27H–27K, inserted by the 2003 Act s.44.

[172] 1991 Act s.95B, inserted by the 2003 Act s.45(2).

investigate under section 181,[173] the Council must, instead of investigating, refer it to the WSRA. Where it appears to the Council that the complaint relates to a matter in respect of which a function under ss.18 or 22A[174] is or may be exercisable by any person, the Council must (unless it considers that person already has notice of the matter) refer it to him. Where it appears to the Council that the complaint relates to a matter which does or might constitute an offence, the Council must refer the matter to the National Assembly or the Secretary of State. Where it appears to the Council that the complaint relates to a matter which constitutes a dispute of a kind which can be referred to the WSRA under any provision of the 1991 Act, the Council must, if the complainant consents, refer the matter to the WSRA. The Council need not investigate a matter if it appears to it that it is unlikely that the complaint could be resolved by action taken by the undertaker, or the undertaker has not been given a reasonable opportunity to deal with it, or (in cases relating to ss.18 or 22A, or a possible criminal offence) it would be inappropriate to do so.

After investigating a complaint, the Council may make a report to the WSRA, the Secretary of State or the National Assembly. Where a representation is made to the WSRA, the Secretary of State or the Assembly, appearing to be or to amount to a complaint and to have been made by or on behalf of the complainant, it must be referred to the Council.[175]

The Council has a general power to investigate any other matter which appears to it to be a matter relating to the interests of consumers, after consulting the WSRA, the Secretary of State and the National Assembly.[176]

(d) The National Rivers Authority

This body corporate, established by the Water Act 1989 and continued **1–034**
by Pt 1 of the Water Resources Act 1991,[177] was primarily responsible for the standards of quality of water in rivers, streams, coastal and estuarine waters and is also concerned with the prevention of water pollution. The Authority was not therefore concerned with sewerage matters other than the discharge of sewage and trade effluent into

---

[173] See below, pp.110–111.

[174] See above, pp.24–26, 27.

[175] 1991 Act s.29, substituted by the 2003 Act s.46(1); s.30 of the 1991 Act was repealed by the 2003 Act s.46(2).

[176] 1991 Act s.29A, inserted by the 2003 Act s.47.

[177] ss.1–18.

rivers and streams, and in cases of pollution it could institute proceedings where it considered an offence had been committed.

Between 1974 and 1989, the water authorities were responsible for both the operation of the sewerage system and for enforcing the law on water pollution offences. This dual role was ended by the establishment of the Authority, which described itself as "the strongest Environmental Protection Agency in Europe" and a very effective "Guardian of the Water Environment."[178] It adopted an increasingly confrontational approach to its enforcement role.[179] The Authority was merged with other bodies[180] to form the Environmental Agency, with effect from April 1, 1996.[181]

(e) The Environment Agency

1–035 The Environment Agency, established by Pt 1 of and Sch.1 to the Environment Act 1995, is a body corporate and carries out the functions transferred or assigned to it by or under the 1995 Act.[182] These include functions concerning water resources management, the control of pollution of water resources, flood defence, fisheries, navigation, harbour or conservancy authorities, waste regulation, pollution control, radioactive substances and special category effluent. Its principal aim (subject to and in accordance with the provisions of the 1995 Act or any other enactment and taking into account the likely costs) in discharging its functions is so to protect or enhance the environment, taken as a whole, as to make the contribution considered appropriate by ministers towards attaining the objective of achieving sustainable development. Ministers are to give guidance to the Agency with respect to objectives which they consider it appropriate for the Agency to pursue in the discharge of its functions.[183] Its pollution control powers are exercisable for the purpose of preventing, or minimising or remedying or mitigating the effects of, pollution of the environment and it must follow developments in technology and

---

[178] *Annual Report and Accounts 1992–93*, inside front cover.

[179] S. Ball and S. Bell, *Environmental Law*, 2nd edn (London: Routledge, 1994) pp.112–117; W. Howarth, "The Law of the National Rivers Authority and Making Water Polluters Pay: England and Wales" [1994] *Env. Liability* 29.

[180] Waste regulation authorities and Her Majesty's Inspectorate of Pollution.

[181] Environment Act 1995 Pt 1.

[182] See s.2. In Wales, the functions are discharged by the Environment Agency Wales, which is both part of the Corporate Agency for England and Wales and an Assembly Government Sponsored Body (AGSB). The Welsh Assembly Government indicates annually the strategic priorities and targets it wishes the Agency to focus upon (see *http://www.wales.gov.uk* [Accessed July 29, 2010]).

[183] 1995 Act s.4, as amended by the Natural Environment and Rural Communities Act 2006, Sch.11, Pt.1 Para.140.

techniques for this purpose. It may be required to carry out assessments or prepare reports for ministers.[184]

The Agency is under a duty, to such extent as it considers desirable, and without prejudice to its general environmental and recreational duties under s.7, generally to promote:

(a) the conservation and enhancement of the natural beauty and amenity of inland and coastal waters and of land associated with such waters;

(b) the conservation of flora and fauna which are dependent on an aquatic environment; and

(c) the use of such waters and land for recreational purposes.[185]

It is also under a duty to take all such action as it considers necessary or expedient for the purpose of conserving, redistributing or otherwise augmenting, and of securing the proper (including the efficient) use of, water resources in England and Wales.[186]

There are also general environmental and recreational duties: to further (or as regards the exercise of pollution control functions, have regard to) the conservation and enhancement of natural beauty and the conservation of flora, fauna and geological or physiographical features of special interest; to have regard to the desirability of preserving for the public any freedom of access to areas of woodland, mountains, moor, heath, down, cliff or foreshore and other places of natural beauty, and any facility for visiting any building, site or object of archaeological, architectural, engineering or historic interest; and to take such steps as are reasonably practicable and consistent with the purposes of the Agency's statutory functions for securing that the Agency's rights to use water, or to use land used with water, are exercised so as to ensure that it is made available for recreational purposes.[187] The Secretary of State may approve codes of practice with respect to the environmental and recreational duties under ss.6(1), 7 and 8.[188] The Agency is also under a duty to exercise its functions under Pt 4 of

---

[184] 1995 Act s.5, as amended by the Pollution Prevention and Control Act 1999 s.6(1), (2) Sch.2 paras 14, 15 Sch.3.

[185] 1995 Act s.6(1).

[186] 1995 Act s.6(2), as amended by the Water Act 2003 s.72.

[187] 1995 Act s.7.

[188] 1995 Act s.9, as amended by SI 1999/416 art.3(d) Sch.1 para.17(1), (2) and the Natural Environment and Rural Communities Act 2006 Sch.11 Pt 1 para.142. See the Water and Sewerage (Conservation, Access and Recreation) (Code of Practice) Order 2000 (SI 2000/477).

the Water Industry Act 1991 and a series of regulations to secure compliance with the Water Framework Directive.[189]

1–036 The Agency also has general incidental powers and functions,[190] including the protection against pollution of any waters belonging to the Agency or any water undertaker or from which either is authorised to take water, of any reservoir belonging to or operated by the Agency or a water undertaker, and of any underground strata from which either is authorised to abstract water; and carrying out works with or on behalf of water or sewerage undertakers.[191] All the regulatory functions[192] of the Environment Agency are subject (in England) to sections 21 and 22 of the Legislative and Regulatory Reform Act 2006.[193] S.21 provides that any person exercising a specified regulatory function must have regard to the principles that regulatory activities should be carried out in a way which is transparent, accountable, proportionate and consistent, and should be targeted only at cases in which action is needed. S.22 enables a minister of the crown to issue a code of practice.

The Agency must establish Environment Protection Advisory Committees for the different regions of England and Wales.[194] A minister may delegate functions to the Agency.[195] There is a general duty for the Agency to have regard to costs and benefits in exercising powers, unless and to the extent that it is unreasonable for it to do so in view of the nature or purpose of the power or in the circumstances of the particular case.[196] The Secretary of State or National Assembly may give directions, including such directions as are considered appropriate for the implementation of international obligations.[197]

The Agency may make schemes imposing charges and has a general incidental power to impose charges.[198]

---

[189] Water Environment (Water Framework Directive) (England and Wales) Regulations 2003 (SI 2003/3242) reg.3 and Sch.2.

[190] 1995 Act s.37(1).

[191] 1995 Act s.10(1)–(3).

[192] Defined in the 2006 Act s.32(2). It does not include any function of conducting civil or criminal proceedings.

[193] Legislative and Regulatory Reform (Regulatory Functions) Order (SI 2007/3544) art.2 and Sch., as amended by SI 2009/2981.

[194] 1995 Act s.12 and Sch.3. There are also regional and local fisheries advisory committees (s.13) and regional and local flood defence committees (ss.14–19 Sch.5), as amended by the Water Act 2003 ss.66 and 67.

[195] 1995 Act s.38.

[196] 1995 Act s.39.

[197] 1995 Act s.40.

[198] 1991 Act ss.41–43.

(f) Sewerage undertakers

There are now 10 companies appointed as sewerage undertakers, originally under the 1989 Act, and operating under the regime of the Companies Acts.[199] The previous water authorities were described as: **1–037**

> "a publicly owned utility acting as monopoly supplier of a necessary commodity, enjoying certain statutory powers and subject to certain obligations, but . . . not acting as an instrument or agent of government."[200]

These remarks would apply a fortiori to the successor undertakers. An undertaker is, however, a state authority against which EC directives are capable of direct enforcement.[201]

The assets, including public sewers and sewage pumping stations, functions and liabilities of the former water authorities in respect of sewerage were transferred to the ten "successor companies"[202] on September 1, 1989 (the "Transfer Date") under s.4 of the 1989 Act and the Water Authorities (Transfer of Functions) (Appointed Day) Order 1989,[203] under schemes made by the authorities with the approval of the Secretary of State. The Secretary of State also nominated a "holding company" for each "successor company".[204] Shares in the holding companies were initially all owned by H.M. Treasury, but were offered for sale to the public upon terms set out in a Prospectus and Memorandum of Association prepared for each company under the terms of the 1989 Act and in compliance with the Companies Acts on November 1, 1989. In the case of each holding

---

[199] Anglian Water Services Ltd; Dwr Cymru Cfyngedig (Welsh Water); Northumbrian Water Ltd; Severn Trent Water Ltd; Southern Water Services Ltd; South West Water Ltd; Thames Water Utilities Ltd; United Utilities Water plc; Wessex Water Services Ltd; Yorkshire Water Services Ltd. On the political background to privatisation, see D. Kinnersley, *Coming Clean: The Politics of Water and the Environment* (London: Penguin Books, 1994), Chs 4–6.

[200] Per Bingham M.R. in *A.B. v South West Water Services Ltd* [1993] Q.B. 507, 532. The authority was accordingly not within one of the categories of cases where exemplary damages can be awarded, viz. "oppressive, arbitrary or unconstitutional action by the servants of the government" (per Lord Devlin in *Rookes v Barnard* [1964] A.C.1129, 1226).

[201] *Griffin v South West Water Services Ltd* [1995] I.R.L.R.15.

[202] Specified by the Water Authorities (Successor Companies) Order 1989 (SI 1989/1465).

[203] SI 1989/1530. The sewerage undertakers inherited the liability of the predecessor water authorities: see *Dear v Thames Water Co and Others* (1993) 33 Con. L.R. 43. As to the initial financial arrangements, see the Water Act 1989 ss.84–96.

[204] Water Act 1989 s.83(1); the Water Reorganisation (Holding Companies of Successor Companies) Order 1989 (SI 1989/1531). These companies are plcs.

company, a target investment limit for the remaining government shareholding was specified by the Secretary of State, and was not to exceed 0.5 per cent of the ordinary voting rights.[205] In most areas the same company was appointed to be both water and sewerage undertaker in succession to a former water authority. This was not the case, however, where statutory water companies existing prior to the passing of the 1989 Act continued in existence.

1–038 The initial appointments have been for 25 years.[206] The structure of separate "holding companies" and "appointed companies" enables the former to diversify.[207] Only the latter are subject to the regulatory regime enshrined in the 1991 Act. However, the business as undertaker must be kept at arm's length from the other activities of the group.[208] The special "golden" shares in each holding company held by the Secretary of State for the Environment were redeemed on December 31, 1994, opening the way for mergers and takeovers to occur among the companies.[209]

The general duties of the sewerage undertakers are specified by s.94 of the Water Industry Act 1991, under which they must provide and maintain sewers adequate for the drainage of their area and they must properly dispose of the contents of the sewers, and also similarly receive and dispose of trade effluent in accordance with the terms of Ch.3 of Pt 4 of the 1991 Act. When exercising their functions, they must observe the requirements of ss.3 and 4 in preserving and enhancing the natural environment and means for public recreation and access.

Under s.95 of the 1991 Act, performance standards for the provision of sewerage services may be specified by the Secretary of State.

1–039 The matters that may be contained in regulations made by the Secretary of State include:

---

[205] See the 1989 Act s.89, and the Water (Target Investment Limit) Order 1990 (SI 1990/1083).

[206] The notice period required for termination of an appointment as a sewerage undertaker (Licence Condition) was modified from 10 years to 25 years in order to provide greater regulatory stability: OFWAT, Letter to Managing Directors, MD 182, October 15, 2002.

[207] See OFWAT Information Note No.9, *Diversification by Water Companies* (January 1992, Revised September 2001).

[208] Guidelines on "transfer pricing" (i.e. the prices paid by the appointed business to the non-appointed business and associates) were issued by the Director in 1994. These prevent cross-subsidisation: see "OFWAT Annual Report 1993" (1993–94 H.C.416), p.10, and s.2 of the 1991 Act (above, pp. 21–23). The guidelines were revised in 2000 and 2005 (*Regulatory Accounting Guidance 5.04—Guideline for Transfer Pricing in the Water Industry*).

[209] "OFWAT Annual Report 1994" (1994–95 H.C. 431), p.52. Changes of ownership between 1996 and 2003 are set out in OFWAT, DEFRA, "The development of the water industry in England and Wales" (2006), p.104.

(a) provision for contraventions of prescribed requirements to be treated as breaches of the duty under s.94;

(b) prescription of such standards of performance in connection with the provision of sewerage services as, in his opinion, ought to be achieved in individual cases;[210] and

(c) provision that a sewerage undertaker which fails to meet a prescribed standard shall pay a prescribed amount to any person affected who is of a prescribed description.[211]

The procedure for making regulations is set out in s.96 of the 1991 Act.[212] The Secretary of State has made the Water Supply and Sewerage Services (Customer Service Standards) Regulations 2008,[213] setting standards as to keeping appointments; complaints, account queries and requests about payment arrangements; flooding from sewers; the timing and means of payment to customers; and giving notice to customers of their rights. In some cases, provision is made for specified payments for customers if standards are not met, without affecting other legal liabilities. In the case of flooding from sewers that enters a customer's building, the undertaker must for each incident remit sewerage charges for the year or pay £1,000 (whichever is the lesser), with a minimum payment of £150. This obligation does not arise where the entry of effluent is caused by exceptional weather, industrial action by the undertaker's employees, an action of the customer, or any defect, inadequacy or blockage in his drains or sewers; or the undertaker could not

---

[210] Regulations under this head may include a requirement for an undertaker to inform a person of his rights under the regulations; provide for any dispute to be referred by either party to the WSRA; provide for the procedure for the reference and the enforceability of the WSRA's determination; and prescribe circumstances in which a sewerage undertaker is to be exempted from requirements of the regulations: 1991 Act s.95(4). Where the WSRA determines any dispute in accordance with the regulations it must give its reasons: s.95(5), inserted by the Competition and Service (Utilities) Act 1992 Sch.1 para.24, and amended by the Water Act 2003 s.36(2).

[211] 1991 Act s.95(1)–(3).

[212] As amended by the Competition and Services (Utilities) Act 1992 s.30 and Sch.2, para.25 and the Water Act 2003 ss.36(2) and 42. Regulations may be made on the application of the WSRA, which must first commission research to discover the views of persons likely to be affected and serve copies of the application on affected undertakers, persons or bodies likely to represent persons likely to be affected, the Consumer Council for Water and such other persons or bodies as the Secretary of State may consider appropriate. Regulations may be made other than on such an application only if the Secretary of State considers that they will contribute towards the attainment of policies relating to public health or the environment, or for other exceptional reasons; a similar process must be followed.

[213] SI 2008/594 (revoking SI 1989/1159, as amended).

practicably have identified the customer as having been affected and a claim is not made within three months. In the case of flooding from sewers that enters a customer's land or property, but not a building, similar obligations arise, except that the payment is 50 per cent of the sewerage charges for the year or £500 (whichever is the lesser) with a minimum of £75, and a payment need not be made if the customer was not materially affected. Effluent is not taken to have entered a building or land while in a drain or sewer. Any disputes as to the right to a payment may be referred by either party to the WSRA.

Sewerage undertakers are expressly empowered by s.142 of the Act to make charges for their services, without statutory restrictions on any amounts. However, the amounts are subject to close regulation by the Director under the Conditions of Appointment of each undertaker.[214] Initial charging limits were set by the Secretary of State for 10 years from 1989. Price increases thereafter are controlled by a percentage formula RPI + K, where "RPI" is the rate of inflation in November prior to the beginning of the charging year in April and "K" is the individual price limit set for each company for each year, "reflecting what each company needs to charge in order to finance the provision of its services and meet its obligations". K can itself be negative. OFWAT's 2002–2003 Annual Report refers to the formula as "RPI-X", a "price cap that limits changes in overall prices to inflation (RPI) plus or minus a factor determined by the regulator".[215] A "Periodic Review" of charging limits took place in 1994, with new limits effective from April 1, 1995.[216] Further Periodic Reviews took place in 1999,[217]

---

[214] See DoE, Welsh Office, *Instruments of Appointment of the Water and Sewerage Undertakers* (HMSO, 1989), and Conditions B (Charges), C (Infrastructure Charges), and D (Charges Schemes).

[215] p.4; OFWAT Information Note No.3, "Water and sewerage bills—how they are controlled" (July 1995, Revised September 2001). See also Note No.8 on "Price limits—what they are and how can they be changed?" (October 1991, Revised June 2002).

[216] Such a review was mandatory after 10 years but could be held after five at the option of the Director or the appointees (on this occasion, the Director). See OFWAT Information Note No.17, "1994 Review of water charging limits—the periodic review" (February 1993, Revised January 1996). The outcome of the Periodic Review was set out in OFWAT, "Future Charges for Water and Sewerage Services" (1994). Two water companies objected, but on a reference, the Monopolies and Mergers Commission came to an almost identical conclusion: OFWAT News Release PN 19/95, July 28, 1995. On the Periodic Review, see D. Legge, (1994) *Utilities Law Review* 85 and (1994) *Utilities Law Review* 115. See also below, pp.133–140.

[217] OFWAT, "Final determinations. Future water and sewerage charges 2000–05". A £9bn programme of environmental improvement was agreed.

2004[218] and 2009.[219] the Licence Conditions having been modified to provide for five years between such Reviews.[220] Infrastructure charges levied on new properties connected for sewerage services are not controlled under this formula but under separate limits; these are also considered in the Periodic Reviews. Provision is made in Condition B of undertakers' licences for interim determinations of the price limits for individual companies. This may be at the instigation of OFWAT or at the request of the company, and must be either in response to "relevant changes of circumstances"[221] or "notified items".[222] If a company is unhappy with the price limit set on a Periodic Review or an interim determination, it can require a reference to the Competition Commission.[223]

Each sewerage undertaker must establish a procedure for dealing with complaints by customers or potential customers, after consulting the appropriate regional committee, and with the approval of the WSRA. The WSRA may direct an undertaker to review or modify its procedure. The undertaker's duty to establish a procedure or to comply with a direction is enforceable under s.18 of the 1991 Act.[224] **1–040**

---

[218] OFWAT, "Future water and sewerage charges 2005–10. Final determinations" (December 2004). Key features were price limits of 4.2% a year on average (before inflation) and a £16.8bn capital programme for further environmental and service improvements (including tighter standards at over 1,000 sewage treatment plants and improvement of over 2,000 overflows and £1bn for safeguarding homes against the risk of sewer flooding). No companies appealed to the Competition Commission.

[219] OFWAT, "Future water and sewerage charges 2010–15: Final determinations" (November 2009). Key features were price limits of 0.5% a year on average (before inflation) and a £22bn capital programme (including £547m for upgrade to sewage treatment works and £985m to limit pollution from combined sewer overflows, emergency overflows and storm tanks, £1.2bn to reduce the risk and incidence of sewer flooding, and £108m to tackle issues of odour at sewage treatment works. Bristol Water was the only company to appeal.

[220] See OFWAT, Letter to Managing Directors, MD 137, September 1, 1998.

[221] A new or changed legal requirement, including regulations made by the EU or the Secretary of State (RCC 1); variations in the proceeds of land disposals from what was assumed when OFWAT last set price limits (RCC2); failure to achieve outputs for which funding was allowed when OFWAT last set price limits (RCC3); for three companies, changes in the movement in the construction price index relative to RPI from that assumed when OFWAT last set price limits (RCC4).

[222] i.e. areas of uncertainty that could have an impact on companies' turnover, identified by OFWAT; currently, variation in numbers of customers opting for a meter; increases in bad debt and debt collection costs arising from the ban on disconnections; and increased administration costs arising from arrangements for vulnerable customers.

[223] See Information Note No.8, "Price limits—what are they and how can they be changed" (October 1991, revised June 2002).

[224] 1991 Act s.116A, inserted by the Competition and Service (Utilities) Act 1992 s.33, as amended by the Water Act 2003 s.36(2) and Sch.7, para.27(3).

Each undertaker is required by its Conditions of Appointment to produce a Code of Practice for domestic customers, subject to the approval of the WSRA.[225]

A sewerage undertaker is by s.155 of the 1991 Act given powers to acquire compulsorily land required for the purposes of, or in connection with, the carrying out of its functions, but any order made by an undertaker would be subject to confirmation by the Secretary of State, and the usual procedure of the Acquisition of Land Act 1981 would apply.

(g) Infrastructure providers

1–041 Part 2A of the Water Industry Act 1991[226] enables the Secretary of State and Welsh Ministers to make regulations about the provision of infrastructure by a third party for the use of water or sewerage undertakers. The regulations may confer regulatory functions on the WSRA and apply provisions of Pt 2 of the Act with or without modification. The regulations will specify the activities to which they apply[227] and define "infrastructure", and can make provision only in relation to projects or works that in the minister's opinion are of a size or complexity that threatens the undertaker's ability to provide services for its customers. They may enable the minister or the WRSA to specify infrastructure projects that must be put out to tender; specify tender criteria; enable the minister or WRSA to designate as an "infrastructure provider" a person who appears to be wholly or partly responsible for a project put out to tender and confer powers or duties on the provider and relieve the undertaker of duties.

(h) Local authorities

1–042 Sewerage services in this country were traditionally a principal function of local authorities, and those at district level in particular. The principal legislation began with the Public Health Act of 1848 and the major consolidating and reforming Public Health Act of 1875, establishing the former boroughs, urban and rural sanitary districts.

---

[225] Condition 6, "OFWAT Annual Report for 1993" (1993–94 H.C. 416), p.20. They are reviewed every three years unless substantial changes to policy are required earlier: "Understanding Ofwat" (May 2007), p.11.

[226] ss.36A–36G, inserted by the Flood and Water Management Act 2010 s.35.

[227] These can include designing, constructing, owning and operating infrastructure to be used by undertakers ("it would include complex, novel or exceptionally large-scale construction projects that may expose customers to new financial risks": Explanatory Note).

These were followed by the county boroughs, non-county boroughs and urban and rural districts of the Local Government Acts of 1888, 1894 and 1933. Their sewerage services were reformed by the Public Health Act 1936, but were transferred in 1974 to the water authorities,[228] which were, in their turn, succeeded by the appointed companies under the privatisation statute of 1989. However, many powers in relation to the drainage of individual premises have been left with the modern district councils (metropolitan and non-metropolitan), the London boroughs and, from April 1, 1996, the county or county borough councils in Wales. In England, collection of waste is also the responsibility of the district councils, but the controls over the disposal of waste and the licensing of waste disposal sites are the concern of county councils.

The prevention of river pollution was formerly a district council function, but this is now the principal concern of the Environment Agency, which is responsible for monitoring the discharge of sewage and trade effluent into rivers and streams. The principal statute concerning river pollution was formerly the Control of Pollution Act 1974, but most of the relevant provisions of the 1974 Act were replaced by the Water Act 1989,[229] now Pt 3 of the Water Resources Act 1991.[230]

The prevention of nuisances, requirements for adequate drainage for individual premises of various kinds, the maintenance and cleansing of sanitary conveniences, the cleansing of stopped up, etc. drains and other detailed provisions of a similar kind remain the responsibility of district councils and London boroughs, virtually unaffected by the 1989 Act. They may also act as agents for sewerage undertakers,[231] although the latter remain statutorily responsible for the discharge of the relevant functions.[232]

---

[228] The transfer of property, rights and liabilities was effected by the Local Authorities (England) (Property etc.) Order 1973 (SI 1973/1861) arts 8, 9, 18, as amended by SI 1974/406, and the Local Authorities (Wales) (Property etc.) Order 1973 (SI 1973/1863) arts 8, 9, 18, as amended by SI 1974/404. See the *Local Government Reorganisation in England, Transfer of Property—Memorandum* (HMSO, 1973) and *Supplementary Memorandum* (HMSO, 1974), and DoE Circular 100/73, *Water Act 1973: Water Authorities and Local Authorities.*

[229] See in particular ss.103–124.

[230] ss.82–104.

[231] See below, pp.140–141.

[232] *King v Harrow LBC* [1994] E.G.C.S. 76; *R. v Yorkshire Water Services Ltd, The Times*, July 19, 1994 (undertaker fined total of £15,000 for two pollution incidents deemed to have been caused by it, although day-to-day operations were entrusted to an agent local authority).

(i) The Ombudsmen

1–043 Under the Parliamentary Commissioner for Administration Act 1967, complaints of maladministration causing injustice by any officer in central government departments can be referred to the Commissioner (popularly known as the Ombudsman). He may then investigate the complaint and issue a report suggesting remedial action to be taken should he find the complaint well-founded. The complaint may be made by a member of the public, but must be directed through a Member of Parliament.

Similarly, complaints of maladministration causing injustice by a member of the public against a local authority may be made to one of the Local Commissioners for Administration under the Local Government Act 1974, whereupon similar action may be taken.

The Environment Agency,[233] the WSRA and the Consumer Council for Water are subject to the jurisdiction of the Parliamentary Commissioner. The successor sewerage companies have, however, not been made subject to his jurisdiction. The Consumer Council for Water performs in general the functions of an ombudsman in relation to water and sewerage services under the Water Industry Act 1991, although the way it handles complaints is subject to review by the Parliamentary Commissioner.

THE URBAN WASTE WATER TREATMENT (ENGLAND AND WALES) REGULATIONS 1994

1–044 It is convenient at this point to introduce the Urban Waste Water Treatment (England and Wales) Regulations 1994,[234] which implement the Urban Waste Water Treatment Directive.[235] These regulations

---

[233] Except in relation to its flood defence functions, which fall under the jurisdiction of the Local Government Ombudsman or the Public Services Ombudsman for Wales: Parliamentary Commissioner Act 1967 Sch.2, as substituted by SI 2010/239, Sch.; Local Government Act 1974, substituted by the Environment Act 1995 Sch.22 para.18.

[234] SI 1994/2841.

[235] Dir.91/271, as amended by Commission Directive 98/15 of February 27, 1998 (substituting a new Table 2 of Annex I to the Directive). The Directive was amended by Regulation 1137/2008 enabling the Commission to amend specified requirements of sections A, B and (of Annex I) (being "non-essential elements") in accordance with the regulatory procedure with scrutiny in Article 5a of Decision 1999/468. On the background to the Directive, see the 10th Report of the House of Lords Select Committee on the Environment, *Municipal Waste Water Treatment* (1990–91 H.L. 50), and A.W. Gurwitz, "Municipal Waste Water and Sewage Sludge Management in the EC" (1991) XIV (2) *Boston College International & Comparative Law Review* 403. On the Regulations, see *ENDS Report* 240, January 1995, p.40.

introduce new standards to be met at specified times in the collection, treatment and disposal of urban waste water. They constitute a new body of law, using terms many of which are not the familiar expressions used hitherto in this area, which supplement the existing structure by imposing new duties on (as appropriate) the Secretary of State, the WSRA, the Environment Agency and the sewerage undertakers.

Key matters regulated include "collecting systems" for "urban waste water" and the treatment of discharges of urban waste water into receiving waters. The latter requirements vary when the waters are a "sensitive area" or a "high natural dispersion area", and according to the "population equivalent" of the "agglomeration" from which discharges take place. Special rules apply to discharges of "industrial waste water". The detailed rules will be considered at the appropriate point in this book. A table summarising the implementation requirements is reproduced in the Appendix. The main definitions are set out here.

(a) Collecting system

A "collecting system" is a "system of conduits which collects and conducts urban waste water".[236] It will be noted that no distinction is drawn here between sewers and drains. **1–045**

(b) Waste water[237]

"Urban waste water" means "domestic waste water or the mixture of domestic waste water with industrial waste water and/or run-off rain water". **1–046**

"Domestic waste water" means "waste water from residential settlements and services which originates predominantly from the human metabolism and from household activities".

"Industrial waste water" means "any waste water which is discharged from premises used for carrying on any trade or industry,[238] other than domestic waste water and run-off rain water".

(c) Sensitive areas and high natural dispersion areas[239]

These areas are to be identified by the Secretary of State according to criteria set out in, respectively, Pt I and Pt II of Sch.1 to the **1–047**

---

[236] SI 1994/2841 reg.2(1).
[237] SI 1994/2841 reg.2(1).
[238] These terms are not defined.
[239] SI 1994/2841 reg.3, as amended by SI 2003/1788 reg.4.

Regulations. The identification is to be reviewed by the Secretary of State or the National Assembly for Wales no later than December 31, 1997, and thereafter at intervals of no more than four years. Where the Secretary of State (or National Assembly) decides, on a review, that any area identified as a sensitive area or as a high natural dispersion area should no longer be identified as such, or vice versa, he must give notice in writing to the Environment Agency informing it of the decision and the date on which it takes effect. He must also publish the notice, ensure that revised maps are deposited with the Agency and take such other steps as he considers appropriate to publicise his decision.[240] The Secretary of State (or National Assembly) and the Agency must each ensure that their website makes available to the public maps of all areas of water currently identified as sensitive areas or high natural dispersion areas, and the dates on which any area of water was so identified or ceased to be so identified. The Agency must also keep such maps and information available for public inspection.[241]

A body of water must be identified as a "sensitive area" if it is in one of three groups:

(a) natural freshwater lakes, other freshwater bodies, estuaries[242] and coastal waters[243] which are found to be eutrophic[244] or

---

[240] Urban Waste Water Treatment (England and Wales) (Amendment) Regulations 2003 (SI 2003/1788) reg.2.

[241] SI 2003/1788 reg.3.

[242] i.e. "the transitional area at the mouth of a river between fresh-water and coastal waters, the outer (seaward) limits of which are shown on maps kept in accordance with Regulation 12": reg.2(1). In *R. v Secretary of State for the Environment, ex p. Kingston-upon-Hull City Council; R. v Secretary of State for the Environment, ex p. Bristol City Council* [1996] Env. L.R. 248, decisions of the Secretary of State in setting estuary boundaries (which affected the level of treatment required) were quashed as he had taken into account an irrelevant consideration, the potential cost of treatment.

[243] i.e. "the waters outside the low-water line or the outer limit of an estuary": reg.2(1).

[244] "Eutrophication" means "the enrichment of water by nutrients, especially compounds of nitrogen and/or phosphorus, causing an accelerated growth of algae and higher forms of plant life to produce an undesirable disturbance to the balance of organisms present in the water and to the quality of the water concerned." Part I also specifies elements that "might be taken into account when considering which nutrients should be reduced by further treatment". The term "eutrophication" must be interpreted in the light of the directive's objective, which goes beyond the mere protection of aquatic ecosystems and seeks to conserve man, fauna, flora, soil, water, air and landscapes: *Commission v France* (C-280/02) [2004] E.C.R. I-8573 at [13]–[17]; there must be a relationship of cause and effect between the enrichment by nutrients and the accelerated growth of algae, and between that growth and the undesirable disturbance to the balance of organisms: *Commission v France* at [19]; Member States are only required to identify the areas where discharges contribute significantly to eutrophication or the

which in the near future may become eutrophic if protective action is not taken;

(b) surface freshwaters intended for the abstraction of drinking water which could contain more than the concentration of nitrate laid down in the Drinking Water Directive[245] if action is not taken;

(c) areas where further treatment other than secondary[246] or equivalent treatment is necessary to fulfil Council Directives.[247]

A "marine water body or area" can be identified as a high natural dispersion area "if the discharge of waste water does not adversely affect the environment as a result of morphology, hydrology or specific hydraulic conditions which exist in that area". However, the Secretary of State must take into account the risk that discharged load may be transferred to adjacent areas where it can cause detrimental environmental effects, and must recognise the presence of sensitive areas outside England and Wales. Elements to be taken into consideration are:

> "open bays, estuaries and other coastal waters with a good water exchange and not subject to eutrophication or oxygen depletion or which are considered unlikely to become eutrophic or to develop oxygen depletion due to the discharge of urban waste water."[248]

By 2008, the Secretary of State had designated 367 sensitive areas in England, comprising 132 waters which suffer from eutrophication, eight drinking water supplies with excess nitrate levels, 180 seaside waters where disinfective treatment was needed to protect the health

---

risk of eutrophication: *Commission v France* at [25]. Demonstrating an increase in algae does not necessarily establish an undesirable disturbance to the balance of organisms: *Commission v UK* (C-390/07) [2009] All E.R.(D) 224 (Dec) (where the ECJ rejected most complaints that the UK had in breach of its obligations failed to identify specified areas as sensitive areas).

245 Dir.75/440, concerning the quality required of surface water intended for the abstraction of drinking water in the Member States, as amended by Dir.79/869.

246 i.e. "treatment of urban waste water by a process generally involving biological treatment with a secondary settlement or other process in which the requirements established in Table 1 in Sch. 3 are respected": reg.2(1).

247 Sch.1 Pt I.

248 Sch.1 Pt I.

of bathers, and 47 shellfish waters where such treatment was needed to protect them.[249]

(d) Population equivalent

1–048 This is a:

> "measurement of organic biodegradable load, and a population equivalent of 1 (1 p.e.) is the organic biodegradable load having a five-day biochemical oxygen demand (BOD 5) of 60g of oxygen per day (the load shall be calculated on the basis of the maximum average weekly load entering the treatment plant during the year, excluding unusual situations such as those due to heavy rain)."[250]

(e) Agglomeration

1–049 This means:

> "an area where the population and/or economic activities are sufficiently concentrated for urban waste water to be collected and conducted to an urban waste water treatment plant or to a final discharge point."[251]

Provision is also made in the Regulations for samples and records, and the deposit of maps and certificates with the Environment Agency.[252] The Agency must monitor or procure the monitoring by a competent authority or appropriate body:

(a) of discharges from urban waste water treatment plants to verify compliance with Sch.3 of the Regulations[253];

---

[249] See *http://www.defra.gov.uk* [Accessed July 30, 2010]. The seaside waters are also identified under the Bathing Water Directive and the shellfish waters under the Shellfish Waters Directive: see p.171. The Directive term for "high natural dispersion areas" is "less sensitive areas". 85 such areas were originally identified across the UK (see *ENDS Report 232*, May 1994, pp.35–36); most were revoked in 1998 and the remainder by July 2002, following the government's decision to require secondary treatment for all coastal waters (see DEFRA, *Raising the Quality*, September 23, 1998, paras 50–52).
[250] reg.2(1).
[251] reg.2(1).
[252] regs 10, 12, as amended by SI 2003/1788 reg.4(3) and SI 2010/675 Sch.26 Pt 2 para.10(5).
[253] See below, pp.157–158.

(b) of amounts and composition of sludges disposed of to surface waters (other than by dumping from ships);

(c) of waters subject to discharges from such plants provided under Reg.5[254] in cases where it can be expected that the receiving environment will be significantly affected;

(d) to verify that specified discharges and the disposal of sludge to surface waters (other than by dumping from ships) do not adversely affect the environment.[255]

The Secretary of State must every two years publish a situation report on the disposal of urban waste water and sludge in England and Wales, and provide information to the Commission on a programme for the implementation of the Directive.[256]

---

[254] See below, pp.157–158.

[255] reg.11(1). Dumping from ships is to be monitored by the licensing authority under s.24 of the Food and Environmental Protection Act 1985. Such dumping was to be phased out by December 31, 1998: reg.9.

[256] reg.13. A report on the UK implementation programme was sent to the European Commission in November 1994: *This Common Inheritance: U.K. Annual Report 1995* (Cm. 2822, 1995), p.53. The UK has published two reports on implementation of the Directive, as required by art.16, March 1996, updated March 2002: see *http://www.defra.gov.uk* [Accessed July 30, 2010] ("Urban Waste Water Treatment"). The Commission maintains a summary of implementation measures on its website (http://europa.eu [Accessed July 30, 2010]). The UK had not made a timely report in time for the Commission's 5th Implementation Report (2009). The ECJ has declared the UK to be in breach of Art.4(1) and (3) of the Directive by failing to take the measures necessary to ensure that adequate treatment was provided in respect of Brighton, Broadstairs, Lerwick, Margate and a number of locations in Northern Ireland: *Commission v UK* (405/05) [2007] E.C.R. I-10.

Chapter 2

OWNERSHIP OF SEWERS

INTRODUCTORY

2–001 Whether a particular sewer belongs to a private individual or to a sewerage undertaker is a matter of importance in view of the positive duty laid upon sewerage undertakers in respect of sewers owned by them by s.94 of the Water Industry Act 1991, inter alia,

> "so to cleanse and maintain those sewers as to ensure that [its] . . . area is . . . effectually drained; and . . . to make provision for the emptying of those sewers and . . . for effectually dealing . . . with the contents of their sewers."

This duty applies generally only to sewers vested in a sewerage undertaker, i.e. to "public sewers". Owners of private sewers have certain common law and statutory liabilities in respect of them, from which they will however be freed if they can repudiate ownership. A sewerage undertaker is under a general duty to provide a public sewer for the domestic drainage of premises in its area where a notice to that effect is served upon it by an owner, occupier or local authority affected and the premises either have buildings upon them or will have when projects in hand are completed.[1] When meeting such a sewer requisition, the sewerage undertaker may require financial undertakings and guarantees.[2]

The question of ownership falls to be considered under two principal headings: first, the circumstances in which a sewer vests in a sewerage undertaker (such a sewer being known[3] and hereinafter described as a "public sewer") and, secondly, the principles according to which the ownership of private sewers is determined.

PUBLIC SEWERS: THE PRESENT POSITION

2–002 According to s.219(1) of the 1991 Act,[4] "public sewer" means (subject to s.106(1A)[5]),

---

[1] Water Industry Act 1991 s.98, as amended by the Government of Wales Act 1998 Sch.18 Pt IV.

[2] Water Industry Act 1991 s.99. See below, pp.86–87.

[3] Water Industry Act 1991 s.219(1).

[4] As amended by the Water Act 2003 s.99(6).

[5] See below, p.217.

> "a sewer for the time being vested in a sewerage undertaker in its capacity as such, whether vested in that undertaker by virtue of a scheme under Sch. 2 to the Water Act 1989 or Sch. 2 to this Act or under section 179 above or otherwise. . . ."

The apparent simplicity of this definition, however, masks issues of considerable complexity. The position as regards a *new* sewer is reasonably straightforward. This vests in the sewerage undertaker if:

(i) it is a sewer, lateral drain or disposal main laid by the undertaker itself in exercise of a power conferred by Pt 6 of the Water Industry Act 1991[6] or otherwise[7];

(ii) it is a sewer, lateral drain or sewage disposal works in respect of which a declaration of vesting is made by the undertaker under Ch.2 of Pt 4 of the 1991 Act[8]; or

(iii) it is laid in the area of the undertaker under Pt 11 of the Highways Act 1980 (making up private streets) and is not a sewer belonging to a road maintained by a highway authority.[9]

Provision is also made by Sch.2 to the 1991 Act for schemes for the transfer of property from a company holding an existing appointment as sewerage undertaker to a new appointee.

However, the position as regards identifying the sewers transferred to sewerage undertakers in 1989 is more complex.

All those sewers which, on September 1, 1989, the "transfer date"[10] **2–003**
for the purposes of the 1989 Act, were vested in one of the former water authorities, vested on that date in the successor company appointed in each case to act as sewerage undertaker. Naturally, the determination of which sewers were so vested will turn upon the interpretation of the legal provisions in force prior to the "transfer date" and these therefore continue to be of relevance.

---

[6] See ss.158 and 159 of the 1991 Act, replacing powers conferred by s.153 and Sch.19 of the Water Act 1989, and below, pp.92–101.

[7] 1991 Act s.179(1), (7), as amended by the Water Act 2003 s.97(7). This is subject to any provision to the contrary contained in an agreement between the relevant undertaker and the person in whom an interest in the pipe or works is or is to be vested: s.179(1A), inserted by the Water Act 2003 Sch.8 para.41.

[8] 1991 Act s.179(2)(a). See Ch.4, below. This provision also applies to lateral drains by virtue of the Water Act 2003 s.97(7), amending the 1991 Act s.179(2)(a) and (7)(b).

[9] 1991 Act s.179(2)(b). See the discussion of the equivalent provision of the Public Health Act 1936, below, p.53–54.

[10] The Water Authorities (Transfer of Functions) (Appointed Day) Order 1989 (SI 1989/1530).

There have in turn been four legislative regimes governing the identification of public sewers. The first was established by the Public Health Act 1875, s.13 of which provided that, subject to some exceptions, all sewers vested in the local authority.[11] The second was established by the Public Health Act 1936, s.20 of which provided that the local authorities continued to be responsible for all sewers constructed prior to October 1, 1937, but that, from that date, only those sewers a local authority constructed or in respect of which the authority made a specific declaration of vesting would vest in that authority.[12] The third was established by the Water Act 1973,[13] which transferred responsibility from local authorities to water authorities with effect from April 1, 1974. The fourth, and current, regime was established by the Water Act 1989,[14] which transferred responsibility from water authorities to sewerage undertakers, with effect from September 1, 1989, the relevant provisions being re-enacted in the Water Industry Act 1991. At each transfer, provision was made in the legislation for the sewers vested in the existing body to pass to its successor, and rules were set out identifying which newly built sewers would vest in the successor body. The latter rules were significantly different as between the 1875 and 1936 Acts, but have followed similar principles since.

PUBLIC SEWERS: SEWERS TRANSFERRED FROM WATER AUTHORITY TO SEWERAGE UNDERTAKER

2–004 The sewers transferred from the water authority to the sewerage undertaker comprised: (a) sewers created after April 1, 1974 that had vested in the water authority by virtue of s.20 of the Public Health Act 1936, as substituted by Sch.8 para.33 of the Water Act 1973; and (b) sewers created before April 1, 1974 that it had inherited from the local authority on that date. These will be considered in turn.

(a) Sewers created between April 1, 1974 and September 1, 1989

2–005 Section 20 of the Public Health Act 1936, substituted by the Water Act 1973,[15] set out three circumstances in which a sewer created on

---

[11] See below, pp.55–60.
[12] See pp.55–66.
[13] See the Public Health Act 1936 s.20, as substituted by the Water Act 1973 Sch.8. See pp.52–55.
[14] Sch.8 and s.153.
[15] Sch.8 para.33.

or after April 1, 1974 would become a "public sewer". These were as follows.

(i) Sewers constructed or acquired by the water authority

The first category was: **2–006**

> "All sewers and disposal works constructed by the water authority at their expense or vested in the authority in pursuance of arrangements under section 15 of the Water Act 1973, or otherwise acquired by the authority."[16]

Accordingly, a sewer became vested in the water authority if it was constructed either by the authority itself or by the local authority[17] acting pursuant to arrangements made under s.15 of the Water Act 1973.[18] The reference to the "acquisition" of a sewer includes all forms of acquisition, as by operation of the maxim *quicquid plantatur solo, solo cedit*.[19]

(ii) Sewers in private streets

The second category was: **2–007**

> "All sewers constructed under [Part 11 of the Highways Act 1980][20] except sewers belonging to a road maintained by the highway authority."[21]

This paragraph refers to the procedure for the making up of private streets at the expense, partial or complete, of the frontagers, under Pt 11 of the Highways Act 1980.[22] These provisions enable the "street works authority"[23] to require a private street to be sewered, levelled,

---

[16] Public Health Act 1936 s.20(1)(a), substituted by the Water Act 1973 Sch.8 para.33.
[17] Usually a district or London borough council or the Common Council of the City of London: Water Act 1973 s.15(10) (as originally enacted); Sch.4A para.9, as substituted by the Water Act 1983 s.6(2).
[18] See s.15(2)(c) of the Water Act 1973 as originally enacted. A new s.15 was substituted by the Water Act 1983 s.6(1): this made no mention of the vesting of sewers constructed by the local authority.
[19] *Royco Homes v Eatonwill Construction Ltd, Three Rivers DC (Third Party)* [1979] Ch. 276.
[20] This replaced, with effect from January 1, 1981, a reference to Pt 9 of the Highways Act 1959 in the version of s.20 originally substituted by the 1973 Act.
[21] Public Health Act 1936 s.20(1)(b), substituted by the Water Act 1973 Sch.8 para.33.
[22] There is now only one such procedure, that under "the code of 1892"; the former procedure by way of "the code of 1875" was abolished by the Local Government Act 1972. See below, pp.153–154.
[23] See below, pp.153 n.47.

paved, metalled, flagged, channelled, made good[24] or lighted to the satisfaction of the authority; any one or more of these operations can be required to be executed at the same time. Once a sewer was constructed under these provisions, it became a public sewer and vested in the water authority. Where the street works authority had expressed itself as satisfied with a particular system of sewering, it could not require the owners of the private street in question to construct a further sewer, should this subsequently become necessary.[25]

Highway drains vest in the highway authority,[26] and consequently the exception in the present paragraph provided that, where the private street works action was confined to the construction of a highway drain or sewer, any sewer so constructed would vest in the highway authority and would not be a "public sewer".

(iii) Declarations of vesting

2–008 The third category was:

> "All sewers and sewage disposal works with respect to which a declaration of vesting under the foregoing provisions of this Act has taken effect."[27]

Section 17 of the Public Health Act 1936 enabled the water authority to adopt any sewer in or serving its area by a declaration of vesting, provided that the sewer's construction had not been completed before October 1, 1937.

(b) Sewers constructed before April 1, 1974

2–009 The three categories just discussed were:

> "In addition to the sewers and sewage disposal works vested in a water authority by virtue of section 254 or 68 of the Local Government Act 1972, as either section applies for the purposes of the Water Act 1973."[28]

---

[24] This particular operation did not appear in the code of 1875; otherwise the two codes were similar.

[25] *Bonella v Twickenham Local Board* (1888) 20 Q.B.D. 63; *Poole Corp v Blake* [1956] 1 Q.B. 206.

[26] See below, Ch.6.

[27] Public Health Act 1936 s.20(1)(c), substituted by the Water Act 1973 Sch.8 para.33.

[28] Public Health Act 1936 s.20(1), as substituted.

Accordingly, sewers vested in local authorities prior to April 1, 1974 were transferred to the water authorities on that date.[29] The determination of what sewers were so vested in local authorities rested upon s.20 of the Public Health Act 1936 *in its original form.*

PUBLIC SEWERS: THE PUBLIC HEALTH ACT 1936 IN ITS ORIGINAL FORM

This had *five* classifications of sewer for the purpose. Two of these were to all intents and purposes identical with the second and third categories of the substituted s.20 discussed above,[30] but the other three are as mentioned here, and therefore all sewers coming within any of these provisions are still public sewers. The three paragraphs of s.20(1) in its original form considered here were as follows: **2–010**

(a) Sewers within the meaning of the Public Health Act 1875 and sewage disposal works which, by virtue of the provisions of that Act, were, immediately prior to October 1, 1937,[31] vested in the local authority

In order to appreciate the effect of this provision, it is necessary to consider the relevant provisions of the Act of 1875, and the effect of the considerable case law arising therefrom, and the meaning of "sewer", as explained in Ch.1, must also be borne in mind. **2–011**

(i) Meaning of "sewer" in 1875 Act

The word "sewer" was defined by s.4 of the 1875 Act to include "sewers and drains of every description, except drains to which the word 'drain' interpreted as aforesaid applies, and except drains vested in or under the control of any authority having the management of **2–012**

---

[29] Water Act 1973 ss.14(2) and 34(1) Sch.6 Pt I paras 4, 5, applying the Local Government Act 1972 ss.254 and 68. See the Local Authorities (England) (Property etc.) Order 1973 (SI 1973/1861) Art.8, as amended by SI 1974/406; and the Local Authorities (Wales) (Property etc.) Order 1973 (SI 1973/1863) Art.8, as amended by SI 1974/404. See *Thames Water Authority v Enfield LBC* (unreported, April 1, 1982) where it was held that land on which there was the empty shell of sewage disposal works did not pass to the water authority as it was neither "sewage disposal works" within art.8(3) of SI 1973/1861, nor property vested in the council for the purpose of functions exercisable for the purposes of sewerage or sewage disposal within art.9(3); and *London Electricity Board v Redbridge LBC* (1985) 84 L.G.R. 146, where it was held that liabilities transferred by art.18(2) included potential liabilities for negligence in the laying of a sewer in 1914 by the local authority's predecessor-in-title.

[30] pp.53–54.

[31] The date of the commencement of the 1936 Act: see s.347(1).

roads and not being a local authority under this Act"; "drain" in turn was defined in the same section to mean[32] "any drain of and used for the drainage of one building only, or premises within the same curtilage, and made merely for the purpose of communicating therefrom with a cesspool or other like receptacle for drainage, or with a sewer into which the drainage of two or more buildings or premises occupied by different persons is conveyed." Speaking generally, therefore, by virtue of these definitions, a sewer was, for the purposes of the 1875 Act, any drain (or "line of pipes," to use a neutral expression), which served more than one building, or premises[33] not within the same curtilage.[34] Even by reducing the provisions to this comparatively simple proposition one does not, however, explain the position fully, for the courts have had to consider the meanings in this connection of the term "building," and of the expression "within the same curtilage".

"Building" and "house" are not here necessarily synonymous, and it has been held to be a question of fact whether two semi-detached houses are a single building,[35] and the court, in a later case,[36] refused to lay down any general rule on the point. "Curtilage" is a legal term of ancient vintage, but none the less does not seem to be capable of very precise definition; in *Harris v Scurfield*,[37] it was said[38] "there is no definition of a curtilage which would include the case of a number of houses separately occupied by different people, simply because

---

[32] *Not* "include", as in the definition of "sewer". Strictly, a definition introduced by the word "includes" is not a definition at all; it leaves the word explained with its "ordinary" or dictionary meaning and adds to that meaning other terms not ordinarily included in the dictionary meaning. "Means", however, has an exclusionary effect—the definition is to be substituted for the word or words in the statute.

[33] In *City of Bradford Metropolitan DC v Yorkshire Water Services* [2001] EWHC Admin 687, the Divisional Court left open the question whether an unadopted street could constitute "premises" for this purpose; the court held that the fact that a pipe used for draining one building was joined by a pipe constructed for the purpose of protecting another building from water from the surface of the highway did not turn it into a sewer from the junction. The decision on a similar point arising in *Wincanton RDC v Parsons* [1905] 2 K.B. 34 was to be explained on this basis.

[34] Whether or not the sewer was laid in private land, if it were so laid, there would be no right to connect thereto, without the consent of the landowner.

[35] Two such houses were held to be a single building for this purpose in *Hedley v Webb* [1901] 2 Ch. 126, but the converse had been held for the purposes of the Lands Clauses Consolidation Act 1845, on slightly different facts, in *Harvie v South Devon Railway Co* (1874) 32 L.T. 1.

[36] *Humphrey v Young* [1903] 1 K.B. 44. In *Birch v Wigan Corp* [1953] 1 Q.B. 136, a single house was held not to be capable of being part of a building for the purposes of the closing order provisions of the Housing Act 1936 but this would not necessarily apply in the present context.

[37] (1904) 68 J.P. 516.

[38] per Alverstone L.C.J. at p.517.

there is a common access and to some extent common accommodation." In one case,[39] two blocks of buildings belonging to the same owner and containing 46 sets of apartments, were separated by a passageway some 20 feet wide, one end of which was open to a public highway. On the particular facts of the method of construction of these buildings, the court held that the two blocks were premises within the same curtilage. On the other hand, an arcade with a number of houses and shops on either side, and roofed over, with gates at either end, was held not to be buildings or premises within the same curtilage for the present purposes.[40] In the Scottish case of *Sinclair-Lockhart's Trustees v Central Land Board*[41] the Court of Session concluded that "the ground which is used for the comfortable enjoyment of a house or other building may be regarded in law as being within the curtilage of that house or building . . ." It may, thus, in general be taken that the "curtilage" of a building is that land used for its normal enjoyment.

The whole question of the meaning of drain for the purposes of the 1875 Act was reconsidered by the House of Lords in *Weaver v Family Housing Association (York) Ltd*.[42] Their Lordships in considering whether a row of eight houses could be regarded as one building, said that all the following matters were relevant, although they were not all to be given equal weight:

- structural unity;
- unit of ownership;
- occupation by separate tenants, without intercommunication;
- existence of a single comprehensive system of drainage;
- separate cold stores;
- separate outside lavatories.

Whilst refusing to interfere with the finding of the court below that **2–013**
these were separate buildings, their Lordships said that it was essentially a question of fact.

In a subsequent case,[43] Walton J. applied the cases discussed above including *Weaver*, and found that two separately occupied cottages,

---

[39] *Pilbrow v St Leonard's Shoreditch Vestry* [1895] 1 Q.B. 433.
[40] *St. Martin's-in-the-Field Vestry v Bird* [1895] 1 Q.B. 428.
[41] (1950) 1 P&CR 195, affirmed (1951) 1 P&CR 320.
[42] (1975) 74 L.G.R. 255.
[43] *Cook v Minion* (1978) 37 P&CR 58.

built onto one another and owned by the same landlord, were a single building, and that the water closets in the garden serving the cottages were within the curtilage of the building. "Curtilage" said his Lordship, was an "enclosure", or "land within an enclosure".

The essential point under this heading, therefore, is that the particular conduit (in order to be a public sewer) should drain two or more buildings (or "premises").[44] The connection of a second building to an existing drain serving one building only, although done illegally and without the consent of the local authority, was nevertheless capable of operating to convert the drain into a public sewer as from the point of junction.[45] On the other hand, if one of the two premises drained by a public sewer was subsequently disconnected therefrom, such an action would not normally operate so as to make the sewer once more a drain.[46]

Moreover, because a particular line of pipes served a number of premises, it did not necessarily follow that that conduit must be a public sewer from end to end.[47] That portion of the conduit which received the drainage of one building only would be a drain,[48] while the remainder could be a public sewer. If the conduit had been constructed by the local authority, or by a private individual with the approval of the local authority,[49] with the intention of it receiving the drainage of more than one building, it would normally be a public sewer, although no buildings might have been actually connected thereto.[50]

---

[44] *Travis v Uttley* [1894] 1 Q.B. 233; *Holland v Lazarus* (1897) 66 L.J.Q.B. 285.

[45] *St Matthew, Bethnal Green, Vestry v London School Board* [1898] A.C. 190, and compare *Holland v Lazarus* (1897) 66 L.J.Q.B. 285. Both these decisions were on the provisions of the Metropolis Management Acts, but there seems to be no reason why the principle therein applied should not apply also to cases under the Public Health Acts.

[46] *St Leonard, Shoreditch, Vestry v Phelan* [1896] 1 Q.B. 533; but see also *Kershaw v Smith* [1913] 2 K.B. 455, in which Avory J. refused to agree with the principle "once a sewer always a sewer", and held that a sewer which by reconstruction had become a drain serving but one building, could be no longer vested in the local authority as a public sewer. Where there was no such reconstruction, however, it was held that a sewer did not cease to be a sewer for the purposes of the 1936 Act just because it was not used as such: *Blackdown Properties Ltd v Minister of Housing and Local Government* [1967] Ch. 115. "Vesting" does not mean complete ownership, but merely the giving of an interest sufficient to enable the local authority to perform its duties; if those duties cease by a change in the factual situation then the vesting comes to an end; see also *Bradford v Eastbourne Corp* [1896] 2 Q.B. 205, and article by J.F. Garner at 20 Conv. N.S. 208.

[47] As was suggested in *Travis v Uttley*, above.

[48] *Beckenham UDC v Wood* (1896) 60 J.P. 490.

[49] *Turner v Handsworth UDC* [1909] 1 Ch. 381.

[50] *Turner v Handsworth UDC* and *Beckenham UDC v Wood*, above.

(ii) "Vesting" under 1875 Act

Having decided that the particular line of pipes in question was a "sewer" within s.4 of the Act of 1875, it is then necessary to consider the effect of s.13 of that Act (now repealed), which read as follows: **2–014**

> "All existing and future sewers within the district of a local authority, together with all buildings, works, materials and things belonging thereto,[51] except—
>
> (1) Sewers made by any person for his own profit, or by any company for the profit of the shareholders; and
> (2) Sewers made and used[52] for the purpose of draining, preserving, or improving land under any local or private Act of Parliament, or for the purpose of irrigating land; and
> (3) Sewers under the authority of any commissioners of sewers appointed by the Crown;
>
> shall vest in and be under the control of such local authority:
>
> Provided that sewers within the district of a local authority which have been or which may hereafter be constructed by or transferred to some other local authority or by or to a sewage board or other authority empowered under any Act of Parliament to construct sewers shall (subject to any agreement to the contrary) vest in and be under the control of the authority who constructed the same, or to whom the same have been transferred."

The second and third[53] exceptions from the general proposition in this section are virtually self-explanatory,[54] and do not normally give rise to difficulties, but the exception of sewers made "by any person for his own profit" has been the subject of considerable judicial interpretation. Whether or not a particular sewer was made for profit is essentially

---

[51] The position of sewage works, etc. is discussed below, Ch.7.

[52] The test here is probably the *primary* use for which the sewer in question was made. Difficulties may arise in practice where a land drain is also used for the conveyance of sewage.

[53] The second exception clearly deals with land drainage; the third deals with sewers that are not normally the concern of the local authority as such (except with the consent of the appropriate government department under e.g. s.327 of the Act of 1875). The proviso to the section does not cause difficulty, this relating to public sewers constructed by a public body for public use.

[54] It is largely a question of fact and degree as to whether a land drain has become a sewer. If the ditch takes a considerable amount of surface water from houses, this may make it a sewer: *Ferrand v Hellas Land & Building Co* [1893] 2 Q.B. 135; but see *R. v Godmanchester L.B.* (1886) L.R. 1 Q.B. 328.

a question of fact.[55] Thus, a sewer constructed by a builder laying out a building estate was still capable of not having been made for profit, although the builder proposed to sell off the houses, when constructed, and make a profit out of the transaction.[56] On the other hand, "profit" in the section does not necessarily mean a direct money payment, and a land drain constructed for the purpose of enabling the land to be used more economically would normally be held to be one made for profit.[57]

To summarise the effect, therefore, of this first class of sewers vested in the local authority under s.20 of the 1936 Act in its original form, it seems that every "line of pipes" which was a "sewer" and was constructed prior to October 1, 1937, for the drainage of more than one building, or for premises not within the same curtilage, and which was not made for profit, vested in the former local authority under the 1875 Act, and would have become vested in the local authority under s.20, subsequently becoming vested in the water authority under s.20 of the 1936 Act in its new form.[58]

(b) All combined drains constructed before October 1, 1937,[59] which, by virtue of the provisions of the 1875 Act, would immediately prior to that date have been vested in the local authority as sewers but for the provisions of some enactment or statutory scheme relating to the construction of combined drains, or of an order made under such an enactment or scheme[60]

2–015 The class of "combined private drains" caused much difficulty in the pre-1936 Act law. The strict application of the terms "sewer" and

---

[55] *Southstrand Estate Development Co v East Preston RDC* [1934] Ch. 254; unfortunately, it is only too often in this branch of the law that one finds that a particular matter is to be treated by the courts as a "question of fact". The result is that every such problem must be considered in relation to all the relevant circumstances, and reference to previously decided cases, except perhaps to indicate which circumstances are likely to be considered relevant, is not of any great assistance.

[56] *Ferrand v Hallas Land & Building Co* [1893] 2 Q.B. 135; *Pinnock v Waterworth* (1887) 3 T.L.R. 563; the fact that the builder intends to reimburse himself for his expenses in constructing the sewer does not affect the position; *Vowles v Colmer* (1895) 64 L.J. Ch. 414, which was followed in *Solihull RDC v Ford* (1932) 30 L.G.R. 483. " 'Made for profit' is not the same thing as 'made for use'," said Huddleston B. in *Bonella v Twickenham Local Board* (1887) 18 Q.B.D. 577.

[57] *Croysdale v Sunbury-on-Thames UDC* [1898] 2 Ch. 515. A sewer constructed for the purpose of draining agricultural land will also normally be held to have been one made for profit and hence not a sewer within the section: *Phillimore v Watford RDC* [1913] 2 Ch. 434, and see *Vare v Joy* (1920) 124 L.T. 148.

[58] Subject to the possible exception of "single private drains", considered under class (b), below.

[59] The date of commencement of the 1936 Act: see s.347(1).

[60] 1936 Act s.20(1)(a), as originally enacted.

"drain" in s.4 of the Public Health Act 1875 and the vesting rules set out in s.13 of that Act[61] meant in principle that, whenever a second house was connected to a drain, the drain from the point of connection would automatically become a sewer vested in the local authority, which would become responsible for its maintenance. A variety of steps could be taken by local authorities to avoid or mitigate that outcome. These included powers to prohibit "combined drains" altogether by requiring new houses to be connected directly to an existing sewer[62]; or, conversely, where it was convenient for two or more houses to be drained in combination, for this to be done by a "combined drain" which was deemed not to be a sewer and responsibility for whose maintenance remained with the houseowners.[63] The 1936 Act provided that a combined drain that would have been a sewer under the 1875 Act had it not been for an enactment or statutory scheme should, by virtue of s.20(1)(a), from October 1, 1937 vest in the local authority as a public sewer. However, provision was made by s.24 of the Act for the local authority to recover the costs of maintenance of these particular pipes from the owner(s) of the premises served by them.[64] Where such pipes were constructed by persons other than the local authority after October 1, 1937, they would now be private sewers unless and until they were adopted by the local authority.

The expression "combined drain" was not defined in the 1875 Act, nor was a definition included in the 1936 Act; it must therefore be construed as a technical term, referring to the common practice of builders and others engaged in the construction of drains. Generally speaking, buildings may be said to be drained in combination where a common line of pipes takes the effluent from the internal drains of the several buildings through private land to a cesspool, cesspit or "other receptacle for drainage", or to a sewer.

---

[61] See p.59.

[62] See the Public Health Act 1875 s.25; *Woodford UDC v Stark* (1902) 66 J.P. 536.

[63] Powers of this nature were found in local Acts and planning schemes under the Housing, Town Planning etc. Act 1909, the Town Planning Act 1925 s.1 and the Town and Country Planning Act 1932: see *Lumley's Public Health*, 11th edn (1937), pp.64–65. Responsibility for maintaining a combined drain could also be assumed by the relevant owner(s) by agreement. A combined drainage agreement is valid and enforceable by the local authority (*Butt v Snow* (1903) 67 J.P. 454) with whom it is made, but only against the original owner, as the stipulations in the agreement will be positive in character and would not, therefore, run with the land as would restrictive covenants (see, e.g. *Haywood v Brunswick Building Society* (1882) 8 Q.B.D. 403). By incorporating such agreements in the local authority's planning scheme under the Town and Country Planning Act 1932, this difficulty of enforceability was overcome.

[64] This power was repealed by the Water Act 1989 Sch.27 Pt I. See the 5th edition of this book at pp.68–71.

It is also necessary to consider the relationship of s.20(1)(a) of the 1936 Act to s.19 of the Public Health Acts Amendment Act 1890. Section 19 was also:

> "aimed at relieving local authorities of the burden of maintaining drains which had become sewers merely because a second house connection had been made, but was so badly drafted that it led to much doubt and litigation."[65]

Indeed, it was the confusion that surrounded the scope of this provision that led to the provisions in private Acts and schemes already discussed that dealt expressly with the status of combined drains, making clear that they were not sewers for the purposes of the 1875 Act.

Section 19 of the 1890 Act[66] read as follows:

2–016 "(1) Where two or more houses belonging to different owners are connected with a public sewer by a single private drain, an application may be made under section 41 of the Act of 1875[67] (relating to complaints as to nuisances from drains), and the local authority may recover any expenses incurred by them in executing any works under the powers conferred on them by that section from the owners of the houses in such shares and proportions as shall be settled by their surveyor or (in case of dispute) by a court of summary jurisdiction.

(2) Such expenses may be recovered summarily or may be declared by the urban authority to be private improvement expenses under the Public Health Acts, and may be recovered accordingly.

(3) For the purposes of this section the expression 'drain' includes a drain used for the drainage of more than one building."

The term "single private drain" in this section was not given a statutory definition, but it received much judicial consideration.[68] Suffice it

---

[65] *Lumley's Public Health*, 11th edn (1937), p.57. "The truth is, that the whole of our sanitary legislation is in a state which I hardly like to characterise in the language that naturally suggests itself": per Wills J. in *Bradford v Eastbourne Corp* [1896] 2 Q.B. 205, 216.

[66] The section had to be adopted by the local authority concerned, this being an adoptive Act; the section was repealed by the 1936 Act.

[67] Under this section the local authority, on complaint made to it of a nuisance in a drain, privy, cesspool, etc., could take certain action to secure the abatement of the nuisance, and if necessary take default action, its expenses in so doing being recoverable from the owner of the premises concerned.

[68] See *Lumley's Public Health*, 11th edn (1937), pp.58–60.

here to summarise the cases by describing the expression as a drainage pipe provided for a single house or for a group of houses in common, which is exclusive and private to that house or those houses.[69] It is important to note that a "single private drain" for the purposes of the 1890 Act, unlike "combined drains" under appropriately worded local legislation and statutory schemes, was not deemed by that Act to be a drain and not a sewer for the purposes of the definitions in s.4 of the 1875 Act. The exact relationship between s.19 of the 1890 Act and ss.4 and 13 of the 1875 Act was accordingly left unclear. One question was whether s.19 applied in the case of sewers that had already become vested in the local authority by virtue of ss.4 and 13 of the 1875 Act, or only prospectively. The Divisional Court in *Bradford v Eastbourne Corp*[70] held that s.19 did apply retrospectively to existing sewers. The court emphasised that this conclusion might have been difficult to reach had "vesting" involved giving absolute property to the local authority, but the concept of "vesting" was in fact more limited.[71] Thus, for example, the authority had no power to stop up a sewer vested in them or physically to disconnect drains therefrom.[72]

Another major uncertainty was whether any pipe that fell within the definition of a "single private drain" was no longer a sewer under the 1875 Act[73]; or whether it retained its status as a sewer, but subject

---

[69] *Kingston-upon-Hull Corp v North Eastern Railway Co* [1916] 1 Ch. 31; the houses had to be in separate ownership for s.19 of the 1890 Act to apply.

[70] [1896] 2 Q.B. 205.

[71] *Att Gen v Dorking Union* (1882) 20 Ch. D. 595: "We must remember that the vesting of the sewers in the local authority gives them a very limited right of ownership": per Jessel M.R. at p.604.

[72] *Ogilvie v Blything Union Rural Sanitary Authority* (1891) 65 L.T. 338; (1892) 67 L.T. 18. "It has been clearly held that the vesting is not a giving of the property of the sewer and in the soil surrounding it to the local authority, but gives such ownership and such rights only as are necessary for the purpose of carrying out the duties of a local authority with regard to the subject matter": per Lord Russell C.J. in *Bradford v Eastbourne Corp* [1896] 2 Q.B. 205 at p.211. In *Newcastle-under-Lyme Corp v Woolstanton Ltd* [1947] 1 All E.R. 218, it was held that a gas undertaking has no natural right of support (apart from statute) for the land surrounding its gas mains, but only an implied right of support for the mains themselves (and see Ch.5 below); it seems that this principle applies equally to public sewers.

[73] An approach encouraged by the contrasting use of the terms "single private drain" and "public sewer" in s.19 itself. A number of judges stated the relevant question was whether a pipe was a single private drain or a sewer: see, e.g. Scrutton L.J. in *Hill v Aldershot Corp* [1933] K.B. 259 at p.263; but this is better regarded as shorthand for the question which statutory regime applied than a concluded view that a single private drain could not also be a sewer. Cf. Scrutton L.J.'s statement in *Hill* at p.267 that the provisions of s.19 "are independent of the definitions of the Act of 1875, and certain 'sewers' under the Act of 1875 are yet repairable by or at the expense of the private owner if they are 'single private drains' as defined by the Act of 1890." See also Wills J. in *Bradford v Eastbourne Corp* [1896] 2 Q.B. 205 at pp.214–215; and Bankes L.J. in *Kingston-upon-Hull Corp v North Eastern Railway* [1916] 1 Ch. 31,38.

to the qualification that the local authority was entitled to exercise its powers under s.19. The latter seemed to be the better view.[74] Accordingly, a "single private drain" serving two houses was in fact a "sewer" for the purposes of the 1875 Act, whether or not s.19 of the 1890 Act applied, vested in the local authority under the 1875 Act and therefore remained vested in the local authority under s.20(1) of the Public Health Act 1936 (class(i)). Any lingering argument that the 1890 Act at least in part divested the property in a sewer that was otherwise vested in the local authority under the 1875 Act would in any event be covered by s.20(1)(a) of the 1936 Act (class (ii)).

2–017 A similar position would appear to arise in connection with the common form provision in many local Acts,[75] in force before the passing of the 1936 Act, by which the effect of the section of the 1890 Act above discussed was made applicable to a "single private drain" serving two or more houses owned by the same person, or by different persons.[76] Such a provision also would not, it is submitted, have affected the vesting of the sewer under the Act of 1875.[77]

Other local Acts may contain different provisions which would be affected by this paragraph[78]; these obviously cannot be dealt with in detail in the present context.

Before leaving the subject of combined drains, it should, perhaps, be mentioned that the term is not here used in the sense sometimes used by engineers and other technicians, namely, to indicate that the particular drain is used for the conveyance of both foul and surface water.

---

[74] In *Pemsel and Wilson v Tucker* [1907] 2 Ch. 191, a "single private drain" within the meaning of s.19 of the Act of 1890 was held none the less to have vested in the local authority as a sewer; the 1890 Act did not operate to prevent this vesting, and the owner of the property concerned therefore could not convey to a purchaser the property in the sewer.

[75] "Enactment" includes any enactment in a provisional order confirmed by Parliament: s.343(1) of the 1936 Act.

[76] See, e.g. s.49 of the Kingston-upon-Hull Corporation Act 1903, considered by the court in *Kingston-upon-Hull v North-Eastern Railway Co.*

[77] See s.49 of the Kingston-upon-Hull Corporation Act 1903.

[78] Under the Metropolis Management Acts, the term "drain" was defined to include "any drain for draining any group or block of houses by a combined operation under the order of any vestry" (see s.250 of the Metropolis Management Act 1855). The Public Health Acts applied to central London only with modifications; cases decided on the statutes relating to London should therefore be read and applied with caution and reserve. A number of local Acts provided that the local authority should be enabled to order the provision of combined drainage; such cases, outside the Metropolis, might have operated prior to the 1936 Act, to prevent such combined drains from vesting in the local authority (see, e.g. s.81 of the Wimbledon Corporation Act 1914, discussed in *Grant v Derwent* [1929] 1 Ch. 390).

(c) Sewers and sewage disposal works[79] constructed by the local authority at their expense or acquired by them

It will be observed that this class of public sewer refers only to sewers **2–018** properly so-called,[80] but includes sewers constructed either prior or subsequent to the commencement of the 1936 Act. Moreover, it would include a sewer constructed by the predecessors in title of the local authority, either as landowner or as sanitary authority, by virtue of the reference to "acquisition". In *Royco Homes Ltd v Eatonwill Construction Ltd*,[81] it was held that a sewer which had been constructed by private individuals which lay under a roadway which subsequently became vested in the local authority, as highway authority, prior to 1974 thereupon became a public sewer, as having been "acquired" by them. Because the soil was acquired, the line of pipes within it was also acquired upon the principle *quicquid plantatur solo, solo cedit.*

The sewer need not have been constructed by the local authority in its capacity of local sanitary authority; it may, for example, have been constructed for the purpose of draining the authority's housing estate, under the Housing Act 1957: in such a case, the proviso in s.20(2)[82] would normally apply, and the sewer did not become a public one until the authority had declared it to be such. No particular formality had to be observed in the making of such a declaration; an ordinary resolution of the authority was probably sufficient. This provision applied also to sewers constructed by a local authority outside their own district, under ss.15 and 16 of the 1936 Act.[83]

The proviso did not appear in the re-enacted version of s.20, but in view of the terms of s.20(1)(a) this is immaterial as the paragraph refers to sewers constructed by the water authority not by the local authority. There was therefore no question of a sewer constructed by the local authority after April 1, 1974 becoming a public sewer, unless and until it was "adopted" by the water authority or arrangements were made under s.15 of the 1973 Act.

A sewer constructed by the local authority, but at the expense of some other person,[84] did not vest in the authority under this provision,

---

[79] 1936 Act s.20(1)(b), as originally enacted.

[80] See above, pp.3–12

[81] [1979] Ch. 276.

[82] A sewer constructed by a local authority after October 1, 1937 for the purpose only of draining property belonging to them was not to be deemed to be a public sewer for the purposes of the Act until it was declared by the authority to be a public sewer.

[83] Now repealed.

[84] e.g. under s.36 of the 1936 Act (see s.36(3)); or by agreement with the owner or occupier of the premises concerned, under s.275.

and (if constructed after the commencement of the Act) remained a private sewer.

PUBLIC SEWERS: EFFECT OF PUBLIC OWNERSHIP

2–019 In summary a "public sewer" under the 1991 Act is broadly any sewer vested in a sewerage undertaker in its capacity as such[85] whether by transfer from the former authorities including the effect of "historical" provisions considered above, or by construction *de novo*. Any other sewer is a private sewer, and will be vested not in a sewerage undertaker, but in some other public or private body or individual.

If a particular conduit is in law a public sewer, it will be vested in the sewerage undertaker, but its ownership thereof will be limited, as above explained[86] to the purposes of fulfilling its functions as undertaker. Further, it will not be able to interfere with private rights enjoyed in respect of the particular conduit before it became a public sewer,[87] nor may it physically disconnect any drains from the public sewer (except under s.113 of the Water Industry Act 1991).[88] However, the following consequences will apply in the event of a conduit being in law a public sewer:

(a) the sewerage undertaker will be under a duty to maintain, cleanse and empty it[89];

(b) provided he has a means of access thereto, an adjoining landowner will have a right to cause the drains of his premises to connect thereto[90];

(c) the sewerage undertaker will not be able to take proceedings (e.g. in nuisance) in respect of any effluent therefrom;

(d) the *local* authority may be able to prevent building over the sewer[91] and the sewerage undertaker will be able to take proceedings if anyone interferes with its property.[92]

Thus, for example, in Diagram 2 in Appendix A[93], the drain, although it serves more than one premises, is *not* a public sewer (whether

---

[85] ss.219(1).
[86] See above, p.63.
[87] See, e.g. *R. v Staines Local Board* (1888) 60 L.T. 261.
[88] *Ogilvie v Blything Union R.S.A.* (1891) 65 L.T. 338.
[89] 1991 Act s.94, below, pp.130–133.
[90] 1991 Act s.106, below, pp.226–231.
[91] See below, pp.142–143.
[92] Below, pp.143–144.
[93] See p.291

constructed before or after October 1, 1937); indeed it is not a sewer at all, as it does not lead to a proper outfall (above, page 9). Therefore, if flooding occurs at the shaded area, the sewerage undertaker would not itself be liable, but the local authority could probably commence nuisance proceedings against the persons responsible, who will presumably be the owners of A, B and C. If there is a highway drain connected at point E, this will not affect the position, as the frontagers would be liable. However, if Lovers' Lane were adopted by the highway authority, and the flooding was shown to be due to the surface water from the highway, that authority would (presumably) be held liable.

Further, if a new house is built on plot D, the owner will have no right to cause his house drains to connect with this existing drain; he would have to negotiate terms with the owners of A, B and C.

LATERAL DRAINS

The Water Act 2003[94] introduces new provision for "lateral drains" to be requisitioned from or adopted by sewerage undertakers. This will ensure that appropriate standards can be applied to their provision and maintenance. **2–020**

The term "lateral drain" means:

"(a) that part of a drain which runs from the curtilage of a building (or buildings or yards within the same curtilage) to the sewer with which the drain communicates or is to communicate; or

(b) (if different and the context so requires) the part of a drain identified in a declaration of vesting made under section 102 above or in an agreement made under section 104 above."[95]

PRIVATE SEWERS AND DRAINS

A sewer which is not a public sewer must be a private sewer, and there is no point, in law, of distinguishing between a private sewer and a drain.[96] "Sewer" will normally be used to describe a conduit **2–021**

---

[94] ss.95–99.

[95] 1991 Act s.219(1): definition inserted by the Water Act 2003 s.97(9).

[96] A drain, *stricto sensu*, cannot be vested in the sewerage undertaker in its capacity as such, although it may, of course, belong to the undertaker in its capacity as landowner, or by virtue of its draining the undertaker's own property. See also definition of "private sewer" in s.343(1) of the 1936 Act and s.219(1) of the 1991 Act. By virtue of ss.95–99 of the Water Act 2003, "lateral drains" may be requisitioned from or adopted by the sewerage undertaker.

draining more than one property, and "drain" will be used to signify a channel draining a single property,[97] but the distinction has no legal significance. The all important question is whether a particular sewer is a *public* sewer.

In practice, however, the subsidiary question may arise, in whom is a particular private sewer or drain vested? If the sewer drains the premises and runs through the land of but a single owner, it is normally clear that such owner is the owner of the sewer; if the sewer is used to drain the property of another person, the legal position (in the absence of any express agreement or provision in the relevant title deeds) will be presumed to be that the owner of the tenement has granted an easement of drainage through his property—provided the requirements for presuming such an easement are present. Thus (apart from an express grant), the right must have continued for the statutory period for prescription of 20 years,[98] the dominant owner must have enjoyed the easement claimed as a benefit for his property of which he is owner in fee simple, the use of the sewer must be claimed "as of right",[99] and the right claimed must be to drain through a well-defined channel.[100]

It is frequently important to decide whether a particular person has an easement to lay a private sewer or drain through another person's land,[101] for if the conduit is there with the permission of the

---

[97] Buildings drained "in combination" are, however, said to be served by a combined "drain".

[98] Prescription Act 1832. User for 20 years may be defeated by evidence proving that no easement had in fact been granted (for all prescription depends on a presumed grant), but user for 40 years is indefeasible, except by proof that the user had originally been by agreement or consent (see s.2 of the Act of 1832). A right to cause sewage to flow across another's land or into a public sewer cannot be acquired secretly without the knowledge of the owner of the servient tenement: *Liverpool Corp v Coghill* [1918] 1 Ch. 307.

[99] The user must therefore have commenced "*nec vi nec clam nec precario*", i.e. permission must not have been obtained by force, or the user must not have commenced secretly and in such circumstances that the owner of the servient tenement could not have been aware of the drain in question, or with the permission of the owner of the servient tenement, as in such last-mentioned case, the right would be limited to the terms of such permission. On these points, see such cases as *Union Lighterage Co v London Graving Dock Co* [1902] 2 Ch. 557, and *Lyell v Hothfield* [1914] 3 K.B. 911.

[100] This proposition follows, it is submitted, from the law relating to the acquisition of rights to watercourses; thus, in *Acton v Blundell* (1843) 12 M. & W. 324, it was held that a landowner could have no rights in water percolating in an undefined channel through his land in such manner as to enable him to prevent an adjoining owner from diverting such water.

[101] The right to lay a drain and to cause drainage to flow through such drain will normally carry with it the ancillary right to enter on the land and effect necessary works of repair, maintenance or renewal to the drain; see *Pomfret v Ricroft* (1669) 1 Saund. 321. It would not, of course, under such a right be competent to increase the size of the drain. In *Simmons v Midford* [1969] 2 Ch. 415, it was held, on the facts of that case, that a grant of an easement of drainage amounted to an exclusive right to use the line of pipes in question.

landowner in such circumstances that an easement has been created, that landowner will not be able to require the removal of the conduit without making payment of compensation to the person entitled to use the drain.[102] However, when taking proceedings for the abatement of a nuisance[103] in a private sewer or drain, or caused thereby, the local authority is not concerned to ascertain whether the persons whose premises are drained by the conduit in question have a legal right to cause their drainage to flow through such conduit[104]; they will be the persons by "whose act, default, or sufferance"[105] the nuisance has arisen or is continuing, and abatement proceedings may, therefore, properly be taken against them.[106] On the other hand, the landowner who stops up a private sewer laid through his land without his consent may be liable in nuisance abatement proceedings brought by the local authority, as he would then be the person who had caused the nuisance.[107] The owner of a private sewer or drain may be liable in private nuisance to another landowner who has sustained injury as a consequence of his failure to cleanse the sewer, etc.[108]

---

102 An easement is a legal interest provided it is created by grant (express, implied or presumed from long use) and limited for an interest equivalent to an estate in fee simple absolute in possession or a term of years absolute: Law of Property Act 1925 s.1(2)(a). If the easement of drainage in question is a legal interest, it will be enforceable against subsequent purchasers of the servient tenement. If it has been limited in such a manner that it is capable of subsisting only as an equitable interest in the land, it will none the less still be enforceable against subsequent owners, provided it is registered as an equitable easement under s.2(5) of the Land Charges Act 1972 (Class D (iii)). Easements granted for drains to serve an estate to be developed subsequent to the time of the grant should be limited so as to take effect within the perpetuity period: *Dunn v Blackdown Properties Ltd.* [1961] 1 Ch. 433. However, in the case of deeds coming into effect after 1964, an easement which is in fact exercised within the perpetuity period will not be invalidated simply because it could have first been exercised after the end of that period; one is now entitled to "wait and see" if there will be a breach of the perpetuity rule: Perpetuities and Accumulations Act 1964 s.3.

103 Under the Environmental Protection Act 1990 Pt 3 or s.59 of the Building Act 1984.

104 *Brown v Bussell* (1868) L.R. 3 Q.B. 251.

105 See s.79(7) of the 1990 Act (definition of "person responsible" for a statutory nuisance).

106 If the drain is really a public sewer vested in the sewerage undertaker, apparently no nuisance proceedings can be taken against a person draining into it, and in respect of whom it might otherwise be said that he was causing a nuisance: *Fordom v Parsons* [1894] 2 Q.B. 780. The judgment of Kennedy J. in *Wincanton RDC v Parsons* [1905] 2 K.B. 34, however, suggests that the fact that the conduit in question was a public sewer would not necessarily constitute a defence in nuisance proceedings. It is submitted that this decision, in so far as this point is concerned, would not be followed (see *Lumley's Public Health*, 12th edn, Vol. III, p.2278).

107 *Riddell v Spear* (1879) 43 J.P. 317; but it should be noted that in this case the sewer in question had become a public sewer before the action complained of was taken.

108 *Sedleigh-Denfield v O'Callaghan* [1940] A.C. 880.

Chapter 3

CONSTRUCTION OF PUBLIC SEWERS

DUTY TO PROVIDE SYSTEM OF PUBLIC SEWERS

(a) The basic duty

3–001 Under s.94(1)(a) of the Water Industry Act 1991, it is the duty of every sewerage undertaker:

> "to provide, improve and extend such a system of public sewers (whether inside its area or elsewhere) . . . as to ensure that that area is and continues to be effectually drained . . ."

this provision being in effect a repetition of the former s.14 of the Water Act 1973, which itself derived from s.14 of the Public Health Act 1936 and indirectly from s.15 of the 1875 Act. In performing this duty, a sewerage undertaker must have regard to its existing and likely future obligations to allow for the discharge of trade effluent into its public sewers and to the need to provide for the disposal of trade effluent which is so discharged.[1]

The duty under s.94 is supplemented by reg.4 of the Urban Waste Water Treatment Regulations 1994.[2] Thus, the duty under s.94(1)(a) is to include a duty to ensure that collecting systems[3] which satisfy the requirements of Sch.2 to the regulations are provided:

(a) where the urban waste water[3a] discharges into receiving waters which are a sensitive area,[3b] by December 31, 1998, for every agglomeration with a population equivalent of more than 10,000; and

(b) without prejudice to (a), by December 31, 2000, for every agglomeration with a population equivalent of more than 15,000; and by December 31, 2005, for every agglomeration[3c] with a population equivalent of between 2,000 and 15,000.

---

[1] ss.94(2). "Trade effluent" has the same meaning as in Ch.3 of Pt 4 of the 1991 Act: s.94(5), to be amended by the Water Act 2003, s.88(2), providing that s.139 (see p.258) shall have effect for the purposes of s.94 as it has effect for the purposes of Ch.3 of Pt 4. As to trade effluent, see further pp.247–257.

[2] SI 1994/2841.

[3–3c] These expressions are defined in reg.2(1); see above, pp.45–49.

These requirements do not apply where either the Environment Agency certifies that the establishment of a collecting system is not justified because it would produce no environmental benefit; or the Secretary of State certifies that this is not justified because it would entail excessive costs. In either case, individual systems or other appropriate systems must be provided that the Authority certifies achieve the same level of environmental protection.[4]

The requirements for collecting systems specified by Sch.2 are that systems shall take into account waste water treatment requirements, and that the design, construction and maintenance of such systems shall be undertaken in accordance with the best technical knowledge not entailing excessive costs, notably regarding:

(a) volume and characteristics of urban waste water;

(b) prevention of leaks; and

(c) limitation of pollution of receiving waters due to storm water overflows.

(b) Consequences of default

Under the Public Health Act 1875 it was provided that where a local **3–002** authority failed to provide its district with adequate sewers or to maintain those provided, a complaint could be made to the Local Government Board which could then make a default order requiring the authority to perform its statutory duties.

Under the 1875 (and s.1936) legislation, the existence of the default power was held to exclude the grant of *mandamus*.[5] Furthermore, it was held in a number of cases that no action for damages or a mandatory injunction lay for breach of duty or negligence in respect of harm arising from the inadequacy of a sewerage system constructed by the responsible authority itself and which was adequate originally.[6] It was

---

[4] reg.4(1)–(3).

[5] *Pasmore v Oswaldtwistle UDC* [1898] A.C. 387 (*mandamus* not available to compel a local authority under the 1875 Act to provide an adequate sewerage system).

[6] *Glossop v Heston and Isleworth Local Board* (1879) 12 Ch. D. 102 (mandatory injunction refused); *Att Gen v Dorking Union Guardians* (1882) 20 Ch. D. 595; *Robinson v Workington Corp* [1897] 1 Q.B. 619 (claim for damages rejected where the case was admitted to be one of non-feasance in that the defendants had not replaced an existing, inadequate, sewer; the duty was owed to the district as a whole not any individual and the default power was the only remedy); *Pride of Derby and Derbyshire Angling Association v British Celanese Ltd* [1953] 1 Ch.149 (general principle recognised, see Evershed M.R. at pp.169–179, but distinguished as here the defendant corporation was itself discharging polluting effluent from its own sewage disposal works into the River Derwent); *Smeaton v Ilford Corp* [1954] 1 Ch. 450 (corporation not liable in nuisance arising simply from the overloading of its sewers).

unclear whether the principle recognised in these cases was an aspect of a wider principle that a local authority was not liable for "non-feasance" as distinct from "misfeasance".[7] In any event the sanitary authority could be held liable if it caused, adopted or continued a nuisance.[8]

In the *Pride of Derby* case, Denning L.J. stated *obiter*[9] that, where the sanitary authority as local authority was itself responsible for or permitted additional building that rendered a sewerage system inadequate, "they are themselves guilty of the nuisance"[10]; the old "non-feasance" cases had "little or no application in the present day" as in the 19th century local authorities had no powers to control additional buildings.[11] However, his Lordship also accepted that no evidence had been given of the building or planning activities of Derby Corporation and so it was not right to base the decision on the point. It is submitted that these dicta are unsound; in particular, a local authority cannot be said to have "caused" a nuisance through the grant of a planning permission. In any event the dicta cannot apply now that the functions of sewerage undertaker and planning authority have been separated.[12]

3–003 So far as modern sewerage undertakers, which are limited companies vested with statutory functions rather than public authorities, are concerned it is provided that the duty under s.94 of the 1991 Act is enforceable under s.18 of that Act by the Secretary of State or (with the consent of or in accordance with a general authorisation given by the Secretary of State) by the Water Services Regulation Authority. Section 18 enables the Secretary of State or the WSRA to make a final or provisional "enforcement order".[13] Section 18(8) provides that:

> "Where any act or omission constitutes a contravention of a condition of an appointment under Chapter 1 of this Part or of a statutory or other requirement enforceable under this section, the only remedies

[7] The existence of any such general doctrine outside highway cases was denied by Evershed M.R. and Denning L.J. in the *Pride of Derby* case at pp.175–176, 187–189, respectively.
[8] See the *Pride of Derby* case; and see below, pp.113–114, 155–156, 206–207.
[9] pp.189–191.
[10] p.190.
[11] pp.190–191.
[12] See *Dear v Thames Water* (1993) 33 Con. L.R. 43, where Judge Bowsher Q.C. (Official Referee) held that the *Glossop* case, above n.6, was still good law, and not to be regarded as qualified by the principle of *Leakey v National Trust*, below, p.77 (alternatively, if the cases could be reconciled, it was within the application of the reasonableness test).
[13] See above, pp.24–26.

for that contravention, apart from those available by virtue of this section, shall be those for which express provision is made by or under any enactment and those that are available in respect of that act or omission otherwise than by virtue of its constituting such a contravention."

This makes the s.18 remedies for breach (inter alia) of duties under s.94 exclusive, apart from any other remedies expressly provided under statute, and any causes of action arising from the same act or omission but not relying in terms on the fact of non-compliance with s.94.[14] Contravention of an enforcement order is actionable by a person affected who sustains loss or damage, subject to a defence that the company has taken all reasonable steps and exercised all due diligence.[15] The relevant enforcement authority (i.e. the Secretary of State or the WSRA, as the case may be) may seek an injunction.[16] If the Secretary of State is satisfied that there has been a contravention, he *must* make an enforcement order unless one of the exceptions applies. If he is not so satisfied, it is unclear whether a person who claims to have been prejudiced by a breach of duty may challenge that decision on application for judicial review.[17]

Sections 23 and 24 of the 1991 Act provide for the issue of special administration orders by the High Court in certain cases of default.[18]

---

[14] See *Dear v Thames Water* (1993) 33 Con. L.R. 43, where Judge Bowsher QC, Official Referee, held that the forerunner of s.18 (the Water Act 1989 s.20) precluded an action against a sewerage undertaker in respect of any alleged negligence or nuisance occurring after August 31, 1989, in respect of any matters coming within the enforcement procedure. It is submitted that an application for judicial review based on a breach of s.94 would also be barred by s.18(8). See further *Marcic v Thames Water*, below, pp.74–80.

[15] 1991 Act s.22(1)–(3).

[16] 1991 Act s.22(4), (5), as amended by the Water Act 2003 s.36(2).

[17] cf. *R. v Secretary of State for the Environment, ex. p. Jaywick Sands Freeholders Association Ltd* [1975] J.P.L. 663, where the Divisional Court stated *obiter* that there were grounds for quashing the Secretary of State's decision to refuse to exercise his default power under s.322(1) of the Public Health Act 1936 (see below, pp.283–284) where there had been a delay of over 20 years in providing sewers (and water supply) for 773 holiday chalets. The matter would have been remitted to the Secretary of State had responsibility not by then been transferred from the local authority (Clacton U.D.C.) to the water authority. Lord Widgery C.J. said that "the Secretary of State did not have the power to direct the water authority to do the work as it was not the defaulting authority in the first place" (p.663). Note, however, that this case concerned a default *power* and so does not necessarily apply to the s.18 powers. In *R. v Secretary of State for the Environment, ex p. Friends of the Earth Ltd* [1996] Env. L.R. 198, the Court of Appeal entertained but rejected on the merits an application for judicial review of the Secretary of State's decision to accept undertakings under s.19 of the 1991 Act: see p.25, n.126, above.

[18] See above, pp.27–29.

Such an order is issued where the court is satisfied upon petition by the Secretary of State or, with the consent of the Secretary of State, by the WSRA that, inter alia, there has been or is likely to be a contravention by a sewerage undertaker of a requirement imposed by s.94 sufficiently serious to justify its deprivation of its appointment.[19]

3–004 The position of a water authority in respect of the period April 1, 1974 to August 31, 1989 was different. There was no provision for a default power in the Water Act 1973, and the general duty to provide for the effectual draining of the area under s.14 (unlike other powers[20]) was not made subject to the Minister's default power in s.322(1) of the Public Health Act 1936. Accordingly, the s.14 duty was in principle enforceable by *mandamus*, although liability in negligence or for breach of statutory duty arising out of non-compliance was limited.[21]

For the individual consumer, or potential consumer, some further aid might be found in provisions of the 1991 Act concerning complaints.[22]

Like that under the former s.14 of the 1973 Act, the duty of sewer provision under s.94 of the 1991 Act does not include the provision of land drains or drains required for agricultural purposes. The duty is only to provide *public sewers*, which is to say those which will vest in the sewerage undertaker under s.179 when constructed.[23]

(c) Civil liability of sewerage undertakers

3–005 It is well established that a sewerage undertaker may be liable in nuisance in respect of positive acts that cause loss or damage.[24] As

---

[19] s.25(2).

[20] See the Water Act 1973 s.14(2).

[21] *Dear v Thames Water* (1993) 33 Con. L.R. 43. In *Weaver v West Yorkshire Water Authority* [1981] C.L.Y. 2874, the public sewer running beneath the plaintiff's house became blocked at an interceptor trap by foreign bodies (including newspapers) put into the system by third parties. The plaintiff's cellar was consequently flooded with sewage and she declined an offer to remove and seal up the trap. The sewer was adequate for the houses it served. The plaintiff lost an initial claim that the pipe concerned was not a public sewer (see *Weaver v Family Housing Association (York) Ltd* (1975) 74 L.G.R. 255), but then sought redress against the water authority by an ordinary action for damages and for an injunction under s.14 requiring diversion of the sewer. Glidewell J. held that the facts did not disclose a breach of the section and that an individual had no right to bring an action for damages in such a case even had there been a breach (cf. the *Glossop* case, above, p.71, n.6). An application for judicial review (unreported, C.A. July 17, 1985) also failed because the Court of Appeal, upholding the Divisional Court, held that on the facts there was no evidence that the drainage was not effectual and, therefore, no grounds for judicial review were disclosed.

[22] See above, pp.32–33.

[23] s.219(1).

[24] See above, p.72.

explained above, the decision in *Glossop v Heston and Isleworth Local Board*[25] and the cases which followed it established, however, that no action for damages lay in negligence or nuisance in respect of harm arising from the inadequacy of a sewerage system constructed by the defendant board and which was adequate originally. Furthermore, such an action against a sewerage undertaker would appear to be barred by s.18 of the Water Industry Act 1991.[26]

Nevertheless, the Court of Appeal in *Marcic v Thames Water Utilities Ltd*[27] held that there may be liability where an undertaker fails to take reasonable steps to remedy a nuisance caused by the inadequacy of sewerage arrangements. In this case, sewers in Stanmore provided by Thames Water had become inadequate to deal with the increasing quantity of water and sewage discharged into them.[28] From 1992, the sewers regularly discharged both surface water and foul water into the front of the claimant's house and from there into the back garden, damaging the fabric of the house. The claimant successfully took steps to prevent it getting inside his home. Many thousands of premises in the area of Thames Water faced the risk of internal or external flooding. While there were practicable steps that Thames Water could take to deal with the problem that affected the claimant, the system of priorities used by it gave priority to properties at risk of internal flooding, of which there were some 18,000. Accordingly, there was no prospect of the work necessary to protect the claimant's property being carried out in the foreseeable future. The claimant declined to complain to the Director General of Water Services under s.18 of the Water Industry Act 1991, but brought a claim for damages at common law and under the Human Rights Act 1998. At first instance[29] Judge Havery QC held:

(i) that causes of action based on *Rylands v Fletcher*,[30] nuisance, negligent non-feasance and breach of statutory duty were barred

---

[25] (1879) 12 Ch. D. 102, above, p.71, n.6.

[26] above, pp.72–73.

[27] [2002] EWCA Civ 64; [2002] Q.B. 929. See W. Howarth (2002) 14 J.E.L. 353.

[28] The expert evidence referred to two causes of flooding: (1) flooding caused by an accumulation of surface water at times of heavy rainfall which the sewers were unable to remove because they had become full to overflowing; and (2) flooding caused by overflow from the surcharged surface and foul water sewers. The former would occur if there were no sewerage system in place; the latter was directly attributable to the existence of the sewers which transmitted surface and foul water from other areas served by the system and discharged this on to the claimant's property. The Court of Appeal noted that different legal principles were applicable to the two but the judge had proceeded on the basis that the only relevant flooding was (2), and this had not been challenged: per Lord Phillips M.R. [2002] Q.B. 929 at [18] and [19].

[29] [2001] EWHC Technology 421; [2002] Q.B. 929.

[30] (1868) L.R. 3, H.L. 330.

by the decision in *Glossop v Heston and Isleworth Local Board*[31];

(ii) that an action for breach of statutory duty did not lie at the suit of an injured person unless an enforcement notice had been made under ss.18 and 22 or the Water Industry Act 1991;

(iii) that policy excluded the existence of a duty of care under the principles of *Stovin v Wise (Norfolk CC third party)*[32];

(iv) that Thames Water's failure to carry out works to end the repeated flooding of the claimant's property constituted an interference with his right to respect for his home under ECHR Art.1 and of his entitlement to peaceful enjoyment of his possessions under Art.1 of the First Protocol. On the "limited evidence" presented, Thames Water had failed to show that its scheme of priorities struck a fair balance between the competing interests of the claimant and of other customers, and its failure to act was incompatible with Convention rights. The judge declined in the exercise of his discretion to award a mandatory injunction, but held that Thames Water was liable in damages, to be assessed. In further proceedings,[33] Judge Havery Q.C. held that the damages could include damages for the diminution in value of the house caused by the continuing risk of future flooding. The measure of damages should reflect the difference between: (1) the hypothetical value of the house on the completion date of remedial works assumed to have been started on the date of commencement of the Human Rights Act 1998 (October 2, 2000); and (2) the actual value of the house on that date.

Thames Water appealed against the finding of liability; the claimant cross-appealed against the findings that Thames Water was not liable at common law. The Court of Appeal allowed the cross-appeal and dismissed the appeal. It held:

---

[31] (1879) 12 Ch. D. 102, above, p.71, n.6.

[32] [1996] A.C. 923. Here, the House of Lords held that, where it was sought to base a duty of care simply on the existence of a statutory power, the minimum preconditions for doing so "if it can be done at all, are, first that it would in the circumstances have been irrational not to exercise the power, so that there was in effect a public law duty to act, and secondly, that there are exceptional grounds for holding that the policy of the statute requires compensation to be paid to persons who suffer loss because the power was not exercised": per Lord Hoffmann at p.953. But see now *Gorringe v Calderdale MBC* [2004] UKHL 15, [2004] 1 W.L.R. 1057.

[33] The judge also rejected submissions that he should change his judgment on liability.

(i) that it was doubtful that the principle of *Rylands v Fletcher* applied in respect of overflows from sewers maintained by a sewerage undertaker,[34] but it was not necessary to express a concluded view on the point[35];

(ii) that any action for breach of statutory duty was barred by ss 18 and 22 of the Water Industry Act 1991[36];

(iii) that in principle the law of private nuisance imposed liability in these circumstances on the ground that, while Thames Water had not created the nuisance, it knew (or should have known) that the inadequacy of its sewerage system was causing a nuisance, and it had failed to take reasonable steps to bring it to an end[37]; no defence of statutory authority was made out, as the flooding was not the inevitable consequence of the exercise by Thames Water of its duties and powers[38] and this common law claim was not barred by ss 18 and 22 of the 1991 Act as it did not involve the averment of violation of the Act[39]; and the *Glossop* line of authority[40] could not survive the development of the law of nuisance in *Goldman v Hargrave*[41]; and

[34] Following Denning L.J. in *Pride of Derby and Derbyshire Angling Association Ltd v British Celanese Ltd* [1953] Ch. 149, 189, who said that "the use of land for drainage purposes by the local authority is 'such a use as is proper for the general benefit of the community', and is on that ground exempt from the rule in *Rylands v Fletcher*, see *Rickards v Lothian* [1913] A.C. 263, 280 *per* Lord Moulton, approved by the House of Lords in *Read v J. Lyons & Co. Ltd.* [1947] A.C. 156, 169, 187, *per* Lord Simon and *per* Lord Uthwatt; and also on the ground of statutory authority, see *Hammond v St Pancras Vestry* (1894) L.R. 9 C.P. 316, 322, *per* Brett J."

[35] at [45], [46].

[36] at [61].

[37] at [48]–[56]: *Sedleigh-Denfield v O'Callaghan* [1940] A.C. 880, 894, per Viscount Maughan; *Goldman v Hargrave* [1967] 1 A.C. 645 (the Privy Council held that the occupier of land on which a fire had started by natural causes was under a duty to take such steps as were reasonable in his individual circumstances to prevent the fire spreading to the land of his neighbour); *Leakey v National Trust for Places of Historic Interest or Natural Beauty* [1980] Q.B. 485 (the Court of Appeal applied *Goldman v Hargrave* in concluding that an occupier owed a duty to his neighbour in respect of a hazard (a mound of soil which collapsed) arising naturally on his land); *Holbeck Hall Hotel Ltd v Scarborough BC* [2002] Q.B. 836 ("measured duty of care" owed to prevent damage to a neighbour's land from lack of support due to natural causes); *Delaware Mansions Ltd v Westminster City Council* [2002] 1 A.C. 321 (duty of landowner not to permit tree roots to cause damage by encroaching on a neighbour's land).

[38] Following *Allen v Gulf Oil Refinery Ltd* [1981] A.C. 1001.

[39] at [62].

[40] See above, p.71, n.6.

[41] at [63]–[80], [97]–[103].

(iv) that the judge had rightly found there to have been a breach of the claimant's Convention rights.[42]

3–006 A crucial issue was therefore whether Thames Water had done all that was reasonable in the circumstances. Here, once the claimant had established that Thames Water had caused a nuisance, the burden of proof lay on Thames Water to prove that it had done so. As to the evidence, it had not set out to prove that it had taken all reasonable steps to prevent causing a nuisance to the claimant, but only that "their system of priorities was a fair way of devoting limited resources to the widespread problem of nuisances emanating from their sewers". The Court of Appeal agreed with the trial judge that it had failed to do so. If it had done so this "arguably" would have established that it had done everything that was reasonable, but:

> "We say 'arguably' because we cannot readily accept that a body with the actual and potential resources of Thames is in a postion to rely on the lack of resources to justify not merely taking no immediate steps, but take no steps at all to abate a nuisance such as that suffered by Mr Marcic."[43]

The court rejected Thames Water's submission here that the *Leakey* duty could not extend so far as to require it to exercise its statutory powers, including the power to acquire land compulsorily.[44] Accordingly, Thames Water was liable in damages for the full period covered by the claim.

In coming to this conclusion, the court seemed to attach no weight to the point that it would cost Thames Water £1,000 million to alleviate the flooding problems of all its customers who were in a similar position to the claimant or whose properties were at risk of internal flooding once every 10 years. This would entail wiping out Thames' profits for a number of years, an increase in sewerage charges (assuming the regulator were to approve) or a combination of both. The exact basis on which it was right for the courts to hold that a sewerage undertaker's choices reflected in its system of priorities was unreasonable was left unclear, the trial judge (upheld on this point by the Court of Appeal) merely holding that Thames Water had adduced insufficient evidence on the facts of this particular case.

---

[42] at [105]–[110].
[43] at [87].
[44] at [88]–[96].

Interestingly, the court also suggested an alternative approach, which would require the existing principles to be modified to allow the application of *Rylands v Fletcher*, under which:

> "those who pay to make use of a sewerage system should be charged sufficient to cover the cost of paying compensation to the minority who suffer damage as a consequence of the operation of the system."[45]

This position appears attractive at first sight. However, there is room for debate as to whether the costs to individual householders of inadequate sewerage arrangements of making them adequate, should fall on (1) the undertaker's shareholders; (2) all the occupiers in the particular geographical area where additional development has caused overloading; (3) all the occupiers in the area of the sewerage undertaker in question; (4) all occupiers in the UK; (5) taxpayers; or (6) some combination of these. It is not obvious that the policy here should be determined by the courts rather than Parliament.

The House of Lords unanimously allowed an appeal by Thames Water on both grounds of liability.[46] The House held that the statutory scheme under ss.18 and 94 of the 1991 Act barred both the claim at common law and the claim under the Human Rights Act 1998. Mr Marcic was seeking to "sidestep the statutory enforcement code".[47] The *Goldman* and *Leakey* cases exemplified the standard of conduct expected today of ordinary occupiers of land, but Thames Water was not an ordinary occupier. The common law of nuisance "should not impose on Thames Water obligations inconsistent with the statutory scheme. To do so would run counter to the intention of Parliament as expressed in the Water Industry Act 1991. . . . [T]he cause of action in nuisance asserted by Mr Marcic is inconsistent with the statutory scheme."[48] **3–007**

It was clear that one important purpose of the enforcement scheme in the 1991 Act was that individual householders should not be able to launch proceedings in respect of the failure to build sufficient sewers.[49] The claim under the Human Rights Act 1998 was barred by the same reasoning. Under the statutory scheme, it was for the

[45] at [113], [114].

[46] [2003] UKHL 66, [2004] 2 A.C. 42.

[47] at [22], per Lord Nicholls of Birkenhead; Lord Hoffmann and Lord Hope delivered concurring speeches. Lords Steyn and Scott agreed with Lords Nicholls and Hoffmann.

[48] at [33], [34].

[49] at [35]. cf. Lord Hoffmann at [63]–[64]: decisions as to the level of capital expenditure and charges to consumers were decisions "which the courts are not equipped to make in ordinary litigation".

industry regulator, and not the courts, to determine whether the system of priorities established by the undertaker was fair. The statutory scheme as a whole was Convention-compliant, striking a reasonable balance between the interests of customers whose properties were prone to sewer flooding and the interests of all the other customers of the sewerage undertaker.[50] Although this had no bearing on the outcome, the House noted that in 2002 the Director General of Water Services had approved additional investment to enable works to be done freeing 250 properties, including that of Mr Marcic, from the risk of external flooding; that work had been done.

Overall, the conclusion of the House of Lords is persuasive, and consistent with earlier authorities, leaving a complaint to the WSRA as the available remedy in these cases.[51] While the cases relied on concerned undertakers that were public bodies, the position of privatised companies subject to a detailed regulatory regime seems sufficiently analogous. The fact that Parliament has not intervened to reverse the decision notwithstanding that there has been continued attention paid to the problem of sewer flooding[52] perhaps provides a further indication that the decision was right.

3–008 The parameters of the *Marcic* decision are (at the time of writing) (June 2010) in the course of being explored in litigation against Thames Water by some 1,300 residents of Isleworth and Twickenham in respect of odours and mosquitoes from the Mogden Sewage Treatment works in Isleworth. The claims are based on nuisance, negligence and Arts 8(1) and First Protocol, Art 1 of the ECHR. A number of preliminary issues have been determined by Ramsey J.,[53] with some of these taken to the Court of Appeal.[54] The key issues

---

[50] paras [37]–[46], following the approach of the European Court of Human Rights in *Hatton v UK*, Judgment of July 8, 2003, concerning the effect of the government's policy on night flights from Heathrow on those living near the airport, emphasising that the role of the domestic policy maker should be given special weight.

[51] See also comments by J. O'Sullivan, [2004] C.L.J. 552 (noting that it "would have been preferable had Thames Water's privatised status not been ignored completely", although this was not to say that the result was wrong; D. Howarth, [2004] J. Env. L. 252 (providing an economic analysis of the decision, and criticising it on the grounds that the courts had more experience in deciding property rights than the Director, and that the Director would have been able to maintain an overall balance in response to a decision upholding the claimant's right to sue by enabling the undertakers to increase the sewerage charges of householders who benefit from new infrastructure spending); H. Wilberg, (2004) 120 L.Q.R. 574.

[52] See pp.211–213. The Flooding and water Management Bill 2009–2010 would have provided an appropriate vehicle had a different solution been thought appropriate.

[53] *Dobson v Thames Water Utilities Ltd* [2007] EWHC 2021 (TCC); [2008] 2 All E.R. 362. See also *Ministry of Defence v Thames Water Utilities Ltd* [2006] EWCA Civ 1620 (ordinary claim for restitution not inconsistent with the statutory regime).

[54] [2009] EWCA Civ 28; [2009] 3 All E.R. 319.

concerned the extent to which these claims were barred by *Marcic*. Ramsey J. held that (i) the claimants *were* seeking to enforce duties that arose under s.94(1)(b) of the 1991 Act[55]; but (ii) their claims in nuisance, negligence and under the Human Rights Act 1998, insofar as they were based on negligence in the operation of the sewage treatment works, were *not* barred to the extent that, as a matter of fact and degree, the exercise of adjudicating on the cause of action was not inconsistent with, and did not involve conflicts with, the statutory regime under the 1991 Act.[56] Here, the claim was based not on *Leakey*[57] but on *Allen v Gulf Oil Refining Ltd*,[58] where the House of Lords had held that a defence of statutory authority is subject to a condition:

> "that the statutory powers are exercised without 'negligence', that word here being used in a special sense so as to require the undertaker, as a condition of obtaining immunity from action, to carry out the work and conduct the operation with all reasonable regard and care for the interests of other persons."[59]

Furthermore, the claim in *Marcic* was based on a breach of the first aspect of section 94(1)(a), being essentially one that Thames Water "ought to build new sewers"[60]; members of the House at least implied that claims were permitted where there was a failure to cleanse and maintain, the second aspect of s.94(1)(a).[61] Accordingly, a boundary had to be drawn between matters solely actionable under section 18 of the 1991 Act, as in *Marcic*, and those actionable apart from the existence of any statutory duty. This distinction could be difficult to draw.[62] Policy matters or matters requiring capital works were likely, and operational matters less likely, to lead to an inconsistency with the statutory scheme.[63] His Lordship expressed the provisional view

---

[55] See p.131. Ramsey J. rejected the claimants' argument that the duty under s.94(1)(b) was confined to getting rid of the contents of the sewers and did not extend to environmental protection: see paras [42]–[84].
[56] paras [86]–[155]. His Lordship held that *Marcic* would bar a claim in nuisance absent negligence, but no such claim was relied upon: paras [86]–[88].
[57] See p.77.
[58] [1981] A.C. 1001.
[59] per Lord Wilberforce at p.1011.
[60] per Lord Nicholls, [2004] 2 A.C. 42 at [34].
[61] See Lord Hoffmann at [53], discussed by Ramsey J. in *Dobson* at [121]–[131].
[62] Ramsey J. at [140].
[63] Ramsey J. at [143] and [145].

that a claim that there were inadequate odour control measures was likely to conflict with the statutory regime, while claims of inadequate monitoring of odours and management failings and of a failure to take preventative measures in relation to mosquitoes were not likely to conflict. The extent of any inconsistency could only be determined at trial.[64] Similarly, *Marcic* did not bar a claim that the defendant had neglected to press for capital funding for odour-related expenditure; in general, the ability to fund expense would not provide a defence to an allegation of negligence.[65] Finally, his Lordship set out guidance on the principles governing the award of damages in such a case and on the approach to limitation.[66]

REQUISITION NOTICES

3–009 Under s.98(1) of the Water Industry Act 1991, a sewerage undertaker is under a duty to provide a public sewer for the drainage for domestic purposes of premises in a particular locality in its area where it is required so to do by a notice served upon it by one or more persons entitled to make such a demand. A notice may be served by:

(a) an owner of any premises in the locality concerned;

(b) an occupier of such premises;

(c) a local authority within whose area the locality is in whole or part located;

(d) where the whole or any part of that locality is situated within a new town, the new towns residuary body or the development corporation for the new town; and

(e) an urban development corporation where the locality is situated in whole or part within an area designated as an urban development area under Pt 16 of the Local Government, Planning and Land Act 1980.[67]

---

64 paras [144]–[147].

65 paras [160]–[178].

66 paras [179]–[259]. A number of the issues on damages were taken to the Court of Appeal ([2009] 3 All E.R. 319), which ruled that an award of damages for nuisance to the property owner would normally constitute just satisfaction for a claim by the owner under Art.8(1) of ECHR; whether this also would also be so in respect of a claim by an occupier with no interest in the property (who did not have standing to sue in nuisance) would depend on the facts.

67 s.98(2), as amended by the Government of Wales Act 1998 Sch.18 Pt IV and the Housing and Regeneration Act 2008 Sch.8 para.58.

The duty to provide a public sewer to be used for the drainage for domestic purposes of premises in a particular locality only arises if the premises, the drainage of which would be by means of that sewer, are premises on which there are buildings, or will be buildings when proposals made by any person for the erection of any buildings are carried out. The conditions specified in s.99 of the 1991 Act (as to meeting the costs)[68] must also be satisfied.[69] The reference in s.98 to "domestic purposes" is a reference to such "domestic sewerage purposes" as are specified in the requirement under the section in relation to existing or future buildings and, in the case of future buildings, to times after their erection.[70] "Domestic sewerage purposes", in relation to any premises, means any one or more of the following:

(a) the removal, from buildings on the premises and land occupied with and appurtenant to the buildings, of the contents of lavatories;

(b) the removal from such buildings and land of water which has been used for cooking or washing, other than in connection with a laundry business or the business of preparing food and drink for consumption otherwise than on the premises; and

(c) the removal from such buildings and land of surface water.[71]

The Water Act 2003[72] extended requisitioning rights to cover the provision of lateral drains.[73] Accordingly, it is the duty of a sewerage undertaker (in accordance with s.101) to provide a lateral drain to communicate with a public sewer and to be used for the drainage for domestic purposes of premises in its area if:

(a) the undertaker is required to provide it by a notice served by one or more of the persons entitled under subs.(2A) to require the provision of the lateral drain;

(b) the premises the drainage of which would be by means of that lateral drain are premises on which there are buildings, or will be when proposals made by any person for the erection of any buildings are carried out; and

---

[68] See below, pp.86–87.
[69] s.98(1)(b), (c).
[70] s.98(5), as amended by the Water Act 2003 s.95(5).
[71] s.117(1).
[72] ss.95, 97.
[73] For the definition, see above, p.67.

(c) the conditions specified in s.99 (as to meeting the costs)[74] are satisfied in relation to that requirement.[75]

3–010 The persons entitled to require the provision of a lateral drain are:

(a) the owner of the premises the drainage of which would be by means of that lateral drain;

(b) the occupier of those premises;

(c) any local authority within whose area those premises are situated;

(d) where the premises are situated in a new town, the new towns residuary body and the town development corporation; and

(e) where the premises are situated in an urban development area, the urban development corporation.[76]

Under the relevant provisions as originally enacted, where a requisition notice was served upon a sewerage undertaker in due order under s.98, the sewerage undertaker had, in effect, a period of six months from the day upon which any financial conditions which may be set were satisfied or that upon which the points at which private sewers and drains leading from the premises would connect with the public sewer are agreed, whichever shall be the later, in which to meet the requisition before it would be considered to be in default.[77] The points of connection with the public sewer should be agreed between the parties, i.e. those making the requisition and the sewerage undertaker,[78] or in default be determined by a single arbitrator appointed by agreement or, if this is not achieved, by the President of the Institution of Civil Engineers.[79]

These provisions were remodelled by the Water Act 2003.[80] The sewerage undertaker will not be in breach of a duty under s.98 unless the period of six months beginning with the "relevant day" has

---

[74] See below, pp.86–87.

[75] 1991 Act s.98(1A), inserted by the 2003 Act s.95(2).

[76] 1991 Act s.98(2A), inserted by the 2003 Act s.95(3) and amended by the Housing and Regeneration Act 2008 Sch.8 para.58.

[77] s.101(1), as originally enacted.

[78] s.101(3), as originally enacted.

[79] s.101(4), as originally enacted.

[80] ss.95(7), substituting a new s.101 in the 1991 Act with effect from May 28, 2004. The substitution did not apply in respect of requirements notified under s.98 before the substitution came into force: s.95(8).

expired, and the undertaker has not before the end of that period so laid (as the case may be):

(i) the public sewer to be provided as to enable drains and private sewers to be used for the drainage of premises in the locality to communicate with the public sewer; or

(ii) the lateral drain to be provided as to enable the drain to be used for the drainage of premises to communicate with a public sewer vested in that undertaker, at the place or places determined under the section.[81]

The six-month period may be extended by agreement or, where there is a dispute as to whether it should be extended, by the WSRA on a reference to it.[82] The place or places determined under the section are to be determined by agreement between the undertaker and the person(s) making the requisition. In default of agreement, either party may refer the matter to the WSRA, for determination under the 1991 Act s.30A. The WSRA is to identify the place(s) at which it is reasonable, in all the circumstances: **3–011**

(i) for the drains or private sewers to communicate with the public sewer; or

(ii) in relation to the provision of a lateral drain, for the drain to communicate with a public sewer vested in the undertaker and for the remainder of the drain of which the lateral drain forms part to connect with the lateral drain.[83]

The "relevant day" means the day after:

(a) the day on which the financial conditions specified in s.99 are satisfied; or

(b) the day on which the place or places where either drains or private sewers will communicate with the public sewer, or the lateral drain will communicate with a public sewer and the remainder of the drain will connect with the lateral drain, are determined under subs.(3),

---

[81] s.101(1).
[82] s.101(2).
[83] s.101(3), (4).

whichever is the later.[84]

The duty of the sewerage undertaker to provide a public sewer (or lateral drain) under the provisions of s.98 of the 1991 Act is stated by s.98(3)[85] to be owed to the person making the requisition or to each of the persons joining in doing so. Any breach of this duty which causes loss or damage to be sustained by a person to whom the duty is owed is actionable at the suit of that person[86]; it is, however, a defence to such an action for the sewerage undertaker to show that it took all reasonable steps and exercised all due diligence in seeking to avoid the breach.[87]

3–012 The detail of the financial conditions for compliance is set out in s.99 of the 1991 Act.[88] The sewerage undertaker may reasonably require from the person or persons requisitioning a public sewer undertakings binding them to pay to it in each of the 12 years following the provision of the sewer an amount not exceeding the "relevant deficit"[89] as defined for the year in question, if there should be one, in respect of the cost of making the sewerage provision requisitioned.[90] In the case of a requisition for a lateral drain, the undertaker may require undertakings that bind the person(s) making it, to pay to the undertaker following provision of the lateral drain, on such terms as may be specified in the undertaking, an amount not

---

[84] s.101(5).

[85] As amended by the Water Act 2003 s.95(4), adding references to lateral drains.

[86] s.98(4).

[87] s.98(4). The reference to a "water" undertaker in the original version of s.98(4) was replaced by a reference to a "sewerage" undertaker by the Competition and Service (Utilities) Act 1992 Sch.2 para.26, correcting an obvious drafting error.

[88] As amended by the Water Act 2003 s.95(6).

[89] The relevant deficit upon a sewer for any year is "the amount (if any) by which the drainage charges payable for the use during that year of that sewer are exceeded by the annual borrowing costs of a loan of the amount required for the provision of that sewer": s.100. For this purpose the "annual borrowing costs" is the aggregate amount for the year representing the interest payments and capital repayments "if an amount equal to so much of the costs reasonably incurred in providing that sewer as were not incurred in the provision of additional capacity had been borrowed, by the sewerage undertaker providing the sewer", upon (a) the basis of payments and repayments by twelve equal annual instalments and (b) an interest rate calculated upon such a basis as may have been determined by the undertaker with the approval of the Director or, in default, by the Director himself: s.100(2)(3).

[90] The cost of provision includes costs arising from provision of such other public sewers and pumping stations as may be rendered necessary by the provision of the new sewer and a proportion (if any), which is reasonable, of the costs incurred in the provision of any resulting necessary additional capacity in any other public sewer which was provided in the previous 12 years pursuant to s.98 or s.71 of the Water Act 1989 or s.16 of the 1973 Act or any equivalent local statutory provision: s.100(5), (6).

exceeding the costs reasonably incurred in or in connection with its provision.[91]

The person(s) concerned (unless a public authority) may be reasonably required by the undertaker to secure their undertakings if it was by virtue of s.98(2)(a) or (b) or 98(2A)(a) or (b) that the provision of the sewer or lateral drain was required.[92] Where a deposit is demanded under s.99 by way of security by a sewerage undertaker, interest may be payable by the undertaker upon the sums so retained.[93] Disputes upon financial undertakings under s.99 may be referred to the WSRA, for determination under s.30A, by either party to the dispute.[94]

Provision is made by the Water Act 2003[95] for an alternative mechanism whereby the offset payment may be made following provision of the sewer as a single payment, rather than over 12 years. This is an amount not exceeding the "discounted aggregate deficit on that sewer". This is the sum of the estimated relevant deficits for each of the 12 years following the provision of the sewer.[96] These are calculated by reference to drainage charges reasonably likely to occur and annual borrowing costs.[97] The deficit is discounted to determine its net present value applying such factor, and in accordance with such other provision, as may be determined by the WSRA. Such a determination may be for a particular public sewer or in relation to the provision of public sewers generally.

PROVISION OF PUBLIC SEWERS OTHER THAN BY REQUISITION

The Environment Act 1995,[98] inserting s.101A in the Water Industry **3–013**
Act 1991, introduced a new obligation for sewerage undertakers to provide a public sewer in specified circumstances. Without prejudice to the duty under s.98 of the 1991 Act,[99] it is the duty of a sewerage undertaker to provide a public sewer to be used for the drainage for

---

91 s.99(2A), inserted by the Water Act 2003 s.95(6)(b).

92 s.99(1)(b), (3); subs.(3) substituted by the 2003 Act s.95(6)(c).

93 Interest is payable on each sum of 50p so deposited for every three months during which it is held by the undertaker. The rate is determined by the undertaker with the approval of the WSRA or, in default, by the WSRA himself: s.99(4), (5) subs.(5) as amended by the 2003 Act s.95(6)(d).

94 s.99(6) as amended by the Water Act 2003 s.93(1)(b).

95 s.93, amending s.99 of the 1991 Act and inserting a new s.100A.

96 1991 Act s.100A.

97 s.100(2) to (6), (8) and (9) apply for the purposes of s.100A.

98 Sch.22, para.103.

99 Above, pp.82–84.

domestic sewerage purposes of premises in a particular locality[100] in its area if three conditions are satisfied.[101] These are:

(a) that the premises in question[102] (or any of them) are premises on which there are buildings[103];

(b) that the drains or sewers used for the drainage for domestic sewerage purposes of the premises in question do not, either directly or through an intermediate drain or sewer, connect with a public sewer; and

(c) that the drainage of any of the premises in question is giving, or likely to give, rise to such adverse effects to the environment or amenity that it is appropriate, having regard to guidance issued by the Secretary of State[104] and all other relevant considerations, to provide a public sewer for the drainage for domestic sewerage purposes of the premises in question.[105]

---

[100] This does not mean *all* the premises in a particular locality, but "refer to those premises, within a particular locality, being considered for public sewerage by the undertaker and, where there is a s.107A(7) dispute, the [Environment Agency]. And the number and identity of such premises may change in the course of those considerations": per Laws L.J. at [26] in *Environment Agency v Anglian Water Services Ltd* [2002] EWCA Civ 05. The Court of Appeal rejected an alternative construction to the effect that, if a duty arose in respect of any premises in a particular locality, it extended to all the premises in that locality.

[101] s.101A(1).

[102] The expression "premises in question" in (a), (b) and (c) (s.101A(2)(a), (b) and (c)) refers to "premises in a particular locality" in s.101A(1).

[103] As originally enacted, each of the buildings (with exceptions) had to be erected before, or substantially completed by, June 20, 1995; this limitation was repealed by the Water Act 2003 s.94, with effect from May 28, 2004.

[104] Issued under s.101A(4) after consultation with the WSRA the Environment Agency and such other bodies or persons as he considers appropriate: s.101A(5). See DoE/WO, "Guidance on the Provision of a Public Sewer under Section 101A of the Water Industry Act 1991" (April 1996). There is nothing in the guidance which suggests a decision maker is bound to accept it or accord it greater weight than other relevant considerations: *R. (on the application of Dwr Cymru Cyfyngedig) v Environment Agency* [2009] EWHC 435 (Admin) at [29].

[105] s.101A(2). The question of appropriateness must accordingly be considered in respect of all the premises under consideration for inclusion in the "particular locality". This was made clear by Tomlinson J. at first instance in the Anglian Water Services case: *R. (on the application of Anglian Water Services Ltd) v Environment Agency* [2000] N.P.C. 113 and was endorsed implicitly by the Court of Appeal: see Laws L.J. at [18]–[28]. The undertaker and/or the Agency may include premises in the duty to sewer which were not the subject of the initial application, and which are not themselves giving, or likely to give, rise to adverse environmental effects: see Harrison J. in *R. (on the application of Dwr Cymru Cyfyngedig) v Environment Agency of Wales* [2003] EWHC 336 (Admin) at [25] (points accepted by both sides); if the Agency is contemplating the inclusion of such premises, it should ensure that the undertaker is aware of this and should seek to ensure that it has what it considers to be the relevant information in relation to those premises, whether from the undertaker or otherwise. On the fact of the case, however, the Agency was entitled to act on the information it had: paras [25]–[29].

Without prejudice to the generality of (c), regard is to be had, so far as relevant, in determining whether it is appropriate for a sewer to be provided, to:

(a) the geology of the locality in question or any other locality;

(b) the number of premises with buildings which might reasonably be expected to be drained by means of that sewer;

(c) the costs of providing that sewer;

(d) the nature and extent of adverse effects to the environment or amenity if the premises or locality are not drained by a public sewer;

(e) the extent to which it is practicable for those effects to be overcome other than by the provision of public sewers (through s.101A or otherwise), and the costs of so overcoming those effects.[106]

The duty under s.101A(1) is enforceable under s.18 of the 1991 Act.[107] Any dispute between a sewerage undertaker and an owner or occupier of premises in its area as to whether the duty under s.101A(1) arises, the domestic sewerage purposes for which a sewer should be provided, or the time by which any such duty should be performed, is to be determined by the Environment Agency, whose decision is final.[108] An undertaker is only to be taken to be in breach of its duty where, and to the extent that, it has accepted, or the Environment Agency has determined, that it is under such a duty and that the time by which the duty is to that extent to be performed has passed.[109]

In applying s.101A, the duty to provide a public sewer will not arise where the sewerage undertaker decides that the environmental problems can be resolved practicably by other private means[110]; these **3–014**

[106] s.101A(3).

[107] See above, pp.24–26. A decision by an undertaker that a duty arises under s.101A can be withdrawn if it is satisfied that the earlier decision was susceptible to be quashed on public law grounds had a person with a sufficient interest sought a quashing order: *R. (on the application of Dwr Cymru Cyfynedig (Welsh Water)) v Environment Agency* [2009] EWHC 435 (Admin) (on the facts the first decision was lawful; there had been no failure to take account of take-up (under (b)) or costs, it seeming to be the case that the undertaker was simply minded to adopt a different method of calculating economic benefits).

[108] s.101A(7)–(9).

[109] s.101A(10).

[110] e.g. septic tank, cesspool, private sewerage treatment plant.

are not confined to reconstruction of the existing private sewerage arrangements. This point arose in *R. (on the application of Anglian Water Services Ltd) v Environment Agency*,[111] where the latter approach was accepted to be erroneous; in this case, four decisions by the Agency to overturn the undertaker's view that the duty under s.101A did not arise in a number of cases were quashed on the grounds variously: (1) that while the Agency's policy not to accept cesspools as a viable long-term sewerage option was not itself flawed as inflexible, it had been applied inflexibly on the facts of two of the cases[112]; (2) that it had unlawfully imposed on the undertaker a burden of establishing that the residents would agree to collaborate on and provide land for alternative private arrangements, as this left the Agency's coercive powers out of account; (3) that it had acted unreasonably and unfairly towards the undertaker in the light of previous representations in including a particular area as part of a "particular locality"; (4) that in deciding whether certain houses were part of a "particular locality" it failed to consider whether the provision of public sewerage to them was the appropriate solution.

Appeals in two of the cases were taken, raising grounds (2), (3) and (4) in *Environment Agency v Anglian Water Services Ltd.*[113] The appeals were dismissed, the judge being upheld on grounds (2) and (4) (although the Court of Appeal adopted a different approach to the interpretation of "premises in a particular locality" in s.101A(1)), but not on ground (3).

A fresh determination by the Agency that Anglian Water Services Ltd was under a duty to provide a public sewer for one of these locations was also quashed.[114] The undertaker's preferred solution remained the provision of a communal private treatment plant. This was rejected by the Agency for reasons of: (1) difficulties associated with the siting of the plant and/or its operation and maintenance; (2) the absence of any power to insist upon connection by residents to a communal plant; and (3) the cost of the private treatment plant option. Reason (1) was based on letters from residents which had not been disclosed to Anglian: this omission was held to constitute procedural

---

[111] [2000] N.P.C. 113.

[112] cf. *R. (on the application of Dwr Cymru Cyfyngedig) v Environment Agency of Wales* [2003] EWHC 336 (Admin) where the Agency's policy of generally favouring public sewers over cesspools was not on the facts applied inflexibly. The court also rejected the submission that the Agency had failed to carry out the balancing exercise under s.104A.

[113] [2002] EWCA Civ 05.

[114] *R. (on the application of Anglian Water Services) v Environment Agency* [2003] EWHC 1506 (Admin).

unfairness. Reason (2) was a correct statement of the law but was a legally irrelevant consideration as, otherwise, the simple refusal of residents to co-operate in a private scheme would always be decisive. If there was no duty to provide a public sewer, residents would have to choose whether to join a communal scheme or continue to rely on their individual arrangements. A challenge to Reason (3) failed as Anglian had had an adequate opportunity to comment on costings.

This new provision was introduced as a last-minute amendment to **3–015** the Environment Bill in the House of Commons "to make easier the provision of first-time connection to mains sewerage of existing premises."[115] It is to be seen in the context of the repeal of s.151 of the 1991 Act which authorises the Secretary of State to make grants to support the provision of sewerage services in rural areas.[116] The power of the sewerage undertaker to charge for any services provided in the course of carrying out its duty under s 101A(1) is to be exercised through a charges scheme applicable to the undertaker's customers generally.[117]

POWER TO CONSTRUCT LATERAL DRAINS FOLLOWING PROVISION OF A PUBLIC SEWER

The Water Act 2003[118] inserts a new section in the 1991 Act (s.101B) **3–016** providing that, where an undertaker provides a public sewer in accordance with a duty under ss98 or 101A of the 1991 Act, the undertaker may, at the request of specified persons, also provide at the same time one or more lateral drains to be used for the drainage for domestic purposes of premises in its area and to communicate with the sewer.[119] A request may be made:

(a) in the case of a public sewer to be provided under s 98, by the person who requires its provision under that section; and

(b) in the case of a public sewer to be provided under s 101A, by the owner or occupier of any premises in respect of which the

---

[115] Sir Paul Beresford, Parliamentary Under Secretary of State for Environment, Vol. 262 H.C.Deb., 28th June 1995, col. 1047.

[116] See DoE, "Review of Rural Water and Sewerage" (1994).

[117] 1991 Act ss.142(3A) and 143(3A), inserted by the Environment Act 1995 Sch.22 paras 114, 115. See below, pp.133–140.

[118] s.95(9), in force from May 28, 2004. The section does not apply in respect of a public sewer to be provided pursuant to a requirement notified under s.98 before that date; or a duty under s.101A which the undertaker had accepted or the Agency had determined it was under before that date: s.95(10).

[119] s.101B(1).

duty arises under that section, although any request may only be for the provision of a lateral drain to his premises.[120]

The person making the request must pay to the undertaker, following provision of the lateral drain, the costs reasonably incurred in or in connection with its provision.[121] Any dispute as to whether a lateral drain should be provided or as to its costs may be referred by either party to the WSRA for determination under s 30A of the 1991 Act.[122] Any lateral drain provided under this section is to belong to the undertaker.[123]

RIGHTS TO LAY SEWERS

3–017 Under ss.158 and 159 of the Water Industry Act 1991, sewerage undertakers are empowered to lay and maintain pipes in pursuance of their statutory functions,[124] both within and without their designated areas.[125] The provisions make a distinction between "street works" and works on, over or under "other land" and these categories must be considered separately.

(a) Power to carry out street works

3–018 Sections 158 and 161(1) of the 1991 Act empower a sewerage undertaker:

(a) to lay a sewer or disposal main[126] in, under or over any street and to keep it there;

---

[120] s.101B(2).
[121] s.101B(3).
[122] s.101B(4).
[123] s.101B(5).
[124] These powers are applicable to the functioning of both water undertakers and sewerage undertakers.
[125] s.192(3). By subs.(3A), inserted by the Competiton and Service (Utilities) Act 1992 s.47, in the case of the exercise of a power under ss.158 or 159 to construct a public sewer other than a storm water overflow sewer outside an undertaker's area, the undertaker must give notice to, and obtain the consent of, the undertaker for the other area (or the WSRA if consent is refused).
[126] The Water Act 2003 s.97(4), in force from May 28, 2004, extended the definition of "relevant pipe" under s.158(7) to apply, in relation to the exercise of a power to lay a pipe under s.158(1)(a) or a power related to that power under s.158(1)(c), to any lateral drain which the undertaker is to lay by virtue of ss.98 or 101B of the 1991 Act; or, in relation to any other power under s.158(1), any lateral drain which belongs to or is vested for the time being in the undertaker.

(b) to inspect, maintain, adjust, repair or alter any sewer or disposal main in, under or over any street;

(c) to carry out in a street all such works as are necessary to ensure that water in a waterworks used, or potentially to be used, by a water undertaker for purposes of water supply is not polluted or contaminated[127]; and

(d) to carry out any works requisite for or incidental to any of these purposes including, in particular,

(i) breaking up or opening a street,
(ii) tunnelling or boring under a street,
(iii) breaking up or opening a sewer, drain or tunnel, and
(iv) moving or removing earth and other materials.

By s.158(11) of the 1991 Act,[128] where a company replaces a relevant undertaker as sewerage undertaker under an inset appointment, any pipe serving the relevant premises is deemed to be a "sewer" for the purposes of ss.158 and 159.[129] The New Roads and Street Works Act 1991[130] now defines the term "street" as meaning:

> "the whole or part of any of the following, irrespective of whether it is a thoroughfare—
>
> (a) any highway, road, lane, footway, alley or passage,
> (b) any square or court, and
> (c) any land laid out as a way whether it is for the time being formed as a way or not."

A highway must be a way over which members of the public have a right to pass and re-pass on their lawful occasions, but it need not necessarily be maintainable at the public expense and this may be taken to be the case also for the purposes of the 1991 Act.

When carrying out street works a sewerage undertaker must comply with the street works code set out in Pt 3 of the New Roads and Street Works Act 1991[131] relating to the break-up of streets. In most circumstances notice must be given to the highway authority

---

[127] 1991 Act s.161(1).
[128] Inserted by the Competiton and Service (Utilities) Act 1992 s.40(6).
[129] See above, p.15 on inset appointments.
[130] s.48(1). This definition is applied for the purposes of the Water Industry Act 1991 by s.219(1).
[131] See *Cross on Local Government Law*, 9th edn (London: Sweet & Maxwell), paras 17–68—17–76.

before the works are commenced[132] and openings made in the road must be adequately guarded and lit at night; proper traffic signs must also be placed and operated as may be required[133]; and unnecessary delay and obstruction must be avoided.[134] In carrying out such works a sewerage undertaker is under an express duty:

(a) to do as little damage as possible; and

(b) to pay compensation for any loss or damage resulting therefrom.[135]

3–019 Where dispute arises upon matters of compensation, the amount is to be settled by a single arbitrator appointed by agreement between the parties or, in default, by the WSRA.[136] This duty relates primarily to property damage done during the performance of works. It is however clear that a sewerage undertaker will be under a general duty of care to any member of the public who sustains injury as a consequence of its performance of works upon the public highway.[137] In exercising its power to construct a sewer in, under or over a street, a sewerage undertaker will also be under a general duty to do so in a proper and reasonably careful manner. If the sewerage undertaker's negligence in constructing the sewer causes subsidence or otherwise damages the highway, it will be liable in damages to any lawful user of the highway who suffers injury in consequence.[138]

Moreover, if a sewerage undertaker fails properly to maintain a sewer it will be liable to any lawful user of the highway who suffers damage as a result.[139] On the other hand, if the sewer itself is properly laid and maintained, no liability will arise from the mere fact of the presence of the sewer in the highway because it is there pursuant to statutory authority.[140] If a properly laid and protected sewer should

---

[132] New Roads and Street Works Act 1991 s.54, as amended by the Traffic management Act 2004, s.49.

[133] New Roads and Street Works Act 1991 s.65.

[134] New Roads and Street Works Act 1991 s.66.

[135] Water Industry Act 1991 Sch.12 para.1(2).

[136] Water Industry Act 1991 para.1(3), as amended by the Water Act 2003 s.36(2).

[137] See, e.g. *Kimber v Gas Light & Coke Co* [1918] 1 K.B. 439.

[138] See, in relation to former authorities, *Smith v West Dudley Local Board* (1878) 3 C.P.D. 423 and *Shoreditch Corp v Bull* (1904) 68 J.P. 415.

[139] See, in relation to former authorities, *Skilton v Epsom and Ewell UDC* [1937] 1 K.B. 112.

[140] Such an action must be founded upon negligence: *Lambert v Lowestoft Corp* [1901] 1 K.B. 590 and *Thompson v Brighton Corp* [1894] 1 Q.B. 332. Similar considerations will apply if a sewer is laid in the bed of a watercourse, but no responsibility could attach to the sewerage undertaker if the sewer is initially properly laid but subsequently obstructs the flow of water in the river due to some change in the river not the responsibility of the undertaker: *Radstock Co-operative and Industrial Society Co Ltd v Norton-Radstock UDC* [1968] Ch. 605.

be damaged as a result of some misuse of the highway above it (e.g. by driving an exceptionally heavy vehicle along it in circumstances amounting to negligence), it seems probable that the sewerage undertaker in whom the sewer is vested could recover damages from the person responsible.[141]

Certain special provisions are made in respect of works upon streets under the control of railway undertakers[142] or a navigation authority.[143] The general power of a sewerage undertaker to undertake street works is inapplicable to a street which is not a highway maintainable at public expense within the meaning of the Highways Act 1980 and is controlled, managed or maintainable by railway undertakers or a navigation authority or forms part of a level crossing belonging to such a company or authority or other person, except with the consent of such company, authority or person. This restriction does not, however, apply to emergency works within the meaning of the New Roads and Street Works Act 1991.[144] In other circumstances consents given under this provision may be made subject to reasonable conditions but may not be unreasonably withheld. Disputes as to the granting or withholding of such consents are to be resolved by a single arbitrator appointed by agreement or, in default of such agreement, by the President of the Institution of Civil Engineers. Contravention of the restrictions without reasonable excuse is a criminal offence for which an offender will incur liability to a fine not exceeding level 3 on the standard scale.

A further specific restriction is imposed by Sch.13 of the Water **3–020**
Industry Act 1991. It is provided that powers to perform works conferred by the 1991 Act do not authorise the carrying out of actions without consent of certain specified undertakings which, whether directly or indirectly, would injuriously affect works or property vested in such an undertaker in that capacity as such or with the use of

---

141 See *Driscoll v Poplar Board of Works* (1897) 62 J.P. 40. It might also be possible to recover damages from the highway authority where a sewer is damaged by the use of exceptionally heavy equipment for highway repairs: see *Gas Light and Coke Co v Vestry of St Mary Abbots* (1885) 15 Q.B.D. 1.

142 For this purpose "railway undertakers" means the British Railways Board, Transport for London or any subsidiary, or any other person authorised by or under any enactment to construct, work or carry on a railway (1991 Act s.219(1), as amended by SI 2003/1615 Sch.1 para.15).

143 1991 Act Sch.13 para.3(1).

144 1991 Act Sch.13 para.3(2). As to "emergency works" under the New Roads and Street Works Act 1991, see *ibid.*, s.52.

any such works or property.[145] Any disputes upon such consent are to be referred to a single arbitrator appointed by agreement or, in default thereof, by the President of the Institution of Civil Engineers.[146] The undertakings specified for this purpose are those of:

(a) the Environment Agency, the Civil Aviation Authority, the Coal Authority and the provider of a universal postal service;

(b) a water or sewerage undertaker;

(c) any undertaking consisting in the provision of an electronic communications network;

(d) an airport to which Pt V of the Airports Act 1986 applies;

(e) a public gas supplier within the meaning of Pt I of the Gas Act 1986 or a gas transporter;

(f) an undertaking licensed to generate, supply or participate in the transmission of electricity under Pt I of the Electricity Act 1989;

(g) a navigation, harbour or conservancy authority or an internal drainage board;

(h) the British Railways Board, Transport for London or any subsidiary, or any other enterprise authorised to construct, work or carry on any railway;

(i) any public utility carried on by a local authority under any Act or any order having the force of an Act;

(j) the undertaking of any licensed operator, within the meaning of the Coal Industry Act 1994; and

---

[145] 1991 Act Sch.13 para.1(1). It is further provided that no power to perform works under the 1991 Act authorises works prejudicial to the performance of statutory functions by any of the specified undertakers (Sch.13 para.2). Further, nothing in the 1991 Act confers power to interfere without consent with any sluices, floodgates, sewers, groynes, sea defences or other works used for the drainage, preservation or improvement of any land under any local statutory provision or with any works used by any person for the irrigation of land (s.186(1)). Where, other than in the exercise of compulsory powers, a sewerage undertaker proposes to construct or alter an inland water not forming part of a main river for the purposes of Pt 4 of the Water Resources Act 1991 or to alter works thereon or in, the undertaker must first consult with the internal drainage board for the district (s.186(5)).

[146] Sch.13 para.1(3), (4).

(k) the undertaking of a person as licence holder under Ch.1 of Pt 1 of the Transport Act 2000 (air traffic services).[147]

(b) Powers to carry out works upon other land

Under ss.159 and 161(2) of the Water Industry Act 1991, a sewerage undertaker[148] has power in respect of land not in, under or over a street: **3–021**

(a) to lay a sewer or disposal main,[149] above or below the surface;

(b) to inspect, maintain, adjust or alter a sewer or disposal main;

(c) to carry out works requisite for the aversion of pollution or contamination of water in a water works[150];

(d) to carry out works requisite for or incidental to any such works.

This power was originally inserted in parenthesis in s.16 of the 1875 Act and was at that time made subject to a requirement that the power should be exercised only where the (then) local authority's surveyor had stated that passing through the private land in question was necessary.[151] This requirement no longer specifically applies. Before power under the paragraph may be exercised, "reasonable notice" of the proposed exercise must be given to the owner and occupier of the land concerned.[152] The precise form of notice is not stated by the Act but "reasonable notice" is defined to mean:

(i) in case of operations to lay a sewer or disposal main, a three-month period;

(ii) in case of alteration of an existing pipe, a period of 42 days.[153]

---

147 Sch.13 para.1(5), as amended by the Coal Industry Act 1994 Sch.9 para.42; the Environment Act 1995 Sch.22 para.127; SI 2001/1149 Sch.1 para.88(1), (2), (3); SI 2003/1615 Sch.1 para.15; the Communications Act 2003 Sch.17 para.111(1), (2) and the Transport Act 2000 Sch.5 para.14; and modified by the Utilities Act 2000 s.76(7).

148 As to the powers of companies by virtue of inset appointments, see above, pp. 15, 93.

149 Extended by the Water Act 2003 s.97(5), referring to s.158(7): see above, p.92.

150 This provision is of primary relevance to water undertakers but may have some significance for sewerage undertakers.

151 See, e.g. *Lewis v Weston-super-Mare Local Board* (1888) 40 Ch. D. 55.

152 1991 Act s.159(4). Shaw's Form PH85 is appropriate.

153 1991 Act s.159(5).

These time limits do not, however, apply in cases of emergency or where a sewerage undertaker is under a duty to provide a public sewer following a requisition under s.98 of the 1991 Act.[154]

Under former equivalent powers it was held that a public sewer so constructed need not necessarily lead at either end (or at both ends) to a public sewer, although it normally will do so; it might be constructed to serve as a link between two private sewers.[155] Presumably in such a case the authority must acquire rights from the owner of at least one of the private sewers to allow effluent from the public sewer to flow through that private sewer. This position was confirmed by the decision of the Court of Appeal in *British Waterways Board v Severn Trent Water Ltd*,[156] where it was held that s.159 did not include an implied power for a sewerage undertaker to discharge the contents of the sewer on to or into someone else's land or watercourse without their consent. There was nothing in the wording of s.159 to support the existence of such a power. The contention that an implied power existed for the benefit of a sewerage undertaker was inconsistent with the fact that the 1991 Act conferred an express power[157] to discharge water, subject to conditions, on a water undertaker. Finally, it could not be argued that it was necessary for the discharge of a sewerage undertaker's function for such a power to be implied, given the possibilities of obtaining the right to discharge by agreement, subject to the payment of compensation, or discharging on to the undertaker's own land or land acquired by it compulsorily.

3–022 Also under earlier equivalent powers, it was held that where construction of a sewer necessarily involved the demolition of a building such action lay within the authority conferred.[158] It also appears that for this purpose a right of water to a mill is also "land".[159]

No land need be acquired in order to lay a sewer under these provisions and, if a recalcitrant owner were to object to the performance of such works, a notice under s.159 would generally suffice without need of recourse to compulsory purchase procedures.[160] Nonetheless, the performance of such works has an effect equivalent to compulsory purchase and provision is therefore made by the 1991 Act for the

---

154 1991 Act s.159(6).

155 *Moore v Frimley and Camberley UDC* (1965) 63 L.G.R. 194.

156 [2001] EWCA Civ 276; [2002] Ch. 25.

157 s.165(1).

158 *Hutton v Esher UDC* [1974] Ch.167.

159 *Cleckheaton UDC v Firth* (1898) 62 J.P. 536. The Act does not specifically define "land", but Sch.1 to the Interpretation Act 1978 states that the term includes buildings and other structures, land covered with water, and any estate, interest, easement, servitude or right in or over land.

160 See *Thornton v Nutter* (1867) 31 J.P. 419 in respect of equivalent earlier provisions.

payment of compensation. If the value of private land over which powers conferred by ss.159, 161(2) and 163 of the 1991 Act have been exercised or land held with such land[161] is depreciated by the exercise of such powers by a sewerage undertaker, then the persons entitled to an interest so depreciated will be entitled to equivalent compensation from the undertaker.[162] Further, if a person entitled to an interest in such land sustains loss or damage attributable to the exercise of such powers by a sewerage undertaker, which whilst not a depreciation of the value of the interest is a matter in respect of which disturbance compensation would have been payable in case of a compulsory acquisition under s.155,[163] compensation will also be payable.[164] Compensation will also be payable where damage or injurious affection is caused by its performance of works to land which is not the land immediately concerned.[165] The amount of compensation in respect of depreciation in value is assessed in accordance with the rules set out in s.5 of the Land Compensation Act 1961, subject to any necessary modifications.[166] Any dispute as to the amount of compensation is to be settled by the Upper Tribunal (formerly the Lands Tribunal) in the light of ss 2 and 4 of the Land Compensation Act 1961, again subject to any necessary modifications.[167] If the interest in respect of which compensation is to be paid is burdened with a mortgage:

---

[161] This definition is given by Sch.12 para.2(5).

[162] Sch.12 para.2(1). See, e.g. *Collins and Collins v Thames Water Utilities Ltd* [1994] 49 E.G.116, where the Lands Tribunal held on the facts that the value of a house had not been depreciated by the construction of a sewer under part of the back garden. Judge Marder Q.C., President, inclined to the view but did not decide that the Tribunal could take into account any enhancement of value as a result of the works: here, the house was now on mains drainage, replacing a septic tank. The existence of compulsory powers is not to be ignored in assessing compensation for the diminution in the value of the land affected; accordingly, there is no room for any "ransom value": *Kettering BC v Anglian Water Services plc* [2002] R.V.R. 266, Lands Tribunal.

[163] See below.

[164] Sch.12 para.2(2). The onus lies on the claimant to establish that loss or damage was in fact caused: see, e.g. *Hodder v South West Water Services Ltd* [2002] R.V.R. 365, Lands Tribunal, where the claim was not established on the evidence. Facts occurring after the date of valuation may be taken into account when assessing compensation for disturbance: *Wickham Growers Ltd v Southern Water plc* (1996) 73 P. & C.R. 351.

[165] Sch.12 para.2(3).

[166] Sch.12 para.3(2).

[167] Sch.12 para.3(1), as amended by SI 2009/1307 Sch.1 para.224(a). A reference to the Upper Tribunal is regarded as an action to recover compensation for the purposes of s.9(1) of the Limitation Act 1980, which accordingly imposes a six-year period within which the reference must be made: see *Hillingdon LBC v ARC Ltd* [1999] Ch. 139 (decided in respect of a claim for compensation for compulsory purchase); applied in respect of a claim under Sch.12 in *Lillis v North West Water Ltd* [1999] R.V.R. 12, Lands Tribunal (holding, nevertheless, that on the facts reliance on the limitation period was barred on the basis of estoppel by convention).

(i) the assessment is made as if the interest were not so burdened;

(ii) a claim may also be made by the mortgagee but without prejudice to the claim of the holder of the interest;

(iii) no compensation is payable in respect of the interest of the mortgagee *per se*, as distinct from the interest which is subject to the mortgage; and

(iv) any such compensation will be paid to the mortgagee, or the first if there is more than one, and then applied as if it were the proceeds of sale.[168]

A claim for compensation may also be made where physical factors caused by the use of public works result in depreciation in the value of an interest in land.[169]

3–023 In respect of all land compensation claims in respect of works by sewerage undertakers, the Secretary of State has power by regulation to authorise advance payments.[170]

Each water and sewerage undertaker must submit to the Secretary of State for his approval a code of practice with respect to its exercise of any powers confirmed by or by virtue of sections 159 or 161(2). Approval is expressed by a statutory instrument.[171] Breach of a code does not affect the undertaker's powers, or itself entitle any person to be paid any amount under section 181(4) or give rise to any civil or criminal liability, but the WSRA must take any contravention into account in determining whether to give a direction under that subsection.[172]

If a pipe is laid without the required notice to the owner of the land, the undertaker will be liable in trespass.[173] Conversely, interference

---

[168] Sch.12 para.3(3).

[169] Pt 1 of the Land Compensation Act 1973; see, e.g. *Butcher and Butcher v North West Water Ltd* [1997] R.V.R. 287 (reduction in value of a dwelling caused by noise during maintenance and smells arising from a new sewerage outlet on neighbouring land).

[170] Sch.12 para.2(4). See the Water and Sewerage (Works) (Advance Payments) Regulations 1989 (SI 1989/1379).

[171] e.g. Water and Sewerage Undertakers (Pipelaying and Other Works) (Code of Practice) Order 1999 (SI 1999/3070).

[172] 1991 Act s.182. As to s.181, see pp.110–111.

[173] See *Severn Trent Water Ltd v Barnes* [2004] EWCA Civ 570; [2004] E.G.L.R. 95, where the Court of Appeal held that the damages should be awarded in respect of a sum (1) equivalent to the statutory compensation that would have been payable had proper procedures been followed; and (2) a sum for the loss of the opportunity to negotiate; but not (3) a further sum for restitutionary damages in respect of some part of the profits that were made by using the pipe; and *Ramdhun v Thames Water Utilities Ltd* [2010] EWHC 1014 (QB).

by the landowner with a pipe properly laid may give rise to liability in trespass on his part.[174]

(c) Powers of entry in relation to the performance of works

A person so authorised in writing by a sewerage undertaker may enter premises[175] for the purposes of determining whether it is appropriate or practical for the undertaker to exercise any power conferred by ss.158, 159, 161(1), (2), 163 and 165 of the 1991 Act; or for determining how such a power should be exercised; or for the actual exercise of such a power.[176] The works so authorised include experimental borings to ascertain the nature of the subsoil and the removal for analysis of samples of water, effluent, land or articles necessary for determining the appropriateness of the exercise of powers. Such powers of entry may, however, only be exercised at a reasonable time and upon seven days' notice to the occupier or in an emergency.[177] However, under Pt II of Sch.6 to the 1991 Act,[178] a Justice of the Peace who is satisfied upon sworn information in writing that there are reasonable grounds for the exercise of a power conferred by, inter alia, s.168 and that: **3–024**

(a) the exercise of the right or power in relation to the premises has been refused;

(b) such a refusal is reasonably apprehended;

(c) the premises concerned are unoccupied;

(d) the owner is temporarily absent from the premises;

(e) the case is one of urgency; or

(f) an application for admission would defeat the object of the proposed entry,

---

174 See *Bromley LBC v Morritt* (1999) 79 P. & C.R. 536.

175 Including land where entry is needed to gain access to other land where works are to be performed, etc.: *Dwr Cymru Cyfyngedig v Williams*, *The Times*, October 9, 1991, D.C.

176 1991 Act s.168.

177 1991 Act Sch.6 Pt II para.6.

178 para.7. In *Severn Trent Water Ltd v Slack and Hazard* [2001] EWHC Admin 1094, Elias J. left open the question of whether this procedure complied with ECHR Art.6; as all the points that the respondents had wished to raise had been raised before the justices, it was not open to them to challenge the procedure on the basis that it might in other circumstances cause unfairness.

may[179] by warrant authorise the sewerage undertaker to designate a person to exercise the powers in relation to the premises concerned, by force if need be. Such a warrant will remain in force until such time as the purposes for which it was issued have been fulfilled.

(d) Powers to acquire land

3–025 A sewerage undertaker may be authorised by the Secretary of State to purchase land in England and Wales which is required for the performance of its functions; such an authorisation may include the creation of new rights and interests and the extinguishment of pre-existing rights.[180] The land compulsorily acquired by a sewerage undertaker may include land required for giving in exchange for, or for any right in, land which forms part of a common, open space or a fuel or field garden allotment.[181] Compulsory purchases by a sewerage undertaker are generally governed by the procedures under the Acquisition of Land Act 1981 with certain specific exceptions.[182]

(e) Restrictions upon disposal of land

3–026 A sewerage undertaker may not dispose of an interest in or right over any land which was transferred to it in accordance with a scheme under Sch.2 of the 1989 Act or, in the case of a statutory water company, was held by it in the financial year ending with March 31, 1990[183]; or has since then been held by the company in connection with the performance of its functions as a sewerage undertaker; or was transferred from a company so holding it in accordance with a

---

[179] This does not confer a general discretion on the justices; once one of the conditions in para.7(1) is established, the warrant should be authorised, provided the specified procedural requirements have been fulfilled: *Severn Trent Water Ltd v Slack and Hazard* [2001] EWHC Admin 1094. The court also indicated, obiter, that if the justices were concerned that to grant a warrant might damage a site of special scientific interest unless certain precautions were taken, this could be a relevant consideration in determining whether the condition in para.7(1)(a) was established.

[180] 1991 Act s.155(1), (2). These powers are transferred to the National Assembly in Wales in respect of such parts of Wales as are outside the catchment areas of the rivers Dee, Wye and Severn, and are exercisable by the National Assembly concurrently with the Secretary of State within those areas: SI 1999/672 Sch.1.

[181] 1991 Act s.155(3).

[182] In particular in relation to the acquisition of mineral rights, in which case, by virtue of s.188 of the Act, Sch.14 of the 1991 Act is substituted for Sch.2 of the Acquisition of Land Act 1981. Note also that certain modifications are made by Sch.9 to the 1991 Act in cases where a right over land is acquired by the creation of a new right.

[183] i.e. including the transfer date (September 1, 1989): The Water Authorities (Transfer of Functions) (Appointed Day) Order 1989, SI 1989/1530.

scheme under Sch.2 of the 1991 Act, except with the consent of, or in accordance with a general authorisation given by, the Secretary of State. Such consent or authorisation must be set out in a notice served by the Secretary of State and may be made subject to conditions.[184] Such conditions may include requirements that:

(a) prior to disposal an opportunity of acquiring the land or right must be offered to a specified person;

(b) the company has complied with the conditions of its appointment relating to disposal of lands or any interest in or right in or over that land;

(c) in a case of land in a National Park, the (Norfolk or Suffolk) Broads or in an area of outstanding natural beauty or special scientific interest, the undertaker should consult with Natural England (in England) or the Countryside Council for Wales and/or enter into such agreements under s.39 of the Wildlife and Countryside Act 1981[185] or such covenants under s.156(6) of the 1991 Act[186] as the Secretary of State may determine;

(d) provision requiring determinations under or for the purposes of the consent or authorisation to be made, in the cases mentioned in (c), either by the Natural England or the Countryside Council for Wales or only after consultation with that Natural England or the Council.[187]

(f) Environmental duties of sewerage undertakers

Sewerage undertakers as such will be less significant landowners than **3–027** water undertakers, although they may often of course be in fact the same body, but may still hold considerable areas of land and therefore be vested with considerable environmental responsibilities. The 1991 Act provides by s.3[188] that in formulating or considering any proposals

---

[184] 1991 Act ss.156(1)–(3), 219(1) (definition of "protected land").

[185] Or under s.7 of the Natural Environment and Rural Communities Act 2006. These are management agreements.

[186] s.156(6) provides for the entry into a covenant between a company and the Secretary of State relating to freedom of access to the land by members of the public or other persons or the use or management of the land. Such a covenant binds all persons deriving title from or under that company and will be enforceable by the Secretary of State accordingly.

[187] 1991 Act s.156(4), (5) subs.(4) as amended by the Natural Environment and Rural Communities Act 2006 Sch.11 Pt 1 para.131.

[188] As amended by SI 2002/794 Sch.2 and the Water Act 2003 ss.36(2) and 82.

relating to any of its functions, or the functions of the Environment Agency, a sewerage undertaker is under a duty to comply with specified requirements. There are two sets of requirements, the second being subject to the first. The first set is:

(a) a requirement, so far as may be consistent with the purposes of any enactment relating to the undertaker's functions (and in the case of the Secretary of State, the National Assembly and the WSR, the general duties under s.2 of the 1991 Act),[189] so to exercise any powers conferred with respect to the proposals as to further the conservation and enhancement of natural beauty and the conservation of flora, fauna and geological or physiographic features of special interest and, in the case of the exercise of such a power by a company holding an appointment as a relevant undertaker, as to further water conservation;

(b) a requirement to have regard to the desirability of protecting and conserving buildings (which include structures), sites and objects of archaeological, architectural or historic interest; and

(c) a requirement to take into account any effect which the proposals would have on the beauty or amenity of any rural or urban area or on any such flora, features, buildings, sites or objects.

The second set is:

(a) a requirement to have regard to the desirability of preserving for the public any freedom of access to areas of woodland, mountains, moor, heath, down, cliff or foreshore and other places of natural beauty;

(b) a requirement to have regard to the desirability of maintaining the availability to the public of any facility for visiting or inspecting any building, site or object of archaeological, architectural or historic interest; and

(c) a requirement to take into account any effect which the proposals would have on any such freedom of access on or the availability of any such facility.[190]

---

[189] See above, pp.21–23.

[190] 1991 Act s.3(1)–(4). These duties also apply to the Secretary of State, the National Assembly and the WSRA in formulating or considering any such proposals.

Every relevant undertaker is also under a duty to take such steps as are reasonably practicable and consistent with statutory purposes for securing that any rights to the use of water or land associated with water are exercised so as to ensure that the water or land is made available for recreational purposes and is so made available in the best manner. This is subject to obtaining the consent of any navigation, harbour or conservancy authority to any interference with navigation.[191] In deciding what measures in fact to adopt in particular connection with public access to water and land associated with water, an undertaker is under a duty to take into account the needs of the chronically sick or disabled.[192] There is, however, no express or implied duty to make recreational facilities available free of charge.[193]

Rather stricter obligations are imposed upon sewerage undertakers **3–028**
with reference to certain sites of special interest under s.4 of the 1991 Act. The areas so protected fall into two broad groups. The first are those which Natural England or the Countryside Council for Wales notifies to the undertaker as of special interest by reason of its flora, fauna or geological or physiographical features and which is likely to be affected by its activities.[194] The second group are those in a National Park or the Norfolk and Suffolk Broads[195] which a National Park authority or the Broads Authority considers to be of particular importance in terms of the general environmental duties set out in s.3 of the 1991 Act and which may be affected by the activities of, inter alia, a sewerage undertaker. In either situation the National Park authority or Broads Authority must notify the fact, and the reasons why, to the undertaker and to any other body whose works or operations might affect the land.[196] Following receipt of a notification, the sewerage undertaker, or other body concerned, must consult with the notifying body before carrying out any works, operations or activities which appear to the undertaker to be likely to destroy or damage any flora, fauna or geological or physiographical features by reason of which the land is of special interest or significantly to prejudice access or environmental factors within the meaning of s.3 of the Act which render land in a National Park or the Broads of importance.[197]

---

[191] 1991 Act s.3(5). In the nature of things this is clearly a matter of more relevance to water undertakers than to sewerage undertakers.

[192] 1991 Act s.3(6).

[193] 1991 Act s.3(8).

[194] 1991 Act s.4(1), as amended by the Natural Environment and Rural Communities Act 2006 Sch.11 Pt 1 para.129.

[195] As defined in the Norfolk and Suffolk Broads Act 1988 (1991 Act s.4(6)).

[196] 1991 Act s.4(2).

[197] s.4(3).

A general exception is provided in cases of emergency, provided that what is done and the nature of the emergency are notified to Natural England, the Countryside Council for Wales, the National Park authority or the Broads Authority, as might be appropriate in a given case, as soon as possible.[198] The possible necessity for emergency works without time for consultation is evident and this provision takes account of it although the exception is very widely phrased. The general duty of consultation is stated to exist in respect of works, etc. "which appear to that" undertaker to be potentially damaging. The subjectivity of this standard may give rise to uncertainty in practice. Some relief is offered however by s.5 of the 1991 Act. Under that section the Secretary of State has powers by order to issue or approve codes of practice giving guidance, inter alia, to sewerage undertakers upon such matters and encouraging what appears to him to be desirable practices. In making such an order, the Secretary of State must consult the Environment Agency, Natural England, the Countryside Council for Wales, the Historic Buildings and Monuments Commission for England, the Sports Council, the Sports Council for Wales, all such water and sewerage undertakers and other persons which he may consider appropriate.[199] Such a code does not in itself form part of the requirements of ss.3 and 4, nor does contravention of it give rise to civil or criminal liability but the Secretary of State will be under a duty to take into account whether there has been or is likely to be a contravention in determining when and how to exercise his powers under the 1991 Act.[200] These powers include, of course, ultimately the power to deprive a company of its appointment as a sewerage undertaker. The *Code of Practice on Conservation, Access and Recreation* has effect under these provisions.[201]

(g) Power of statutory undertakers to alter public sewers

3–029 The Environment Agency or the Civil Aviation Authority or any internal drainage board, dock undertakers, railway undertakers, airport operation or licence holder under Pt 1, Ch.1 of the Transport Act 2000

---

[198] s.4(4), as amended by the Natural Environment and Rural Communities Act 2006 Sch.11 Pt 1 para.129.

[199] 1991 Act s.5(4), as amended by the Environment Act 1995 Sch.22 para.98; SI 1999/416 Sch.1 para.15(1), (2); and the 2006 Act Sch.11 Pt 1 para.130.

[200] 1991 Act s.5(2), as amended by SI 2002/794 Sch.2.

[201] See the Water and Sewerage (Conservation, Access and Recreation) (Code of Practice) Order 2000 (SI 2000/477), replacing SI 1989/1152.

may, after giving reasonable notice to the sewerage undertaker concerned, at its own expense and on substituting an equivalent, take up, divert or alter the level of specified sewers, drains, culverts or other pipes. These must be vested in the sewerage undertaker, and pass under or interfere with: (i) any watercourse vested in or under the control of the Agency or board; (ii) any property of the Civil Aviation Authority; (iii) any river, canal towing path or works forming part of the undertaking of those dock undertakers; (iv) the railway of the railway undertakers; (v) the airport in question; or (vi) any property of a licence holder used by the holder for the purpose of carrying out activities authorised by the licence. Any difference of opinion as to what is "an equivalent" may be referred to arbitration.[202]

(h) Duty to remove pipes

Where a sewerage undertaker keeps a sewer or disposal main[203] or other apparatus, on, under or over land and a person with an interest in that land or adjacent land requires it to alter or remove the pipe or apparatus upon the ground that this is necessary to facilitate a proposed improvement of the land, the undertaker must in most cases comply unless the demand is unreasonable.[204] No definition of "unreasonableness" for this purpose is given and the issue, if it comes in a practical form, will presumably be determined on a case by case basis. A notice of requirement for the alteration or removal of a pipe cannot impose a duty upon an undertaker to alter or remove any pipe or apparatus in, under or over a street.[205] **3–030**

Where a sewerage undertaker carries out works pursuant to such a notice it will be entitled to recover its reasonable expenses in doing so from the person who made the requirement[206] and may make it a condition of compliance that reasonable security be provided in respect of the payment of such expenses.[207] Where such a security is deposited, the undertaker must pay interest upon each sum of 50p so deposited for each three months period in which it remains deposited

---

[202] 1991 Act s.184, as amended by the Environment Act 1995 Sch.22 para.119, and the Transport Act 2000 (Consequential Amendment) Order 2001 (SI 2001/4050) Sch. para.8.

[203] i.e. a "relevant pipe": 1991 Act s.158(7), applied by s.185(9).

[204] 1991 Act s.185(1), (2). "Improvement" includes any development or change of use but not improvements with respect to water supply or the provision of sewerage services (s.185(9)).

[205] s.185(3).

[206] s.185(5).

[207] s.185(4).

with it. The rate of interest will be determined by the undertaker, with the approval of the WSRA or, in default, by the WSRA itself.[208] The duty of the sewerage undertaker to comply with such a demand is enforced by the WSRA through an enforcement order under s.18 of the 1991 Act.[209]

(i) Planning controls in respect of sewerage works

3–031 Where the operations or activities of a sewerage undertaker amount to "development" within the meaning of section 55 of the Town and Country Planning Act 1990, the fact that they are authorised by the 1991 Act does not exempt them from the requirement for planning permission.[210] Under the Town and Country Planning (General Permitted Development) Order 1995,[211] a number of classes of development by or on behalf of a sewerage undertaker are "permitted development" and so do not require an express grant of planning permission.[212] These are:

"A (a) development not above ground level required in connection with the provision, improvement, maintenance or repair of a sewer, outfall pipe, sludge main[213] or associated apparatus[214];

(b) the provision of a building, plant, machinery or apparatus in, on, over or under land for the purpose of survey or investigation[215];

(c) the maintenance, improvement or repair of works for measuring the flow in any watercourse or channel;

(d) any works authorised by or required in connection with an order made under section 73 of the Water Resources Act

---

[208] s.185(6).

[209] s.185(8). As to s.18 enforcement orders, see above, pp.24–26.

[210] s.190.

[211] SI 1995/418, replacing SI 1988/1813, as amended.

[212] Unless a direction has been given under Art.4 of the order restricting what would otherwise be permitted development.

[213] i.e. "a pipe or system of pipes (together with any pumps or other machinery or apparatus associated with it) for the conveyance of the residue of water or sewage treated in a water or sewage treatment works as the case may be, including final effluent or the products of the dewatering or incineration of such residue, or partly for any of those purposes and partly for the conveyance of trade effluent or its residue: Sch.2 Pt 16.A.3.

[214] "Associated apparatus" means "pumps, machinery or apparatus associated with the relevant sewer, main or pipe": Sch.2 Pt 16.A.3.

[215] Subject to the condition that after 6 months (or, if sooner, on the completion of the survey or investigation), all such operations cease, and all such buildings, etc. are removed and the land restored as soon as reasonably practicable to its former condition (or any other condition agreed with the local planning authority): Sch.2 Pt 16.A.2.

1991 (power to make ordinary and emergency drought orders);

(e) any other development in, on, over or under their operational land, other than the provision of a building but including the extension or alteration of a building."[216]

The grant of planning permission in respect of proposed works may be open to challenge on conventional judicial review grounds.[217]

(j) Sewer maps

Sewerage undertakers are under a duty to keep records of the locations and particulars of all sewers, lateral drains and disposal mains vested in them; all sewers or lateral drains in respect of which a vesting declaration has been, or deemed to have been, made by the undertaker under Ch.2 of Pt 4 of the Water Industry Act 1991 but has not taken effect and all drains or sewers to which an agreement to make such a declaration made, or deemed to have been made, under s.104 of the 1991 Act relates.[218] For each pipe particulars must be noted of whether it is a drain, sewer or disposal main, of the nature of the effluent flowing through it and of whether it is vested in the undertaker or, if not, whether it is the subject of a vesting declaration under Ch.2 of Pt 4 of the 1991 Act or any agreement under s.104 of the 1991 Act.[219] Separate records must be kept by the sewerage undertaker in relation to each local authority the area of which is in whole or part coincident with its own. Copies of such records are required to be supplied, and updated, to the local authorities concerned without charge and such records must also be made available for inspection by members of the public, free of charge, at all **3–032**

---

[216] 1995 Order Sch.2 Pt 16 Class A. Development is not permitted by Class A(e) if: (a) it would consist of or include the extension or alteration of a building so that (i) its design or external appearance would be materially affected; (ii) the height or the cubic content of the original building would be exceeded by more than 25%; or (iii) the floor space of the original building would be exceeded by more than 1,000 square metres; or (b) it would consist of the installation or erection of any plant or machinery exceeding 15 metres in height or the height of anything it replaces, whichever is the greater.

[217] See, e.g. *R. v Kent CC and Southern Water Services Ltd, ex p. Foreness Point Environmental Action Group*, unreported, June 16, 2000 (challenge to planning permission in respect of works for the provision of secondary treatment rejected on the merits; the council had taken account of the effect on tourism of continued discharges of offensive matter during overflow conditions, and the effect of the works on visual amenity).

[218] 1991 Act s.199(1), as amended by the Water Act 2003 s.97(8).

[219] 1991 Act s.199(2).

reasonable times at an office of the undertaker.[220] Similarly a local authority must make available to the public for inspection, without charge at reasonable hours at its office, information so supplied in the form of a map.[221]

In the keeping of such records there may obviously arise difficulties in the seeking out of the requisite information and the 1991 Act seeks to some extent to take account of this. A sewerage undertaker is not required to record drains, sewers or disposal mains laid prior to September 1, 1989 (the "Transfer Date")[222] if it had no knowledge of or reasonable grounds to suspect their presence or it is not reasonably practicable for it to discover their course.[223] Moreover, a sewerage undertaker is not under a duty at any time within the 10 years running from September 1, 1989 (the "Transfer Date") to record any drain, sewer or disposal main laid before that date unless particulars of it were shown immediately prior to that date upon a map kept by a local authority under the former equivalent s.32 of the 1936 Act or it is the subject of a vesting declaration or an agreement therefore within that period.[224] The duties thus imposed upon sewerage undertakers may be enforced by the Secretary of State through an enforcement order under s.18 of the 1991 Act.[225]

(k) Complaints in respect of works on private land

3–033 Where a sewerage undertaker exercises its powers under or by virtue of ss.159 or 161(2) of the 1991 Act to perform works upon private land, complaints in respect of the works may be addressed to the WSRA, which is then in general be under a duty to investigate them.[226] Such complaints would clearly include violations of codes of practice with respect to such works.[227] Exceptions to the duty of

---

[220] 1991 Act ss.199(3), (4), 200.

[221] 1991 Act ss.199(4), 200. "Local authority" for the purposes of the Inner Temple and the Middle Temple includes respectively their Sub-Treasurer and Under Treasurer (s.200(5)).

[222] The Water Authorities (Transfer of Functions) (Appointed Day) Order 1989 (SI 1989/1530).

[223] s.199(7).

[224] s.199(8).

[225] s.199(9). As to s.18 enforcement orders, see above, pp.24–26.

[226] s.181(1), as amended by the Water Act 2003 s.36(2).

[227] i.e. in particular codes made under s.182; see the (two) Water and Sewerage Undertakers (Pipelaying and Other Works) (Code of Practice) Orders 1999 (SI 1999/1546 and SI 1999/3070). Such a contravention would not affect the undertaker's powers, or itself entitle any person to be paid any amount under s.181(4) (see below) or give rise to any civil or criminal liability but would be a matter to be taken into account by the Director in determining whether to give a direction under s.181(4): s.182(3).

investigation are provided where the complaint appears to the WSRA to be vexatious or frivolous, where he is not satisfied that the matter has been drawn to the attention of the sewerage undertaker concerned with a reasonable opportunity for investigation and action or the complaint was first made to the WSRA or the Consumer Council for Water more than 12 months, or such longer period as the WSRA in a special case may allow, since the matter came to the complainant's attention.[228] A sewerage undertaker is under a duty to provide the information and assistance which the Director might reasonably require in the course of such an investigation.[229]

If, upon investigation of a complaint the WSRA is satisfied that a sewerage undertaker has failed adequately to consult the complainant before and during the exercise of its statutory powers or has inflicted loss, damage or inconvenience upon the complainant by acting unreasonably in the manner of the exercise of its powers, he may direct the undertaker to pay compensation up to the sum of £5,000 to the complainant.[230] Before making such an award any representations made to the WSRA by the complainant and/or the undertaker must be considered.[231]

Such compensation may not, however, be awarded in respect of loss, damage or inconvenience which is compensatable under any other enactment, unless the sum so recoverable would not seem an adequate reflection of the unreasonableness of the undertaker's conduct.[232]

NEW CONNECTIONS WITH PUBLIC SEWERS

Section 110A of the Water Industry Act 1991[233] provides that the **3–034**
WSRA may require an established undertaker to permit a "main connection"[234] into its sewerage system by another undertaker or a person who has applied for an appointment or variation of an appointment under s.8 of the 1991 Act replacing a company as undertaker.[235]

---

228 Water Industry Act 1991 s.181(2), as amended by the Water Act 2003 s.36(2) and Sch.7 Pt para.27(4).

229 s.181(3). This duty may be the subject of an enforcement order under s.18 (s.181(6)).

230 s.181(4).

231 s.181(3)(b).

232 s.181(5).

233 Inserted by the Competition and Service (Utilities) Act 1992 s.45, and as amended by the Environment Act 1995 Sch.22 para.104 and the Water Act 2003 s.36(2).

234 i.e. a connection between a sewer or disposal main and a sewer or disposal main, or a connection which allows a sewer or disposal main to discharge directly into a sewage disposal works: s.110A(3).

235 See above, pp.14–15.

The WSRA must first consult the Environment Agency, and must have regard to the desirability of:

(a) facilitating effective competition within the sewerage services industry;

(b) the existing undertaker's recovering its expenses and securing a reasonable return on capital;

(c) the existing undertaker's being able to meet its existing and likely future obligations to provide sewerage services without having to incur unreasonable expenditure in carrying out works;

(d) not putting at risk the ability of the existing undertaker to meet such obligations.

Chapter 4

CONSTRUCTION OF SEWERS BY PRIVATE INDIVIDUALS[1]

INTRODUCTORY

The construction of a drain or sewer for the purpose of draining one's land or premises is a natural incident of the ownership of that land which will not normally give rise to a cause of action in third parties. Liability in private nuisance might, however, arise if: **4–001**

(i) the work interferes with neighbouring land, e.g. by physical damage, encroachment, disturbance of easements or other natural rights;

(ii) there is unreasonable interference with the comfort or convenience of the occupier;

(iii) there is negligence or malicious interference with the natural drainage of neighbouring land, such interference not being an inevitable consequence of the reasonable use and development of the land with due care for the avoidance of harm.[2]

Failure to take reasonable steps to maintain a private sewer may also give rise to liability in private nuisance on ordinary principles.

A landowner will not, however, be liable for damages where non-negligent and proper construction work sets natural agencies in motion which drain subterranean water and cause subsidence.[3] In contrast, liability may arise where the support of land is removed as a consequence of construction of drains or sewers concomitant upon mineral extraction.[4] Once the landowner has caused sewage or other matter to collect on his land (in the drain pipes, or in a cesspool or

---

[1] The expression "private individual" is used in this chapter as including any body corporate other than a sewerage undertaker. "Sewers" includes drains and sustainable drainage systems (SUDS).

[2] *Home Brewery Co Ltd v William Davis & Co (Leicester) Ltd* [1987] Q.B. 339.

[3] *Popplewell v Hodkinson* (1869) L.R. 4 Exch. 248; it was an essential feature of the case that the natural agencies in question could not reasonably have been foreseen. See also *Stephens v Anglian Water Authority* [1987] 1 W.L.R. 1381.

[4] *Stephens v Anglian Water Authority* [1987] 1 W.L.R. 1381 at p.1384.

tank), he may be held strictly liable for damage to property caused by any escape.[5] Liability under this principle—an application of the rule in *Rylands v Fletcher*—will attach irrespective of the proof of any negligence but it is now a prerequisite of liability that the damage is foreseeable[6] and the law recognises a number of special defences.[7]

The right to cause sewage matter to flow under or across another's land is thus one which must be acquired by prescription[8] or by express or implied grant or reservation. The details of such matters form part of the law of easements. In the present context we are concerned rather with relations between the sewerage undertaker and a private individual proposing to construct a sewer[9]; the construction of drains by private individuals is considered later.[10]

THE CONSTRUCTION OF PRIVATE SEWERS

4–002 There is no express provision in the 1936 or 1991 Acts requiring a private individual proposing to construct a sewer to submit plans thereof to, or to obtain the approval of, the local authority or the sewerage undertaker, but such proposals are in effect regulated as a consequence of the following provisions:

---

[5] *Rylands v Fletcher* (1868) L.R. 3 H.L. 330; see, e.g. *Jones v Bedwellty UDC* (1916) 80 J.P. Jo. 192. "I think it clear that the principle of *Rylands v Fletcher* would apply to the owner of a sewer, whether he himself made the sewer or not . . . His duty at common law would be to see that the sewage in his sewer did not escape to the injury of others": per Parker J. in *Jones v Llanrwst UDC* [1911] 1 Ch. 393; *Humphries v Cousins* (1877) 2 C.P.D. 239: "It was the defendant's duty to keep the sewage which he was himself bound to receive from passing from his own premises to the plaintiff's premises, otherwise than along the old accustomed channel": per Denman J. at p.244.

[6] *Cambridge Water Co v Eastern Counties Leather plc* [1994] 2 A.C. 264, H.L. *Humphries v Cousins*, above, seems inconsistent with this principle and must be taken to have been overruled on this point: cf. Lord Goff at pp.302, 306.

[7] Including act of God and act of a stranger: see generally W.V.H. Rogers, *Winfield and Jolowicz on Tort*, 18th edn (2010), pp.778–789. The House of Lords in *Transco plc (formerly BG plc and BG Transco plc) v Stockport MBC* [2003] UKHL 61, [2004] 2 A.C. 1, held that the *Rylands v Fletcher* principle remained part of English law, but restated its scope: see Lord Bingham of Cornhill at [11].

[8] See above, Ch.2, pp.67–69.

[9] A private individual has none of the special powers discussed in Ch.3, above, pp.92–102. Thus, the breaking up of the surface of a street for the purpose of laying a private sewer (as distinct from making a communication with a public sewer) may be done only by agreement with the highway or other appropriate authority.

[10] See Ch.9, below, pp.223–236. The difference between private sewers and private drains is that between sewers and drains generally; see above Ch.1, pp.3–12 and Ch.2.

(a) New buildings

Part H of the Building Regulations 2000[11] imposes requirements as to drainage and waste disposal in respect of any new building or an extension to a building.[12] Furthermore, a *Protocol on Design, Construction and Adoption of Sewers in England and Wales* has been agreed by DEFRA, DTLR, the National Assembly for Wales, the House Builders Federation and Water UK.[13] This is aimed at putting into practice a common approach for designing and constructing all sewers to ensure that they fall within an adoptable standard, and to prevent the proliferation of private sewers with their associated problems of ownership and maintenance. Accordingly, the essential elements of Approved Document to Pt H of the Building Regulations 2000 have been harmonised with the guidance in the *Sewers for Adoption* (6th edition, 2006) published by WRC plc on behalf of Water UK. The protocol applies to domestic foul sewage arising from any type of development. It emphasises the need for developers and sewerage undertakers to work in close liaison, the latter being consulted ideally before a planning application is made.[14] Since 2001, undertakers have been working to align practices across the country. **4–003**

(b) Existing buildings

If any private sewer or drain[15] of an existing building is "insufficient"[16] **4–004**
or, in the case of a sewer or drain communicating directly or indirectly with a public sewer, is so defective as to admit subsoil water, or if it is in such a condition as to be prejudicial to health or a nuisance,[17] the local authority may, in any such case, by notice[18] require the defect to

---

[11] SI 2000/2531, as amended by SI 2001/3335, Sch.

[12] See below, pp.227–229.

[13] April 2002, http://www.defra.gov.uk [Accessed August 4, 2010]. See also Environment Agency, Scottish Environmental Protection Agency, Environment and Heritage Service, Pollution Prevention Guidelines 4, "Treatment and disposal of sewage where no foul sewer is available" (PPG 4, July 2006, http://publications.environment-agency.gov.uk [Accessed August 3, 2010]).

[14] As to connections with existing public sewers, see ss.106 and 107 of the Water Industry Act 1991, Ch.9, below, p.226–232.

[15] Or cesspool, soil pipe, rain-water pipe, spout, sink or other necessary appliance: Building Act 1984 s.59(1)(b), below, Ch.9, p.241.

[16] This term is not defined or explained in the Act.

[17] As to the effect of this phrase see below, p.245.

[18] The notice must indicate the nature of the works to be executed and state the time within which they are to be executed: 1984 Act s.99(1). It must be in writing (s.92). As to authentication and service of documents, see ss.93, 94. The requirement as to writing is mandatory: *Epping Forest DC v Essex Rendering* [1983] 1 W.L.R. 158, H.L., a decision on the equivalent s.283 of the Public Health Act 1936. There is no prescribed form but see Shaw's Form PN23D.

be remedied or the nuisance abated.[19] In the event of failure to comply with a notice under this section, the authority may itself act in default and recover its expenses in so doing from the owner of the property for the time being. On completion of the work the expenses become a charge upon the premises.[20] In practice this section provides the local authority with a most effective means of control over the condition, etc. of private drains and sewers.

(c) Special cases

4–005 The sewerage undertaker may, in certain circumstances, require any person[21] proposing to construct a drain or sewer to construct it according to the different specifications of the authority. The authority may specify alterations "as regards material or size of pipes, depth, fall, direction or outfall or otherwise".[22] This power may be exercised by the undertaker only when it considers[23] that the "proposed drain or sewer is, or is likely to be, needed to form part of a general sewerage system which that undertaker provides or proposes to provide".[24] A requirement imposed under s.112 may not be inconsistent with, or more onerous than, standards published for the purposes of s.106B.[25]

Failure to comply with the sewerage undertaker's requirements will be a breach of a duty owed to the undertaker and any loss or damage which it suffers in consequence will be actionable at its suit.[26] A person aggrieved by the requirements may appeal within 28 days to the WSRA.[27]

Where a person[28] reconstructs a drain that communicates with a sewer or another drain, or executes any works to such a drain or

---

[19] Building Act 1984 s.59. See further below, pp.240–242.
[20] Building Act 1984 s.107, and below, Ch.11, pp.277–278.
[21] "Person" here must include a county council, and therefore it seems that a sewerage undertaker may take action under this section against the county council acting under the private street works code contained in the Highways Act 1980 Pt 11.
[22] 1991 Act s.112(1). The words "or otherwise" normally suggest that the *ejusdem generis* rule is to be applied, but it is submitted that the rule is not applicable in the present context, as the terms used are of different *genera* (see, e.g. *R. v Payne* (1866) 35 L.J.M.C. 170, and *Maxwell on the Interpretation of Statutes*, 12th edn, pp.297–306; *Craies on Statute Law*, 7th edn, pp.178–186).
[23] A decision on this point would be open to challenge on conventional grounds for judicial review, including irrationality.
[24] 1991 Act s.112(1).
[25] 1991 Act s.112(8) inserted (from a day to be appointed) by the Flood and Water Management Act 2010 s.42(4). See pp.218–219.
[26] 1991 Act s.112(5).
[27] 1991 Act s.112(2), (3), as amended by the Water Act 2003 s.36(2).
[28] The section applies to any person, including apparently a contractor, and it is not confined to cases where a new sewer is being constructed.

premises served by such a drain so as permanently to discontinue its use, he must take certain steps. He must disconnect and seal unnecessary or disused drains at such points as the local authority may reasonably require.[29] In addition he must give at least 48 hours' notice to the local authority before complying with this requirement.[30] It it the aim of this provision to prevent abandoned drains becoming a health hazard. The local authority is not given any powers to take action itself in default of compliance with this provision, but failure to give the notice referred to renders the offender liable to a fine on conviction. It is also an offence, again punishable by fine, for any person knowingly to fail to comply with the duty created by s.62(1). In the case of a demolition of a building, the local authority has further powers of control.[31]

(d) Planning control

Direct detailed control over the construction of private sewerage **4–006**
or drainage schemes is maintained under the Town and Country Planning Act 1990. These controls are enforceable by the local planning authority which for this purpose will be the unitary, district or London borough council in England, or county or county borough council in Wales.[32]

Under this Act the construction of works such as private sewerage schemes, being engineering operations in, on or over land, amounts to development.[33] Express planning permission from the local planning authority is therefore required before it may be undertaken.[34] Guidance has been given by the DETR and the Welsh Office emphasising that the first presumption in drawing up sewerage proposals for any development must always be to provide a system of foul drainage discharging into a public sewer. If this is not feasible, a package sewage treatment plant should be considered. Only if this is not feasible, taking account of cost and/or practicability, should the case of septic tank(s) be considered. If non-mains sewerage and/or sewage

---

[29] Building Act 1984 s.62(1).
[30] Building Act 1984 s.62(4).
[31] Building Act 1984 s.80.
[32] See Town and Country Planning Act 1990 ss.1, 62 and Schs 1, 1A, as amended by the Local Government (Wales) Act 1994 s.18 and Sch.4.
[33] See definition of "development" in s.55 of the 1990 Act. The 1990 Act provides no definition of the phrase "engineering operations" except to extend it to include the formation or laying out of means of access to highways: see s.336(1).
[34] See further below, pp.160–162, on the requirements applicable in respect of sewage disposal works.

disposal proposals incorporating septic tanks are likely to lead to a significant environmental, amenity or public health problem, that will normally be sufficient to justify refusal of planning permission. Relevant factors are listed.[35]

(e) Other provisions

4–007 The general law places few, if any, major obstacles to the construction of a private sewer or connecting drain. However care must be taken that all necessary easements or other rights[36] can be obtained from other landowners. It is also important to avoid creating a common law nuisance as a result of the construction. If it is intended to connect a new drain or private sewer to an existing *private* drain or sewer, the consent of the owners of the land through which that existing conduit runs must be obtained. The owner of the land from which the existing effluent originates will have obtained an easement and the burden thereby placed on the servient owner cannot be increased without his consent.[37]

The construction of works for the supply of sewage to land for agriculture purposes by owners of limited interests in land (e.g. a tenant for life under the Settled Land Act 1925) is deemed to be an improvement of land within the Improvement of Land Act 1864,[38] and the construction of sewers and drainage is an authorised improvement, the cost of which may be expended out of capital moneys and is not liable to be replaced by instalments under the Settled Land Act 1925.[39]

THE ADOPTION OF SEWERS AND LATERAL DRAINS

4–008 Provided the appropriate procedure is followed, the sewerage undertaker may at any time "adopt" any sewer situated within its area or which serves the whole or any part of that area,[40] or any part of a sewer,[41] or any sewage disposal works so situated or which serve the whole or any part of that area, the construction whereof was not

---

[35] DETR Circular 03/99, WO Circular 10/99, "Planning Requirements in respect of the Use of Non-Mains Sewerage incorporating Septic Tanks in New Developments".

[36] The construction of a private sewer or drain on another's land without permission will constitute trespass: *Phillips v Lacey*, unreported, March 9, 1987; cf. *Grant v Derwent* [1929] 1 Ch. 390.

[37] See such cases as *Bracewell v Appleby* [1975] Ch. 408.

[38] Public Health Act 1936 s.33.

[39] Settled Land Act 1925 s.83 and Third Schedule Pt I.

[40] The provision applies only to sewers, not to drains (other than lateral drains); but see also s.104 of the 1991 Act, below, pp.123–125.

[41] 1991 Act s.102(3).

completed before October 1, 1937.[42] This procedure was extended by the Water Act 2003[43] to enable the adoption of any lateral drain[44] which communicates or is to communicate with a public sewer which is so situated or serves the whole or any part of that area.

(a) Effect of a declaration

The effect of any such declaration is to cause the sewer or lateral drain to vest in the undertaker as from the date of such declaration.[45] It should be noted, however, that any person who, immediately before the making of a vesting declaration, was entitled to use the sewer or lateral drain, shall be entitled to use it (or any sewer or lateral drain substituted therefor), to the same extent as if the declaration had not been made.[46] A sewerage undertaker may not be liable for any damage caused by an improperly or negligently constructed sewer which had vested in it by virtue of statute[47] "whether with or against their will"[48]; nor would it matter that the damage occurred after the vesting of the sewer in the undertaker. However, it would seem that any such immunity from liability would not protect an undertaker who had adopted a defective private sewer under the present provision, as in such circumstances it could be held to have taken positive action with regard to the sewer. **4–009**

(b) Procedure

When a sewerage undertaker proposes to adopt a sewer or lateral drain by a declaration of vesting under the section,[49] the following procedure must be observed: **4–010**

---

42 1991 Act s.102, as amended by the Water Act 2003 s.96. The date mentioned was the date of commencement of the 1936 Act: see s.347(1) thereof. As to the general vesting of sewers and works in undertakers, see pp.50–67 above.

43 s.96(1).

44 See above, p.67.

45 cf. Ch.2, above, pp.50–51.

46 1991 Act s.102(6), as amended by the Water Act 2003 s.96(1)(e), extending its application to lateral drains.

47 e.g. under s.13 of the 1875 Act; above, p.59.

48 per Atkin J. in *Morris v Mynyddislwyn UDC* (1917) 81 J.P. 262. In the Court of Appeal it was simply held on this point that the pipe in question did not constitute a nuisance: [1917] 2 K.B. 309. See further *Marcic v Thames Water Utilities Ltd*, above, pp.75–80.

49 The owner himself, or any of the owners, may make application to the undertaker requesting a declaration to be made (1991 Act s.102(2)). It is suggested that a declaration of vesting should be made in respect of the sewers on any new private estate when the building has been completed, provided of course the sewers have been properly constructed. Where the sewers can be said to form part of a street, adoption of the street may include adoption of the sewer, but in any case of doubt the procedure of the present section should be followed.

(i) Notice[50] of the proposal must be given to the owner or owners of the sewer, lateral drain or works in question.[51]

(ii) In the rare case where the sewer, etc. in question is situate outside the area of the "adopting" sewerage undertaker it must give notice[52] of its proposal to the undertaker in whose area the sewer is situated, and may not proceed to make the vesting declaration until *either* the other undertaker has consented thereto, *or* the Secretary of State, on application to him,[53] has "dispensed with the necessity for such consent, either unconditionally or subject to such conditions as he may think fit to impose". If a vesting declaration is made, notice must be given to the other undertaker.[54]

(iii) No vesting declaration may be made (except on the application of such body) in respect of any sewer, or of any part thereof, which is vested in another sewerage undertaker, a local authority,[55] a county council,[56] any railway undertakers[57] or dock undertakers.[58]

When the notice under (i) above has been served, the adopting sewerage undertaker may not proceed further until *either* two months[59] have

---

[50] The notice must be in writing: 1991 Act s.219(1) (definition of "notice"), and must be served in the prescribed manner (1991 Act s.216). In *Epping Forest DC v Essex Rendering* [1983] 1 W.L.R. 158, the House of Lords decided that the requirement as to writing is mandatory. The notice itself need not be in any particular form, but Shaw's Form PN4 is appropriate.

[51] 1991 Act s.102(4)(a), as amended by the Water Act 2003 s.96(1)(c).

[52] See preceding note; the same notice will serve for this purpose also.

[53] No provision is made in the section for an inquiry, but the Secretary of State has power to convene one under the 1991 Act s.215, as amended by the Environment Act 1995 Sch.22, para.123.

[54] 1991 Act s.103(1), (2), as amended by the Water Act 2003 s.96(2)(a) to apply to lateral drains situated within the area of another sewerage undertaker or which, though situated within its own area, communicates or is to communicate with a public sewer situated within or serving the whole or any part of the area of another sewerage undertaker.

[55] i.e. a district or London borough council or the Common Council of the City of London and a county or county borough council in Wales: 1991 Act s.219(1), definition as amended by the Local Government (Wales) Act 1994 Sch.11 Pt I para.2(2).

[56] This will be of particular importance with reference to highway sewers: see Ch.6, below, p.147.

[57] i.e. the British Railways Board, Transport for London or any subsidiary, any other person authorised by or under any enactment to construct, work or carry on any railway: 1991 Act s.219(1).

[58] Provided the sewer, etc. in question is situated in or on land which belongs to them and is held or used by them for the purposes of their undertaking: 1991 Act s.103(3), as substituted by the Water Act 2003 s.96(2)(b), which extended the provision to cover lateral drains vested in one of these bodies.

[59] i.e. two calendar months: Interpretation Act 1978 Sch.1.

elapsed[60] without an appeal against its proposals being lodged[61] *or* until any such appeal has been determined.[62] Any owner of a sewer etc.[63] aggrieved by the proposal of the undertaker to make a vesting declaration, may appeal to the WSRA within two months after the notice of the proposal was served upon him; and a similar right of appeal is open to any owner who is aggrieved by the refusal of a sewerage undertaker to make a vesting declaration under the section on his application.[64]

The relationship between "adoption" and the other means whereby a sewer may become a public sewer, should not be overlooked. Thus, in Diagram 3 in Appendix A[65], the whole of the drainage system serving the 13 houses in Lovers' Close (having been constructed after 1936 by a private developer) could be adopted by the sewerage undertaker by resolution under s.102; the lengths F-C and E-B would then become public sewers. On the other hand if the roadway of Lovers' Close is made up under the private street works code (Highways Act 1980 Pt 11), the sewers in the highway (i.e. length F-C) alone will vest in the sewerage undertaker under s.179(2)(b) of the 1991 Act, leaving length E-B as a private sewer.

(c) Relevant considerations

When the sewerage undertaker considers the question whether to make a vesting declaration in respect of a particular sewer, etc., or when the Director considers an appeal under the section, regard must be had to all the circumstances of the case. More specifically the following matters must be taken into account[66]: **4–011**

(a) whether the sewer, or works in question is or are adapted to, or required for, any general system of sewerage or sewage disposal which the undertaker has provided, or proposes to provide, for the whole or any part of its area;

---

[60] Presumably, from the date of service of the notice.

[61] See below, n.64.

[62] 1991 Act s.102(4), as amended by the Water Act 2003 s.96(1)(c), extending its application to lateral drains.

[63] Presumably, this means the owner of the sewer, etc. in question; "owner" is defined for the purposes of the 1991 Act in s.219(1) thereof.

[64] 1991 Act s.105(1), as amended by the Water Act 2003 ss.36(2) and 96(5)(a). This right of appeal may be exercised at any time after he has received notice of the authority's refusal of his application, or, if he receives no such notice, at any time after the expiration of two months from the making of his application (1991 Act s.105(3), as amended by the 2003 Act s.96(5)(b)).

[65] See p.292

[66] 1991 Act ss.102(5), 105(7), s.102(5), as amended by the Water Act 2003 s.96(1)(d).

(b) whether the sewer or lateral drain is constructed under a highway or under land reserved by a planning scheme[67] for a street[68];

(c) the number of buildings which the sewer or lateral drain is intended to serve, and whether, regard being had to the proximity of other buildings or the prospect of future development, it is likely to be required to serve additional buildings[69];

(d) the method of construction and state of repair of the sewer, lateral drain or works; *and*

(e) in a case where an owner objects, whether the making of the proposed vesting declaration would be seriously detrimental[70] to him.

These five considerations are not paramount. Although they must be considered particularly they may be outweighed by other material considerations. However it is not clear whether "all the circumstances of the case" covers financial issues such as the burden of repair and maintenance charges. In *R. v Secretary of State for Wales and A.B. Hutten*,[71] the Secretary of State, contrary to his inspector's recommendation, directed a water authority (as predecessor to the present

---

[67] This expression as it appeared in s.17 of the Public Health Act 1936 was not deleted from the present section by the Town and Country Planning Act 1947 or by any corresponding provisions in the Town and Country Planning Acts 1971 or 1990: but it is submitted that it must be understood to refer to a confirmed development plan under the 1990 Act and now local development documents under the Planning and Compulsory Purchase Act 2004 (see *Cross on Local Government Law* (London: Sweet & Maxwell, 1997), paras 22–21C—22–21H). It should be noted that the definition of "planning scheme" in s.343(1) of the 1936 Act was repealed by the Ninth Schedule of the Town and Country Planning Act 1947.

[68] In view of the undertaker's powers of entry and the local authority's power to prevent building over sewers, adoption should not be refused on this ground merely because sewers are in back gardens: *Westfield Drive, Bolton-le-Sands, Re* (DoE Appeal Decision, October 15, 1987, WS/5527/AB/17), cited in J. Bates, *Water and Drainage Law* (London: Sweet & Maxwell, 2010), para.9.48.

[69] This does not set a minimum figure in respect of the present or future number of buildings; each case is treated on its merits: *Portman Close, Dartford, Re* (DoE Appeal Decision, February 5, 1987, WS/5274/AB/1), cited in Bates, para.9.48.

[70] There is no elucidation in the section of this somewhat obscure expression. However, it has been stated on an appeal that it must be shown that there is an increased likelihood either that the sewer would overflow on to his land or that a structural failure of some sort will occur or that some onerous liability may fall on him as a result of the declaration; however, given the other powers available to an undertaker to deal with such matters, adoption is likely to be considered as beneficial to the owner: *Stennet Ave., Spalding, Re* (DoE Appeal Decision, October 8, 1987, WS/5530/AB/22), cited in Bates, para.9.47.

[71] [1987] J.P.L. 711.

sewerage undertaker) to adopt defective private sewers because it was "less inequitable" for the water authority to bear the financial burden of repair and maintenance than for it to be borne by the owners of the private estate served by the sewers. On an application for judicial review, Macpherson J. seems to have held that there was insufficient evidence available to the Secretary of State for him to justify his decision on that ground; the court did not directly decide whether the financial burden was a relevant consideration in such circumstances. It is submitted that the declaration should normally depend upon the condition of the sewers and drains concerned and only in exceptional circumstances should personal factors, including that of financial equity, be a relevant circumstance within s.102.

On an appeal,[72] either against the proposals of the undertaker to make a declaration, or its refusal to make a declaration, the WSRA may allow or disallow the undertaker's proposals, or may make any declaration the undertaker might have made. In addition, it may specify conditions (including conditions as to the payment of compensation[73] by the sewerage undertaker[74]), and may direct that any declaration it had made should not take effect unless any such conditions are accepted.[75]

AGREEMENTS FOR THE ADOPTION OF SEWERS

As amended by the Water Act 2003,[76] s.104 of the Water Industry Act 1991 provides that, subject to subs.(7) and s.146(3), a sewerage undertaker may agree with: **4–012**

---

[72] Appeals may be lodged by simple letter addressed to the WSRA; there are no rules of procedure governing their conduct, except that if the rules of "natural justice" were not observed on a particular appeal, the proceedings could presumably be quashed by the courts.

[73] The undertakers themselves have no power to agree to make compensation to the owner, nor can they be compelled to do so, except on appeal to the WSRA. Even if the owner can prove that he has sustained damage as a consequence of the undertaker having exercised its powers under the section, any right to compensation (except through an appeal to the WSRA) is excluded specifically by the 1991 Act Sch.12 para.4(5), as amended by the Water Act 2003 s.97(10), adding a reference to a lateral drain.

[74] But not payment *to* the undertaker: *Robin's Close, Broadstone, Re* (DoE Appeal Decision, January 19, 1981, WS/5533/AB/1), cited in J. Bates, *Water and Drainage Law* (London: Sweet & Maxwell, 2010), para.9.48.

[75] 1991 Act s.105(5), as amended by the Water Act 2003 s.36(2); the conditions must be accepted, presumably, by the appellant. This power will be used sparingly as it is considered that the fact that the sewer will become available for public use is not a ground for compensation; if the owner has lost any potential profit from the adoption, compensation will only be considered if the sewer was constructed for some purpose beneficial to the owner over and above its normal sanitary purpose, so that it might contain an element of value which public use of the sewer would destroy: *Battenhall Road, Worcester, Re* (DoE Appeal Decision, December 23, 1971, WS/1857/AB/1), cited in Bates, para.9.47.

[76] s.96(4), in force from May 28, 2004.

(a) any person constructing or proposing to construct any sewer, any drain intended to communicate with a public sewer vested in that undertaker, or any sewage disposal works; or

(b) any person at whose expense the undertaker is, by virtue of an agreement under s.160,[77] to carry out work in connection with the construction of such a drain or sewer;

that, if the sewer, drain or works is or are constructed in accordance with the terms of the agreement, the undertaker will, upon completion of the work, at some specified date or on the happening of some future event, declare the sewer, or such part of the drain as constitutes the lateral drain, or works, to be vested in that undertaker.[78] Any person mentioned in (a) or (b) may make an application to the undertaker requesting it to make an agreement under s.104. Such an application must be accompanied and supplemented by all such information as the undertaker may reasonably require.[79] Any agreement is enforceable against the undertaker by the owner or occupier of any premises served by the sewer, lateral drain or works to which it relates.[80] The terms of an agreement which relate to a drain may include, in particular, identification of that part of the drain which constitutes a lateral drain for the purposes of the agreement, and the point or points of connection between that part and the remainder of the drain; a requirement for the installation of an inspection chamber at the expense of the person with whom the undertaker is to make the agreement, at a place specified in the agreement; provision, if the chamber is constructed in accordance with the terms of the agreement, for the undertaker to declare the chamber to be vested in it at the same time as the lateral drain; and provision for the lateral drain, once vested, to communicate with a public sewer at the place or places specified in the agreement.[81] An undertaker cannot make an agreement under s.104 with respect to a sewer, drain or works situated within the area of another sewerage undertaker, or a drain intended to communicate with a sewer which is so situated or is vested in another sewerage undertaker, until the other undertaker has consented or the Secretary of State has dispensed with the necessity

---

[77] This confers a general power for sewerage undertakers to carry out works for sewerage purposes by agreement.
[78] s.104(1).
[79] s.104(2), (3). In specified circumstances, the undertaker may delay its response to an application until a reasonable time after the required information is provided: s.104(4).
[80] s.104(5).
[81] s.104(6A).

for such consent, conditionally or unconditionally.[82] Undertakers must have regard to guidance about agreements issued by the Secretary of State or Welsh Ministers.[83]

Where a person constructing or proposing to construct a drain, sewer or sewage disposal works has applied to the sewerage undertaker in due form for an adoption agreement under s.104 and this has been refused, that person may appeal to the WSRA.[84] Upon such an appeal the WSRA may refuse the application or enter into such an agreement as the undertaker might have entered into either upon terms which it considers reasonable or upon terms offered by the undertaker with suitable modifications.[85] Such an agreement will be entered into "on behalf of" the undertaker. The Director General of Water Services decided that, generally, sewer works should be adopted provided that:

(a) the development and associated sewer works have been planned in a way which provides for efficient drainage of the properties concerned;

(b) the design and standard of construction comply with the standards prevailing at the time the proposal for adoption is made, as set out in *Sewers for Adoption* (4th edn)[86];

(c) the sewer works are in a satisfactory condition (i.e. with no outstanding maintenance problems);

(d) the sewer works are compatible with the undertaker's existing sewer system, so that adoption would not present operational problems for the undertaker; and

(e) there is easy access to the sewers for maintenance purposes, which generally means that the sewer must be laid in the highway or land open to the public.

---

[82] s.104(7), (8).

[83] 1991 Act s.104(9), inserted (from a day to be appointed) by the Flood and Water Management Act 2010 s.42(3).

[84] 1991 Act s.105(2), as amended by the Water Act 2003 s.36(2). The considerations applicable in determining appeals under s.105(1) concerning vesting declarations (above, pp.121–123) apply here with necessary modifications: s.105(7). Subs.(2) is to be substituted (from a day to be appointed) by the Flood and Water Management Act 2010 s.42(2), to provide that a person who has entered or wants to enter an agreement under s.104 may appeal to the WSRA about any matter concerning the agreement (including whether it is concluded, its terms and its operation).

[85] 1991 Act s.105(6), as amended by the Water Act 2003 s.36(2).

[86] Now the 6th edition.

The underlying principle was that adoption by the undertaker should not impose costs on it which could have been avoided; however, the Director also accepted that even necessary and unavoidable costs may be so high that it would be unreasonable for the sewerage undertaker to agree to adopt them.[87]

DUTY TO ADOPT SEWERS

4–013 The Water Act 2003[88] introduces[89] new provisions (ss.105A–105C of the Water Industry Act 1991) enabling the Secretary of State to make regulations that provide for him to make schemes for the adoption by sewerage undertakers of sewers, lateral drains and sewage disposal works situated in their area or which serve the whole or any part of that area. Regulations require an affirmative resolution of each House. They may require undertakers to prepare draft schemes and submit them to the Secretary of State. Each scheme must relate to the area of an undertaker, or part(s) of it, or the areas of more than one undertaker, or part(s) of them. It will then be the duty of an undertaker, in specified circumstances, to exercise its powers under s.102 of the 1991 Act to adopt sewers, lateral drains or sewage disposal works that satisfy specified criteria. The circumstances and criteria are themselves to be specified in the regulations or determined in accordance with the regulations and specified in the scheme. In relation to the exercise of those powers pursuant to the duty, s.102 is applied with modifications and ss.103 and 105 do not apply. The duty under s.105A(4) is enforceable by the Secretary of State under s.18 of the 1991 Act.[90] The owner of a sewer, lateral drain or sewage disposal works or any other person affected aggrieved by (a) the proposal of a sewerage undertaker to adopt a sewer, lateral drain or sewage disposal works pursuant to the duty under s.105A(4), or (b) the failure of an undertaker to make such a proposal, may appeal to the WSRA. The grounds are that the relevant duty is not owed or that the adoption would be seriously detrimental to him; or that the relevant duty is owed; or any other prescribed ground.[91] The Secretary of State must publish each scheme, and may vary any scheme or revoke it, and he must consult each sewerage undertaker which would be affected, the WSRA, the Consumer Council for Water and such other persons as he considers appropriate.[92]

---

[87] "OFWAT Annual Report 1994" (1994–95 H.C. 431), p.29.
[88] s.98.
[89] With effect from April 1, 2007: see SI 2007/1021 art.2(b).
[90] 1991 Act s.105A.
[91] 1991 Act s.105B.
[92] 1991 Act s.105C.

These provisions were inserted at a late stage in the passage of the Water Act 2003, and provide a framework that could be implemented if it were decided as a matter of policy that sewerage undertakers should proceed to take over private sewers, lateral drains and sewage disposal works.[93] Whether such steps should be taken was still under consideration at the time the Water Bill received Royal Assent in 2003. A review in 1986 had concluded responsibility should not be transferred, but a further review of this matter was started in 2003.[94] The Consultation Paper identified a number of problems relating to private sewers and drains. These included a lack of awareness of the legal position amongst the owners of properties served by private pipes which connect to public sewers; the significant incidence of flooding from private sewers (approximately 108,000 reports per year); and disquiet among property owners about their obligation to pay sewerage charges without any reduction to help maintain their private sewers and lateral drains. Options for consideration were the transfer of ownership of or management responsibility for private sewers and lateral drains to a sewerage undertaker or local authority; the adoption of private "lateral" pipes by the sewerage undertaker; new enforcing legislation; and general legislative improvements and guidance.

In the event, the government decided that existing private sewers and lateral drains in England that connect to the public network would be transferred into the ownership of the sewerage undertaker from 2011. The costs would be met by an increase in the sewerage element of bills for the generality of customers.[95] The government launched a further consultation on the methods for implementing transfers.[96] A majority of respondents favoured an overnight automatic transfer.

DUTY TO ADOPT DRAINAGE SYSTEMS

Schedule 5 to the Flood and Water Management Act 2010 introduced a package of measures extending the use of sustainable drainage **4–014**

[93] See H.C. Deb., November 10, 2003, cols 74*ff*.

[94] See DEFRA, Welsh Assembly Government, "Review of Existing Private Sewers and Drains in England and Wales", Consultation Paper, July 2003.

[95] DEFRA News Releases 49/07 (February 22, 2007) and 390/08 (December 15, 2008); DEFRA, "Review of Existing Private Sewers and Drains in England and Wales". "Regulatory Impact Assessment" (2007). Similar decisions have been taken in Wales: Welsh Assembly Government, "Strategic Policy Position Statement on Water" (March 31, 2009).

[96] DEFRA, "Consultation on Private Sewers Transfer—Implementation Options" (July 2007); DEFRA, "Summary of responses to the consultation" (March 2008); and DEFRA, "Impact Assessment of transfer of private sewers and lateral drains to statutory water and sewerage companies" (November 5, 2008).

systems. Construction work with drainage implications will need the approval of an "approving body" before it commences, and this will only be given if the system complies with national standards.[97] In addition, a duty to adopt may arise. Accordingly, an approving body[98] must adopt a drainage system[99] which satisfies the following conditions:

> Condition 1 is that the drainage system was constructed in pursuance of proposals approved under Sch.3 para.7.[100]
>
> Condition 2 is that the approving body is satisfied (a) that the drainage system was constructed, and functions, in accordance with the approved proposals (including any conditions of approval), or (b) that the approving body can issue or has issued a certificate under Schedule 3 paragraph 12(2).[101]
>
> Condition 3 is that the drainage system is a sustainable drainage system, as defined by regulations made by the Minister.[102]

There are then a number of exceptions. Exception 1 relates to single-property systems. The adoption duty does not apply to a drainage system (or any part of a drainage system) which is designed only to provide drainage for a single property.[103]

4–015 Exception 2 relates to roads. The adoption duty does not apply to any part of a drainage system which is a publicly maintained road.[104] If part of an adopted drainage system becomes a publicly maintained road, the adoption lapses in respect of that part.[105] Where a drainage system is adopted and part of the system is a publicly maintained road (and that part therefore need not be adopted); or where a drainage system is entirely on a publicly maintained road (and the adoption duty does not therefore apply to it), the maintaining authority must

---

97 See pp.217–219.

98 i.e. normally a unitary authority or county council in a two-tier area: see p.234.

99 Where part of a drainage system is exempt from adoption a reference in Sch.3 to the adoption of a drainage system includes a reference to adoption of part of a drainage system: para.17(6).

100 See pp.233–234.

101 Sch.3 para.17(3). An approving body must have regard to any guidance issued by the Minister about the application of Condition 2: para.17(4).

102 Sch.3 para.17(5).

103 Sch.3 para.18(1),(2). The Secretary of State or Welsh Ministers may make regulations for determining whether or not a system is to be treated as designed only to provide drainage for a single property: para.18(3).

104 Sch.3 para.19(1). "Publicly-maintained road" means a highway to which the duty under s.41 of the Highways Act 1980 applies, and a reference to a road includes a reference to part of a road: para.19(6).

105 Sch.3 para.19(2).

exercise its functions in respect of the road in accordance with the approved proposals for the drainage system (including any conditions of approval), and with national standards for sustainable drainage.[106]

The Secretary of State and Welsh Ministers may by order provide additional exceptions.[107] The duty to adopt is complemented by the provision that an approving body may voluntarily adopt all or part of a sustainable drainage system, as defined by regulations made by the Secretary of State or Welsh Ministers, to which the duty to adopt does not apply.[108]

Where an approving body adopts a drainage system it becomes responsible for maintaining the system, and in so doing it must comply with national standards for sustainable drainage.[109]

As to the procedure for adoption in pursuance of the duty to adopt, **4–016**
an approving body may adopt a drainage system on its own initiative, or (b) at the request of the person who applied for approval under Sch.3 para.7. A request must be determined within such period as the Secretary of Sate or Welsh Ministers may prescribe by order. Specified notifications must be made and any bond provided under Sch.3 para.12 must be released. The approving body must arrange for the designation under Sch.1 of any part of the drainage system (whether an adopted part or not) which is eligible for designation (and which is not owned by the approving body).[110]

Where an approving body decides to exercise its power to adopt a drainage system to which the duty to adopt does not apply, it must notify:

(a) the sewerage undertaker in whose area the drainage system is;

(b) any person who appears to the approving body to own or occupy land on which the drainage system is (including details of any arrangements under the approved proposals for access and maintenance); and

(c) any person who appears to the approving body to own or occupy land from which water will be drained by the drainage system.[111]

---

[106] Sch.3 para.19(3)–(4).
[107] Sch.3 para.20.
[108] Sch.3 para.21.
[109] Sch.3 para.22.
[110] Sch.3 para.23. Sch.1 enables specified authorities in England and Wales formally to designate structures or features which affect flood or coastal erosion risk, increasing regulatory control where they are not maintained or operated by those formally responsible for managing the risk (see Explanatory Note to Sch.1).
[111] Sch.3 para.24(1), (2).

It must also arrange for the inclusion of the drainage system (including any non-adopted part) in the relevant register under s.21 of the 2010 Act,[112] and the designation under Sch.1 of any part of the drainage system (whether an adopted part or not) which is eligible for designation (and which is not owned by the approving body).[113]

4–017 The Minister must by regulations provide a right of appeal against decisions under Sch.3 about applications for approval (including decisions about conditions), and about the duty to adopt.[114]

---

[112] Under s.21, a lead local flood authority must establish and maintain: (a) a register of structures or features which, in the authority's opinion, are likely to have a significant effect on a flood risk in its area; and (b) a record of information about each of those structures or features, including information about ownership and state of repair.

[113] Sch.3 para.24(3).

[114] Sch.3 para.25.

Chapter 5

MAINTENANCE AND USE OF PUBLIC SEWERS

GENERAL DUTIES OF SEWERAGE UNDERTAKERS

Under s.94(1) of the Water Industry Act 1991 it is the duty of every sewerage undertaker "(a) to provide, improve and extend such a system of public sewers (whether inside its area or elsewhere) and so to cleanse and maintain those sewers and any lateral drains which belong to or vest in the undertaker[1] as to ensure that that area is and continues to be effectually drained"; also "(b) to make provision for the emptying of . . . [public] sewers and such further provision . . . as is necessary from time to time for effectually dealing, by means of sewage disposal works or otherwise, with the contents of those sewers." **5–001**

This duty includes an obligation to have regard to existing and likely future obligations and to make allowance for the discharge of trade effluent[2] into the undertaker's public sewers and the disposal thereof. The modern provision is derived from s.23 of the 1936 Act and it is suggested that here, as in the former case, "maintain" must include all ordinary works of repair,[3] and that "cleanse" must include the clearance of obstructions. The duty to "empty" public sewers would seem to include a duty to provide and maintain a proper outfall,[4] and to cause the sewage or other contents of the sewer to flow in the direction of the outfall. These duties must necessarily be taken to apply to all the public sewers vested in a sewerage undertaker, whether or not laid through private land. Powers of entry are provided for the performance of such works in emergency or at a reasonable time and upon seven days' notice to the occupier by s.168 and Sch.6 Pt II to the 1991 Act. The exercise of such power of entry will, of course, be limited strictly to that which is necessary for the performance of the undertaker's lawful purposes and if the right is exceeded the undertaker and its agents will be liable in damages as trespassers ab initio.[5]

---

[1] The reference to lateral drains was added by the Water Act 2003 s.97(3).

[2] "Trade effluent" has here the same meaning as in Ch.3 of Pt 4 of the 1991 Act (ss.118–141): see s.141(1).

[3] As to the provision of new sewers see Ch.3, above.

[4] As to the duty to provide a proper outfall under former provisions, see *R. v Tynemouth RDC* [1896] 2 Q.B. 451.

[5] The *Six Carpenters Case* (1610) 1 Sm. L.C. 134, cf. Lord Denning "Freedom under the Law" at p.112 and W.V.H. Rogers, *Winfield and Jolowicz on Tort*, 18th edn (2010), pp.698–699.

Under the modern, as under former, provisions the duty to "maintain" must not be exaggerated. In *Radstock Co-operative and Industrial Society v Norton-Radstock UDC*[6] Ungoed-Thomas J. said[7] "I fail to see that the statutory obligation to 'maintain' the sewer includes any such extended obligation to maintain lands or conditions outside the sewer, as the plaintiffs suggest, or that it involves obligations to third parties like the plaintiffs who are complete strangers to the sewer." In that case a public sewer had been properly constructed in a river bed but, with no fault on the part of the responsible authority, the river bed was in course of time washed away and the pipe became exposed and caused eddies in the flow of water which damaged the plaintiff's property. The plaintiff claimed, inter alia, in nuisance but failed both at first instance and in the Court of Appeal.[8]

5–002 A more marginal question might arise were a plaintiff to be injured as a result (for example) of the defective state of a manhole cover situated in private premises.[9] A sewerage undertaker is, of course, under an ordinary duty of care in respect of such a structure,[10] even if it was not aware of the existence of the sewer itself, but it is not clear whether in such a case the court would be prepared to hold a sewerage undertaker liable on the ground that it had not carried out a system of regular inspections of sewers upon private property. Presumably the case would turn on the commonly accepted practice amongst sewerage undertakers in this regard.

The duty imposed by s.94 must be performed in a fashion which does not contravene other provisions of the 1991 legislation, in particular the offence of polluting controlled waters.[11]

The duty to cleanse, maintain and empty public sewers imposed by s.94 of the 1991 Act is expressly made enforceable by the Secretary of State or, with his special consent or general authorisation, the WSRA.[12]

---

[6] [1967] Ch. 1094; this point was not discussed in the Court of Appeal: see [1968] Ch. 605.

[7] at p.1118.

[8] [1968] Ch. 605.

[9] Such a cover will normally form part of the sewer: see the Water Industry Act 1991 s.219(2), providing that references to a sewer "shall include references to . . . any accessories for the [sewer]"; as to the definition of "accessories", see above, p.11, n.62; cf. the Public Health Act 1936 s.90(4).

[10] The standard of care differs according to whether the injured person is a visitor or a person other than a visitor: Occupiers' Liability Act 1957 s.1(3)(a) and 2(2) and Occupiers' Liabilty Act 1984.

[11] See below, pp.172–201.

[12] s.94(3). See above, pp.24–26 on powers to make enforcement orders.

The obligation to comply with a valid provisional or final order under s.18 is owed to "any person who may be affected by a contravention" and such a contravention will be actionable at the suit of any such person who suffers consequent loss or damage.[13] It will be a defence to such a civil action for the sewerage undertaker to show that it "took all reasonable steps and exercised all due diligence to avoid contravening the order."[14] Without prejudice to the possibility of such a civil action, the Secretary of State or the WSRA, as the case might be, may take civil proceedings for the enforcement of a s.18 order by injunction or other appropriate relief.[15] **5–003**

A further remedy for contravention of s.94 of the 1989 Act by a sewerage undertaker is provided by the possibility of a special administration order under ss.23 and 24 of the 1991 Act.[16]

In addition to these statutory remedies, a sewerage undertaker may be liable in civil proceedings for damages or an injunction through the application of the ordinary principles of negligence or nuisance.[17]

THE POWER TO CHARGE FOR SEWERAGE SERVICES

Power to charge for provision of sewerage services is conferred upon sewerage undertakers by s.142 of the 1991 Act. The power so conferred is wide ranging and, except insofar as the Act otherwise provides, allows a sewerage undertaker to: **5–004**

> "fix charges . . . by reference to such matters and adopt . . . such methods and principles for the calculation and imposition of the charges, as appear to the undertaker to be appropriate."[18]

---

[13] s.22(1), (2).
[14] s.22(3).
[15] s.22(4).
[16] See above, pp.27–29.
[17] See, e.g. *Dear v Thames Water Co* (1993) 33 Con. L.R. 43 (where negligence was not proved and the defendants were found not to be responsible for any nuisance arising from the flooding of a watercourse); *Yorkshire Water Services Ltd v Sun Alliance and London Insurance plc* [1998] Env. L.R. 204 (no liability in nuisance in respect of costs incurred in alleviating the risk of flooding following an escape of sewage sludge that blocked a river and also spread into the undertaker's sewage works; the apprehension of damage was insufficient for a claim for damages; therefore no liability for such costs in negligence as this was irrecoverable pure economic loss; furthermore, interference with contractual right to use a public sewer at the sewage works did not constitute interference with the use or enjoyment of the claimant's land so as to give rise to a cause of action in private nuisance). Proceedings based simply on a contravention of s.94 are, however, barred by s.18(8): see above, pp.72–73.
[18] s.142(4).

Charging limits are, however, set by the WSRA.[19]

Charges may be fixed either by agreement with the customers concerned[20] or in accordance with a "charges scheme" under s.143 of the 1991 Act.[21] A "charges scheme" may:

(a) fix the charges to be paid for any services provided[22] by a sewerage undertaker in carrying out its functions;

(b) fix the charges to be paid where, in circumstances specified by the Scheme, a trade effluent notice is served on the undertaker under s.119 of the 1991 Act, a consent required under Ch.3 of Pt 4 of the Act is given by the undertaker, or a discharge is made pursuant to such a consent[23];

(c) provide for the times and methods of payment of the charges it fixes.[24]

A scheme may make variant provisions for different cases, including different circumstances and localities and may contain supplemental, consequential and transitional provisions and may revoke or amend and earlier scheme.[25] Any charges scheme, so far as it recovers the

---

[19] See above, pp.40–41. A review of the principles governing charging was conducted by Anna Walker, "The Independent Review of Charging for Household Water and Sewerage Services" (December 2009), recommending, inter alia, that water prices continue to be regionally based, that charging for water should continue move towards volume consumed and that foul sewerage should continue to be charged for on the same basis as water supply.

[20] From April 1, 2000, it has not been possible to enter agreements in relation to charges for the supply water to or the provision of sewerage services in respect of a dwelling: 1991 Act, s.142(2A), inserted by the Water Industry Act 1999 s.3(1), brought into force by SI 1999/3440. "Dwelling" means a private dwelling-house (which may be a building or part of a building), a caravan or a boat or similar structure designed or adapted for use as a place of permanent habitation: 1991 Act Sch.4A para.1(2), inserted by the 1999 Act Sch.1.

[21] 1991 Act, s.142(2). The power of a sewerage undertaker to charge for any services provided in the course of carrying out its duty under s.101A(1) (see pp.87–88) is exercisable only by or in accordance with a charges scheme: s.142(3A), inserted by the Environment Act 1995 Sch.22 para.114(3).

[22] In *Thames Water Utilities Ltd v Ministry of Defence* [2006] EWCA Civ 1620, the Court of Appeal rejected an argument that the provision that charges could be made for "services provided" meant that it was unlawful to charge for sewerage services to a military barracks by reference to the volume of water entering the sites as distinct from the volume discharged from the sites to sewers; the term "services" was to be construed broadly to cover the undertaker's duties under the legislation.

[23] In such a case the person liable to pay the charges will be the person who serves the notice, the person to whom consent is given, or any person who makes a discharge pursuant to such a consent. Such a charge may comprise a single charge for the whole period of the consent, separate charges in respect of different parts of the period. or both such types of charge (s.143(2), (3)).

[24] s.143(1).

[25] s.143(4).

undertaker's costs of providing a sewer by virtue of its duty under s.101A(1),[26] must cause those costs to be borne by the undertaker's customers generally.[27] Even where such a charges scheme is in force, a sewerage undertaker may still, except in the case of a dwelling, conclude charging agreements with customers in particular cases and enter into agreements as to discharge of trade effluent under Ch.3 of Pt 4 of the 1991 Act.[28]

A charging scheme may now only last for a period of 12 months.[29] **5–005**
It must be approved by the WSRA, which must have regard to any guidance issued by the Secretary of State.[30] The WSRA may not exercise its power to approve charges schemes for the purpose of limiting the total revenues of relevant undertakers from charges fixed by or in accordance with charges schemes.[31] The Secretary of State may make regulations as to provisions to be included in charging schemes.[32] He has exercised this power to make the Water Industry (Charges) (Vulnerable Groups) Regulations 1999,[33] which require charges schemes to include special provision for providing assistance in relation to any premises for specified consumers. A consumer[34] is entitled to this provision[35] if he or another person residing with him in the premises ("the qualifying person") is on a low income[36] and either (a) the qualifying person is entitled to receive child benefit for

---

[26] See above, pp.87–88.

[27] See above, p.91, n.117.

[28] s.143(5), as amended by the Water Industry Act 1999 s.3(2).

[29] By virtue of an amendment to the 1991 Act s.143(1), effected by the Water Industry Act 1999 s.4(2), with effect from December 23, 1999 (see the Water Industry Act 1999 (Commencement No.2) Order 1999 (SI 1999/3440)).

[30] 1991 Act s.143(6)–(8), inserted by the 1999 Act s.4(3). The functions of the Secretary of State under subss.(7) and (8) have been transferred to the National Assembly for Wales, in relation to water and sewerage undertakers whose areas are wholly or mainly in Wales, by the National Assembly for Wales (Transfer of Functions) (No.2) Order 1999 (SI 1999/2787).

[31] 1991 Act s.143(9), inserted by the 1999 Act s.4(3).

[32] 1991 Act s.143A, inserted by the 1999 Act s.5. These powers have been transferred to the National Assembly for Wales, in relation to water and sewerage undertakers whose areas are wholly or mainly in Wales, by SI 1999/2787.

[33] SI 1999/3441, as amended by SI 2000/519, SI 2003/552, and SI 2005/89. The Regulations do not apply to any water or sewerage undertaker whose area is wholly or mainly in Wales: reg.1(2).

[34] The term "consumer" for the purposes of Ch.1 of Pt 5 of the 1991 Act is defined as a person on whom liability to pay charges to the relevant water or sewerage undertaker would fall: 1991 Act s.150B, inserted by the Water Industry Act 1999 Sch.3 para.3.

[35] SI 1999/3441 reg.2.

[36] i.e. is in receipt of any of a number of benefits or tax credits, including council tax benefit, housing benefit, income support, disabled person's tax credit, working families tax credit, income-based job-seeker's allowance, state pension credit, child tax credit (if it includes an element in respect of the individual element of child tax credit), working tax credit and income-related employment and support allowance.

three or more children under 19 who reside in the premises, or (b) the consumer, or another person residing with him in the premises, whether or not the same person as the qualifying person, is diagnosed as suffering from, and is receiving treatment for, one of a list of medical conditions,[37] or, with the support of a registered medical practitioner, from another medical condition, and as a result of that condition is obliged to use a significant additional volume of water. Further conditions must also be satisfied.[38] In these cases, charges must not exceed the undertaker's average charges for household consumers for water supplies or sewerage services.[39] An application for assistance must be made in accordance with the regulations.[40]

For the purpose of levying charges for sewerage services, services are generally taken to be supplied to the occupiers for the time being of premises which are drained by a sewer or drain connecting, directly or intermediately, with a public sewer provided by the undertaker concerned for the carriage off of both foul or surface water or both, or of premises benefitting from facilities draining into a sewer or drain so connected.[41]

A person may remain liable for sewerage charges after vacating premises if he fails to inform the undertaker of the termination of occupation with at least two working days' notice. Liability will then arise for the charges, ending no later than the earliest of:

(i) where information of termination of occupation is given less than two days before, or at any time after, such termination, the twenty-eighth day after information is given;

(ii) the day on which the meter would normally have been read;

(iii) the day on which a new occupier informs the undertaker of his occupation.[42]

---

[37] i.e. desquamation; weeping skin disease; incontinence; abdominal stoma; Crohn's disease; ulcerative colitis; and renal failure requiring dialysis at home.

[38] Including that water charges are fixed by reference to volume (or would be so fixed if the consumer had not been receiving assistance under the Regulations); the consumer and any other qualifying person each occupies the whole or part of the premises as his only or principal home; where premises are not used solely as a person's home, the other use must not be the principal use of the premises; water supplied to the premises is not used for watering a garden, other than by hand, by means of any apparatus or automatically replenishing a pond or swimming pool with a capacity greater than 10,000 litres; and the consumer has applied for assistance.

[39] SI 1999/3441 reg.3.

[40] SI 1999/3441 reg.4.

[41] s.144(1)(b).

[42] s.144(2), (3), (4).

Although the point is not expressly made by the 1991 Act, it may reasonably be presumed that no charges could be levied for remedying faults or defects which were a direct consequence of the sewerage undertaker's own negligence or misfeasance.

Under earlier provisions, it was doubtful whether "cleansing" was included within the same category as "maintenance", the latter broadly involving constructional works but the former not doing so. Consequently, the 6th edition of this book concluded at p.71 that: **5–006**

> "the legislature understood the two terms ['maintain' and 'cleanse'] as being mutually exclusive and . . . [t]he cost, therefore, of the clearance of obstructions, would seem not to be recoverable . . ."

Under the present (1991 Act) provision the position is somewhat clarified. Section 94(1) provides for duties to "provide [etc.] . . . a system of public sewers . . . and . . . to cleanse and maintain [them] . . . and to make provision for the emptying of those sewers . . ." Section 142(1)(a) then empowers sewerage undertakers "to fix charges for any services provided in the course of carrying out its functions." Such "functions" are those defined by s.94 and there would thus seem to be no reason why the "cleansing" of sewers should not now be considered a chargeable "service" under the 1991 Act.

A sewerage undertaker is not entitled to recover a charge simply in respect of becoming the supplier of sewerage services to domestic premises or to require payment for a declaration of vesting under Ch.2 of Pt 4 of the 1991 Act or in respect of any agreement to make such a declaration.[43] Nor may a charge be levied upon a highway authority in respect of the drainage of a highway or the disposal of the contents of any such drain or sewer.[44] A sewerage undertaker may, however, levy a connection charge in respect of the connection to a public sewer[45] of premises which have never at any previous time been connected to a sewer used for the drainage, for domestic sewerage purposes, of those premises by a sewerage undertaker (or predecessor acting under statute).[46] Such a charge may include an infrastructure charge in respect of capital and maintenance costs, and is not confined to the

---

[43] s.146(1)(b), (3).
[44] s.146(4).
[45] By virtue of s.106(1A), inserted by the Water Act 2003 s.99(2), this extends to include a public lateral drain: see below, p.217.
[46] s.146(2)(b).

costs of the physical connection.[47] The term "premises" will usually include buildings, but is not necessarily limited to them; it also includes part of a building where a building is converted—it is a question of fact and degree whether the result is or includes the construction of premises which have never previously been connected.[48] Where a new public sewer connection is requisitioned, the sewerage undertaker may also require financial guarantees.[49]

5–007 It was originally provided that the level of charging for sewerage services was not after March 31, 2000 to be fixed by reference to a rating valuation list. Charges so fixed were not to be recoverable in respect of services supplied after that date.[50] However, no alternative system could be established and this restriction was removed by s.8 of the Water Industry Act 1999.

A sewerage undertaker may choose to fix its charges by reference to volume.[51] Where this is done, or notice of such intent has been given, the undertaker has power to install a meter to measure the discharge of effluent in a drain or private sewer connecting with a public sewer and also to enter upon premises for the maintenance, repair, disconnection or removal of such meters.[52] The power of entry for purposes of installation, maintenance, etc. will be conferred by the undertaker upon designated persons, who may enter premises only at a reasonable time and after seven days' notice has been given to the occupier.[53] However, if it is shown to a Justice of the Peace upon sworn information in writing that there are grounds for the installation, maintenance, repair, disconnection or removal of a meter and that the exercise of the power has been refused or such refusal is reasonably anticipated, the premises are unoccupied, the occupier is temporarily absent, the case is urgent or an application for admission would defeat the object of the entry, the Justice may by warrant authorise entry, by force if need be.[54]

---

[47] *Thames Water Utilities Ltd v Hampstead Homes (London) Ltd* [2002] EWCA Civ 1487; [2003] 1 W.L.R. 198 (conversion of two office blocks previously connected for domestic supply provided by a water undertaker into 109 flats held to involve the creation of new premises never previously connected for the purposes of s.146(2)(a), which is in similar terms to s.146(2)(b)).

[48] *Thames Water Utilities*.

[49] See below.

[50] 1991 Act s.145. A "rating valuation list" is one maintained for rating purposes under ss.41 or 52 of the Local Government Finance Act 1988 s.67 of the General Rate Act 1967 or other enactments.

[51] 1991 Act ss.142, 144A, 144B, 149, as amended by the Water Industry Act 1999 Sch.3 para.2 (authorising the Secretary of State to make regulations).

[52] 1991 Act s.162, as amended by the Water Industry Act 1999 s.10 and the Water Act 2003 s.36(2) and Sch.8 para.37.

[53] 1991 Act s.172 and Sch.6 Pt II.

[54] 1991 Act Sch.6 Pt II.

The expenses of installing and connecting a meter, maintaining, repairing, disconnecting or removing a meter, and associated works will generally be borne by the sewerage undertaker but an occupier must, in particular, bear the element of the expense arising from compliance with a request to position the meter in a place other than that reasonably proposed by the undertaker.[55] Once a meter has been installed it is a criminal offence to tamper with it.[56]

Where a consumer exercises his right[57] to elect for charging for water by reference to volume, the relevant sewerage undertaker is under a corresponding obligation to fix charges in respect of foul water drainage provided by the undertaker in respect of those premises by reference to that volume. Conversely, when a consumer exercises (within 12 months) his right to change back from charging by volume, the same applies to the sewerage undertaker.[58] Where water is supplied to any premises in which, or in any part of which, a person has his home, charges in respect of those premises have previously been fixed without reference to volume, and prescribed conditions are satisfied,[59] a water or sewerage undertaker may not by virtue of any charges schemes begin to fix the charges in respect of those premises by reference to volume, unless the consumer has so elected or gives consent or there has been a change in the occupation of the premises and no charges have yet been demanded from the new consumer.[60] **5–008**

Where sewerage services are provided by a person other than a sewerage undertaker, the WSRA may by order prescribe maximum charges which may be levied by such a person who makes direct or indirect use of the services of a sewerage undertaker in the supply of such services.[61] Such an order may require the person providing the sewerage services to furnish the person provided with them with specified information, and may also provide that, in the event of the failure to furnish that information, the maximum charges he is entitled to recover shall be such as may be fixed by the order.[62] Where

---

[55] s.148(1)–(4A), as amended by the Competition and Service (Utilities) Act 1992 s.53(2), (3) and the Water Industry Act 1999 s.9, prohibiting charges for the installation of meters at private dwelling houses, and Sch.3 para.1.

[56] ss.175–177 as amended by the Water Act 2003, s.36(2) and Sch.8 para.40.

[57] Under s.144A of the 1991 Act, inserted by the 1999 Act s.6.

[58] 1991 Act s.144A(9), (10).

[59] See the Water Industry (Prescribed Conditions) Regulations 1999 (SI 1999/3442), as amended by SI 2007/2457. These do not apply to any water or sewerage undertaker whose area is wholly or mainly in Wales, as to which see the Water Industry (Prescribed Conditions) (Undertakers Wholly or Mainly in Wales) Regulations 2004 (SI 2004/701).

[60] 1991 Act s.144B, inserted by the 1999 Act s.7.

[61] 1991 Act s.150(1), (2), as amended by the Water Act 2003 s.36(2).

[62] 1991 Act s.150(2A), (2B), inserted by the Water Act 2003 s.59.

such an order is made it is the duty of the WSRA to publish it in a manner which he considers appropriate for the purpose of bringing it to the attention of persons likely to be affected.[63]

A sewerage undertaker may not levy charges in contravention of any local statutory provision expressly precluding the making of charges for the supply of specified services.[64]

5–009 The Secretary of State may by regulations provide for billing disputes (i.e. disputes between a customer and a sewerage undertaker concerning the amount of the charge the undertaker is entitled to recover for the provision of sewerage services other than by carrying out trade effluent functions) to be referred to the WSRA for determination.[65]

Recovery of charges and/or expenses in performance of works will normally be as for a simple contract debt in any court of competent jurisdiction, generally the County Court. The legality of the charges levied and/or the expenses claimed will be matters which the court may take into account in proceedings for recovery. The statutory authority of a sewerage undertaker may also, of course, be tested independently in the courts by persons affected by their proposed or actual exercise.

PERFORMANCE OF SEWERAGE FUNCTIONS BY LOCAL AUTHORITIES

5–010 A sewerage undertaker may enter into an arrangement whereby a local authority, the new towns residuary body, a New Town development corporation or an urban development corporation in an urban development area will carry out sewerage functions in the whole or part of the undertaker's area.[66] Such an arrangement may provide for the exercise by the authority, etc. of any of the undertaker's functions and powers which may be specified; no such arrangement will however affect the availability of remedies against the undertaker in respect of sewerage functions or failures in their performance.[67] Except insofar as a specific arrangement may otherwise provide, a

---

[63] 1991 Act s.150(3).

[64] 1991 Act s.142(5).

[65] 1991 Act s.150A, inserted by the Competition and Service (Utilities) Act 1992 s.36 and amended by the Water Act 2003 s.36(2).

[66] 1991 Act s.97(1), (5), as amended by the Government of Wales Act 1998 ss.129(2), 152 Sch.15 para.17 Sch.18 Pt IV, and the Housing and Regeneration Act 2008 Sch.8 para.57.

[67] 1991 Act s.97(2), (3). The liability of the local authority as agent can be no geater than the liability of the undertaker, apart from any acts of individual misfeasance: *Dear v Thames Water* (1993) 33 Con. L.R. 43.

local authority acting under such an arrangement may itself delegate its sewerage functions under s.101 of the Local Government Act 1972.[68]

Where an arrangement applies for a local authority which is operating executive arrangements under the Local Government Act 2000[69] to carry out sewerage functions on the undertaker's behalf, those functions are to be treated as functions of the authority for the purposes of s.13 of the 2000 Act.[70] Furthermore, if or to the extent that those sewerage functions are the responsibility of the authority's executive, s.97(4) does not apply and ss.14 to 16[71] and any regulations under ss.17 to 20 of the 2000 Act are to apply in relation to those sewerage functions only in so far as the arrangements do not provide otherwise.[72]

THE ALTERATION AND CLOSURE OF PUBLIC SEWERS

Under s.116 of the 1991 Act,[73] a sewerage undertaker has power to discontinue and prohibit the use of any public sewer[74] vested in it. Under the 1991 Act, the duty is imposed upon sewerage undertakers by s.94 to "provide, improve and extend . . . a system of public sewers (whether inside their area or elsewhere) . . . to ensure that that area is and continues to be effectually drained"[75]; and their power to perform works on land includes that "to inspect, maintain, adjust, repair or alter any relevant pipe".[76] This power would seem prima facie to include also powers of necessary closure, e.g. when a public sewer has been replaced. These powers may only, however, be exercised in pursuance of the duty under s.94 to secure effectual drainage in the area of the undertaker concerned and, clearly, the **5–011**

---

[68] 1991 Act s.97(4).

[69] All county, county borough, district and London borough councils, other than small district councils, were required by the 2000 Act to adopt one of three forms of executive: elected mayor and cabinet, leader and cabinet, elected mayor and council manager: see ss.10, 11.

[70] This provides that functions not specified in regulations made by the Secretary of State or National Assembly are to be the responsibility of the executive.

[71] These provide for the discharge of functions under the three specified models for executive arrangements.

[72] 1991 Act s.97(4A), inserted (for England) by SI 2001/2237 art.27(a), and (for Wales) by SI 2002/808 art.26(a).

[73] As amended by the Competition and Service (Utilities) Act 1992 s.35(12) and the Water Act 2003 s.36(2).

[74] By virtue of the 1991 Act s.106(1A), inserted by the Water Act 2003 s.99(2), this extends to include a public lateral drain: see below, p.217.

[75] s.94(1)(a).

[76] ss.158(1)(b) and 159(1)(b).

alteration or closure of a public sewer (or public lateral drain) in such a fashion as to deprive a part of the area of effectual drainage would be a breach of the statutory duty of the undertaker under s.94.

A discontinuance or prohibition under s.116 may be for all purposes, for the purpose of foul water drainage or for surface water drainage. Before a person lawfully using a sewer for any purpose is deprived of the use of the sewer for that purpose, the undertaker must provide a sewer equally effective for his use and, at the undertaker's own expense, carry out work necessary to make that person's drains or sewers communicate with the replacement sewer provided. Any dispute as to the effectiveness of a sewer provided may be referred by either party to the WSRA for determination under s.30A of the 1991 Act.[77]

Compensation is payable by the undertaker to any person who sustains damage by reason of the exercise of this power in relation to a matter as to which that person has not himself been in default.[78]

THE PRESERVATION OF PUBLIC SEWERS

5–012 The integrity of public sewers may be threatened by a number of external influences, in particular by the impact of external works and by the abuse of the pipes themselves. The latter issue is considered below.[79]

(a) Buildings over sewers

5–013 The Building Regulations 2000[80] impose specific requirements in respect of the erection of a building or an extension to a building or underpinning work over any sewer, drain or disposal main shown on the map of sewers.[81] Work carried out in contravention of the Regulations may be removed by the local authority at the building

---

[77] s.116(4), inserted by the Competition and Service (Utilities) Act 1992 s.35(12). See above, p.31. This provision extends to public lateral drains.

[78] Under the 1991 Act, Sch.12 para.4(1). See *Yorkshire Water Services Ltd v Sun Alliance and London Insurance plc* [1998] Env. L.R. 204, where a communication to a company that the flow of effluent to a public sewer had to be reduced to a minimum following an escape of sewage sludge that had blocked a river and affected sewage works was held not on the facts to be a prohibition under s.116.

[79] See pp.143–144.

[80] SI 2000/2531 Sch.1 para.H4, inserted by SI 2001/3335 reg.2(12) and Sch. This replaced the Building Act 1984 s.18.

[81] See, pp.225–226. The restriction applies only to buildings for which plans must be submitted under the Regulations.

owner's expense[82] and such construction will normally constitute an offence under the Regulations.

The term "building" is not defined generally for the purposes of the 1984 Act, but it is normally understood as signifying any construction or erection capable of enclosing some area of ground.[83] Section 121 of the 1984 Act, however, provides a limited definition for the purposes of Pt I of the Act and any other enactment that relates to building regulations. Accordingly, "building" means "any permanent or temporary building, and, unless the content otherwise requires, it includes any other structure or erection of whatever kind or nature (whether permanent or temporary)." It also includes "part of a building". In the case of the superseded statutory provisions dealing with building over sewers, the underlying purpose was clearly the prevention of damage to sewers, and to provide the sewerage undertaker with ready access thereto and it was suggested that "a building to be within the section must be one which, by reason of its weight or otherwise, may cause an injury to the sewer over which it has been built, or one which, by reason of its size or otherwise, prevents access being gained to the sewer".[84]

(b) Injuries to sewers

In addition to the safeguards contained in the Building Regulations 2000, a sewerage undertaker has sufficient ownership in a public sewer[85] to entitle it to bring an action for nuisance for damages or an injunction in a case of injury to its sewers.[86] In practice, however, it **5–014**

[82] Provided that the work is in actual contravention of the Act or the Regulations and also provided that the appropriate procedure is observed: see s.36 of the 1984 Act.

[83] See, e.g. *Slaughter v Sunderland Corp* (1891) 60 L.J.M.C. 91.

[84] *Urban Housing Co Ltd v City of Oxford* [1939] 3 All E.R. 839, per Bennett J. at p.850, where he suggested that two walls, each 7 feet high and 9 inches thick were not "buildings" within the meaning of the earlier 1875 Act. Sir Wilfrid Greene M.R., however, in the Court of Appeal in the same case ([1940] Ch. 70 at p.86, upholding the judgment of Bennett J.) said that he would have been disposed to take the view that these walls were buildings within the section, as "there must be, on the face of it, some slight interference, or might be some slight interference owing to their presence, with the facility of repairing or re-laying the sewers". Both these observations were, however, obiter. Such walls might well constitute a "structure or erection" for the purposes of the s.121 definition.

[85] See Ch.2, pp.66–67.

[86] See, e.g. *Cleckheaton UDC v Firth* (1898) 62 J.P. 536, although in that case it was held that the defendant was legally entitled to do the act complained of. In *Gas Light and Coke Co v St Mary Abbotts Kensington Vestry* (1885) 15 Q.B.D. 1, an injunction was granted to prevent the highway authority from using a heavy steam roller for repairs in such a manner as would injure gas mains laid in the highway at a depth and protected sufficiently against all ordinary traffic, and in *Driscoll v Poplar Board of Works* (1897) 62 J.P. 40, the same principle was applied in an action for damages.

may more commonly be convenient for the local authority in the area concerned to take proceedings in public nuisance against the person responsible,[87] as most injuries to public sewers will result in such a nuisance.[88]

Such an action would be brought by the local authority and would not directly involve the sewerage undertaker, unless, in an unusual case, as defendant. If the sewerage undertaker felt impelled to take action on its own behalf, it seems that it would be limited to the rights arising from its ownership of the sewer in question.

(c) Support of sewers: removal of coal

5–015 Where support is withdrawn from land in connection with the lawful working and getting of coal and/or other minerals worked with coal, causing damage to a public sewer, the responsible person[89] will be liable to make a payment to the sewerage undertaker in which the sewer concerned is vested for the subsidence damage.[90]

THE USE OF PUBLIC SEWERS

5–016 Not all liquids and substances may be permitted to flow into a public sewer, certain restrictions being imposed by both statute and common law.

(a) Prohibition upon polluting emissions from public sewers

5–017 The detail of pollution control is considered below.[91] However, in the present context it must be said that it is a criminal offence under s.85 of the Water Resources Act 1991 for any person to cause or knowingly permit any matter, other than trade or sewage effluent, to enter "controlled waters"[92] by discharge from a drain or sewer in

---

[87] If the person responsible cannot be found, however, the owner of the sewer or drain concerned, i.e. the sewerage undertaker, may be liable in public nuisance: *Rhymney Iron Co v Gelligaer UDC* [1917] 1 K.B. 589.

[88] See, e.g. *Riddell v Spear* (1879) 40 L.T. 130.

[89] i.e. the licensed operator or, if there is no such operator with responsibility for the area in question, the Coal Authority.

[90] See the Coal Mining Subsidence Act 1991, as amended by the Coal Industry Act 1994 ss.42–48 and Sch.9 para.41. In most cases a "damage notice" must be served under s.3 of the Act in accordance with the Coal Mining Subsidence (Notices and Claims) Regulations 1991 (SI 1991/2509).

[91] See Ch.8, below.

[92] See below, pp.167–202.

contravention of a prohibition imposed under s.86[93]; or to cause or knowingly permit any trade or sewage effluent to be discharged into any controlled waters or, from land in England and Wales, through a pipe, into the sea outside the seaward limits of controlled waters[94]; or to cause or knowlingly permit trade or sewerage effluent to be discharged, in contravention of a s.86 prohibition, from a building or any fixed plant on to or into any land or into any waters of a lake or pond which are not inland freshwaters.[95] Discharges of sewage effluent into "controlled waters"[96] which a sewerage undertaker did not knowingly cause or permit but which it was bound (unconditionally or otherwise) to receive into the sewer or works matter included in the discharge, will normally be deemed to have "caused the discharge".[97] Upon summary conviction the offence will carry a penalty of imprisonment for a term not exceeding three months or to a fine not exceeding £20,000 or both; or upon conviction on indictment, to imprisonment not exceeding two years or to a fine or both.[98]

(b) Other material not to be passed into public sewers

It is a criminal offence under s.111 of the Water Industry Act 1991 to "throw, empty or turn, or suffer to permit to be thrown or emptied or to pass, into any public sewer, or into any drain or sewer communicating with a public sewer"[99] any of the following: **5–018**

"(a) any matter likely to injure the sewer or drain or to interfere with the free flow of its contents, or to affect prejudicially the treatment and disposal of its contents[100]; or

---

93 Water Resources Act 1991 s.85(2). A relevant "prohibition" for these purposes is one contained in a notice issued by the Environment Agency prohibiting a person from making or continuing a discharge or imposing conditions upon its continuation or a proscription by regulation of particular substances or concentrations thereof (s.86(1), (2), as amended by the Environment Act 1995 Sch.22 para.128).

94 s.85(3).

95 s.85(4).

96 Specifically discharges under s.85(3), (4).

97 s.87(1)–(1C), inserted by the Competition and Service (Utilities) Act 1992 s.46. See below, p.178.

98 s.85(6). As to defences by way of authorisations for discharges, see s.88.

99 The term "public sewer" extends to include a public lateral drain by virtue of the 1991 Act s.106(1A), inserted by the Water Act 2003 s.99(2): see below, p.217.

100 See *Liverpool Corp v Coghill (H) & Son Ltd* [1918] 1 Ch. 307 where the particular effluent had a deleterious effect on the land on which the sewage matter was eventually deposited. In this case also it was suggested obiter, by Eve J., that an authority could not grant a right to a person to cause effluent to flow into public sewers in such a manner as to cause a public nuisance.

(b) any chemical refuse or waste steam, or any liquid of a temperature higher than forty-three Degrees Celsius,[101] being refuse or steam which, or a liquid which when so heated, is, either alone or in combination with the contents of the sewer or drain, dangerous or the cause of a nuisance, or prejudicial to health; or

(c) any petroleum spirit,[102] or carbide of calcium."

(c) Trade effluent

5–019 Under Ch.3 of Pt 4 of the Water Industry Act 1991[103] which is further considered below,[104] no trade effluent (unless it is of a type which may lawfully be discharged into a public sewer) may be discharged from trade premises into a public sewer otherwise than in accordance with a Trade Effluent Notice.

(d) Common law

5–020 In addition to the above statutory provisions, the sewerage undertaker may sue for damages or an injunction if it can be shown that an injury is being caused as a consequence of any effluent, etc. being permitted to flow into a public sewer vested in it. Liability will not however arise if the person responsible has a prescriptive right therefor. Moreover, if the injury is sufficiently serious, proceedings may be brought in respect of public nuisance. Normally the statutory remedies should prove adequate, but it seems that the courts would grant an injunction to prevent any contravention in a proper case where the penalties could be shown not to be an adequate deterrent.[105]

---

[101] Changed from 110°F by the Water Act 2003 Sch.7 para.39(a).
[102] Defined by s.111(5) as meaning "any such (a) crude petroleum; (b) oil made from petroleum, or from coal, shale, peat or other bituminous substances; or (c) product of petroleum or mixture containing petroleum, as, when tested in the manner prescribed by or under the Petroleum (Consolidation) Act 1928, gives off an inflammable vapour at a temperature of less than twenty-three degrees Celsius substituted for "seventy-three degrees Fahrenheit" by the Water Act 2003 Sch.7 para.39(b). In addition to the above control, it is customary to insert in a licence to store petroleum spirit under s.1 of the Petroleum (Consolidation) Act 1928 (which licence is issued by the fire and rescue authority (in Greater London or a metropolitan county) or the county council or county borough council: 1928 Act s.2, as amended) a condition to the effect that no spirit or vapour shall be allowed to escape into any drain or sewer.
[103] ss. 118–141.
[104] See Ch.9, below, pp.247–257.
[105] See *Att Gen v Sharp* [1931] 1 Ch. 121, and *Att Gen v Bastow* [1957] 1 Q.B. 514.

Chapter 6

HIGHWAY DRAINS

HIGHWAY DRAINS AS PUBLIC SEWERS

In this chapter the expression "highway drain" is used as meaning any conduit or ditch (artificial or natural) which takes off or conveys the surface water from a highway[1] maintainable at the public expense.[2] Since, in this context, there are no legal consequences attaching to the distinction, it is unnecessary to distinguish between a sewer and a drain. **6–001**

The drains which take off the surface water from a highway—which "belong" to the highway in question[3]—and which serve no other purpose will normally be vested in the highway authority[4] as such, and there will in most cases be no question of them being vested in the sewerage undertaker as public sewers under s.179 of the Water Industry Act 1991. Where, however, a highway drain also conveys foul or surface water from premises in the vicinity of the highway, or where it is desired to connect the drains of such premises to a highway drain, the status of the latter may well be very important; in particular it will have to be ascertained whether or not the drain is a public sewer.

Highway drains constructed subsequent to October 1, 1937, by the highway authority, will be public sewers if they have been constructed under some statutory provision relating to the sewering of private streets.[5] They will also be public sewers if they were constructed before April 1, 1974 by a highway authority which was at that time also the local sanitary authority and provided they then drained other property not belonging to the local authority.[6]

---

[1] This term is used in its widest sense as comprising "all portions of land over which every subject of the Crown may lawfully pass" (Pratt and Mackenzie's *Law of Highways*, 21st edn, p.1).

[2] Private streets are considered below, pp.153–154.

[3] The expression used in s.264(1) of the Highways Act 1980.

[4] By s.263 (as amended) of the Highways Act 1980, every highway maintainable at the public expense vests in the highway authority. All such highways are now vested in the county (in Wales, from April 1, 1996, county or county borough) and metropolitan district councils, outside London under ss.1 and 265 of the 1980 Act, although in England urban roads, footpaths and bridleways may be maintained by the district council. The main exceptions are trunk and special roads, vested in the Secretary of State (1980 Act s.1).

[5] Successively, the 1936 Act s.20(1)(c) (original form); 1936 Act s.20(1)(b), as inserted by the Water Act 1973 Sch.8 para.33, and amended by the Highways Act 1980 Sch.24 para.4(a); Water Act 1989 s.153(3)(b); Water Industry Act 1991 s.179(2)(b).

[6] 1936 Act s.20(1)(b), and proviso to s.20(2), in their original form, before the amendment effected by the Water Act 1973.

6–002 If such drains drained the highway alone, or if they were constructed, whether before or after the April 1, 1974, by a highway authority which was not the local sanitary authority, they will not be public sewers, unless the former water authority made a declaration of vesting,[7] on the application of the highway authority or, since September 1, 1989, such a declaration has been made by the sewerage undertaker.[8] On the other hand a statute transferring liability for a highway from one local authority to another only affected "functions with respect to highways", and therefore did not transfer responsibility for a land drain to the new highway authority.[9]

A highway drain constructed prior to October 1, 1937, which belonged to a highway, in respect of which the highway authority was not the local sanitary authority,[10] was excluded from the definition of "sewer" contained in s.4 of the 1875 Act,[11] and any such drain did not, therefore, vest in the local authority or (now) the sewerage undertaker as a public sewer under s.20 of the 1936 Act.[12] If the highway of which the drain formed part was vested in or under the control of a highway authority which was also the local sanitary authority, the drain would have been a sewer vested in the local authority (and therefore a public sewer under the 1936 Act) under the 1875 Act in accordance with the normal principles applicable to other drains.[13]

The fact that surface water from a highway was caused to flow into a public sewer would not affect its status,[14] and under s.115(1)(b) of the 1991 Act, a "relevant authority"[15] is entitled to use any public sewer[16] vested in the sewerage undertaker for the conveyance of

---

[7] Or unless such a declaration had been made by the sanitary authority before April 1, 1974.

[8] Successively, the 1936 Act s.17(9); s.17(9), as amended by the London Government Act 1963 Sch.18 Pt II, and the Water Act 1973 s.14(2); and the 1991 Act s.103(3).

[9] *Att Gen v St Ives RDC* [1961] 1 Q.B. 366.

[10] Apparently a drain "belonging to" a main road which was formerly vested in the county council, and which was transferred to the district council, which was also the local sanitary authority, would not thereby become a public sewer: *Williamson v Durham RDC* [1906] 2 K.B. 65. This position is preserved by s.264 of the Highways Act 1980.

[11] See Ch.2, above, pp.55–58.

[12] See Ch.2, above, pp.54, 55–56 and *Irving v Carlisle RDC* (1907) 71 J.P. 212.

[13] Ch.2, above, pp.59–60.

[14] *Wilkinson v Llandaff and Dinas Powis RDC* [1903] 2 Ch. 695.

[15] i.e. a county council or any local authority except a non-metropolitan district council: 1991 Act s.115(9). "Local authority" means the council of a district or of a London borough or the Common Council of the City of London or, in relation to Wales, the council of a county or county borough: 1991 Act s.219(1), definition as amended by the Local Government (Wales) Act 1994 Sch.11 Pt I para.2(2).

[16] By virtue of the 1991 Act s.106(1A), inserted by the Water Act 2003 s.99(2), this includes a public lateral drain: see below, p.217.

surface water from roads repairable by the authority.[17] Similarly any highway drain or sewer[18] may be used by the sewerage undertaker for the purpose of conveying surface water from premises or streets.[19] Further, the fact that a certain amount of water flowed off a highway into a land drain, would not affect the status of that drain or make it part of the highway.[20] The unauthorised connection of a house drain to a highway drain which is not a public sewer does not affect the status of the highway drain or cause it to become a public sewer.[21] A private individual has no right to cause his drains or sewers to be connected to a highway drain and he would be liable in respect of any nuisance arising as a consequence of any such connection.[22]

A "walkway" in, through or under a building created by agreement under s.35 of the Highways Act 1980 (as amended) or its predecessor in the Act of 1971, has some of the characteristics of a highway. The agreement made between the local authority and the owner(s) of the building should make provision for the drainage of the building (see s.35(3)(a)), and it is suggested that it should be made clear in the agreement that any such drains should remain in private ownership.

MEANING OF "HIGHWAY DRAIN"

The term "highway drain" is not a term of art, and yet, for the purpose of deciding questions of liability for the cleansing thereof, or in respect of accidents occasioned by such drains, it is important to decide what forms part of a highway drain and what does not. As between the highway authority and the sewerage undertaker, a drain in a highway will be the responsibility of the former only if it is not a public sewer as above explained, and if it forms part of the road or highway, or is vested in the highway authority as such. **6–003**

Whether or not a particular drain forms part of the highway, and whether such objects as gullies, gratings and manhole covers in the highway are part of a drain belonging to the highway, are questions

---

[17] Subject to such terms as may be agreed between the authorities. In default of agreement, the matter may be referred to the Secretary of State, whose decision in the matter is to be final (s.115(4), (5)). A sewerage undertaker must accept any use by a highway authority which is in accordance with a drainage system approved under Sch.3 to the Flood and Water Management Act 2010 (as to which see pp.233–236): s.115(5A), inserted by the 2010 Act Sch.3 para.16(3).

[18] Vested in a "relevant authority".

[19] 1991 Act s.115(1)(a).

[20] *Att Gen v St Ives RDC* [1961] 1 Q.B. 366.

[21] *Rickarby v New Forest RDC* (1910) 26 T.L.R. 586.

[22] See, e.g. *Wincanton RDC v Parsons* [1905] 2 K.B. 34.

of fact.[23] Generally speaking, a manhole cover of a public sewer laid under the highway will be treated as part of the sewer and not part of the highway,[24] unless the drain or sewer itself is a highway drain originally constructed solely for the purpose of draining the highway. Gullies and gratings leading to a public sewer will form part of that sewer,[25] unless they were provided solely for the purpose of draining the highway, in which event they will normally be treated as forming part of the highway.[26]

In a case decided by the Court of Appeal in New Zealand,[27] based on English decisions, it was said that a sewer authority "is not liable in nuisance for the dangerous state of sewers or drains in a highway unless (1) it constructed them, or (2) it is the owner of them, or (3) it has the control or management of them."

CLEANSING OF HIGHWAY DRAINS

6–004 Under s.100(1) of the Highways Act 1980, the highway authority for a highway may, for the purpose of draining it or of otherwise preventing surface water from flowing on to it, "scour, cleanse and

---

[23] See, e.g. *Papworth v Battersea Corp (No.2)* [1961] 1 K.B. 583. The question may also arise in connection with private streets not maintainable at the public expense. If the gully forms part of the street, its cleansing will not be the responsibility of the sewerage undertaker, but if the gully is to be regarded as part of the sewer to which it drains, and that sewer is a public one, the sewerage undertaker will be responsible for the cleansing of the gully. References to a drain or sewer include references to any "accessories", which include manholes, ventilating shafts, pumps and other machinery or apparatus designed or adapted for use in connection with the maintenance of the sewer or other pipe, for the purposes of the 1991 Act, but it is not clear that this expression includes gullies (see s.219(1), (2) of the 1991 Act). Again, alterations to the sewerage system of a private street may be included in private street works expenses chargeable to the frontagers, but the cost of construction of new gullies leading to an existing sewer necessitated by the widening of the street was held not to be so recoverable from the frontagers in *East Barnet UDC v Stacey* [1939] 2 K.B. 861.

[24] See s.219(1), (2) (cited in the preceding note), and *Winslow v Bushey UDC* (1908) 72 J.P. 259, where the local sanitary authority was held liable in respect of an accident which occured in the highway and was caused by a defective manhole cover forming part of their sewer; but in *Thompson v Brighton Corp* [1894] 1 Q.B. 332, the highway authority was held not liable (in accordance with the principle of non-feasance) nor was the sewer authority, where the cause of the accident was the defective state of the highway surrounding the manhole; and see Ch.3, above, pp.94–95. Under s.58 of the Highways Act 1980, the highway authority can no longer plead non-feasance as a defence, but the special defences in s.58(2) of that Act will be relevant.

[25] *White v Hindley Local Board* (1875) L.R. 10 Q.B. 219.

[26] *Papworth v Battersea Corp*. This distinction is, however, by no means clearly drawn in the cases, and the question is essentially one of fact.

[27] See *Patone Borough v Daubney* [1954] N.Z.L.R. 305, per Cooke J. at p.325.

keep open all drains situated in the highway" or in land adjoining[28] or lying near to the highway. The same section gives the highway authority power to construct or lay such drains as it considers necessary and to erect barriers to divert surface water into or through any existing drain. Any surface water may be discharged into or through the drain and into any inland waters, whether natural or artificial, or any tidal waters. If any owner or occupier of land suffers damage, the authority must pay compensation, to be assessed, if the parties agree, by arbitration or, in case of dispute, by the County Court.[29] The authority also has power for the purpose of the drainage of a highway or proposed highway for which they are or will be the highway authority, to exercise any powers exercisable by a sewerage undertaker under ss.158, 159, 163, 165 and 168 of the Water Industry Act 1991.[30]

This useful section confers a power, not a duty. Accordingly the highway authority could not be compelled, whether by a claim for judicial review seeking a mandatory order or otherwise, to keep their drains clean. Before the Highways (Miscellaneous Provisions) Act 1961, the highway authority were not liable for damage caused by their failure to keep their drains clean because such amounted to acts of non-feasance and the authority were only liable for acts of misfeasance.[31] The defence of non-feasance is now no longer available to highway authorities,[32] and they are now under an express duty to maintain any highway maintainable at the public expense which is vested in them,[33] and this duty must include, it is submitted, the maintenance of any drains which are part of the highway. It would therefore seem that an action for damages would lie at the

---

[28] This includes abutting on: Highways Act 1980 s.329(1). Strict physical contact is not essential and land may adjoin and abut if it is in "close proximity"; however the court may not enlarge the meaning to include all deriving benefit from the drain: *Buckinghamshire CC v Trigg* [1963] 1 W.L.R. 155; *Cobstone Investments Ltd v Maxim* [1985] Q.B. 140, C.A.

[29] Highways Act 1980 s.308.

[30] Highways Act 1980 s.100(5), as amended by the Water Act 1989 Sch.25 para.62(4) and the Water Consolidation (Consequential Provisions) Act 1991 s.2(1) Sch.1 para.36. In specified cases notice must be given to the sewerage undertaker and other councils: s.100(6), as amended by the Water Act 1989 and s.100(6A), (6B), inserted by the Local Government (Wales) Act 1994 Sch.7 Pt I.

[31] See *Irving v Carlisle RDC* (1907) 71 J.P. 212, where the highway authority failed to clean out a ditch and as a result an adjoining occupier sustained damage; and *Masters v Hampshire CC* (1915) 84 L.J.K.B. 2194, where road gullies not connected to any sewer were allowed to become overgrown with grass. In both of these cases, the defendant highway authority was held not liable, the burden of the complaint being in each case based on non-feasance.

[32] Highways Act 1980 ss.41 and 58.

[33] Highways Act 1980 ss.41 and 51.

suit of a person injured by a failure to maintain a highway drain, unless the authority could use one of the defences in s.58 of the 1980 Act.[34]

The power given by s.100 in no way overrides or displaces the common law duty of the owner or occupier of land adjoining the highway so to cleanse and scour any ditches on his land as not to permit them to cause a nuisance on the highway.[35] It is, moreover, an offence to alter, obstruct or interfere with any highway drain without the consent of the highway authority.[36]

6–005 In cleansing their highway drains, or in causing the surface water to flow off the highway, the highway authority may not cause a nuisance,[37] for here it would be doing positive acts of misfeasance.[38] Furthermore, it may not cause or permit any polluted water to flow into a natural stream or watercourse contrary to the Water Resources Act 1991.[39]

The expression "drains" used in this section is defined to include[40] a ditch, gutter, watercourse, soak-away, bridge, culvert, tunnel and pipe. It has been decided, giving a wide definition to the word drain, that a pipe need not be connected to any defined channel for it to be within the section.[41] However a "dumb well" (or "swallow hole", as such a feature is termed in some parts of the country), into which waste water is allowed to flow and there to penetrate into the surrounding soil,[42] or a disused gravel pit or stagnant pond,[43]

---

[34] Following *Griffiths v Liverpool Corp* [1967] 1 Q.B. 374, it seems that the authority should institute a proper system of inspection of all highways vested in it, including drains forming part of such highways.

[35] *Att Gen v Waring* (1899) 63 J.P. 789.

[36] Highways Act 1980 s.100(4).

[37] *Pemberton v Bright* [1960] 1 W.L.R. 436, and contrast *Burton v West Suffolk CC* [1960] 1 Q.B. 72. See also s.117(5)(b) of the 1991 Act, which does not, however, strictly apply in the present context.

[38] *Pearce v Croydon RDC* (1910) 74 J.P. 429; it will be an actionable nuisance if the surface water off the highway is caused to flow over private land otherwise than in accordance with the existing rights. See also *Thomas v Gower RDC* [1922] 2 K.B. 76.

[39] Water fouled by tar from the surface of the highway was held to be polluted water within this meaning: *Dell v Chesham UDC* [1921] 3 K.B. 427. Pure water, or surface water carrying sand or silt, etc. may be discharged into a natural stream: *Durrant v Branksome UDC* [1897] 2 Ch. 291. See also below, Ch.8, pp.167–201.

[40] Highways Act 1980 s.100(9). Note the use of the word "include" rather than "mean"; the definition is therefore not exhaustive.

[41] *Att Gen v Copeland* [1902] 1 K.B. 690.

[42] *Croft v Rickmansworth Highway Board* (1888) 39 Ch. D. 272.

[43] *Croysdale v Sunbury-on-Thames UDC* [1898] 2 Ch. 515.

or the overflow pipe from a catchpit,[44] is not a drain within the section.[45]

THE SEWERING OF PRIVATE STREETS

Under the private street works code and advance payments code **6–006** contained in Pt 11 of the Highways Act 1980,[46] the "street works authority"[47] may execute a variety of works in any street which is not a highway maintainable at the public expense. Provided the procedure of the code is correctly followed, the cost of such work may be charged to the frontagers to the street.[48] It is customary for a number of these works to be done at one and the same time, but this is not an essential feature of the procedure, and any one or more of the works mentioned in the section may be done at one time.[49] One of these works is the "sewering" of the street, where the same is not already sewered to the satisfaction of the authority. There is now no indication as to how "sewer" is to be defined for the purposes of the private street works code contained in the Highways Act 1980, as the expression is not defined in that Act. Formerly the definitions of s.4 of the 1875 Act applied to private street works generally. In practice "sewering" is never regarded as being confined to the provision of a proper system of road drainage for the highway,[50] but includes the provision of a sewer for the drainage from the premises fronting

---

[44] *Ballard v Leek Urban Council* (1917) 87 L.J. Ch. 146.

[45] Therefore, the highway authority is not entitled to use such features for the reception of drainage off the highway, except by agreement with the landowners and occupiers concerned. "Unless the pond can be treated as part of the drainage system under the control of the [highway authority], these sections do not empower [the authority] to discharge the surface water into the plaintiff's pond": per Stirling J. in *Croysdale v Sunbury-on-Thames UDC* [1898] 2 Ch. 515 at p.520.

[46] The private street works code means the Highways Act 1980 ss.205–218, and the advance payments code means ss.219–225 of the 1980 Act: s.203(1). There were originally two private street works codes: one (the "code of 1875") originated in the Public Health Act 1875 and the other (the "code of 1892") in the Private Street Works Act 1892. The latter came to apply in most areas; the former was repealed by the Local Government Act 1972.

[47] i.e. the county (or, in Wales from April 1, 1996, county borough council) or metropolitan district council for streets outside London; the London borough council or the Common Council for streets in London: Highways Act 1980 ss.203(3), 329(2A).

[48] "Street" is defined in s.331(1) of the 1980 Act, and see also definition of "private street" in s.203(2).

[49] This is clear from the wording of the sections.

[50] A conduit provided for carrying off surface water from roads was held to be a sewer within s.4 of the 1875 Act, in *Durrant v Branksome UDC* [1897] 2 Ch. 291. It might even be arguable that, in view of the absence of any definition of "sewer", the provision of road drainage is not included in the term "sewering"; the term "channelling" would, however, appear to be adequate for this purpose. The provision of separate sewers for the reception of sewage and of surface water respectively, is provided for in s.206 of the 1980 Act.

on the street[51] and the expression may include both foul water and surface water conduits.[52] Any sewer constructed under either of these provisions becomes a public sewer on completion, unless it belongs to a road maintained by the highway authority.[53] If these provisions are to be invoked it must be proved that the street has at no time been sewered to the satisfaction of the authority.[54]

Under the similar, but now repealed, provisions of the Public Health Act 1875, a failure to express dissatisfaction with the sewer at, or within a reasonable time of, its construction prevented the authority from subsequently operating these provisions to require the provision of a new sewer at the expense of the frontagers.[55] This is not to say that an expression of satisfaction with the foul sewers of a street later precludes an authority's resolution dealing with the separate surface water drainage of the streets.[56]

It is perhaps somewhat anomalous that it is the street works authority as highway authority who should be able to decide whether or not a street has been sewered to its satisfaction, as the effect of a positive decision to that effect is to vest the sewer not in itself, but in the sewerage undertaker. Moreover, in non-metropolitan counties, the anomaly is compounded if arrangements have been made under s.97 of the Water Industry Act 1991, for administration may then be undertaken on behalf of the sewerage undertaker not by the county council, but by the district council. Close co-operation between the authorities will clearly be desirable.

---

[51] The authority may, by s.207(2) of the 1980 Act, decide to apportion the expenses according to the "degree of benefit" principle, and include premises which do not strictly front on the street, but to which access is obtained from the street.

[52] In *Bognor Regis UDC v Boldero* [1962] 2 Q.B. 448, it was held that the magistrates were entitled to determine that the local authority was not acting reasonably where it was proposed to construct two sewers at different times, instead of laying both sewers at the same operation.

[53] 1991 Act s.179(2)(b). See Ch.2, above.

[54] It is a question of fact whether or not the authority had in fact been so satisfied, but such will be implied by the court if a reasonable time after the sewer had become vested in the authority it took no action to secure its alteration or re-construction: *Bonella v Twickenham Local Board* (1887) 20 Q.B.D. 63, and *Wilmslow UDC v Sidebottom* (1906) 70 J.P. 537. These cases were followed in *Poole Corp v Blake* [1956] 1 Q.B. 206, when the court held that s.9 of the Private Street Works Act 1892, empowering the local authority to do incidental works as well as those covered by s.6, did not have the effect of overruling *Bonella's Case*. In its resolution to sewer the street, the local authority should include a statement to the effect that it was not "satisfied": *Ware UDC v Gaunt* [1960] 1 W.L.R. 1364.

[55] *Fulham District Board of Works v Goodwin* (1876) 1 Ex. D. 400; *Bonella v Twickenham Local Board* (1887) 20 Q.B.D. 63; *Bloor v Beckenham UDC* [1908] 2 K.B. 671. This has been held to be the case even where the sewer never became a working sewer, because it had no outfall: *Hornsey Local Board v Davis* [1893] 1 Q.B. 756.

[56] *Poole Corp v Blake* [1956] 1 Q.B. 206.

Chapter 7

SEWAGE DISPOSAL AND SEWAGE DISPOSAL WORKS

INTRODUCTORY

By virtue of s.94 of the Water Industry Act 1991, a sewerage undertaker is under a duty not only to drain its area, but also "to make provision for the emptying of [its public] . . . sewers and such further provision (whether inside its area or elsewhere) as is necessary from time to time for effectually dealing, by means of sewage disposal works or otherwise, with the contents of those sewers."[1] In performing this duty a sewerage undertaker must have regard to its existing and likely future obligations to allow for the discharge of trade effluent into its public sewers and to the need to provide for disposal of trade effluent so discharged.[2] This provision is the successor of s.14 of the Water Act 1973. **7–001**

The remedies by which the duty under s.94 may be enforced have been considered above.[3] It must, however, also be remembered that the functions given by this section may not be exercised by the sewerage undertaker in such a manner as might cause a nuisance.[4] The only practicable methods of dealing with the contents of public sewers are by providing a proper outfall to a river or the sea (without contravening the anti-pollution provisions of the Water Resources

---

[1] s.94(1)(b).

[2] s.94(2). "Trade effluent" has the same meaning as in Ch.3 of Pt 4 of the Water Industry Act 1991: s.94(5), to be amended by the Water Act 2003 s.88(2), providing that s.139 (see p.248) shall have effect for the purposes of s.94 as it has effect for the purposes of Ch.3 of Pt 4. As to trade effluent, see further pp.247–257.

[3] i.e. ss.18, 23 and 24 of the 1991 Act, see above, pp.24–29.

[4] For examples of a nuisance arising out of a sewage farm see *Bainbridge v Chertsey UDC* (1914) 84 L.J. Ch. 626, and *Cornford v Havant and Waterloo UDC* (1933) 31 L.G.R. 142. The limits of liability in nuisance are illustrated by *Yorkshire Water Services Ltd v Sun Alliance & London Insurance plc* [1998] Env. L.R. 204, where sewage sludge escaped from the undertaker's waste tip, blocking the river and spreading to sewage works also owned by the undertaker. The undertaker was held not liable in nuisance in respect of the costs of works undertaken by the owners of other property in order to alleviate the risk of future flooding as there had to be actual damage not merely the apprehension of damage to sustain a cause of action for damages in nuisance (following *Midland Bank plc v Bardgrove Property Services Ltd* (1992) 37 E.G. 126). Liability in private nuisance may arise out of an isolated escape where there is unreasonable or negligent user and foreseeability of escape: *Colour Quest Ltd v Total Downstream UK plc* [2009] EWHC 540 (Comm) at [408]–[421]. See further, p.72.

Act 1991),[5] or by the provision of disposal works of one type or another. The power of a sewerage undertaker to lay a pipe does not carry with it an implied power to discharge the contents on to private land or into a watercourse without the owner's consent.[6]

A Report by the National Rivers Authority[7] noted that discharges of sewage may arise from a number of different sources, including:

- treated effluent and storm discharges from urban sewage treatment works operated by the sewerage undertakers;
- effluent from sewage treatment plants serving small populations ("package plants");
- combined sewer overflows and emergency overflows from sewerage systems;
- septic tanks; and
- crude sewerage discharges at some estuaries and coastal locations.

7–002 The quality of sewage discharged from *sewage treatment works* depends on the level of treatment accorded. The normal classification is as follows: *preliminary treatment* involves the removal of rags, grit, gross solids, etc.; *primary treatment*, the settlement of solids in suspension; *secondary treatment*, biological treatment to remove organic material; and *tertiary treatment*, treatment to decrease any remaining solids or organic material or to provide disinfection or nutrient removal.[8] Few plants in England and Wales need to proceed beyond the secondary treatment stage; some, mainly in coastal or estuarine locations, only perform primary treatment on sewage received, or discharge preliminary treated effluent direct to sea via a long (offshore) outfall.[9]

---

[5] There is no common law right to cause the contents of sewers to flow into the sea, if a nuisance is thereby caused: *Foster v Warblington UDC* [1906] 1 K.B. 648 and *Hobart v Southend-on-Sea Corp* (1906) 75 L.J.K.B. 305. As to the general prevention see below, Ch.8. As to river pollution prevention in particular, see *George Legge & Son v Wenlock Corp* [1938] A.C. 204.

[6] *British Waterways Board v Severn Trent Water Ltd* [2001] EWCA Civ 276; [2002] Ch. 25; see p.98.

[7] "Discharge Consents and Compliance: The NRA's Approach to Control of Discharges of Water" (HMSO, 1994), p.14.

[8] "Discharge Consents and Compliance", 1994. The terms "primary treatment" and "secondary treatment" are the subject of particular definitions in the Urban Waste Water Treatment (England and Wales) Regulations 1994: see below, pp.157–159.

[9] NRA Report, n.7, p.14.

Package plants are used for small housing developments and commercial and industrial premises where connection to a main sewer is not practical or economic; they provide secondary treatment.

Intermittent discharges from *emergency, combined sewer and storm tank overflows*, although infrequent, can result in significant volumes of sewage being discharged to receiving watercourses.[10]

Septic tanks, which normally serve individual domestic premises, **7–003**
provide primary settlement of sewage together with some anaerobic digestion of the collected sludge; most septic tank effluents are discharged to underground strata by means of a soakaway.[11]

Some sewage outfalls, mostly in coastal or estuarine areas, discharge untreated effluent (or effluent which has only received preliminary treatment) close to shore; others, constructed more recently, are much longer and make use of natural dilution and dispersion for preliminary treated effluent.[12] Many of these discharges will have ceased on implementation of the Urban Waste Water Treatment Directive[13]; some of the outfalls will be retained as discharge points for treated sewage, or for storm or emergency overflows.[14]

The duty under s.94 of the Water Industry Act 1991 is supplemented by the Urban Waste Water Treatment (England and Wales) Regulations 1994,[15] which provide that the duty under s.94(1)(b) shall include a duty to ensure that urban waste water is, before discharge, subject to treatment provided in accordance with reg.5, and to ensure that:

(a) plants built in order to comply with reg.5 are designed (account being taken of seasonal variations of the load), constructed, operated and maintained to ensure sufficient performance under all normal local climatic conditions;

(b) treated waste water and sludge arising from treatment are reused whenever appropriate; and

(c) disposal routes for treated waste water and sludge minimise the adverse effects on the environment.

The requirements of reg.5 are that treatment plants which provide **7–004**
secondary treatment[16] or an equivalent treatment are provided:

---

[10] NRA Report, n.7, p.15.
[11] NRA Report, p.16.
[12] NRA Report, pp.15–16.
[13] See below.
[14] NRA Report, n.7, p.16.
[15] SI 1994/2841 reg.4(4).
[16] i.e. "treatment of urban waste water by a process generally involving biological treatment with a secondary settlement or other process in which the requirements established in Table 1 in Schedule 3 are respected": reg.2(1).

(a) by December 31, 2000 (or, exceptionally, a later date not later than December 31, 2005, agreed with the Commission), in respect of all discharges from agglomerations with a population equivalent of more than 15,000[17];

(b) by December 31, 2005, in respect of all discharges from agglomerations with a population equivalent of between 10,000 and 15,000;

(c) by December 31, 2005, in respect of all discharges to freshwater and estuaries from agglomerations with a population equivalent of between 2,000 and 10,000.[18]

Treatment plants which provide more stringent treatment[19] than this were required to be provided by December 31, 1998, in respect of all discharges from agglomerations with a population equivalent of more than 10,000 into sensitive areas, or into the relevant catchment areas of sensitive areas where the discharges contribute to the pollution of these areas.[20] This duty does not, however, apply where the Environment Agency certifies that it is satisfied as a result of monitoring, that the minimum percentage of reduction of the overall load entering all treatment plants in that area (and in the catchment area the discharges from which contribute to the pollution of that area) is at least 65 per cent for total phosphorous and 75 per cent for total nitrogen.[21] If an area is reclassified from "high natural dispersion area" or to "sensitive area" the target dates become the seventh anniversary of the change of identification or, if specified, a later date.[22]

Less stringent treatments may be provided in respect of discharges of urban waste water from agglomerations with a population equivalent

---

[17] The UK was 90% compliant by December 31, 2000 and expected to be 98% compliant by December 31, 2002: DEFRA website ("Urban Waste Water Treatment").
[18] reg.5(1). For definitions of "agglomeration" and "population equivalent" see above, pp.48–49. The UK government's policy is to apply this standard to all coastal waters, thus going beyond Directive requirements: DEFRA, "Raising the Quality", September 23, 1998, paras 50–52.
[19] i.e. secondary plus tertiary treatment, which may involve disinfection, e.g. by ultraviolet light treatment and/or nutrient removal to help prevent eutrophication and/or removal of specific toxic substances. The nature of the treatment required will be related to the ground on which the sensitive area was designated.
[20] reg.5(2). For the definition of "sensitive area" see above, pp.45–48. This level of treatment affecting identified areas (as at December 31, 2000) had either been provided or was to be in place at the latest by December 31, 2004: DEFRA website ("Urban Waste Water Treatment"). The Directive applies whether the discharge into a sensitive area is direct or indirect: *Commission v Italy* (C-396/00) [2002] E.C.R. I-3949.
[21] 1994 Regulations, reg.5(3).
[22] 1994 Regulations, reg.5(4).

between 10,000 and 150,000 (or, exceptionally, with the agreement of the Commission, more than 150,000) to coastal waters in high natural dispersion areas, and from agglomerations with a population equivalent between 2,000 and 10,000 into estuaries which are in such areas. This is so, provided that the discharges receive at least primary treatment[23] in conformity with the control procedures set out in Sch.3, Pt II to the Regulations, and the Environment Agency certifies that it is satisfied that comprehensive studies have indicated that such discharges will not adversely affect the environment.[24]

Appropriate treatment[25] of urban waste water entering collecting systems was required to be provided by December 31, 2005 in respect of: **7–005**

(a) discharges to freshwaters and estuaries from agglomerations with a population equivalent of less than 2,000; and

(b) discharges to coastal waters from agglomerations with a population equivalent of less than 10,000.[26]

Discharges from treatment plants provided under reg.5, including plants provided other than by sewerage undertakers, must satisfy the relevant detailed requirements of Sch.3, Pt I of the Regulations.[27]

SEWAGE DISPOSAL WORKS

The power to construct sewage disposal works is conferred by implication upon sewerage undertakers by s.94(1)(b) of the Water Industry Act 1991. Such works may be constructed only upon land already **7–006**

---

[23] i.e. treatment by a physical and/or chemical process involving settlement of suspended solids, or other processes in which the BOD5 of the incoming waste water is reduced by at least 20% before discharge and the total suspended solids are reduced by at least 50%: reg.5(8)(b).

[24] reg.5(5). For definitions of "urban waste water", "agglomerations", "population equivalent", "coastal waters", "sensitive areas", "high natural dispersion area", see above, pp.45–49.

[25] i.e. treatment by any process and/or disposal system which after discharge allows the receiving waters to meet the relevant quality objectives and relevant provisions of EC directives: reg.5(8)(a).

[26] reg.5(7). For definitions of "urban waste water", "collecting systems", "estuaries", "agglomerations", "population equivalent" and "coastal waters", see above, pp.45–49.

[27] reg.6(1). The Environment Agency, in exercising its functions under Ch.2 of Pt 3 of the Water Resources Act 1991, must secure compliance with the requirements of reg.5 (reg.6(2)), as well as the limitation of pollution of rising waters due to storm overflows with respect to discharges from a collecting system or treatment plant. See below, p.172.

owned by the sewerage undertaker or acquired or lawfully appropriated for that purpose. The distinction between "sewers" and "sewage disposal works" was a source of some difficulty in cases decided under the 1875 Act, but these were largely resolved by s.90(4) of the 1936 Act (now s.219(2)(b) of the 1991 Act), according to which a "sewage disposal works" includes "the machinery and equipment of those works and any necessary pumping stations and outfall pipes", and these issues are not presently problematic.

(a) Acquisition of land and planning permission

7–007 Acquisition of land for the purpose of constructing a sewage disposal works may be by agreement or by means of a compulsory purchase order made in accordance with the Acquisition of Land Act 1981. The authority for compulsory acquisition of land inter alia for such a purpose is given by s.155 of the Water Industry Act 1991, which empowers a sewerage undertaker, upon authorisation by the Secretary of State,[28] "to purchase compulsorily any land anywhere in England and Wales which is required . . . for the purposes of, or in connection with, the carrying out of its functions." The power of compulsory purchase includes power compulsorily to acquire land required for the purpose of being given in exchange for, or for a right over, other land which under the Acquisition of Land Act 1981 forms part of a common, open space or a fuel or field garden allotment.[29] A compulsory purchase order may be challenged on the ground that the scheme in respect of which the order is made will not comply with mandatory requirements of European directives.[30] Alternatively, a sewerage undertaker may by agreement acquire by purchase, lease or otherwise, an existing sewage disposal works or rights of usage in such works in performance of its general functions under s.94.

Express planning permission will have to be obtained in respect of any development for the purposes of sewage disposal works, etc.

---

[28] As to the position in Wales, see above, p.14, n.71.

[29] 1991 Act s.155(3).

[30] See *Moase v Secretary of State for the Environment, Transport and the Regions* [2001] Env. L.R. 227 (where the challenge based on alleged breaches of the Bathing Water Directive 1976, Dir.76/160, failed on the merits, the court holding that the discharge consent granted by the Environment Agency could be relied upon by the Secretary of State and the sewerage undertaker as evidence that there would be compliance; the court declined to consider a challenge based on alleged breaches of the Urban Waste Water Treatment Directive 1991, Dir.91/271, on the ground that the point had not been raised before the inspector at the inquiry).

above ground level.[31] In the case of applications for development relating to the retention, treatment or disposal of sewage,[32] other than the laying of sewers, the construction of pumphouses in a line of sewers and the construction of certain septic tanks and cesspools,[33] and ancillary works, the local planning authority must consult the Environment Agency.[34] Furthermore, proposals for "waste water treatment plants" with a capacity exceeding 150,000 population equivalent[35] and sludge-deposition sites where the area of deposit exceeds 0.5 hectares or a deposit is to be made within 100 metres of any controlled waters and which would be likely to have significant effects on the environment must be accompanied by an "environmental statement", in accordance with the requirements of the Town and Country Planning (Environmental Impact Assessment) (England and Wales) Regulations 1999.[36] On the other hand, local planning authorities have been encouraged by the Secretary of State to give sympathetic consideration to development proposals aimed at enhancing the treatment of sewage. It was stated that local plans and Pt II of unitary developments plans under the Town and Country Planning Act 1990 should include policies and proposals for treatment works, and the sites should be identified.[37] The Planning Act 2008 provides for planning applications (for "development consent") in respect of nationally significant infrastructure projects to be determined by the Secretary of State or the newly established Infrastructure Planning Commission, and not the local planning authority. One of the categories of such projects is the construction or alteration of a waste water treatment plant in England which is expected to have a capacity exceeding, or to increase capacity

---

[31] See above, pp.108–109. See *R. (on the application of Cavanagh) v East Sussex CC* [2009] EWHC 1234 (Admin), where the court rejected an application for judicial review of the grant of planning permission for a waste water treatment facility on the outskirts of Peacehaven; concerns about odour emissions had properly been addressed through the planning process.

[32] Or trade-waste, slurry (i.e. animal faeces and urine) or sludge.

[33] i.e. those serving single dwelling houses or single caravans or single buildings in which not more than ten people will normally reside, work or congregate.

[34] Town and Country Planning (General Development Procedure) Order 1995 (SI 1995/419) Art.10 and Table, para.(s). See Environment Agency, Scottish Environment Protection Agency, Environmental Heritage Service, Pollution Prevention Guidelines 4, "Treatment and disposal of sewage where no foul sewer is available" (PPG4, July 2006), *http://publications.environment-agency.gov.uk* [Accessed August 3, 2010].

[35] As defined in Directive 91/271, art.2 point (6). Such plants that do not fall within Sch.1 fall within Sch.2 if the area of development exceeds 1,000 sq m; a statement is needed if the development is likely to have significant effects on the environment.

[36] SI 1999/293, as amended, Sch.1, Sch.2.

[37] DoE Circular 17/91, Welsh Office Circular 62/91, "Water Industry Investment: Planning Considerations".

by more than, a population equivalent of 500,000.[38] "Waste water" includes domestic, industrial and urban waste water.[39]

(b) General provisions

7–008 Sewage disposal works, like public sewers[40] may be constructed outside the sewerage undertaker's area by virtue of s.94(1)(b) of the 1991 Act. A sewerage undertaker could also have taken over from a former water authority privately owned sewage disposal works, the construction of which had not been completed prior to October 1, 1937 and which had been adopted by the authority.

(c) Ownership

7–009 Sewage disposal works constructed *de novo* by a sewerage undertaker will automatically vest in that undertaker.[41] In addition, sewage disposal works which were vested in a former water authority on September 1, 1989 (the "Transfer Date")[42] automatically became vested in the successor sewerage undertaker and this necessitates an examination of the former provisions under which disposal works became so vested. The following classes of sewage disposal works would have vested in a water authority:

(a) Those which vested in a local authority under the 1875 Act. Although the term "sewer" under that Act did not include an engine house or pumping station,[43] buildings and works of that nature would have vested in the local sanitary authority under s.13 of the 1875 Act which operated to vest in the authority all sewers "together with all buildings, works, materials and things belonging thereto."[44]

(b) Those actually constructed by the water authority or a predecessor local authority, or acquired by them.[45]

---

[38] 2008 Act s.29(1), (2). s.29 is in force from a day to be appointed.

[39] 2008 Act s.29(3). These terms are as defined in the Urban Waste Water Treatment (England and Wales) Regulations 1994 (SI 1994/2841). See p.45.

[40] See Ch.3, above, p.70.

[41] 1991 Act s.179(1)(b).

[42] The Water Authorities (Transfer of Functions) (Appointed Day) Order 1989 (SI 1989/1530).

[43] *King's College, Cambridge v Uxbridge RDC* [1901] 2 Ch. 768.

[44] A septic tank and outfall privately constructed was held to fall within this expanded definition and to vest in the authority, together with the sewer leading thereto, in *Clark v Epsom RDC* [1929] 1 Ch. 287.

[45] See the expanded definition of "sewage disposal works" in s.90(4) of the 1936 Act.

(c) Those in respect of which a vesting declaration was made by a water authority or their predecessor local authority under s.17 of the 1936 Act.

In present circumstances questions of ownership are perhaps relatively unlikely, but may arise where a sewerage undertaker wishes to use a disposal works as an outfall for a new sewer,[46] or where there arises a question as to responsibility for maintenance.[47]

(d) Maintenance

Having constructed, acquired or otherwise provided, sewage disposal works, it will be the duty of the sewerage undertaker to maintain them in such a manner as not to cause a nuisance.[48] There is no express statutory duty relating to the cleansing, etc. of sewage disposal works parallel to that imposed in respect of public sewers by s.94(1)(a) of the 1991 Act. Nonetheless the duty effectually to drain its area under s.94 will clearly require the efficient maintenance of its sewage disposal works by a sewerage undertaker. **7–010**

(e) Methods of disposal

Apart from discharges of treated (or untreated) sewage mentioned above,[49] sewage sludge (i.e. the residue left after sewage has been treated) may be dumped at sea from a ship, incinerated or disposed of on land, normally by depositing it for agricultural purposes. Sludge dumping at sea was prohibited with effect from the end of December 1998 with, prior to then, progressive reductions in the total amount of toxic, persistent or bioaccumulable materials in sludge so disposed of.[50] The operation of works for the incineration of waste such as sewage sludge, and the deposit of sewage or sewage sludge on land, are subject to the regulatory regime established by the Environmental Permitting (England and Wales) Regulations 2010.[51] This will require a permit from the Environment Agency or the local authority, **7–011**

---

[46] In connection with earlier provisions see *Solihull RDC v Ford* (1932) 30 L.G.R. 385.
[47] *Willoughby v Chapman*, unreported, but see article at (1955) 119 J.P.N. 442.
[48] There also may be liability under the statutory nuisance procedures: see pp.207–209.
[49] pp.155–157.
[50] Urban Waste Water Treatment (England and Wales) Regulations 1994 (SI 1994/2841) reg.9. This activity was licensed under Pt 2 of the Food and Environmental Protection Act 1985.
[51] SI 2010/675.

according to the circumstances. Deposits directly on land for agricultural purposes are governed by the Sludge (Use in Agriculture) Regulations 1989.[52] The National Rivers Authority's policy was to liaise with sewerage undertakers and farmers in relation to the disposal of sewage sludge to land, and influence the location, quantity and timing of applications in order to prevent pollution of water resources.[53]

The government "considers the controlled application of sewage sludge to agricultural land to be the best practicable environmental option in most circumstances. The addition of organic matter improves soil structure, workability and water holding capacity as well as bringing savings in fertiliser costs."[54] Following the prohibition of the dumping of sewage sludge at sea, the quantity of sludge disposed of on land has naturally increased, the proportions in 2005 being: to farmland, 39 per cent; incineration, 51 per cent; landfill, 16 per cent; and other, 2 per cent.[55] The total produced has also increased, from almost 1m tonnes in 1992 to 1.4m tonnes in 2005.[56] A Safe Sludge Matrix has been agreed between the British Retail Consortium (representing major retailers) and Water UK (representing the UK's Water and Sewage Operators).[57] This provides guidance on the safe use of sewage sludge in agriculture.

AGREEMENTS WITH OTHER SEWERAGE UNDERTAKERS

7–012 Besides providing sewage disposal works itself, or causing the contents of its sewers to flow into the sea or some other natural outfall,

---

[52] SI 1989/1263, as amended by SI 1990/880, implementing the EC Directive on the protection of the environment, and in particular of the soil, when sewage sludge is used in agriculture, Dir.86/278. For an example of a prosecution where the conduct fell outside the 1989 Regulations, see "ENDS Report" 230, March 1994, pp.46–47.
[53] NRA, "Policy and Practice for the Protection of Groundwater" (HMSO, 1992), s.E.
[54] DEFRA website, "Consultation paper on Sewage Sludge: Proposals to amend the statutory controls for agricultural use" (2002).
[55] See *http://www.defra.gov.uk* [Accessed August 3, 2010].
[56] See *http://www.defra.gov.uk* [Accessed August 3, 2010].
[57] ADAS, BRC, Water UK, "The Safe Sludge Matrix, Guidelines for the Application of Sewage Sludge to Agricultural Land", 3rd edn (2001) and "Guidelines for the Application of Sewage Sludge to Industrial Crops" (2001) (http://www.adas.co.uk [Accessed August 3, 2010]). These guidelines were more restrictive than previous arrangements, including the phasing out of the use of untreated sludge, and involved significant investment by the water companies: European Commission, "Disposal and recycling routes for sewage sludge. Part I—Sludge use acceptance report" (October 2001), pp.32–35. See also the DoE, "Code of Practice for Agriculture Use of Sewage Sludge", 2nd edn (*http://www.defra.gov.uk* [Accessed August 3, 2010]).

a sewerage undertaker might agree with a neighbouring undertaker for the disposal of its sewage through the sewage system of that other undertaker. In view of the extensive areas now served by sewerage undertakers, the likely need for such an agreement must seem slight.

At common law the "sending" sewerage undertaker would be in the same position as the owner of a dominant tenement in respect of an easement, and could, therefore, only use the sewer and/or sewage disposal works of the "receiving" undertaker by agreement or in pursuance of a prescriptive right so to do.[58]

CONSERVANCY SERVICES

In addition to the disposal of sewage through a sewerage system, **7–013**
the sewerage undertaker has duties under the Control of Pollution Act 1974 (replacing the 1936 Act) to arrange for the disposal of waste from privies[59] serving private dwellings, which is collected by a "waste collection authority"[60] and duly delivered to it.[61] The "waste collection authority" must make such arrangements for the emptying without charge of privies serving one or more private dwellings in its area as it considers appropriate.[62] It must also upon request arrange for the emptying of a cesspool[63] in its area which serves only private dwellings. The authority may make a reasonable charge for the emptying of cesspools, or any other privies which it may agree to empty.[64]

---

[58] See *Att Gen v Acton Local Board* (1882) 22 Ch. D. 221.

[59] A "privy" is defined to mean a latrine which has a moveable receptacle: Environmental Protection Act 1990 s.45(12).

[60] i.e. district and London borough councils, the Common Council of the City of London, the Sub-Treasurer of the Inner Temple and the Under Treasurer of the Middle Temple, and county and county borough councils in Wales: 1990 Act s.30(3), as amended by the Local Government (Wales) Act 1994 Sch.9, para.17(3).

[61] Control of Pollution Act 1974 s.14(9), (10), as amended by the Water Act 1989 Sch.25 para.48(5). These provisions were generally repealed by the Environmental Protection Act 1990 Sch.16 Pt II, but not in respect of "industrial waste" (see the Environmental Protection Act 1990 (Commencement No.11) Order 1992, SI 1992/266 Art.3). The Controlled Waste Regulations 1992 (SI 1992/588) Sch.3 para.7, provides that sewage which has been removed from a privy or cesspool is to be treated as "industrial waste".

[62] 1990 Act s.45(5)(a).

[63] "Cesspool" includes for this purpose a settlement tank or other tank for the reception or disposal of foul matter from buildings.

[64] 1990 Act s.45(5)(b), (6). The service may be performed by the authority itself or by a contractor. Where a contractor caused a nuisance through the manner of emptying cesspools, the employing local authority was held liable therefor: *Robinson v Beaconsfield UDC* [1911] 2 Ch. 188.

Although the emptying of cesspools, and privies not serving private dwellings, is a matter for arrangement as to financial terms between the authority and the occupier requesting the service, it seems that the amount of the charge must not only be reasonable per se, but also comparable with charges made for similar services to similar premises.[65]

[65] If authority is needed for this rather obvious principle, see the reasoning in *Pegg & Jones Ltd v Derby Corp* [1909] 2 K.B. 311.

Chapter 8

THE DISCHARGE OF SEWAGE EFFLUENTS

INTRODUCTORY

In this chapter it is intended to deal with the discharge of sewage effluents (treated or untreated) from public sewers or sewage disposal works vested in a sewerage undertaker: discharge of effluents from private premises into public sewers is discussed elsewhere in this book, but discharges from private premises otherwise than into public sewers are considered here. In the nature of things, sewage effluent can only be discharged to a watercourse or the sea. Discharge from public sewers to a watercourse does not now give rise to any very complicated problems, in view of the modern statutory provisions found in Pt 3 of the Water Resources Act 1991, creating pollution offences in respect of "controlled waters".[1] The position was also now affected by the provisions of the Urban Waste Water Treatment (England and Wales) Regulations 1994.[2] The provisions of the Water Resources Act 1991 concerning offences and the granting of consents to discharges have been replaced, with effect from April 6, 2010, by provision of the Environmental Permitting (England and Wales) Regulations 2010.[3] **8–001**

It should be noted that the power of a sewerage undertaker to lay a pipe does not carry with it an implied power to discharge the contents on to private land or into a watercourse without the consent of the owner.[4]

THE DEFINITION OF "CONTROLLED WATERS"

The control of pollution provisions of the Water Resources Act 1991 were applicable to a range of waters defined as "controlled" for the purposes of the Act. The offences arising out of "water discharge activities" established by the Environmental Permitting (England and **8–002**

---

[1] ss.82–104.
[2] SI 1994/2841.
[3] SI 2010/675. See below.
[4] *British Waterways Board v Severn Trent Water Ltd* [2001] EWCA Civ 276; [2002] Ch. 25; see p.98.

Wales) Regulations 2010 have a similar application, although the term "controlled waters" is not used. "Controlled waters" are defined by s.104(1) and fall into four broad divisions:

(a) territorial waters extending three miles[5] out from the territorial waters baseline of England and Wales;

(b) coastal waters within the territorial waters baseline as far inland as the limit of the highest tide or, in the case of rivers and watercourses,[6] as far as the fresh-water limit, including the waters of any adjoining enclosed docks;

(c) inland freshwaters, i.e. so much of any relevant river or watercourse[7] as is above the fresh-water limit and any relevant lake or pond[8];

(d) ground waters contained in underground strata or in a well or borehole, including similar or associated works, sunk into such strata or any excavation in which the water level depends wholly or mainly upon supply from such strata.

Any reference to the waters of any lake or pond or of any river or watercourse includes a reference to the bottom, channel or bed of any lake, pond, river or watercourse which is for the time being dry.[9]

The fresh-water limits of relevant rivers or watercourses are to be indicated upon maps deposited by the Secretary of State with the Environment Agency. Any changes which require to be made in such indications can be made through the deposit of revised

---

[5] i.e. international nautical miles of 1,852 metres: s.104(3).

[6] "Watercourse" includes (subject to ss.72(2) and 113(1)) all rivers, streams, ditches, drains, cuts, culverts, dykes, sluices, sewers and passages through which water flows, except mains and other pipes which belong to the Environment Agency or a water undertaker or are used by a water undertaker or any other person for the purpose only of providing a supply of water to any premises: 1991 Act s.221(1). A man-made ditch may accordingly be a watercourse if water flows through it: *Environment Agency v Brock plc* [1998] Env. L.R. 607.

[7] Defined as meaning "any river or watercourse (including an underground river or watercourse and an artificial river or watercourse) which is neither a public sewer nor a sewer or drain which drains into a public sewer": Water Resources Act 1991 s.104(3). It includes a watercourse which overflows or which dries up: *R. v Dovermoss Ltd* (1995) 159 J.P. 448, C.A. (Cr.D.).

[8] Defined as meaning "any lake or pond which (whether it is natural or artificial or above or below ground) discharges into a relevant river or watercourse or into another lake or pond which is itself a relevant lake or pond"; "lake or pond" includes a reservoir of any description: 1991 Act s.104(3).

[9] 1991 Act s.104(2).

maps.[10] Such maps must be made available by the Agency for inspection by the public free of charge at all reasonable times.[11]

In addition to those stated waters the Secretary of State may provide by order[12] that other territorial waters or lakes or ponds which would not otherwise be "controlled" shall be so.[13] Furthermore, the expression "controlled waters" has effect for the purpose of giving effect to Directive 2006/113 as if it included all waters which are coastal or brackish waters for the purposes of that Directive[14]; and the expression "inland freshwaters" in s.104(1) includes all waters which need to be classified under regulations to give effect to Directive 75/440,[15] all waters which are fresh waters for the purposes of Directive 2006/44,[16] (for the purposes of Ch.1 of Pt 3 of the Water Resources Act 1991 (ss.82–84)) any lake or pond (other than a relevant lake or pond) which needs to be classified in order to give effect to Directive 76/160, and (for all other purposes) any such lake or pond which has been so classified under that Chapter.[17]

The Secretary of State may by regulations prescribe a system for classifying the quality of any description of controlled waters.[18] The criteria so specified are to consist of some or all of: **8–003**

(a) general requirements as to the purposes for which the specified waters are to be suitable;

---

[10] Water Resources Act 1991 s.192(1), as amended by the Environment Act 1995 Sch.22 para.128.

[11] Water Resources Act 1991 s.192(2), as amended by the Environment Act 1995 Sch.22 para.128.

[12] Water Resources Act 1991 s.104(4).

[13] Water Resources Act 1991 s.104(4). Or that a lake or pond or watercourse is to be treated as if it were not a relevant lake or pond or watercourse. See the Controlled Waters (Lakes and Ponds) Order 1989 (SI 1989/1149) providing that a reservoir which does not discharge into a relevant river or watercourse or a relevant lake or pond, and which does not contain water treated with a view to complying with reg.23 of the Water Supply (Water Quality) Regulations 1989 (SI 1989/1147), is to be treated as a relevant lake or pond. All lakes and ponds are to be treated as "controlled waters" in so far as s.85 (now the Environmental Permitting Regulations 2010) relates to the discharge of waste water from urban waste water treatment plants: Urban Waste Water Treatment (England and Wales) Regulations 1994 (SI 1994/2841), reg.6(5), as amended by SI 2010/675 Sch.26 Pt 2 para.10(3)(d).

[14] Surface Waters (Shellfish) (Classification) Regulations 1997 (SI 1997/1332), reg.6(2), as amended by SI 2009/1266 reg.2.

[15] Surface Waters (Abstraction for Drinking Water) (Classification) Regulations 1996 (SI 1996/3001) reg.7(2).

[16] Surface Waters (Fishlife) (Classification) Regulations 1997 (SI 1997/1331), reg.6(2), as amended by SI 2009/1264 reg.1.

[17] Bathing Waters (Classification) (England) Regulations 2003 (SI 2003/1238), reg.2(1), revoked by SI 2008/1097 reg.19(1) with effect from March 24, 2015.

[18] Water Resources Act 1991 s.82.

(b) specifications as to substances or the concentrations thereof which are permissible or impermissible in the specified waters; and

(c) other specific requirements as to other characteristics of those waters.

The Secretary of State may then serve a notice on the Environment Agency specifying one or more of the prescribed classifications, and a date in relation to each specified classification; this notice establishes the "water quality objectives" for any waters which are, or are included in, waters of a prescribed description.[19] Such objectives may be reviewed by the Secretary of State after five years or at any time upon the request of the Environment Agency, after consultation with such water undertakers or "other persons" as it considers appropriate,[20] the latter general category presumably including sewerage undertakers. The Secretary of State must give notice of any proposed variation of water quality objectives and consider any representations or objections made in respect of it and not withdrawn.

It is the general duty of the Secretary of State and the Agency to utilise their powers to ensure, so far as is practicable, the achievement of the water quality objectives established under the Water Resources Act 1991.[21] The Agency is also under a duty to monitor the extent of pollution in controlled waters and to consult where it seems appropriate with the Scottish Environment Protection Agency.[22]

8–004 The Secretary of State has established statutory water quality objectives in respect of: (1) the quality of inland surface water for abstraction of drinking water[23], (2) the presence of dangerous substances[24];

---

[19] 1991 Act s.83, as modified by SI 1992/337 reg.4, SI 1996/3001 reg.7(1), SI 1997/1331 reg.6(2), SI 1997/1332 reg.6(1) and SI 1997/2560 reg.5, and amended by the Environment Act 1995 Sch.22 para.128.

[20] 1991 Act s.83(3).

[21] 1991 Act s.84(1), as amended by the Environment Act 1995 Sch.22 para.128, and SI 2010/675 Sch.26 Pt 1 para.8(4). On the significance of this duty, see "ENDS Report" 241, February 1995, p.9.

[22] 1991 Act s.84(2), as amended by the Environment Act 1995 Sch.22 para.128.

[23] Based on the Surface Waters (Abstraction for Drinking Water) (Classification) Regulations 1996 (SI 1996/3001) (revoking SI 1989/1148), implementing the Drinking Water Directive, Dir.75/440.

[24] Based on the Surface Waters (Dangerous Substances) (Classification) Regulations 1989 (SI 1989/2286), 1992 (SI 1992/337), 1997 (SI 1997/2560) and 1998 (SI 1998/389), implementing the framework directive on Pollution caused by Certain Dangerous Substances Discharge into the Aquatic Environment of the Community, Dir.76/464 and further (daughter) directives. See DoE Circular 7/89, "Water and the Environment".

(3) the quality of bathing waters[25]; (4) the quality of inland freshwaters which need protection or improvement to support fish life[26]; and (5) the quality of controlled waters which are coastal or brackish waters and which need protection or improvement in order to support shellfish life and growth.[27] The pollution of bathing waters has given rise to particular difficulties.[28] Where EC Directives impose requirements, s.83 of the Water Resources Act 1991 is modified by regulations to impose a duty on the Secretary of State to exercise the powers under that section to classify appropriately under the regulations such waters as are necessary to give effect to the relevant Directive.[29]

---

[25] Based on the Bathing Waters (Classification) Regulations 1991 (SI 1991/1597), as amended by SI 2003/1238 reg.2(2), implementing the Bathing Water Directive 1976, Dir.76/160. "Bathing waters" are as defined in Art.1.2 of the Directive: i.e. "all running or still fresh waters or parts thereof and sea water", in which bathing is "explicitly authorised by the competent authorities of each Member State" or is "not prohibited and is traditionally practised by a large number of bathers". 495 bathing waters have been identified in England and Wales for the purposes of the Directive. The extent of compliance is monitored by the Environment Agency: see annual reports on *Bathing Water Quality*. These regulations are to be revoked and replaced by the Bathing Water Regulations 2008 (SI 2008/1097), implementing Directive 2006/7 concerning the management of bathing water quality, which repeals Directive 76/160.

[26] Surface Waters (Fishlife) (Classification) Regulations 1997 (SI 1997/1331), as amended by SI 2003/1053 and SI 2009/1264, implementing Dir.2006/44.

[27] Surface Waters (Shellfish) (Classification) Regulations 1997 (SI 1997/1332), as amended by SI 2009/1266, implementing Directive 2006/113.

[28] See also the "ENDS Report" 229, February 1994, p.10, noting research that found a significantly greater risk of falling ill after bathing in waters that breach EC standards; it was a matter of controversy whether compliance with the existing standards was sufficient to ensure that bathers did not fall ill: "ENDS Report" 239, December 1994, pp.29–31, summarising the First Report of the House of Lords Select Committee on the European Communities, *Bathing Water* (1994–95 H.L. 6). See also the Committee's Seventh Report, "Bathing Water Revisited" (1994–95 H.L. 41), summarised in "ENDS Report" 243, p.36. The UK was found by the European Court of Justice to have breached its duty to implement the directive (*Commission v UK* (C-56/90) [1993] E.C.R. I-4109), in respect of bathing areas in Blackpool and adjacant to Formby and Southport. A declaration that the UK had failed to comply with the requirements of the Directive was granted in *Commission v UK* C-42 [2002] Env. L.R. DG 6. In 2009, DEFRA stated that compliance with EC minimum water quality standards had risen to 98.3% (79% in 1990) (*http://www.defra.gov.uk* [Accessed August 4, 2010]). In 2007 and 2008, standards had been lower as a result of heavy rainfall causing pollution from agriculture and urban areas to run off and leading to the operation of Combined Sewer Overflows. On the definition of "bathing water" see *Moase v Secretary of State for the Environment, Transport and the Regions* [2001] Env. L.R. 227, where the Court of Appeal held that the inspector had been entitled to conclude that water off a rocky, inaccessible beach with no infrastructure to promote bathing was not bathing water. See further, W. Howarth and D. McGillivray, *Water Pollution and Water Quality Law* (Crayford: Shaw & Sons Ltd, 2001), pp.311–320.

[29] See SI 1996/3001 reg.7(1); SI 1997/1331 reg.6(2); SI 1997/1332 reg.6(1); cf. SI 1992/337 reg.4; SI 1997/2560 reg.5; SI 1998/389 reg.5.

The Secretary of State also has power to develop statutory water quality objectives to replace formally agreed but non-statutory river quality objectives which have been in place since the 1970s.[30]

Finally, it is the Agency's duty in exercising its functions under the Environmental Permitting (England and Wales) Regulations 2010 (formerly Ch.2 of Pt 3 of the Water Resources Act 1991) (broadly) to secure compliance with reg.5 of the Urban Waste Water Treatment (England and Wales) Regulations 1994; the limitation of pollution of receiving waters due to storm water overflows from collecting systems and urban waste water treatment plants; and the phasing out of the discharge of sludge to surface waters by December 31, 1998.[31]

POLLUTION OFFENCES IN RESPECT OF "CONTROLLED WATERS"

These offences have been replaced by new similar provisions of the Environmental Permitting (England and Wales) Regulations 2010.[32] An account of them has, however, been retained as the case law may constitute persuasive authority on particular points of interpretation.

(a) Offences

8–005 Under s.85 of the Water Resources Act 1991 it was a criminal offence for any person[33] to "cause" or "knowingly permit"

---

[30] See *Discharge Consents and Compliance: The NRA's Approach to Control of Discharges to Water: Report of the National Rivers Authority* (HMSO 1994), p.9. Objectives were to be set on a pilot basis, based on the Surface Waters (River Ecosystems) (Classification) Regulations 1994 (SI 1994/1057). The programme has, however, not been taken forward: see Howarth and McGillivray, *Water Pollution and Water Quality Law*, 2001, p.807.

[31] SI 1994/2841 reg.6 as amended by SI 2010/675, Sch.26, Pt 2, Para.10(3). See pp.163–164 above. For definitions of "collecting systems" and "urban waste water", see above, p.45.

[32] SI 2010/675; Sch.26 Pt 2 para.10 repealed ss.85–91, 96(3), 99, 103 and other specified provisions of the Water Resources Act 1991.

[33] Including an unincorporated association: *R v L* [2008] EWCA Crim 1970 (a prosecution may be brought against the association or individual members). A contractor may be liable where under the term of the relevant contractual arrangement he assumes responsibility to deal with pollution: *Environment Agency v Biffa Waste Services Ltd* [2008] EWCA Crim 1102.

(a) any poisonous, noxious or polluting[34] matter or any waste to enter "controlled waters"[35];

(b) matter, other than trade or sewage effluent,[36] to be discharged into "controlled waters" from a drain or sewer in contravention of a prohibition under s.86 of the Water Resources Act 1991[37];

(c) any trade or sewage effluent to be discharged into "controlled waters" or, from land in England and Wales, through a pipe, into the sea outside the seaward limits of controlled waters;

(d) any trade or sewage effluent to be discharged, contrary to a s.86 prohibition, from a building or fixed plant on to or into land or into a lake or pond which does not comprise inland freshwaters; or

(e) any matter to enter inland freshwaters which, directly or indirectly or in combination with other factors, tends to impede the proper flow of waters substantially aggravating pollution otherwise caused or its consequences.

It is also an offence to contravene the conditions of a consent.[38]

"Cause" and "knowingly permit" are distinct concepts, the former applying to acts and the latter omissions. Whether a person has "caused" a discharge is a question of fact and, while it is necessary to show that he had acted, it is not necessary to show that he had caused

---

[34] "Polluting" is an ordinary English word, and intended to be different from "poisonous" or "noxious"; the relevant OED definition is "to make physically impure, foul or filthy; to dirty, stain, taint, befoul": *R. v Dovermoss Ltd* (1995) 159 J.P. 448, C.A. (Cr.D.). Whether matter is a pollutant is a question of fact: *National Rivers Authority v Biffa Waste Services* [1996] Env. L.R. 227 (work involving driving diggers along the river bed stirring up existing mud and silt held not to involve the introduction of a pollutant).

[35] 1991 Act s.85(1), as amended by SI 2007/3538 Sch.21 Pt 1 para.21(1), Sch.23 (omitting the word "solid"). "Waste" includes anything that is waste for the purpose of Directive 2006/12 on Waste, and that is not excluded from the scope of that directive by Art.2(1) thereof. See also the Groundwater (England and Wales) Regulations 2009 (SI 2009/2902) reg.13, making it an offence to cause or knowingly permit the discharge of any hazardous substance or non-hazardous pollutant into groundwater, unless in accordance with a permit granted by the Environment Agency.

[36] Defined in the Water Resources Act s.221(1).

[37] 1991 Act s.85(2). As to s.86 prohibitions, see pp.144–145.

[38] 1991 Act s.85(3)–(6). Contravention of a condition can be an offence even where the defendant has not made a discharge into controlled waters: *Taylor Woodrow Property Management Ltd v National Rivers Authority* [1995] Env. L.R. 52, D.C.; holder of discharge consent liable for failing to ensure that what was discharged "shall not contain any oil or grease". A challenge may not be made collaterally to the validity of a condition: *R. v Etterick Trout Co and Baxter* [1994] Env. L.R. 165.

the pollution intentionally or negligently.[39] The question whether the defendant can be held to have caused a pollution incident where the immediate cause of the incident was the act of a third party has caused difficulty in a number of cases. The House of Lords has held, in *Environment Agency v Empress Car Co (Abertillery) Ltd*,[40] that a broad rather than a narrow view is to be taken. Guidance was given by Lord Hoffmann as follows[41]:

"(1) Justices dealing with prosecutions for 'causing' pollution under section 85(1) should first require the prosecution to identify what it says the defendant did to cause the pollution. If the defendant cannot be said to have done anything at all, the prosecution must fail: the defendant may have 'knowingly permitted' pollution but cannot have caused it.

(2) The prosecution need not prove that the defendant did something which was the immediate cause of the pollution. Maintaining tanks, lagoons or sewage systems full of noxious liquid is doing something, even if the immediate cause of the pollution was the lack of maintenance, a natural event or the act of a third party.

(3) When the prosecution has identified something which the defendant did, the justices must decide whether it caused the pollution. They should not be diverted by questions like 'What was the cause of the pollution?' or 'Did something

---

[39] *Alphacell Ltd v Woodward* [1972] A.C. 824, H.L. ("cause" to be used in its ordinary sense); *National Rivers Authority v Yorkshire Water Services Ltd* [1995] 1 A.C. 444, H.L. (possible to conclude that sewerage undertaker had "caused" the entry of polluting matter into controlled waters where the matter had been discharged into a sewer in secret by an unknown third party, and it then passed with other effluent through the undertaker's works into controlled water; there was, however, a good defence under what is now s.87(2), see below, p.178); *R. v CPC (UK) Ltd* [1995] Env. L.R. 131 (jury entitled to find that defendant caused polluting liquid to enter a river where it escaped from pipe with latent defects); *Att Gen's Reference (No.1 of 1994)* [1995] 1 W.L.R. 599, C.A. (Cr. D.) (jury entitled to find that defendants "caused" pollution where (a) the effluent passed through their pumping system or (b) they ran the pumping system in an unmaintained state); *Environment Agency v Biffa Waste Services* [2006] EWHC 1102 (Admin) (contractor who ended tankering operations at site of escape of sewage rightly acquitted of "causing" pollution as the conduct constituted an omission).

[40] [1999] 2 A.C. 22.

[41] At pp.35–36; followed in *Environment Agency v Brock plc* [1998] Env. L.R. 607 (defendant held to have caused pollution where leachate leaked from a (relatively new) hose through a faulty rubber seal; the failure of such seals is an "ordinary fact of life"); *Express Ltd (t/a Express Dairies Distribution) v Environment Agency* [2003] EWHC 448 (Admin) (defendant held to have caused pollution where milk entered controlled water from a tanker-trailer which had been parked on the hard shoulder of the motorway following damage caused by a tyre blow-out).

else cause the pollution?' because to say that something else caused the pollution (like brambles clogging the pumps or vandalism by third parties) is not inconsistent with the defendant having caused it as well.

(4) If the defendant did something which produced a situation in which the polluting matter could escape but a necessary condition of the actual escape which happened was also the act of a third party or a natural event, the justices should consider whether that act or event should be regarded as a normal fact of life or something extraordinary. If it was in the general run of things a matter of ordinary occurrence, it will not negative the causal effect of the defendant's acts, even if it was not foreseeable that it would happen to that particular defendant or take that particular form. If it can be regarded as something extraordinary, it will be open to the justices to hold that the defendant did not cause the pollution.

(5) The distinction between ordinary and extraordinary is one of fact and degree to which the justices must apply their common sense and knowledge of what happens in the area."

A number of the previous cases were consistent with this approach,[42] **8–006**
but in others too narrow an approach had been adopted.[43]

These offences carried a penalty, upon summary conviction, of imprisonment for a term not exceeding three months and/or a fine not exceeding £20,000 and, upon conviction on indictment, of imprisonment for a term not exceeding two years and/or a fine.[44]

---

[42] See the cases cited in n.39.

[43] *Impress (Worcester) Ltd v Rees* [1971] 2 All E.R. 357 (fuel oil storage tank left with unlocked valve opened by unauthorised person; Divisional Court wrong to allow appeal against conviction); *Wychavon DC v National Rivers Authority* [1993] 1 W.L.R. 125 (Divisional Court wrong to hold that operation of sewerage system not itself sufficient to constitute a positive act); *National Rivers Authority v Wright Engineering Co* [1994] 4 All E.R. 281 (defendants should have been convicted in respect of escape of oil caused by vandals).

[44] 1991 Act s.85(6). As to the level of fines appropriate for environmental offences, see *R. v Milford Haven Port Authority* [2000] 2 Cr. App. R(S) 423 (fine of £4m in respect of oil spillage from the *Sea Empress*, which grounded in Milford Haven following a navigational error by the Authority's pilot, reduced on appeal to £750,000; the judge had, inter alia, failed to consider the possible impact of the fine on the Authority's ability to perform its public functions); *R. v Yorkshire Water Services Ltd* [2001] EWCA Crim 2635 (fines totalling £119,000 in respect of four incidents of supplying water unfit for human consumption reduced to £80,000; relevant factors included the degree of culpability involved in the commission of an offence of relatively strict liability, the damage done, the defendant's previous record, the balance between a fitting expression of censure and the counter-productive effect of imposing too great a

It was a defence, however, to charges brought under s.85 to show that an authority had been obtained for the discharge(s) concerned. Such authority might be obtained through:

(a) an authorisation for a prescribed process designated for central control granted under Pt I of the Environmental Protection Act 1990;

(b) a permit granted under the Environmental Permitting (England and Wales) Regulations 2007, except insofar as it authorises a Part B activity[45];

(c) a licence under Pt 2 of the Food and Environment Protection Act 1985;

(d) s.163 of the Water Resources Act 1991 or s.165 of the Water Industry Act 1991 (discharges for works purposes);

(e) any relevant express local statutory provision or statutory order; and

(f) any prescribed enactment.[46]

It was also a defence to such charges to show that the entry or discharge concerned was caused or permitted in an emergency in

---

financial penalty on an already underfunded organisation, the defendant's attitude and performance after the events, and the need to determine an appropriate penalty for each incident, the sum then to be divided among the various manifestations of that incident); *R. v Anglian Water Services Ltd* [2003] EWCA Crim 2243; [2004] 1 Cr. App. Rep. (5) 374 (fine of £200,000 in respect of discharge of semi-treated sewage into a river killing fish and wildlife reduced to £60,000; the company had been grossly irresponsible but the pollution was limited in time and space); *Dwr Cymru Cyfyngedig v Flintshire Magistrates Court* [2009] EWHC 2679 (Admin) (in a rare case, an absolute discharge may be appropriate); *R. v Thames Water Utilities Ltd* [2010] EWCA Crim 202 (£125,000 fine on water company in respect of release of bleach used in cleaning sewage treatment plant into river reduced to £50,000; while the offence was extremely serious (the damage was extensive, and there was no risk assessment or appropriate staff training), there were a number of mitigating features (including prompt and effective measures to rectify the failures; the payment of £500,000 in reparation and an early plea of guilty); the court set out the approach to be followed in such cases.

45 SI 2007/3538. These replaced permits granted under the Pollution Prevention and Control (England and Wales) Regulations (SI 2000/1973) and waste management or disposal licences.

46 1991 Act s.88(1), as amended by SI 2000/1973 Sch.10 Pt I para.9 and SI 2007/3538 Sch.21 Pt 1 para.21(4) and to be amended by the Pollution Prevention and Control Act 1999 Sch.3 (repealing subs.(1)(b)). s.88(1) applies in relation to an authorisation under reg.13 of the Groundwater (England and Wales) Regulations 2009 (SI 2009/2902) as if the reference in (a) to a consent included a reference to an authorisation under those Regulations: reg.14.

order to avert danger to life or health,[47] taking all reasonably practicable steps[48] in the circumstances for the minimisation of the entry and its polluting effects and that particulars of the incident were furnished to the Environment Agency as soon as reasonably practicable.[49] It was not an offence for a person to permit discharge of trade or sewage effluent from a vessel[50] or to permit water from an abandoned mine or an abandoned part of a mine to enter controlled waters,[51] although this did not apply to the owner or former operator where the mine or part in question became abandoned after December 31, 1999.[52] Similarly, no offence was constituted, other than in respect of the entry of any poisonous, noxious or polluting matter into any controlled waters, by the deposit on land of solid refuse of a mine or quarry so that it falls or is carried into inland freshwaters so long as the prior consent of the Environment Agency was obtained for the storage, no other reasonably practicable site was available and all reasonably practicable steps to prevent such entry had been taken.[53] A highway authority did not commit an offence where a drain was kept open by virtue of s.100 of the Highways Act 1980 and a discharge occurs therefrom, unless it be in contravention of a s.86 prohibition.[54]

Where there was a discharge of sewage effluent under heads (c) or **8–007**
(d) of s.85[55] from any sewer or works vested in a sewerage undertaker, if that undertaker did not cause or knowingly permit the discharge, it was nevertheless deemed to have caused it if:

(a) matter included in the discharge was received by it into the discharging sewer or any other sewer or works vested in it;

---

[47] The question is whether the defendant's act in causing the entry was done in an emergency in order to save life or health; the defence is not limited to situations where the entry or discharge is itself effected to avoid danger to life or health: *Express Ltd (t/a Express Dairies Distribution) v Environment Agency* [2003] EWHC 448 (Admin) (defence available in principle where driver of a tanker-trailer carrying milk moved to the hard shoulder of the motorway following a tyre blow-out that damaged the trailer; milk flowed from the trailer in that position into controlled waters).

[48] "Reasonably practicable" turns upon questions of fact and degree in each relevant situation.

[49] 1991 Act s.89(1), as amended by the Environment Act 1995 Sch.22 para.128.

[50] 1991 Act s.89(2).

[51] 1991 Act s.89(3), as amended by the Environment Act 1995 s.60(1).

[52] 1991 Act s.89(3A)–(3C), inserted by the Environment Act 1995 s.60(2).

[53] 1991 Act s.89(4). An application for consent is to be made under s.90A, inserted by the Environment Act 1995 Sch.22 para.142.

[54] 1991 Act s.89(5).

[55] As set out at p.173, above.

(b) it was bound (either unconditionally or subject to conditions which were observed) to receive that matter into that sewer or works.

However, this did not apply if the sewage effluent was previously discharged into the undertaker's system by another sewerage undertaker by virtue of an agreement under s.110A[56]; in this case, the sending undertaker was deemed to have caused the discharge on an analogous basis.[57]

Furthermore, a sewerage undertaker did not commit an offence under s.85 solely by reason of a discharge from one of its sewers or works in contravention of conditions of a consent relating to such discharge if the contravention was attributable to a discharge made by some other person into the sewer or works which the undertaker was either not bound to receive or was only so bound, subject to conditions which were not met and it could not reasonably have been expected to prevent the discharge into the sewer or works.[58] By the same token a person who made or permitted a discharge into a sewer or works vested in a sewerage undertaker did not thereby commit an offence under s.85 of the 1991 Act if such discharge was one which the undertaker was bound to receive either unconditionally or subject to conditions which were in the given case met.[59]

8–008 In addition to these statutory provisions, the Secretary of State has power under s.92 of the 1991 Act to make regulations[60] prohibiting the possession or control of poisonous, noxious or polluting matter unless prescribed anti-pollution precautions or other steps have been carried out. Such precautions and steps may also be required of persons who prior to the making of such regulations already have possession or control of such materials. Such regulations may empower the Environment Agency to determine circumstances of application and to impose relevant requirements upon any person. Provision may also be

---

[56] pp.111–112, above.

[57] Water Resources Act 1991 s.87(1)–(1C), substituted by the Competition and Service (Utilities) Act 1992 s.46.

[58] Water Resources Act 1991 s.87(2). This defence is available in respect of any offence under s.85 and not just where the prosecution alleges contravention of the conditions of a consent: *National Rivers Authority v Yorkshire Water Services Ltd* [1995] 1 A.C. 444, H.L.

[59] Water Resources Act 1991 s.87(3).

[60] The following regulations have effect or have been made under s.92: Control of Pollution (Silage, Slurry and Agricultural Fuel Oil) Regulations 1991 (SI 1991/324), as amended by SI 1996/2044, SI 1997/547, revoked and replaced for England by the Water Resources (Control of Pollution) (Silage, Slurry and Agricultural Fuel Oil) (England) Regulations 2010 (SI 2010/639); Control of Pollution (Oil Storage) (England) Regulations 2001 (SI 2001/2954).

made for appeals to the Secretary of State and for the maximum penalties in cases of contravention, these not exceeding on summary conviction three months' imprisonment and/or a fine not exceeding £20,000 or, upon conviction on indictment, imprisonment for two years or a fine or both.[61]

The National Rivers Authority's prosecution policy in cases of non-compliance was set out in s.11 of "Discharge Consents and Compliance: the NRA's Approach to the Control of Discharges to Water".[62] In the cases where the plant was inadequate to achieve consent requirements, but there was an existing programme of remedial works agreed with the Authority, the Authority would not normally prosecute where the non-compliance did not result from poor management or from problems unconnected with the proposed works; and every effort was being made in the interim to comply; and the breach was not of such magnitude so as to cause persistent pollution or to justify criminal proceedings in the public interest. If there was no existing programme, the discharger would be given the opportunity to produce an acceptable action plan. In cases where there was a management failure to operate the plant correctly, a decision to prosecute depended on the impact of the discharge on the environment and the attitude of the discharger to improving plant management. This remained policy for the Environment Agency.

The Agency has now adopted a revised "Enforcement and Prosecution Policy" applicable across all its activities.[63] The Agency believes in "firm but fair regulation" applying the principles of proportionality, consistency, transparency and the targeting of enforcement action. In deciding whether to prosecute, it will take into account the environmental effect of the offence, the foreseeability of the offence, the intent of the offender, the history of offending, the attitude of the offender, the deterrent effect of a prosecution and the offender's personal circumstances. Where there is sufficient evidence, the Agency will normally prosecute in respect of incidents or breaches which have significant consequences for the environment or which have the potential for such consequences; carrying out operations without a relevant licence; or excessive or persistent breaches of regulatory requirements in relation to the same licence or site;

---

[61] Water Resources Act 1991 s.92(2), as amended by SI 2010/675 Sch.26 Pt 1 para.8(5). The Secretary of State may delegate his appellate functions to an appointed person by virtue of s.114: s.92(3), inserted by the Environment Act 1995 Sch.22 para.144.

[62] HMSO 1994 (Water Quality Series No.17).

[63] See *http://www.environment-agency.gov.uk* [Accessed August 4, 2010] (edition issued August 7, 2008).

failure to comply or to comply adequately with formal remedial requirements; reckless disregard for management or quality standards; failure to supply information without reasonable excuse or knowingly or recklessly supplying false or misleading information; obstruction of Agency staff; or impersonating Agency staff.

(b) Consents

8–009 The procedure for obtaining a discharge consent was set out in Sch.10 to the Water Resources Act 1991.[64] Consents were granted by the Environment Agency; applications had to be publicised unless the Agency determined otherwise, and prescribed persons had to be consulted; conditions could be attached[65]; applications could be called-in by the Secretary of State, who could hold an inquiry; consents could be revoked or modified by the Agency[66]; a consent could be transferred to a person who proposed to carry on the discharges in place of the holder.[67] Appeals lay to the Secretary of State.[68]

---

[64] A new Sch.10 was substituted by the Environment Act 1995 Sch.22 para.183, which removed some of the requirements in respect of publicity: see "ENDS Report" 239, December 1994, p.22. Applications by the Agency for a discharge consent are made to the Secretary of State and are governed by Sch.2 to the Control of Pollution (Applications, Appeals and Registers) Regulations 1996 (SI 1996/2971). Sch.10 is repealed by SI 2010/675, Sch.26 Pt2 Para. 10(2)(q).

[65] Conditions appropriate to the nature of the industry concerned were to be attached to a consent in relation to discharges of biodegradable industrial waste water from plants representing 4,000 p.e. or more belonging to specified industrial sectors: Urban Waste Water Treatment (England and Wales) Regulations 1994 (SI 1994/2841) reg.8, as amended by SI 2010/675 Sch. 26 Pt 1 para.10(4). For definitions, see above, pp.45–49.

[66] Consents must be reviewed and if necessary modified or revoked to comply with reg.6 of the 1994 Regulations, see above, pp.157–159. The Secretary of State may direct the Agency to review consents it has granted: Sch.10 para.9.

[67] Sch.10 para.11, as amended by the Water Act 2003 s.87. By virtue of these amendments, the proposed transferor and transferee must give joint notice to the Agency, which must arrange to amend the consent. Provision is also made for the transfer of a consent on the holder's death to personal representatives and on bankruptcy to the trustee in bankruptcy. The express provision in para.11(4) that a consent and the obligations arising from it are not capable of being disclaimed is repealed by the 2003 Act as unnecessary as the Agency has ample powers to deal with breaches of condition and illegal discharges. Sch.10 para.11 applies to authorisations under the Groundwater (England and Wales) Regulations 2009 (SI 2009/2902) reg.15.

[68] Water Resources Act 1991 s.91, as amended by the Environment Act 1995 Sch.22 para.143. Appeals lay against, inter alia, a refusal, grant subject to conditions or revocation of a consent. By virtue of the Environment Act 1995 Sch.22 para.143, an appeal also lay in respect of variations to a consent and enforcement notices (see below, p.183). The Secretary of State may delegate his functions to an appointed person by virtue of s.114. Most appeals under s.91 in England are determined by an inspector, with cases of major significance determined by the Secretary of State; appeals in Wales are determined by the National Assembly: see Planning Inspectorate, "Water Resources Act 1991 (as amended). Discharge Consent and Associated Appeals—Appeal Procedure Guide", para.7 and App.3. (*http://www.planning-inspectorate.gov.uk* [Accessed August 10, 2010]).

The policies of the National Rivers Authority in granting consents were set out in "Discharge Consents and Compliance: the NRA's Approach to Control of Discharges to Water: A Report of the National Rivers Authority".[69] Its general approach was to set discharge limits which were individually based on local circumstances, tailored to the needs of the receiving water and to key end uses, rather than uniform emission standards applicable to all discharges of a particular type.[70] Consents must be framed so as to secure compliance with statutory water objectives.[71] The Environment Agency largely follows this approach; it has also produced a *Discharge Consents Manual* setting out detailed policies and technical information. A significant number of consents have been carried over from previous legislation. Thus consents granted under earlier legislation continue to have effect.[72] In addition, the National Rivers Authority Report, "Discharge Consents and Compliance: The NRA's Approach to Control of Discharges to Water",[73] identified three "transitional types of consent."

First, there are *deemed consents*. These cover: (1) consent applications under the Rivers (Prevention of Pollution) Act 1961 outstanding on the implementation of the Control of Pollution Act 1974 in 1985[74]; and (2) consent applications in respect of discharges which prior to 1987 were outside the scope of consent controls, notably discharges to coastal waters and pre-1960 discharges to estuaries.[75] Most such discharges are of sewage.

---

[69] Water Quality Series No.17, HMSO, 1994.

[70] Water Quality Series No.17, pp.8–9.

[71] See above, pp.170–173. The grant of a consent may be open to challenge by way of judicial review if there is non-compliance: see *R. v National Rivers Authority, ex p. Moreton* [1996] Env. L.R. 234, where such a challenge was rejected on the merits, the court holding that the NRA was entitled not to impose a condition requiring ultra violet disinfection in respect of a consent for a discharge of sewage into the sea and to conclude that such a condition was not necessary to meet mandatory requirements of the Bathing Waters Directive and otherwise the marginal benefits of imposing such a condition could not be justified as there were other more pressing needs.

[72] See the Control of Pollution (Consents: Transitional Provisions) Regulations 1985 (SI 1985/5) (preserving consents under the Rivers (Prevention of Pollution) Acts 1951 to 1961); the Water Act 1989 Sch.26 para.21 (preserving consents in force immediately before the transfer date for the purposes of Pt 2 of the Control of Pollution Act 1974); and the Water Consolidation (Consequential Provisions) Act 1991 Sch.2 para.1 (preserving consents in force for the purposes of the Water Act 1989).

[73] HMSO, 1994, p.39.

[74] Control of Pollution Act 1974 s.40(4); preserved by the Water Act 1989 Sch.26 para.24(2) and the Water Resources Act 1991 Sch.13 para.3(1). Consents deemed to have been granted to water authorities by the Secretary of State under s.55 of the 1974 Act were preserved by the 1989 Act Sch.26 para.25(6), (7).

[75] See the Control of Pollution (Exemption of Certain Discharges from Control) (Variation) Order 1986 (SI 1986/1623) Art.4 (inserted by the Control of Pollution (Exemption of Certain Discharges from Control) (Variation) Order 1987 (SI 1987/1782))

8–010 Secondly, there are *time limited consents* in respect of 800 sewage works found in the build-up to privatisation to be operating in breach of their consents. Here, the existing consents were varied to set temporary limits at the then current levels of performance. The majority had elapsed by 1994, but some had been extended by the NRA because of unforeseen scheme development problems.

Thirdly, there were *temporary (schedule) consents* granted under the Water Act 1989[76] in respect of combined sewer overflows and emergency overflows found in the run-up to privatisation not to be subject to consent conditions; these temporary consents are due to be replaced by individual consents in due course. Such consents were also granted in respect of a number of sewage treatment works.

In 1985, consents in respect of sewage discharges were relaxed to a requirement that the proportion of samples meeting the limits for sanitary determinants (BOD, suspended solids and ammonia) should not be significantly lower than 95 per cent.[77] Following the Kinnersley Report,[78] the NRA adopted a policy that where consents were reviewed, absolute limits were to be imposed in addition to 95 percentile limits; the undertakers appealed against these limits to the Secretary of State.[79] The DoE issued policy guidance that absolute limits should not apply to sewage works with a population equivalent of less than 2,000, and that they should generally only be introduced for other works as part of the implementation programme for the Urban Waste Water Treatment Directive.[80]

8–011 Notwithstanding these various steps to accommodate the position of sewerage undertakers, a proportion of discharges breach the terms of consent; this in some, but not all, cases leads to prosecutions.[81] The overall rate of compliance did, however, improve.[82] Prosecutions may also arise out of particular pollution incidents.[83]

---

made under the Control of Pollution Act 1974 s.32(3). These deemed consents were preserved by the Water Act 1989 Sch.26 para.22(1), and now the Water Resources Act 1991 Sch.13 para.2(1).

[76] Sch.26 para.25; and see the Water Resources Act 1991 Sch.13 para.4, to be amended by the Environment Act 1995 Sch.22 para.186.

[77] This replaced a tacit assumption that while consents were expressed as requiring 100% compliance, in practice it was acceptable if more than 95% of the samples met the limit.

[78] "Discharge Consents and Compliance Policy: A Blueprint for the Future" (NRA: Water Quality Series No.1, HMSO, 1990).

[79] "Discharge Consents and Compliance" pp.38, 42–43.

[80] "Discharge Consents and Compliance" p.43.

[81] See "ENDS Report" 230, March 1994, p.11.

[82] "Discharge Consents and Compliance", pp.50–51, noting an improvement from 90% in 1990 to 95% in 1992.

[83] See, e.g. "ENDS Report" 230, March 1994, p.47.

The grant of a consent may be open to challenge on the ground that it is inconsistent with mandatory requirements of EC directives concerning water quality; furthermore, the Agency must consider changing a consent if new scientific evidence emerges suggesting that there is such non-compliance.[84]

(c) Samples

Information provided or obtained pursuant to or by virtue of a condition of a "relevant licence"[85] (including information so provided or obtained, or recorded, by means of any apparatus[86]) shall be admissible in evidence in any proceedings, whether against the person subject to the condition or any other person. For this purpose, apparatus shall be presumed in any proceedings to register or record accurately, unless the contrary is shown or the relevant licence otherwise provides. Where by virtue of a condition of a relevant licence, an entry is required to be made in any record as to the observance of any condition of the licence, the fact that the entry has not been made is admissible as evidence that the condition has not been observed.[87] **8–012**

(d) Enforcement notices

By virtue of the Environment Act 1995,[88] the Environment Agency is given power to serve enforcement notices if it is of the opinion that the holder of a discharge consent is contravening, or likely to contravene, any condition of the consent. Non-compliance is an offence. **8–013**

---

[84] *R. (on the application of Moase and Lomas) v Environment Agency* [2001] EWHC Admin 231, where permission to apply for judicial review was refused on the merits.

[85] i.e. an "environmental licence" (defined in s.56, as amended, to cover various licences, including an IPC authorisation, an IPPC permit and discharge consents under ss.88(1)(a), 89(4)(a) or 90 of the Water Resources Act 1991); any consent under Ch.3 of Pt 4 of the Water Industry Act 1991 to make discharges of special category effluent; and any s.129 agreement (see below, pp.255–266). The reference to a condition includes any requirement to which a person is subject under, by virtue of or in consequence of a relevant licence: s.111(5).

[86] This term includes "any meter or other device for measuring, assessing, determining, recording or enabling to be recorded, the volume, temperature, radioactivity, rate, nature, origin, composition or effect of any substance, flow, discharge, emission, deposit or abstraction": s.111(5).

[87] Environment Act 1995 s.111, replacing a tripartite sampling requirement set out in the Water Resources Act 1991 s.209.

[88] Sch.22 para.142, inserting a new s.90B in the Water Resources Act 1991.

(e) Charges

8–014 The powers of the Environment Agency to make charging schemes in respect of environmental licences (including discharge consents) are set out in sections 41 and 42 of the Environment Act 1995.[89]

(f) Integrated pollution control authorisations[90]

8–015 Certain activities were subject to regulation under Pt 1 of the Environmental Protection Act 1990, which established a system of integrated pollution control enforced by the Environment Agency, rather than under the system of discharge consents under the Water Resources Act 1991. IPC applied to the processes and substances prescribed by regulations.[91] After a date determined in accordance with Sch.3 to the regulations, no person could carry on a prescribed process except under an authorisation granted by the Agency under s.6 of the 1990 Act and in accordance with the conditions attached under s.7 of the Act. Implied in every authorisation was a general condition that the person carrying on the process must use the best available techniques not entailing excessive cost (BATNEEC),

(a) for preventing the release of substances prescribed for any environmental medium into that medium or, where that is not practicable by such means, for reducing the release of such substances to a minimum and for rendering harmless any such substances which are released; and

(b) for rendering harmless any other substances which might cause harm if released into any environmental medium.

---

[89] Provision for the suspension or revocation of licences for non payment of charges is made by the Environmental Licences (Suspension and Revocation) Regulations 1996 (SI 1996/508).

[90] Pt 1 of the Environmental Protection Act 1990. See generally S. Ball and S. Bell, *Environmental Law*, 2nd edn (London: Routledge, 1994), Ch.11. The Environment Agency and the Secretary of State must exercise their powers under Pt 1 to prevent the direct or indirect discharge of specified substances to groundwater and to control resulting pollution in accordance with the Groundwater Regulations 1998 (SI 1998/2746) reg.3.

[91] 1990 Act s.2; the Environmental Protection (Prescribed Processes and Substances) Regulations 1991 (SI 1991/472), as amended. Sch.1 to the Regulations listed the prescribed processes, Part A processes being designated for central control and Part B for local control (in relation to releases to air). However, a process is not a "prescribed process" (inter alia) if it cannot result in the release of a "prescribed substance" to water except in a concentration no greater than the background concentration or the amounts prescribed in Sch.5 col.2: reg.4(1). Sch.5 sets out the "prescribed substances" for release to water: these are the "Red list" substances: see below, p.254.

Other conditions were required to be imposed to ensure such matters as compliance with EC directives and statutory water quality objectives. Accordingly, control could be exercised by virtue of IPC in respect of certain releases to water,[92] and for this purpose any release into a sewer was treated as a release into water.[93]

Applications for authorisations were made under Sch.1 to the 1990 Act.[94]

(g) Integrated Pollution Prevention and Control permits

The Integrated Pollution Control (IPC) regime was progressively superseded by the Integrated Pollution Prevention and Control (IPPC) regime that took effect by virtue of the Pollution Prevention and Control Regulations.[95] Authorisations were required under the Regulations in respect of specified installations[96] and mobile plant from the Environment Agency (Part A(1) installations or plant) or the local authority (Part A(2) and Part B installations or plant). Part A(1) covered, inter alia: **8–016**

(a) the incineration of any waste, otherwise than as part of a Part B activity, in an incineration plant with a capacity of 1 tonne or more per hour; and

---

[92] By the 1990 Act s.1(11)(a), any release into (i) the sea or the surface of the seabed; (ii) any river, watercourse, lake, loch or pond (whether natural or artificial or above or below ground) or reservoir or the surface of the river bed or of other land supporting such waters; or (iii) groundwaters, is a release into water.

[93] 1990 Act s.1(11)(c).

[94] As amended by the Environment Act 1995 Sch.22 para.93(1)—(5). See the Environmental Protection (Applications, Appeals and Registers) Regulations 1991 (SI 1991/507), as amended by SI 1991/836, SI 1994/1271, SI 1996/667, 979 and 2678.

[95] SI 2000/1973, as amended, made under ss.1 and 2 of the Pollution Prevention and Control Act 1999, implementing Dir.96/61 on Integrated Pollution Prevention and Control. See *Cross on Local Government Law*, 9th edn (London: Sweet & Maxwell) paras 19–55—19–61 (IPC) and 19–61—19–61F (IPPC). The same obligations apply in respect of the Groundwater Regulations 1998 (SI 1998/2746) as apply in respect of the IPC regime: reg.3, as amended by SI 2000/1973 Sch.10 Pt 2 paras 46, 47.

[96] "Installation" is defined (reg.2(1)) as "(i) a stationary technical unit where one or more activities listed in Part 1 of Schedule 1 are carried out; (ii) any other location on the same site where any other directly associated activities are carried out". As regards activities in ss.1.1–6.9 of Sch.1 Pt 1, "directly associated activity" means "any directly associated activity which has a technical connection with the activity carried out in the stationary technical unit and which could have an effect on pollution" (reg.2(1)). *See United Utilities Water plc v Environment Agency* [2006] EWCA Civ 633; [2006] Env. L.R. 42, where it was held that two sets of premises half a mile apart could not be on the "same site", but where it was noted that this requirement had probably been incorrectly transposed from the IPPC directive. This point was not taken on appeal.

(b) unless falling within Part B, the incineration of hazardous waste[97] in an incineration plant other than of specified hazardous waste in an exempt incineration plant[98];

(c) the disposal of waste in a landfill receiving more than 10 tonnes of waste in any day or with a total capacity of more than 25,000 tonnes, excluding disposals in landfills taking only inert waste[99];

(d) the disposal of hazardous waste (other than by incineration or landfill) in a facility with a capacity of more than 10 tonnes per day;

(e) the disposal of non-hazardous waste in a facility with a capacity of more than 50 tonnes a day by biological or physico-chemical treatments.[100]

The IPPC regime came into effect from January 1, 2001 in respect of new Part A installations and from at various times between April 1, 2004 and April 1, 2007 for existing installations falling within sections 5.1, 5.2 and 5.3; and April 1, 2003 for existing Part B installations within section 5.1.[101] The Environment Agency gave guidance as to the application of the new regime to sewage treatment works.[102] The main changes were that PPC permits will be required for sludge

---

[97] i.e. waste as defined in art.1(4) of Dir.91/689 on hazardous waste.

[98] See Sch.1 Pt 1, Activities, s.5.1, Disposal of waste by incineration. "Sewage sludge" falls within the definition of "specified hazardous waste" but plant for the incineration of sewage sludge falls outside the definition of "exempt incineration plant". Part B covers, inter alia, the incineration of specified hazardous waste in an incineration plant with a capacity of 10 tonnes or less per day and less than 1 tonne per hour, and the incineration of any non-hazardous waste in a plant with a capacity of less than 1 tonne per hour.

[99] Sch.1 Pt 1, Activities, s.5.2, Disposal of Waste by Landfill.

[100] Sch.1 Pt 1, Activities, s.5.3, Disposal of Waste Other Than by Incineration or Landfill. The treatments must result in final compounds or mixtures which are discarded by means of any of the operations numbered D1 to D12 in Annex IIA to the Waste Framework Directive (Dir.75/442/EEC); the treatments must not be specified in any paragraph in that Annex other than paras D8 (biological) and D9 (physico-chemical). *In United Utilities Water plc v Environment Agency* [2007] UKHL 41; [2008] 1 All E.R. 741, the House of Lords held that it is not necessary that the treatment results *directly* in final compounds or mixtures; the general purpose of the legislation is that of environment protection in the course of waste disposal operations and it accordingly applies to treatment processes at intermediate plants.

[101] See SI 2000/1973 Sch.3 paras 2 and 10, as amended by SI 2002/275 reg.2(3), and SI 2003/3296 reg.2(4) (delaying the imposition of certain requirements in respect of activities under s.5.3 to 2006).

[102] "Guidance on Sewage Treatment Works and the Application of the PPC Regulations" (April 2003). See *http://www.environment-agency.gov.uk/news* [Accessed August 10, 2010] (ref.56/03).

treatment activities with the capacity to treat more than 50 tonnes of residual sludge per day (wet weight) for the purpose of disposal; the deposit and keeping of influents brought to a STW by road tanker will be expected to be covered by a waste management licence; pre-treatment of such influents may be subject to either a WML (or exemption) or PCC permit depending on the treatment capacity and nature of the activity; where the discharge from a PPC installation is the dominant flow or load within a STW, a PPC permit may be required for the entire STW, as it may be regarded as a directly associated activity; and biogas utilisation schemes not part of a PPC permitted sludge treatment installation with a thermal rated input greater than 3MW will require their own PPC permit. Activities previously subject to IPC authorisation required PPC permits at the appropriate date.

The regime established by the Pollution Prevention and Control Regulations 2000 has now been incorporated within the Environmental Permitting (England and Wales) Regulations 2010. **8–017**

(h) Environmental permitting

The Environmental Permitting (England and Wales) Regulations 2007[103] introduced a new environmental permitting regime that replaced both waste management licensing and the pollution prevention and control regime. These were in turn replaced by the Environmental Permitting (England and Wales) Regulations 2010,[104] which extended the regime to include in addition the system of consenting of water discharges in Ch.2 of Pt 3 of the Water Resources Act 1991, the groundwater permitting system in the Groundwater (England and Wales) Regulations 2009 and the system of radioactive substances regulation in the Radioactive Substances Act 1993.

(i) Core requirements

The core requirements are that a person must not, except under and to **8–018** the extent authorised by an environmental permit (a) operate a regulated facility; or (b) cause or knowingly permit a water discharge activity[105] or groundwater activity.[106] However, (b) does not apply if the water discharge activity or groundwater activity is an exempt facility.[107]

---

[103] SI 2007/3538, as amended by SI 2009/3381.
[104] SI 2010/675.
[105] For the definition, see below.
[106] Defined in Sch.22 para.3.
[107] SI 2010/675 reg.12(1), (2). reg.12(3) applies to the disposal of radioactive waste.

A "regulated facility" is any of the following: (a) an installation[108]; (b) mobile plant[109]; (c) a waste operation[110]; (d) a mining waste operation[111]; (e) a radioactive substances activity; (f) a water discharge activity; (g) a groundwater activity.[112] These are subject to a number of limitations. The following are not regulated facilities: (a) an exempt facility[113]; (b) an excluded waste operation[114]; (c) the disposal or recovery of household waste from a domestic property within the cartilage of that property by a person other than an establishment or undertaking.[115]

"Exempt facility" means: (a) an exempt waste operation[116]; (b) an exempt water discharge activity[117]; or (c) an exempt groundwater activity.[118] Sch.2 provides for the registration of exemptions by the "exemption registration authority", which is to be the Environment Agency or the local authority.[119]

---

[108] i.e. (except where used in the definition of "excluded plant" in s.5.1 of Pt 2 of this Schedule) (a) a stationary technical unit where one or more activities are carried on, and (b) any other location on the same site where any other directly associated activities are carried on, and references to an installation include references to part of an installation. "Directly associated activity", in relation to an activity other than a SED activity, means an operation which: (a) has a technical connection with the activity; (b) is carried on on the same site as the activity; and (c) could have an effect on pollution: Sch.1 Pt 1 para.1.

[109] i.e. any of the following: Part A mobile plant; Part B mobile plant; waste mobile plant: reg.2(1). (a) refers to plant, other than an installation, used to carry on an activity listed in Part A(1) or A(2) (or A(2) and B) of any section within Pt 2 of Sch.1. (b) refers to plant, not being Part A mobile plant, that is designed to move or be moved whether on roads or other land and that is used to carry on a Part B activity. (c) refers to plant that is designed to move or be moved whether on roads or other land, used to carry on a waste operation, and not an installation, Part A mobile plant or Part B mobile plant: Sch.1 Pt 1 para.1.

[110] i.e. recovery or disposal of waste: reg.2(1). "Disposal" and "recovery" are defined in Sch.9 para.2.

[111] Defined in Sch.20 para.2(1).

[112] reg.8(1).

[113] See below.

[114] i.e. any part of a waste operation not carried on at an installation or by means of Part A mobile plant or Part B mobile plant that (a) is the subject of a licence under Part 2 of the Food and Environment Protection Act 1985 or does not require such a licence by virtue of an order under s.7 of that Act, or (b) relates to waste described in reg.7(1) of the Controlled Waste Regulations 1992: reg.2(1).

[115] reg.8(2).

[116] i.e. a waste operation (a) that (i) is not carried on at an installation, or (ii) is an activity that falls within s.5.3 or 5.4 of Pt 2 of Sch.1 and is carried on at an installation, and (b) that meets the requirements of Sch.2 para.3(1): reg.5(1).

[117] i.e. a stand-alone water discharge activity (one that is not carried on as part of the operation of a regulated facility of another class) that meets the requirements of Sch.2 para.4: reg.5(1).

[118] i.e. a stand-alone groundwater activity (one that is not carried on as part of the operation of a regulated facility of another class) that meets the requirements of Sch.2 para.5: reg.5(1).

[119] As specified in Sch.2 para.2. The exemption registration authority must carry out appropriate periodic inspections of establishments and undertakings carrying on exempt waste operations in respect of which it is the exemption registration authority: Sch.2 para.15.

Furthermore, a regulated facility of any of classes[120] (c), (d), (f) and (g) may be carried on as part of the operation of a regulated facility of another class.[121]

(ii) Permits

On the application of an operator,[122] the regulator may grant an environmental permit authorising the operation of a regulated facility and that operator as the person authorised to operate that regulated facility.[123] The regulator is the authority on whom functions are conferred by reg.32, or by a direction under reg.33. Regulation 32 provides for the distribution of functions between the Environment Agency and local authorities.[124] This turns, first, on the nature of the activity conducted, which may be a "Part A(1) activity", a "Part A(2) activity" or a "Part B activity" within the sections set out in Pt 2 of Sch.1 to the 2010 Regulations. **8–019**

A "Part A(1) installation" is one where a Pt A(1) activity is carried on, including one also carrying on a Pt A(2) and/or a Pt B activity. A "Part A(2) installation" is one where a Pt A(2) activity is carried on, including one also carrying on a Pt B activity. The definitions of Pt A(1), Pt A(2) and Pt B mobile plant are structured on an analogous basis.[125]

Functions[126] are exercisable by the Environment Agency unless it is provided that they are to be exercisable by a local authority. Functions in relation to a regulated facility comprising a Pt A(2) or Pt B installation or mobile plant are exercisable by the local authority in whose area the regulated facility is or will be operated; however, this does not apply to a waste operation (unless it is a Pt B activity), a mining waste operation, a water discharge activity or a groundwater activity. Functions in respect of a Pt A(2) or Pt B mobile plant are exercisable by the local authority in whose area the operator's principal place of business is, if that is in England and Wales; if it is not in England and Wales, it is the local authority which granted the permit or, if no permit has been granted, the authority in whose area

---

[120] i.e. a class in reg.8(1): reg.8(3).

[121] reg.8(4).

[122] i.e. the person who has control over the operation of a regulated facility, or who will do when it is put into operation, or where it has ceased to be in operation, who holds the permit which authorised its operation: reg.7.

[123] reg.13(1).

[124] i.e. a district or unitary county council or the Council of the Isles of Scilly; a London borough council, the Common Council and the Treasurers; and a county or county borough council in Wales; and in relation to a Part B installation a port health authority: reg.6.

[125] Sch.1 Pt 1 para.1.

[126] These include "relevant functions" as defined in reg.9.

the plant is first operated or is intended to be first operated.[127] The Secretary of State or Welsh Ministers may direct the Agency to exercise local authority functions or vice versa.[128] The procedure governing the grant, variation, transfer and surrender of environmental permits is set out in Sch.5 Pt 1 to the Regulations.

8–020 A permit must specify: (a) every regulated facility to which it relates; and (b) the person authorised to operate that facility. It may be in electronic form and[129] must include a map, plan or other description of the site showing its geographical extent.[130] Conditions may require the operator to carry out works or do other things in relation to land which he is not entitled to do without the consent of another person; that person must give consent and may be entitled to compensation.[131] In specified circumstances, a permit may authorise more than one regulated activity.[132] Once granted, a permit continues in force until revoked, surrendered or replaced with a consolidated permit,[133] and provision is made for those events.[134] A permit may be varied by the regulator, on the application of the operator or on its own initiative.[135] The regulator may, on the joint application of an operator and a proposed transferee, transfer to the proposed transferee the whole or any part of an environmental permit.[136] A rule-making authority[137] may prepare "standard rules" for regulated facilities described in the rules. It must keep them under review and publish them and may revise or revoke them.[138]

A person aggrieved by decisions under the Regulations, for example to refuse a permit, attach a condition or serve a notice, may appeal to the Secretary of State or Welsh Ministers.[139]

---

[127] reg.32.
[128] reg.33.
[129] Except in the case of a mobile plant or a radioactive substances activity.
[130] reg.14. A permit that authorises the operation of a regulated facility "regulated facility A") need not specify any regulated facility of another class that is carried on as part of the operation of regulated facility A: reg.14(2).
[131] reg.15 and Sch.5 Pt 2.
[132] reg.17. Permits may be consolidated: reg.18.
[133] reg.19.
[134] regs 18 and 22–25.
[135] reg.20.
[136] reg.21. This does not apply in the case of the whole or any part of a permit) that authorises the carrying on of a stand-alone water discharge activity or stand-alone groundwater activity: reg.21(3).
[137] i.e. where the regulator is a local authority, the Secretary of State or Welsh Ministers and where it is the Agency, the Agency: reg.2(1).
[138] regs 26–30.
[139] reg.31 and Sch.6.

The regulator must periodically review environmental permits and must make appropriate periodic inspections of regulated facilities.[140] Further detailed provision is made in Schs 7 to 23 in respect of different types of regulated facility.[141]

(iii) Enforcement

A regulator has power to serve enforcement and suspension notices.[142] **8–021** It is an offence for a person, inter alia, to: (a) contravene reg.12(1); (b) to knowingly cause or knowingly permit the contravention of reg.12(1)(a); (c) fail to comply with or to contravene an environmental permit condition; or (d) fail to comply with the requirements of an enforcement, prohibition, suspension or landfill closure or mining waste facility closure notice.[143] It is a defence for a person charged with an offence contrary to reg.38(1), (2) or (3) to prove that the acts alleged to constitute the offence were done in an emergency in order to avoid danger to human health in a case where he took all reasonably practicable steps for minimising pollution, and particulars are given to the regulator as soon as reasonably practicable after they were done.[144] If an offence committed by a person under reg.38 is due to the act or default of some other person, that other person is also guilty of the offence and liable to be proceeded against whether or not proceedings for the offence are taken against the first-mentioned person.[145] On conviction for offences under reg.38(1)–(3), the court may order the cause of the offence to be remedied.[146]

The regulator must maintain a public register of specified information.[147]

---

[140] reg.34.

[141] These are: Sch.7—Part A installations and mobile plant; Sch.8—Part B installations and mobile plant; Sch.9—waste operations; Sch.10—landfill; Sch.11—waste motor vehicles; Sch.12—waste electrical and electronic equipment; Sch.13—waste incineration; Sch.14—SED installations; Sch.15—large combustion plants; Sch.16—asbestos; Sch.17—titanium dioxide; Sch.18—petrol vapour recovery; Sch.18—petrol vapour recovery; Sch.19—waste batteries and accumulators; Sch.20—mining waste operations; Sch.21—water discharge activities; Sch.22—groundwater activities; and Sch.23—radioactive substances activities. These Schedules secure compliance with relevant European directives, and corresponding implementing regulations are revoked by Sch.21 of the 2007 Regulations and Sch.27 of the 2010 Regulations.

[142] regs 36 and 37.

[143] reg.38(1)–(3). Further offences are created by subss.(4) and (5). For penalties, see reg.39. For offences by bodies corporate, see reg.41. The regulator may take proceedings in the High Court to secure compliance with a notice specified in reg.38(3): reg.42.

[144] reg.40(1).

[145] reg.38(6).

[146] reg.44.

[147] Pt 5 (regs 45–56) and Sch.24.

If the regulator considers that the operation of a regulated facility under an environmental permit involves a risk of serious pollution,[148] it may arrange for steps to be taken to remove that risk. It may also arrange for steps to remedy the effects of pollution caused by an offence under reg.38(1)–(3). It may recover its costs.[149] Where the local authority is the regulator in respect of a Pt A installation or mobile plant, the Environment Agency may by notice to the authority specifying the minimum emission limit values or the conditions it considers appropriate for preventing or reducing emissions[150] into water.[151]

(iv) Other provisions

8–022 The Secretary of State or Welsh Ministers or a regulator may require a person to provide information; the Secretary of State or Welsh Ministers may give directions to a regulator or exemption registration authority and require applications to be referred to it or them for determination; may give guidance to a regulator or exemption registration authority; may make a scheme prescribing fees and charges; and may make plans for the setting of limits on the total amount in any period, of emissions from all or any description of source, or the allocation of quotas relating to such emissions.[152] Further requirements apply in respect of waste and extractive waste,[153] and provision is made for the transition from the previous regulatory regimes.[154]

(v) Provisions of Schs 1 to 3 relating to sewers and drains

8–023 A number of the detailed provisions in Schs 1–3 to the Regulations are of particular relevance to the law relating to sewers and drains. Chapter 5 of Pt 2 of Sch.1, dealing with the definitions of Pt A and Pt B *activities*, covers activities in respect of waste management, including the incineration and co-incineration of waste, the disposal of waste by landfill, the disposal of waste other than by incineration or landfill, the recovery of waste, and the production of fuel from waste.

Sch.3 Pt 1 contains detailed descriptions of facilities that are *exempt facilities* if specified conditions are met. These include the use of sludge for the purposes of re-seeding a waste water treatment plant (U6)[155]; the

---

[148] "Pollution" is defined in reg.2(1).
[149] reg.57.
[150] Defined in reg.2(1).
[151] reg.58.
[152] regs 60–66.
[153] Sch.25.
[154] Pt 7 (regs 67–105).
[155] Sch.3 Pt 1 Ch.2 (Use of waste) s.2 para.6. The conditions are that the total quantity of waste used or stored at the plant at any one time does not exceed 1,000 cubic metres; and that the waste was not produced at the plant.

use of effluent to clean a highway gravel bed (U7)[156]; the recovery of waste (including sewage sludge and cesspool waste) at a waste water treatment works (T21)[157]; the deposit of waste on to a railway track from a railway sanitary convenience (D2)[158]; the deposit of waste from a portable sanitary convenience by burying it (D3)[159]; the disposal by incineration of specified waste[160] in a specified incinerator[161] (D6)[162]; and the storage of sludge[163] (S3).[164]

---

[156] Sch.3 Pt 1 Ch.2 s.2 (Use of waste) para.7. The conditions are that: (a) the total quantity of waste used over any 24-hour period does not exceed 10 cubic metres; (b) the highway gravel bed has sealed drainage to ensure that the condition in paragraph (c) can be met; (c) all waste used in and produced by the cleaning operation is collected; and (d) the waste meets any relevant conditions specified in the environmental permit authorising the operation of the water treatment works or waste water treatment plant. Paras 6 and 7 are also subject to the general conditions that (a) the operation is for the purposes of recovering or reusing the waste, unless otherwise stated in the specific conditions; (b) the waste used is suitable for the purposes of the operation; (c) no more waste is used than is necessary to carry on the operation: Ch.2 s.1 para.3.

[157] Sch.3 Pt 1 Ch.3 (Treatment of waste) para.21. The general condition is that the operation is for the purposes of recovering the waste: Ch.3 s.1 para.3. The specific conditions are that: (a) the total quantity of waste brought to the works over any period of 12 months does not exceed 100,000 cubic metres; and (b) the waste is treated and stored in a secure location with sealed drainage.

[158] Sch.3 Pt 1 Ch.4 (Disposal of waste) para.2. The general condition is that the operation is carried on at the place of production: Sch.3 Pt 1 Ch.4 s.1 para.3.The specific condition is that the total quantity of waste deposited per discharge does not exceed 25 litres.

[159] Sch.3 Pt 1 Ch.4 (Disposal of waste) para.3. The general condition is that the operation is carried on at the place of production: Sch.3 Pt 1 Ch.4 s.1 para.3. The specific conditions are that: (a) the total quantity of waste deposited over any 12-month period does not exceed 1 cubic metre; and (b) no waste is deposited within 10 metres of any watercourse or 50 metres of any spring, well or borehole.

[160] i.e. the waste mentioned in Art.2(2)(a)(i) to (viii) of the Waste Incineration Directive, but excluding the waste mentioned in sub-para.(vi) (radioactive waste) of that Article.

[161] It must have a capacity of less than 50kg per hour and a net rated thermal input of less than 0.4 megawatts; and where it is used together with other incinerators (whether or not it is operated simultaneously with them), the aggregate net rated thermal input of all must be less than 0.4 megawatts.

[162] Sch.3 Pt 1 Ch.4 (Disposal of waste) para.6. The general condition is that the operation is carried on at the place of production: Sch.3 Pt 1 Ch.4 s.1 para.3.The specific conditions are that: (a) the total quantity of waste stored prior to incineration does not exceed 5 tonnes at any one time; and (b) the operation is carried on by the person who produced the waste.

[163] i.e. residual sludge from sewage plants treating domestic or urban waste waters and from other sewage plants treating waste waters of a composition similar to domestic and urban waste waters only, and residual sludge from septic tanks and other similar installations for the treatment of sewage only.

[164] Sch.3 Ch.5 (Storage of waste) para.3. The general conditions are that the storage is carried on: (a) at a place other than the place of production; and (b) pending the recovery of the waste: Sch.3 Ch.5 s.1 para.3. The specific conditions are that: (a) the total quantity of waste stored at any one time does not exceed 1,250 tonnes; (b) no waste is stored for longer than 12 months; (c) the waste is stored in a secure location at the place where it is to be used; (d) the waste is stored at least 10 metres from any

Sch.3 Pt 2 contains descriptions and conditions in respect of *exempt water discharge activities*. These include small discharges of sewage effluent.[165] This applies to the discharge from a sewage treatment plant of 5 cubic metres per day or less of sewage effluent into inland freshwaters, coastal waters or relevant territorial waters. The conditions are:

(a) that all works and equipment used for the treatment of sewage effluent and its discharge comply with the requirements specified in guidance issued by the Secretary of State or Welsh Ministers in relation to design and manufacturing standards, construction, installation and operation specifications, and siting and installation;

(b) that the discharge cannot reasonably, at the time it is first made, be made to the foul sewer;

(c) that the discharge does not contain trade effluent;

(d) that all works and equipment used for the treatment of sewage effluent and its discharge are maintained in accordance with the manufacturer's specification;

(e) that records of maintenance work are kept by the person who is the occupier of the land on which the discharge is made ("the occupier") for at least five years after the work is carried out;

(f) that the occupier must notify the exemption registration authority if an exempt water discharge activity ceases to be in operation;

(g) that the occupier must ensure that all works and equipment used for the treatment of sewage effluent and its discharge are appropriately decommissioned when the exempt facility ceases to be in operation so that there is no risk of pollutants entering inland freshwaters or coastal waters;

---

watercourse, 50 metres from any spring or well, or from any borehole not used to supply water for domestic or food production purposes, 250 metres from any borehole used to supply water for domestic or food production purposes; (e) no waste is stored (i) within a zone defined by a 50-day travel time for groundwater to reach a groundwater abstraction that is used to supply water for domestic or food production purposes, (ii) within 0.3 metres of the top of an open storage container or within 0.75 metres of the top of an earthbank tank or lagoon; and (f) after storage, the waste is to be used in accordance with the Sludge (Use in Agriculture) Regulations 1989.

[165] Sch.3 Pt 2 para.2.

(h) that, before an occupier ceases to be in occupation of land on which an exempt water discharge activity is carried on, the occupier must give to the person who will next be in occupation of the land a written notice—

  (i) stating that an exempt water discharge activity is being carried on on the land;
  (ii) containing a description of the exempt facility;
  (iii) stating the conditions that must be satisfied in relation to the exempt facility; and
  (iv) accompanied by any records of maintenance mentioned in para.(e).

Sch.3 Pt 3 contains descriptions and conditions in respect of *exempt groundwater activities*. These include small discharges of sewage effluent.[166] This applies to a discharge from a septic tank or sewage treatment plant of 2 cubic metres per day or less of sewage effluent that results in the input of pollutants to groundwater. The conditions are the same as or analogous to those for exempt water discharge activities, with the addition of the condition that that the discharge does not result in an input of pollutants to groundwater (i) within 50 metres of a point at which water is abstracted from underground strata, or (ii) within a zone defined by a 50-day travel time for groundwater to reach a groundwater abstraction point that is used to supply water for domestic or food production purposes. **8–024**

(vi) Sch.21: Water discharge activities

Sch.21 apples to "water discharge activities".[167] This term applies to any of the following: **8–025**

(a) the discharge or entry to inland freshwaters, coastal waters or relevant territorial waters[168] of any:

  (i) poisonous, noxious or polluting[169] matter;

---

[166] Sch.3 Pt 3 para.3.

[167] Para.1.

[168] These terms are as defined in s.104 of the Water Resources Act 1991: reg.2(1). See above, pp.167–169.

[169] "Pollution", in relation to a water discharge or groundwater activity, means the direct or indirect introduction, as a result of human activity, of substances or heat into the air, water or land which may: (a) be harmful to human health or the quality of aquatic ecosystems or terrestrial ecosystems directly depending on aquatic ecosystems; (b) result in damage to material property; or (c) impair or interfere with amenities or other legitimate uses of the environment: reg.2(1).

(ii) waste[170] matter; or
(iii) trade effluent or sewage effluent[171];

(b) the discharge from land through a pipe[172] into the sea outside the seaward limits of relevant territorial waters of any trade effluent or sewage effluent;

(c) the removal from any part of the bottom, channel or bed of any inland freshwaters of a deposit accumulated by reason of any dam, weir or sluice holding back the waters, by causing it to be carried away in suspension in the waters, unless the activity is carried on in the exercise of a power conferred by or under any enactment relating to land drainage, flood prevention or navigation;

(d) the cutting or uprooting of a substantial amount of vegetation in any inland freshwaters or so near to any such waters that it falls into them and failure to take reasonable steps to remove the vegetation from these waters;

(e) an activity in respect of which a notice under para.4 or 5 has been served and has taken effect.[173]

A discharge or an activity that might lead to a discharge is not a "water discharge activity":

(a) if the discharge is made, or authorised to be made, by or under any prescribed statutory provision; or

(b) if the discharge is of trade effluent or sewage effluent from a vessel.[174]

In determining whether a discharge or an activity is a water discharge activity, no account must be taken of any radioactivity possessed by any substance or article or by any part of any premises.[175]

---

170 "Waste" in the term "waste matter" includes: (a) anything that is waste for the purposes of the Waste Framework Directive and is not excluded from the scope of that Directive by Art.2(1) of that Directive; (b) anything that is waste for the purposes of the Mining Waste Directive and is not excluded from the scope of that Directive by Art.2(2) of that Directive: Sch.21 para.2.
171 These terms are as defined in s.221 of the Water Resources Act 1991: reg.2(1).
172 As defined in the 1991 Act.
173 Sch.21 para.3(1).
174 Sch.21 para.3(2).
175 Sch.21 para.3(3).

Paragraph 4 applies where (a) a person is operating a highway drain[176]; and (b) that activity might lead to a discharge mentioned in para.3(1)(a) or (b). Here, the regulator[177] may serve a notice on the person operating the highway drain requiring the person, from the date the notice takes effect, to hold an environmental permit[178] authorising the carrying on of that activity. Such a notice takes effect on the date specified in it, which must be at least six months after it is served. **8–026**

Under para.5, the regulator may serve a notice on a person who discharges trade effluent or sewage effluent into the waters of any lake or pond[179] which are not inland freshwaters requiring the person, from the date the notice takes effect, to hold an environmental permit authorising the carrying on of that activity. A notice under this paragraph takes effect on the date specified in it, which must be at least three months after it is served.

Paragraph 6 applies for the purpose of determining liability for a water discharge activity that consists of a discharge of sewage effluent from a discharging sewer[180] vested in a discharging undertaker.[181] Accordingly, a discharging undertaker causes a discharge of sewage effluent if:

(a) matter included in the discharge is received by the discharging undertaker into the discharging sewer or into any other sewer or works vested in it;

(b) the discharging undertaker was bound (either unconditionally or subject to conditions which were observed) to receive the matter into the discharging sewer or other sewer or works.[182]

However, this does not apply if, before the discharging undertaker discharges the sewage effluent from the discharging sewer, the sending undertaker,[183] under an agreement with the discharging undertaker under s.110A of the Water Industry Act 1991, discharges **8–027**

[176] i.e. a drain which a highway authority or other person is entitled to keep open by virtue of s.100 of the Highways Act 1980 reg.2(1).
[177] i.e. the authority on whom functions are conferred by reg.32, or by a direction under reg.33: reg.2(1).
[178] As defined in reg.13(1).
[179] As defined in the 1991 Act s.104.
[180] i.e. the sewer or works from which sewage effluent is discharged: Sch.21 para.2.
[181] para.6(1). "Discharging undertaker" means the sewerage undertaker in which a discharging sewer is vested: Sch.21 para.2.
[182] para.6(2).
[183] i.e. a sewerage undertaker which discharges sewage effluent into the discharging sewer or other sewer or works vested in the discharging undertaker: Sch.21 para.2.

the sewage effluent through a main connection[184] into: (a) the discharging sewer; or (b) any other sewer or works vested in the discharging undertaker.[185]

In these circumstances, the sending undertaker causes the discharge if:

(a) matter included in the discharge is received by the sending undertaker into a sewer or works vested in it; and

(b) it was bound (either conditionally or subject to conditions which were observed) to receive that matter into that sewer or works.[186]

A sewerage undertaker is not guilty of an offence under reg.38(1) in relation to a water discharge activity that consists of a discharge of sewage effluent from a sewer or works vested in it if:

(a) the contravention is attributable to a discharge which another person caused or knowingly permitted to be made into the sewer or works;

(b) the undertaker either was not bound to receive the discharge into the sewer or works or was bound to receive it there subject to conditions which were not observed; and

(c) the undertaker could not reasonably have been expected to prevent the discharge into the sewer or works.[187]

8–028 A person is not guilty of an offence under reg.38(1) in relation to a discharge which the person caused or knowingly permitted to be made into a sewer or works vested in a sewerage undertaker if that undertaker was bound to receive the discharge, either unconditionally or subject to conditions which were observed.[188]

(vii) Sch.22: Groundwater activities

8–029 Sch.22 concerns groundwater activities. These are any of:

---

[184] As defined in the Water Industry Act 1991 s.110A.
[185] para.6(3).
[186] para.6(4).
[187] para.6(5).
[188] para.6(6).

(a) the discharge of a pollutant[189] that results in the direct input[190] of that pollutant to groundwater[191];

(b) the discharge of a pollutant in circumstances that might lead to an indirect input[192] of that pollutant to groundwater;

(c) any other discharge that might lead to the direct or indirect input of a pollutant to groundwater;

(d) an activity in respect of which a notice under para.10 has been served and has taken effect;

(e) an activity that might lead to a discharge mentioned in para.(a), (b) or (c), where that activity is carried on as part of the operation of a regulated facility of another class.[193]

However, a discharge or an activity that might lead to a discharge is not a "groundwater activity" if the discharge is (a) made, or authorised to be made, by or under any prescribed statutory provision; or (b) of trade effluent or sewage effluent from a vessel.[194] Furthermore, the regulator may determine that a discharge, or an activity that might lead to a discharge, is not a groundwater activity if the input of the pollutant:

(a) is the consequence of an accident or exceptional circumstances of natural cause that could not reasonably have been foreseen, avoided or mitigated;

(b) is or would be of a quantity and concentration so small as to obviate any present or future danger of deterioration in the quality of the receiving groundwater; or

(c) is or would be incapable, for technical reasons, of being prevented or limited without using:

(i) measures that would increase risks to human health or to the quality of the environment as a whole; or

---

[189] i.e. any substance liable to cause pollution: reg.2(1).
[190] i.e. the introduction of a pollutant to groundwater without percolation through soil or subsoil: Sch.22 para.2.
[191] i.e. all water which is below the surface of the ground in the saturation zone and in direct contact with the ground or subsoil: reg.2(1).
[192] i.e. the introduction of a pollutant to groundwater after percolation through soil or subsoil: Sch.22 para.2.
[193] Sch.22 para.3(1).
[194] Sch.22 para.3(2).

(ii) disproportionately costly measures to remove quantities of pollutants from, or otherwise control their percolation in, contaminated ground or subsoil.

The regulator must keep a record of such determinations.

For the purposes of implementing the Groundwater Directive, the Water Framework Directive, and the Groundwater Daughter Directive,[195] the regulator must, in exercising its relevant functions,[196] take all necessary measures:

(a) to prevent the input of any hazardous substance[197] to groundwater; and

(b) to limit the input of non-hazardous pollutants[198] to groundwater so as to ensure that such inputs do not cause pollution of groundwater.[199]

Particular requirements apply in respect of an application for an environmental permit relating to (a) a discharge mentioned in para.3(1)(a), (b) or (c); or (b) an activity that might lead to such a discharge.[200]

8–030 Despite para.6, provided it does not compromise the achievement of any of the environmental objectives relating to groundwater in Art.4 of the Water Framework Directive, the regulator may grant an environmental permit for a number of specified groundwater activities.[201] The regulator may serve a prohibition notice where any person is carrying on, or proposing to carry on, any activity on or in the ground and that activity might lead to a discharge mentioned in para.3(1)(a), (b) or (c),[202] and may serve a notice requiring an environmental permit to be held authorising the activity.[203]

A highway authority or other person entitled to keep open a highway drain by virtue of s.100 of the 1980 Act who operates a highway drain other than under and in accordance with an environmental permit is

---

195 Dir.2006/60, Dir.80/68 and Dir.2006/118.
196 reg.9.
197 i.e any substance or group of substances that are toxic, persistent and liable to bio-accumulate: Sch.22 para.4(1). These include in particular substances listed in para.4(2).
198 i.e. any pollutant other than a hazardous substance: Sch.22 para.5.
199 Sch.22 para.6.
200 Sch.22 para.7.
201 Sch.22 para.8.
202 Sch.22 para.9.
203 Sch.22 para.10.

not guilty of an offence under reg.38(1) unless the regulator has served a notice on that person under para.10 and the notice has taken effect.[204]

Before January 1, 2012, a person who, other than under and in accordance with an environmental permit, uses a septic tank or sewage treatment plant with a discharge of 2 cubic metres per day or less of sewage effluent that results in the input of pollutants to groundwater is not guilty of an offence under reg.38(1) unless the regulator has served a notice on that person under para.10 and the notice has taken effect.[205]

The Secretary of State or Welsh Ministers may issue guidance to persons causing or liable to cause inputs of pollutants to groundwater.[206] **8–031**

The same rules apply for the purpose of determining liability for a groundwater activity that consists of a discharge of sewage effluent from a discharging sewer vested in a discharging undertaker,[207] as apply to determining such liability for a water discharge activity.[208]

(i) Powers of entry

Extensive powers of entry are conferred on persons authorised by enforcing authorities[209] to enter premises and take any one or more of a wide range of steps, including taking samples, taking possession of articles or substances and requiring the production of information. This must be for the purpose of determining whether any provision of the pollution control enactments[210] is being, or has been, complied with; or exercising or performing one of more of the authority's pollution control functions; or determining whether and, if so, how such a function should be exercised or performed. A person may be **8–032**

---

[204] Sch.22 para.11. Such a notice must not take effect until at least six months after it is served: para.10(3)(a).

[205] Sch.22 para.12. Such a notice must not take effect until at least three months after it is served: para.10(3)(b).

[206] Sch.22 para.13.

[207] Sch.22 para.14.

[208] See above.

[209] i.e. the Secretary of State, the Environment Agency or a local enforcing authority under Pt 1 of the Environmental Protection Act 1990, a local authority for the purposes of Pt 2A of the 1990 Act or Pt 4 of the Environment Act 1995, or a local authority for the purposes of regulations under s.2 of the Pollution Prevention and Control Act 1999 extending to England and Wales: 1995 Act s.108(15).

[210] i.e. functions conferred by a range of Acts, including Pts 1, 2 and 2A of the Environmental Protection Act 1990, Ch.3 of Pt 4 of the Water Industry Act 1991 (special category effluent) and Pt 3 and ss.161–161D of the Water Resources Act 1991: 1995 Act s.108(15).

authorised by the Environment Agency to exercise such powers to carry out an assessment or report in relation to an incident or possible incident involving or having the potential to involve serious pollution of the environment, serious harm to human health or danger to life or health. Except in an emergency, seven days' notice must be given of entry to residential premises or of taking heavy equipment on to any premises, and either consent or a warrant under Schedule 18 must be obtained.[211] The authorised person may seize and cause to be rendered harmless any article or substance found on premises which he has power to enter if he has reasonable cause to believe that it is a cause of imminent danger of serious pollution to the environment or serious harm to human health.[212] Obstruction of an authorised person is an offence.[213]

DECLARATION OF SPECIAL ZONES UNDER THE WATER RESOURCES ACT 1991

8–033 The Water Resources Act 1991 gave power for the creation of various special zones with a view to restriction or prevention of pollution. Two in particular were of significance, *Water Protection Zones* and *Nitrate Sensitive Areas*. The former powers have recently been expanded but the latter repealed.[214]

The Secretary of State (for England) or the Welsh Ministers (for Wales) have power by order to designate an area as a Water Protection Zone and regulate the carrying on in that zone of activities specified or described in order. Activities may be regulated by prohibiting or restricting them or by imposing requirements on persons who carry them on to take such steps as may be specified or described in the order.[215] The power may only be exercised in relation to an area if either: (a) it is appropriate, with a view to preventing or controlling the entry of any poisonous, noxious or polluting matter into controlled waters,[216] to prohibit or restrict the carrying on in that area of activities which the Secretary of State or Welsh Ministers

[211] 1995 Act s.108.
[212] 1995 Act s.109.
[213] 1995 Act s.110.
[214] By the Water Resources Act 1991 (Amendment) (England and Wales Regulations 2009 (SI 2009/3104). Powers to establish Nitrate Sensitive Areas were contained in the 1991 Act ss.94, 95, 96(2) and Sch.12, and repealed by SI 2009/3104 reg.4.
[215] Such requirements may only be imposed for the purpose of enabling the UK to comply with its obligations under the Water Framework Directive (Dir.2000/60) in relation to any applicable environmental objectives.
[216] Water Resources Act 1991 s.104; see pp.167–169.

considers are likely to result in the pollution of any such waters; or (b) it is appropriate, with a view to preventing or limiting any harm[217] that is being or is likely to be caused to controlled waters, to regulate the carrying on in that area of activities which he or they consider are likely to result in such harm. An order may confer determinative powers on the Environment Agency and may create offences.[218] The purpose of such designations clearly extends far beyond pollution by discharges of sewage effluents but, equally, such discharges would obviously fall within their intended limit. The National Rivers Authority proposed that a zone should be designated covering the River Dee catchment; a public inquiry was held, following the receipt of objections, by the Secretary of State and a designation order was ultimately made in 1999.[219] It is expected that further areas will be designated as WPZs in order to achieve the requirements of the Water Framework Directive.

REGISTRATION AND SUPPLY OF INFORMATION UNDER THE WATER RESOURCES ACT 1991

Under s.190 of the Water Resources Act 1991,[220] the Environment **8–034** Agency is under a duty to maintain registers containing particulars as prescribed by order[221] of, or relating to:

(a) notices served respecting water quality objectives;

(b) samples of effluent taken for the purposes of the Act and conclusions derived therefrom;

(c) directions given by the Secretary of State in relation to the Agency's functions under the Act's water pollution provisions;

---

217 "Harm" is defined in s.93(2B), (2C) to mean any adverse impact on the condition of any hydromorphological quality element affecting the controlled waters that would be likely to prevent the achievement of any environmental objectives applicable to those waters (other than an adverse impact under (a)).

218 Water Resources Act 1991 s.93, as amended by SI 2009/3104 (extending the powers to include condition (b)).

219 "Freshwater Quality: Government Response to the 16th Report of the Royal Commission on Environmental Pollution" (DoE, February 1995), p.41; "ENDS Report" 243, p.9; the Water Protection Zone (River Dee Catchment) Designation Order 1999 (SI 1999/915).

220 As amended by the Environment Act 1995 Sch.22 para.169(1)–(4) and SI 2010/675 Sch.26 Pt 1 para.8(2)(o).

221 See the Control of Pollution (Applications, Appeals and Registers) Regulations 1996 (SI 1996/2971) regs 15–17, as modified by SI 1998/1649 and amended by SI 1999/1006 reg.8.

(d) works notices under s.161A;

(e) appeals under s.161C;

(f) convictions for offences under s.161D;

(g) such other matters relating to the quality or pollution of water as may be prescribed by the Secretary of State.

It is further the duty of the Agency under the section to make such registers available for free public inspection at all reasonable times and to afford members of the public reasonable facility at reasonable cost for taking copies of entries upon the register.[222]

Provision is made for the exclusion from registers of information if and so long as in the opinion of the Secretary of State its inclusion would be contrary to the interests of national security,[223] and for the exclusion of specified categories of commercially confidential information.[224]

It is also the duty of the Agency and water undertakers to supply information inter se for the purpose of the performance of their respective statutory duties. These duties do not appear to extend expressly to sewerage undertakers.[225] Other persons may be required by notice to supply information in this connection to the Secretary of State or the Environment Agency and failure of compliance without reasonable excuse is a criminal offence with liability on summary conviction to a fine not exceeding the statutory maximum and, on conviction on indictment, to a fine, up to two years' imprisonment, or both.[226]

CIVIL AND CRIMINAL LIABILITIES UNDER THE WATER RESOURCES ACT 1991

8–035 Apart from the specific provisions upon given liabilities considered above, where an offence under the control of pollution provisions of the Water Resources Act 1991 is due to the act or default of some

---

[222] Water Resources Act 1991 s.190(2), as amended by the 1995 Act Sch.22 para.169(5).

[223] 1991 Act s.191A, inserted by the 1995 Act Sch.22 para.170.

[224] 1991 Act s.191B, inserted by the 1995 Act Sch.22 para.170, and amended by SI 2010/675 Sch.26 Pt 1 para.8(2)(p), (9).

[225] Water Resources Act 1991 s.203, as amended.

[226] Water Resources Act 1991 s.202, as amended by the Environment Act 1995 Sch.22 para.172. Section 202 also has effect as if it conferred power on the Agency to require the furnishing of information reasonably required by it for the purposes of giving effect to Directives 75/440, 79/869, 78/659 and 79/923: SI 1996/3001 reg.7(3), SI 1997/1331 reg.6(3) and SI 1997/1332 reg.6(3). Restrictions on the disclosure of information are imposed by s.204, as amended.

person other than the apparent principal, such other person may be prosecuted whether or not the principal is also charged. In a sewerage connection this will be of obvious relevance where in the circumstances considered above a discharge from a sewer results from the discharge into a sewerage undertaker's sewer of materials which it was not bound to receive or in breach of the conditions imposed upon such receipt.[227] A Magistrates' Court may try any summary offence in this connection upon information laid not more than 12 months after the commission of the offence despite the provision upon time limits for summary proceedings made by s.127 of the Magistrates' Courts Act 1980.[228]

Where a body corporate, including *ex hypothesi*, a sewerage undertaker, is guilty of an offence under the 1991 Act or s.4 of the Water Act 2003 and that offence is proved to have been committed with the consent or connivance, or to be attributable to the neglect, of any director, manager, secretary or similar officer of the body or any person purporting to act in such or a similar capacity, that person will also be liable to prosecution and punishment in respect of the offence.[229] For this purpose the member of a body corporate who directly manages the affairs of the body will be considered to be in the position of the "directors" of the body concerned.[230]

So far as civil liability is concerned, except in so far as it might otherwise be provided, no contravention of the control of pollution provisions of the 1991 Act will confer a civil right of action, other than proceedings for the recovery of a fine, derogate from any right of action or other remedy (civil or criminal) arising from other provisions or compromise any restriction which might be imposed by other, public, local or private, enactment.[231]

---

227 Water Resources Act 1991 s.217(3). See *Express Dairies Ltd v Environment Agency* [2004] EWHC 1710 (Admin), [2005] 1 W.L.R. 223 (landowner liable under s.217 where it permitted licensee to conduct an operation that carried the risk of causing pollution (the escape of cream into a stream); the landowner should have conducted and responded to a risk assessment).

228 Water Resources Act 1991 s.101.

229 Water Resources Act 1991 s.217(1) as amended by the Water Act 2003 Sch.7 Pt 1 para.2. The company itself will be vicariously liable under s.85 (see above, pp.172–173) for the acts or omissions of its employees acting within the course of employment: *National Rivers Authority v Alfred McAlpine Homes East Ltd* [1994] 4 All E.R. 286, D.C. An analogous principle does not apply in respect of unincorporated associations: *R v L* [2008] EWCA Crim 1970; [2009] 1 All E.R. 786.

230 Water Resources Act 1991 s.217(2).

231 Water Resources Act 1991 s.100.

ANTI-POLLUTION WORKS AND OPERATIONS UNDER THE WATER RESOURCES ACT 1991

8–036 The Environment Agency has extensive powers[232] to carry out anti-pollution and operations and other works and operations in respect of harm to controlled waters, and to serve works notices requiring persons to carry out such works and operations. An appeal against a notice lies to the Secretary of State; non-compliance is an offence.[233]

Section 4 of the Salmon and Freshwater Fisheries Act 1975[234] also prohibits putting into any waters or tributaries of waters containing fish, any liquid or solid matter so as to cause the waters to be poisonous or injurious to the fish or the spawning grounds, spawn or food for fish.[235] However, a person is not guilty of an offence in respect of the entry of matter into controlled waters under and in accordance with an environmental permit under reg.13 of the Environmental Permitting (England and Wales) Regulations 2010.[236]

DISCHARGES TO A WATERCOURSE AT COMMON LAW

8–037 Quite apart from statutory provisions, the discharge of sewage effluent or other polluting matter into any stream may amount to a nuisance in respect of which a riparian owner may take proceedings at common law for an injunction and/or for damages. The pollution need not be so bad as to amount to a public nuisance, as any riparian owner is entitled to have a flow of water in any natural stream which is in all respects in its natural state; a similar right may attach to an artificial stream, if the right has been acquired by grant or by prescription. At common law pollution means the addition of something to water which changes its natural qualities, such as the addition of hard water to soft water, the raising of the temperature of the water, or the addition of something which on meeting some other substance already in the water, each in themselves harmless, causes

---

[232] Under ss.161–161D of the Water Resources Act 1991. Sections 161, 161ZA, 161ZB, 161ZC, 161A, 161AA and 161AB were substituted for ss.161 and 161A as previously enacted, by the Water Resources Act 1991 (Amendment) (England and Wales) Regulations 2009 (SI 2009/3104) reg.5, and amended by SI 2010/675 Sch.26 Pt 1 para.8(8). The original version of s.161A and ss.161B–161D were added by the Environment Act 1995 Sch.22 para.162.

[233] See further the Anti-Pollution Works Regulations 1999 (SI 1999/1006), as amended by SI 2009/1307 Sch.2 para.94 and 2009/3104 reg.6.

[234] As amended by the Water Act 1989 Sch.27 Pt I.

[235] As to the Agency's bye-law making powers, see the Water Resources Act 1991 Sch.25 para.6(4), as amended by the Environment Act 1995 Sch.22 para.128.

[236] Water Consolidation (Consequential Provisions) Act 1991 Sch.1 para.30(1), as amended by SI 2010/675 Sch.26 para.9.

pollution.[237] In this context the rule in *Rylands v Fletcher*[238] applies whereby liability will arise where "dangerous" materials are stored upon land and in fact escape therefrom causing foreseeable damage.

Compliance with the provisions of the Water Resources Act 1991 will be no defence in common law proceedings. The standards of the common law are higher than those so far imposed by Parliament; seemingly harmless extraneous matter is none the less capable of being treated as pollution at common law. On the other hand an injunction is a discretionary remedy, and it would not be granted by a court where no prejudice whatever can be shown to the plaintiff's interests.[239]

The discharge of effluent into a watercourse by an undertaker may amount to a nuisance[240]; indeed, an undertaker is expressly prohibited from causing a nuisance in the exercise of its functions[241] by s.117(6) of the Water Industry Act 1991. The fact that the particular watercourse was already polluted from some other source would also be no defence in such proceedings.[242]

It used to be said that at common law a right to pollute a watercourse could be acquired by prescription or by grant as an easement as against a riparian proprietor lower down the watercourse[243] but where such pollution would constitute an offence against the 1991 Act (and a similar principle applied under the earlier statutes), it seems that such a right would not now be upheld by the courts.

STATUTORY NUISANCES

In addition to the above restrictions, statutory or common law, on **8–038**
pollution of watercourses and streams, certain matters are expressly

---

[237] See *Coulson & Forbes on Waters and Land Drainage*, 6th edn (London: Sweet & Maxwell, 1952), p.198, and *Crossley v Lightowler* (1866) L.R. 2 Ch. 476, and other cases there cited. In *Young & Co v Bankier Distillery Co* [1893] A.C. 691, Lord Macnaghten said (at p.698), "A riparian owner is entitled to have the water of the stream, on the banks of which his property lies, flow down as it has been accustomed to flow down to his property, subject to the ordinary use of the flowing water by upper proprietors, and to such further use, if any, on their part in connection with their property as may be reasonable in the circumstances. Every riparian proprietor is thus entitled to the water of his stream, in its natural flow, without sensible diminution or increase and without sensible alterations in its character or quality."

[238] (1866) L.R. 1 Ex. 265.

[239] *Kensit v G.E. Rlwy Co* (1884) 27 Ch. D. 122.

[240] *Pride of Derby and Derbyshire Angling Assn v British Celanese Ltd* [1953] Ch. 149.

[241] Under ss.102–105, 112, 115 and 116 of the 1991 Act.

[242] *Pride of Derby*.

[243] See *Wright v Williams* (1836) 1 M. & W. 77.

dealt with by s.259 of the 1936 Act.[244] These provisions are enforceable not by an undertaker under the 1991 Act but by the local authority.[245] The section provides that the following are statutory nuisances for the purposes of Pt 3 of the Environmental Protection Act 1990:

> "(a) any pond, pool, ditch, gutter or watercourse which is so foul or in such a state as to be prejudicial to health or a nuisance[246];
>
> (b) any part of a watercourse, not being a part ordinarily navigated by vessels, employed in the carriage of goods by water, which is so choked[247] or silted up as to obstruct or impede the proper flow of water and thereby to cause a nuisance, or give rise to conditions prejudicial to health[248];
>
> Provided that in the case of an alleged nuisance under para.(b), nothing in this subsection shall be deemed to impose any liability on any person other than the person by whose act or default the nuisance arises or continues."

In order therefore, for a local authority to act in such a situation, the actual offender must be discovered, either *flagrante delicto*, or by establishing that he has failed to perform a legal duty already imposed on him to clear out the watercourse in question. A riparian owner may be under a limited common law duty to clear out a natural stream,[249]

---

244 As amended by the Environmental Protection Act 1990 Sch.15 para.4.

245 i.e. district and London borough councils, the Common Council of the City of London, the Sub-Treasurer of the Inner Temple and the Under Treasurer of the Middle Temple and the Council of the Isles of Scilly and, after 1st April 1996, county and county borough councils in Wales: 1990 Act s.79(7), as amended.

246 *Att Gen v Leeds Corp* (1870) 5 Ch. App. 583.

247 This expression applies to artificial obstructions such as the piers of a bridge and not just natural obstructions such as weeds; the statutory nuisance caused by the "choking" need not be ever-present and continuous: *R. (on the application of Robinson) v Torridge DC* [2006] EWHC 877 (Admin), [2007] 1 W.L.R. 871.

248 "Prejudicial to health" is defined by s.343(1) of the 1936 Act to mean "injurious, or likely to cause injury to health". It is not necessary to prove that a particular state of affairs is *both* a nuisance and injurious to health: *Betts v Penge UDC* [1942] 2 All E.R. 61.

249 *Leakey v National Trust for Places of Historic Interest or Natural Beauty* [1980] 1 Q.B. 485, per Megaw L.J. at pp.526–527, impliedly disapproving the decision of the Divisional Court in *Neath RDC v WIlliams* [1951] 1 K.B. 115. The test is what it is reasonable to expect of the occupier given the relevant resources, taken on a broad basis, of the parties. See further *Goldman v Hargrave* [1967] 1 A.C. 645, P.C. Very different considerations apply if the defendant creates an artificial watercourse or does anything to make artificial that which was previously natural: *Sedleigh-Denfield v O'Callaghan* [1940] A.C. 880. See now, however, the Water Resources Act 1991 s.90, with specific reference to "deposits and vegetation in rivers".

and in practice it may well be difficult to prove a sufficient act or default to bring a defendant within the proviso to the present section.

Ancillary powers with regard to watercourses, ditches, etc. are given to the local authority by ss.260 to 266 of the 1936 Act, and these are not affected by the 1989 or 1991 Acts.

DISCHARGE TO THE SEA AT COMMON LAW

At common law there is no right for any person (including a local **8–039** authority or sewerage undertaker), to discharge sewage or any polluting matter into the sea, and an injunction may be granted if a nuisance is caused by any such discharge, at the instance of the person injured.[250]

DISCHARGE TO THE SEA: OTHER PROVISIONS

Section 187 of the Water Industry Act 1991 provides that a sewerage **8–040** undertaker may not execute any works below high water mark without the approval of the Secretary of State.

The discharge of sewage from ships into the sea is now regulated by the Merchant Shipping (Prevention of Pollution by Sewage and Garbage from Ships) Regulations 2008.[251] UK ships must be surveyed and given a sewage certificate.[252] Ships constructed on or after October 2, 1983 must be equipped with at least one of a sewage treatment plant, a sewage comminuting and disinfecting system or a holding tank, complying with specified requirements, and an appropriate discharge connection.[253] The discharge[254] of

---

250 *Hobart v Southend-on-Sea Corp* (1906) 75 L.J.K.B. 305, and *Foster v Warblington UDC* [1906] 1 K.B. 648. A local authority may itself be in the position of claimant where its property has been injured as the consequence of pollution of the sea or tidal waters: *Esso Petroleum Co Ltd v Southport Corp* [1956] A.C. 218.

251 SI 2008/3257 (in force from February 1, 2009), implementing Annexes IV and V of the International Convention for the Prevention of Pollution from Ships 1973, as amended. As to the delivery of waste including sewage at a port, see the Merchant Shipping and Fishing Vessels (Port Waste Reception Facilities) Regulations 2003 (SI 2003/1809), as amended by SI 2009/1176.

252 regs 7–20. Non-UK ships cannot normally proceed to sea from a port in the UK without a sewage certificate: reg.19. "Sewage certificate" means an International Sewage Pollution Prevention Certificate referred to in reg.5 of Annex IV to the Convention.

253 regs 21 and 22.

254 i.e. any release howsoever caused from a ship: reg.2(2)(a). This does not include dumping within the meaning of the Convention on the Prevention of Marine Pollution by Dumping of Waste and Other Matters 1972, as amended, or the release of sewage for the purposes of legitimate scientific research into pollution abatement or control: reg.2(3).

sewage[255] from a ship[256] into the sea is prohibited.[257] This does not apply to a ship constructed before October 2, 1983 provided that it is equipped, so far as is practicable, to discharge sewage in accordance with regs 24 or 25.[258] However, sewage may be discharged into the sea through a sewage treatment plant if as a result there are no visible floating solids or discolouration of the water into which it is discharged.[259] Sewage may be discharged through a comminuting and disinfecting system more than three nautical miles from the nearest land,[260] and from a holding tank (whether or not treated) more than 12 nautical miles from the nearest land, subject to further conditions.[261]

The discharge of oil[262] or any mixture containing oil into UK territorial waters or navigable internal waters, from a "place" on land (which would presumably include a sewer), constitutes an offence against s.2 of the Prevention of Oil Pollution Act 1971.[263]

ESCAPE OF SEWAGE AS DEPOSIT OF CONTROLLED WASTE

8–041 Section 33 of the Environmental Protection Act 1990 makes it an offence for any person (inter alia) to deposit controlled waste,[264] or knowingly cause or knowingly permit controlled waste to be deposited in or on any land, unless this is in accordance with a waste management licence; or to treat, keep or dispose of controlled waste in a manner likely to cause pollution of the environment or harm to human health.[265] It has been held that sewage escaping from pipes

[255] i.e. drainage and other wastes from any form of toilets or urinals, drainage from medical premises or spaces containing living animals and other waste waters when mixed with any of these: reg.2(2)(c).
[256] i.e. a ship of 400 gross tonnage (see Schedule) or more or certified to carry more than 15 persons, engaged in international voyages and which is either a UK ship (wherever it may be) or a non-UK ship in UK waters or controlled waters or any other waters which are sea: reg.6(8). An "international voyage" is a voyage from a country to which the Convention applies to a port outside that country or vice versa: reg.2(1). "UK ship" is defined in reg.2(5).
[257] reg.23(1).
[258] reg.23(3).
[259] reg.24.
[260] Defined in reg.4.
[261] reg.25.
[262] "Oil" is defined, somewhat loosely, in s.29(1) of the 1971 Act as meaning "oil of any description" and including "spirit produced from oil of any description and coal tar".
[263] As amended by the Prevention of Oil Pollution Act 1986 s.1.
[264] The definition of "controlled waste" excludes waste that is not "directive waste" for the purpose of the Waste Framework Direction (Dir.75/442).
[265] See *Cross on Local Government Law*, 9th edn (London: Sweet & Maxwell), para.19–123.

maintained by a sewerage undertaker is "controlled waste" for these purposes.[266] While the definition of directive waste excluded, "where they were already covered by other legislation . . . waste waters, with the exception of waste in liquid form,"[267] the Court of Justice on a reference[268] had ruled that the Urban Waste Water Treatment Directive was not "other legislation" within this provision, and that it was for the national court to determine whether there were national rules containing precise provisions organising the management of the waste in question and if they were such as to ensure a level of protection of the environment equivalent to that guaranteed by the Waste Framework Directive. The Divisional Court ruled that there were no such national rules; escapes were by definition unplanned and so outside the scope of the ordinary management regime. The prosecution of TWUL was remitted to the magistrates' court. Offences concerning controlled waste are now dealt with by the Environmental Permitting (England and Wales) Regulations 2010.[269]

THE PROBLEM OF FLOODING FROM SEWERS

The problem of repeated flooding from blocked or overloaded sewers **8–042**
has received increasing attention from the water industry, OFWAT and the courts. The Court of Appeal, in *Marcic v Thames Water Utilities Ltd*,[270] expanded the scope of liability in nuisance for such flooding, holding that Thames Water had not established that its system of priorities for tackling these problems in its area was reasonable or proportionate. This brought into question whether the pace of investment allowed for in successive Price Reviews conducted by OFWAT,[271] in the light of guidance issued by ministers,[272] was sufficient to secure compliance with the law. In 2002, following the decision in *Marcic* and as part of the overall process for Periodic Review 2004, OFWAT issued a Consultation Paper, "Flooding from sewers—a

---

[266] *R. (on the application of Thames Water Utilities Ltd) v Bromley Magistrates' Court* [2008] EWHC 1763 (Admin); [2009] 1 All E.R. 744.
[267] Waste Framework Directive art.2(1)(b)(iv).
[268] Case C-252/05, [2007] 1 W.L.R. 1945.
[269] SI 2010/675.
[270] [2002] Q.B. 929, above, pp.75–79.
[271] See above, pp.40–41. The 1999 price limits included funding to secure a net reduction of 4,500 in the number of properties at risk of sewer flooding at a cost of £140m. The companies sought funding to deal with 7,200 properties: *Flooding from Sewers* (below, n.), p.23.
[272] See DEFRA, "Raising the Quality", September 1998, para.48.

way forward: Consultation".[273] This paper gave figures for the number of properties affected by internal flooding from 1992–93 to 2000–01, which showed a steady reduction to 4,626 in 1996–97, followed by increases to over 7,000 in three of the following four years. There had been a reduction in the overall number of properties at risk of internal flooding from overloaded or blocked sewers.[274] It should be noted, however, that *Marcic* concerned a nuisance arising from *external* flooding, incidents of which are estimated to be about three times as common as internal flooding. Hitherto OFWAT had not monitored the incidence or risk of external flooding and the companies had tended to give little priority to solving external only flooding problems. OFWAT now accepted that there were cases where external flooding was so extensive that it should have equal or higher priority than some internal flooding incidents. The pressure arising from the decision of the Court of Appeal in *Marcic* was subsequently removed by the House of Lords.[275]

Since then, further investment to reduce the risks has been authorised in the 2004 and 2009 Periodic Reviews.[276] The Flooding (formerly "At Risk") Registers are maintained by the 10 water and sewerage companies. In addition to 2:10 and 1:10 registers, 1:20 registers have been introduced, generally to record properties flooded for the first time. Properties flooded in severe weather ("rare events") are recorded but not included in the registers.[277]

Part 1 of the Flood and Water Management Act 2010[278] provides for the strategic overview of flood and coastal erosion risk by the

---

[273] See OFWAT website, *www.ofwat.gov.uk*. See also Water UK, Response to Ofwat Consultation on Flooding from Sewers (2003); and National Audit Office Report, "Out of sight—not out of mind", 2003–04 HC161, January 16, 2004.

[274] P.11 and Appendices 1 and 2. Two registers were kept, one of properties at risk of internal flooding twice in 10 years and the other of properties where the risk is once in 10 years. Approximately 4,500 properties were thought to be subject to 2 in 10 risk, 11,500 to the 1 in 10 risk, although the true numbers were uncertain: p.31.

[275] See pp.79–80.

[276] See pp.40–41; PR04 "Final determinations", pp.206–210, noting the *Marcic* decision, and plans for a reduction in properties at a 1:10 years risk of internal flooding from 8,800 in 2004/05 to 3,100 in 2009/10; PR09 "Final determinations", pp.45–49, noting plans for solving 1:10 problems of internal flooding for 5,277 properties and 1:20 problems for 1,102, and mitigation measures for 2,584 internally flood properties and 1,049 areas at risk of external flooding. With 3,912 properties added to the high risk register, there would be a net reduction of 1,368.

[277] Mott MacDonald, "External Review of Sewer Flooding Risk Registers. Report" (October 2008) (OFWAT website), p.1–1. The report recommended clarification of aspects of arrangements for reporting to OFWAT. OFWAT revised its guidance: see OFWAT, "June return reporting requirements and definitions manual 2010" (OFWAT website).

[278] ss.1–31.

Environment Agency in England and Welsh Ministers in Wales. Unitary authorities and county councils in England and county and county borough councils in Wales as "lead local flood authorities" must put in place strategies for managing flood risk from groundwater, surface runoff[279] and ordinary watercourses in their areas. "Flood" does not include a flood from any part of a sewerage system, unless wholly or partly caused by an increase in the volume of rainwater (including snow and other precipitation) entering or otherwise affecting the system.[280]

STATE LIABILITY FOR BREACH OF EUROPEAN DIRECTIVES

Claims that the state or an emanation of the state such as a sewerage undertaker should be held liable in damages for non-compliance with relevant European environmental Directives have generally not been successful in the context of the discharge of sewage effluent.[281] For example, in *Bowden v South West Water Services*[282] the Court of Appeal held that a trawler fisherman who harvested mussels from the sea bed in Bideford Bay, with one exception, had no cause of action for damages under Community law in relation to losses he suffered when the area of the mussel beds in question was classified to prevent the harvesting and sale of shellfish from it for health reasons. He claimed that the relevant waters were polluted because of the defendant's failure adequately to treat its effluent. The Court held that the plaintiff had no direct rights under the Bathing Water Directive or the Urban Waste Water Directive; he was not directly affected either as a bather nor were his interests directly affected by waste water. It was, however, arguable that a claim could lie under the Shellfish Waters Directive.[283] **8–043**

[279] i.e. rainwater (including snow and other precipitation) which is on the surface of the ground (whether or not it is moving) and has not entered a watercourse drainage system or public sewer: s.6(5).

[280] 2010 Act s.1(3)(a).

[281] See generally W. Howarth and D. McGillivray, *Water Pollution and Water Quality Law* (Crayford: Show & Sons Ltd, 2001), paras 4.15–4.17, 5.5, 5.6, 15.3. Liability would be based on *Francovich v Italy* (C-6 & 9/90) [1991] E.C.R. I–5357.

[282] [1999] Env. L.R. 438.

[283] On these Directives, see above, pp.157–159, 170–172. At first instance, Carnwath J. had also struck out claims for breach of statutory duty under the Water Industry Act 1991, the Water Resources Act 1991 and the Sea Fisheries (Shellfish) Act 1967: [1998] 3 C.M.L.R. 330.

Chapter 9

DRAINAGE OF PREMISES

INTRODUCTORY

9–001 In this chapter it is proposed to deal mainly with drains, as distinct from sewers, and in particular with the drainage of individual buildings and other premises.

In practice, care has to be exercised to consider whether the particular statutory function in question is exercisable by the sewerage undertaker or by the local authority. In general, matters related to a public sewer are the concern of the sewerage undertaker, while matters relating exclusively to drains are the concern of the local authority.

Drains are not vested in the sewerage undertaker or local authority (except (i) where they are owners of property served thereby and (ii) in the case of lateral drains vested in the sewerage undertaker by virtue of the Water Act 2003), but it is the concern of the local authority to ensure that proper means of drainage are provided for new buildings, and that the drains of existing buildings do not cause a nuisance, and also that their contents do not injure the public sewers into which the drains—mediately or immediately—discharge. It is also necessary to consider the circumstances in which the owner or occupier of a building may cause his drains or sewers to be connected to the public sewer vested in the sewerage undertaker, and the use that may be made of any drains so connected.

RIGHTS TO CONNECT DRAINS TO PUBLIC SEWERS

(a) The nature of the rights

9–002 Under s.106 of the Water Industry Act 1991,[1] the owner[2] or occupier of any premises or the owner of any private sewer draining premises[3] is entitled to have his drains or sewer communicate with the public sewer of any sewerage undertaker,[4] provided he has the right (by

[1] As amended by the Competition and Service (Utilities) Act 1992 s.43(2), the Water Act 2003 s.99 and the Flood and Water Management Act 2010 Sch.5 para.16(2).
[2] Defined in s.219(1) of the 1991 Act.
[3] This is also defined in s.219(1), as any sewer which is not a public sewer.
[4] By virtue of the Water Act 2003 s.99(2), this extends, from May 28, 2004, to any public lateral drain which satisfies sewer standards: see below, p.217.

virtue of ownership[5] or easement) to cause his drain or sewer to pass through the intervening land, and he may thereby discharge foul and surface water from those premises or that private sewer; the right does not, however, apply to a sewer vested in the undertaker which has not become a public sewer. Subject to the restrictions mentioned below, and to the prescribed procedure being observed, this right is absolute (the owner or occupier exercising the right must act, however, at his expense) and the person exercising such right will not be responsible if the public sewer is not properly maintained or has an inadequate outfall, or connects with a stream in such a manner as to offend against the control of pollution provisions of the Water Resources Act 1991.[6] There is no right to refuse to allow the exercise of this right unless provision is made for flood prevention works such as on-site attenuation; however, such a requirement may lawfully be imposed by a planning condition.[7]

The Supreme Court[8] by a majority[9] has confirmed that just as the sewerage undertaker cannot refuse a connection on the ground of lack of capacity, the choice as to the point of connection lies with the owner or occupier and not the undertaker. Section 106 confers no express right on the undertaker to select the point of connection or to refuse permission for the connection on the ground that the point of connection is open to objection. Lord Phillips P. rejected an argument that such a right was to be implied as otherwise the relevant provisions would be rendered "insensible, absurd or ineffective to achieve its evident purpose."[10] The history of the right to communicate with a public sewer "does not suggest that the point of connection has ever given difficulty in practice."[11] The only grounds on which connection

---

[5] See above, p.118, n.36.

[6] See above, Ch.8, pp.172–180 now the Environments Permitting Regulations see pp.195–198. This does not mean, however, that a particular effluent which would offend against the Act when it reached the stream may be discharged into the sewer (see proviso (a)(ii) to the present section, below), but that if the effluent from the sewer already pollutes that stream, a particular owner or occupier of premises discharging into the sewer will not be held responsible. On the general principle, see *Ainley & Sons Ltd v Kirkheaton L.B.* (1881) 60 L.J. Ch. 734, and *Brown v Dunstable Corp* [1899] 2 Ch. 378.

[7] *W.E. Black Ltd v Secretary of State for the Environment* [1997] Env. L.R. 1. See also *Tayside Regional Council v Secretary of State for Scotland*, 1996 S.L.T. 473 (fact that public sewer is already overloaded not necessarily valid ground for refusing permission for connection under the Sewerage (Scotland) Act 1968 s.12).

[8] *Barratt Homes Ltd v Dwr Cymru Cyfyngedig (Welsh Water)* [2009] UKSC 13, [2010] 1 All E.R. 965.

[9] Lord Phillips P. and Lords Saville, Walker and Clarke, Lady Hale dissenting. Lord Phillips gave the opinion for the majority.

[10] The phrase used by Lord Bridge as justifying the disregard of particular words in a statute in *McMonagle v Westminster City Council* [1990] 2 A.C. 716 at p.726E.

[11] Lord Phillips P. at [56].

can be refused are those set out in s.106(4),[12] and an issue about the point of connection is not one about the "mode of construction" of the drain or sewer within that subsection.

Under the 1875 Act, it was held that once a communication had been lawfully made under the statutory power which was the predecessor of the present section,[13] any type of effluent (not injurious to health) could be discharged into the public sewer.[14] On the other hand, in two cases[15] in each of which no notice had been given to the local authority pursuant to s.21 of the 1875 Act,[16] a right claimed to connect a foul water drain with a highway (public) sewer, or to change the nature of the effluent to such a sewer from slops to faecal matter, was denied by the court. It is not clear that the decisions would have been the same if the statutory procedure had been followed, but it may be possible to argue that a sewer designed (e.g.) for slop water only cannot be used for other purposes.

9–003 Under the 1991 Act, there are a number of specific restrictions as to what may be discharged to a public sewer, and some public sewers may be reserved for foul, or for surface, water[17] respectively. Subject to the restrictions, it seems that any effluent coming within this expression may be discharged into the public sewer without the consent of the sewerage undertaker.

Section 106(2) provides that this right shall not entitle any person:

"(a) to discharge directly or indirectly into any public sewer—

(i) any liquid from a factory,[18] other than domestic sewage or surface water or storm water, or any liquid from a manufacturing process,[19] or

(ii) any liquid or other matter the discharge of which into public sewers is prohibited by or under any enactment; or

---

[12] See below, pp.219–220.

[13] Act of 1875 s.21.

[14] See the judgment of Charles J. in *Peebles v Oswaldtwistle UDC* [1897] 1 Q.B. 384, at p.392.

[15] *Kinson Pottery Co v Poole Corp* [1899] 2 Q.B. 41, and *Graham v Wroughton* [1901] 2 Ch. 451.

[16] The predecessor to s.34(3) of the 1936 Act.

[17] "Surface water" is defined by s.219(1) of the 1991 Act for the present purpose as including "water from roofs".

[18] This term is to be understood as defined by s.175 of the Factories Act 1961; see s.106(9) of the 1991 Act and s.184(l) of the Factories Act 1961.

[19] But see below, pp.248–249 and, in particular, the definition therein of "trade effluent".

(b) where separate public sewers are provided for foul water and for surface water,[20] to discharge directly or indirectly—

  (i) foul water into a sewer provided for surface water, or

  (ii) except with the approval of the sewerage undertaker, surface water into a sewer provided for foul water; or

(c) to have his drains or sewer made to communicate directly with a storm-water overflow sewer."[21]

It should also be noted that the right relates only to communications to be made from a drain or sewer as defined in the 1991 Act, which would exclude land or agricultural drains, and any person making a communication with a public sewer must comply with the provisions of the section (see s.109).

By virtue of the Water Act 2003 s.99(2),[22] references to a public sewer in s.106[23] include a "public lateral drain which satisfies sewer standards". A "public lateral drain" is a lateral drain[24] which either belongs to the sewerage undertaker or is vested in the undertaker by virtue of a declaration under s.102[25] or an agreement under s.104.[26] "Sewer standards" means such standards of construction and repair as the undertaker would require if the public lateral drain or part of it were to become a public sewer.

(b) Modification of the rights under s.106(1)

The rights arising under s.106(1) are to be modified (from a day to be **9–004** appointed) in respect of a sustainable drainage system construction of which has required approval under Sch.3 to the Flood and Water Management Act 2010.[27] Accordingly, a person may exercise the right under s.106(1) in respect of surface water only if:

(a) the construction of the drainage system was approved under Sch.3; and

---

[20] Under s.116 of the 1991 Act, the undertaker may prohibit the use of any public sewer (or public lateral drain) vested in it, either entirely, or for the purpose of foul water drainage, or for the purpose of surface water drainage (and see Ch.5, above, pp.141–142).

[21] 1991 Act s.106(2). This expression is not defined in the Act.

[22] Inserting subs.(1A) in the 1991 Act s.106 with effect from May 28, 2004.

[23] And ss.107 to 109, 111, 113, 114 to 116, 118, 119, 124, 127, 139 and 146.

[24] See above, p.67.

[25] See pp.118–123.

[26] See pp.123–126.

[27] See below, pp.233–236.

(b) the proposals for approval included a proposal for the communication with the public sewer.

Where these requirements are satisfied, the connection may not be refused:

(a) under s.106(4)[28]; or

(b) on grounds that the drainage system absorbs water from more than one set of premises or sewer, or from land that is neither premises nor a sewer.[29]

The rights are also modified (from a day to be appointed) by s.106B of the 1991 Act.[30] This ensures that lateral drains and sewers are constructed to a proper standard if they are to be adopted by the undertaker. The section provides that a person may exercise the right under s.106(1) in respect of a lateral drain or sewer constructed after the commencement of the section only if Conditions 1 and 2 are satisfied. Condition 1 is that an agreement was entered into under s.104[31] in respect of the drain or sewer. Condition 2 is that the agreement included:

(a) provision about the standards according to which the drain or sewer was to be constructed; and

(b) provision about adoption of the drain or sewer by the sewerage undertaker.

9–005 Provision for the purposes of Condition 2(a) must either:

(a) incorporate or accord with standards published by the Secretary of State of Welsh Ministers; or

(b) depart from those standards by express consent of the parties to the agreement.

Provision for the purposes of Condition 2(b) must:

(a) include provision for adoption to occur automatically upon the occurence of specified events; and

---

[28] See pp.219–220.
[29] 1991 Act s.106A, inserted by the 2010 Act Sch.3 para.16 (2).
[30] Inserted by s.42(1) of the Flood and Water Management Act 2010.
[31] See pp.123–126.

(b) comply with any regulations made by the Secretary of State or Welsh Ministers (which may concern the provision required by para.(a)).

These requirements do not apply to drainage systems required to be approved in accordance with Sch.3 to the Flood and Water Management Act 2010,[32] or in other circumstances specified by the Minister in regulations.

Where a person seeks to exercise the right under s.106(1) in reliance on satisfying Conditions 1 and 2, an undertaker may not refuse connection: **9–006**

(a) whether or not in reliance on s.106(4); and

(b) whether or not the terms of the agreement under s.104 (including terms required by this section) have been complied with.

(c) How the rights may be exercised

In order that a person may exercise the rights given by this section, he must give the sewerage undertaker prior written notice[33] of the proposals, and at any time within 21 days of the receipt of such notice,[34] the undertaker may by notice[35] refuse to permit the communication to be made "if it appears to the undertaker that the mode of construction or condition of the drain or sewer (a) does not satisfy the standards reasonably required by the undertaker; or (b) is such that the making of the communication would be prejudicial to the undertaker's sewerage system"[36] and for the purpose of examining the **9–007**

---

[32] See pp.233–236.

[33] The notice must be in writing (s.219(1) (definition of "notice")) and duly served in accordance with s.216. The form need not follow any particular wording, but Shaw's Form PH58 is appropriate.

[34] This time limit must be strictly applied; a notice under s.106(4) removes a right to connect which is otherwise vested in the owner or occupier, and it is a criminal offence (s.107) to cause a drain or sewer to communicate with a public sewer after notice has been given under s.106(4): per Lord Phillips P. in *Barrett Homes Ltd v Dwr Cymru Cyfyngedig (Welsh Water)* [2009] UKSC 13, [2010], 1 AllE. R. 965 at [60]–[62]. Lords Saville, Walker and Clarke agreed with Lord Phillips.

[35] This also must be in writing and duly signed and served (see preceding note); Shaw's Form PN12 is appropriate.

[36] ss.106(4), as amended by the Water Act 2003 s.99(3). There is no explanation of the expression in (b) afforded by the Act. Clearly the subsection could be invoked to prevent (for example) a 12-inch private sewer being connected to a 4-inch public sewer, but it is doubtful, especially in view of *Smeaton v Ilford Corp* [1954] Ch. 450, whether the power could be used where it is alleged that the effluent to be discharged

mode of construction and condition of the drain or sewer it may, if necessary, require it to be laid open for inspection.[37] Where the sewer or drain satisfies the standards reasonably required by it, a sewerage undertaker may, as a condition of permitting the communication to be made, require that the sewer or that part of the drain forming the lateral drain be vested in it by virtue of a declaration under s.102.[38]

Any question as to the reasonableness of any refusal of the undertaker to permit a communication to be made is to be determined by the WSRA. The undertaker will then have to justify its contention that the communication would prejudice its system or (as the case may be) that the person concerned is not entitled to use the section as one or the other of the above restrictions applies. Similarly, any question arising as to the reasonableness of the requirements of the undertaker regarding the opening of the drain or sewer in question (or a requirement that the sewer or lateral drain be vested in it) may also be determined by the WSRA.[39]

If the communication with a public sewer (or public lateral drain[40]) is made without prior notice having been given to the sewerage undertaker under ss.106 or 108, or before the end of the 21-day period mentioned in s.106(4), the person responsible will be liable to a fine not exceeding level 4 on the standard scale, and the undertaker will be entitled to close the communication and recover its expenses from the person responsible.[41]

(d) The making of the communication

9–008 The physical work of making the communication with the public sewer (or public lateral drain)[42] may be executed by the owner or occupier concerned unless, within 14 days of the notice of his

---

into the sewer would surcharge the sewer or otherwise cause a nuisance. The same result as an exercise of the power under s.106(4) may be achieved by a planning agreement under s.106 of the Town and Country Planning Act 1990: *R. v Canterbury City Council, ex p. Springimage Ltd* (1993) 68 P. & C.R. 171. The amendment made by the Water Act 2003 s.99(3) (effectively adding (a)) is in consequence of the extension of s.106 to public lateral drains.

[37] 1991 Act s.106(5). The requirements of the undertaker should, it is submitted (although this is not expressly stipulated in the statute), be notified in writing; Shaw's Form PN13 is appropriate.

[38] 1991 Act s.106(5A), inserted by the Water Act 2003 s.99(4).

[39] 1991 Act s.106(6), as amended by the Competition and Service (Utilities) Act 1992 s.35(8), and the Water Act 2003 ss.36(2) and 99(5). On the powers of the WSRA to determine questions, see the 1991 Act s.30A, above, pp.31.

[40] See the 1991 Act s.106(1A), above, p.217.

[41] 1991 Act s.109.

[42] See the 1991 Act s.106(1A), above, p.217.

proposals having been served on the sewerage undertaker,[43] the undertaker has given notice[44] to such person to the effect that it intends to make the communication itself.[45]

Whichever party actually executes the works, the same powers as are conferred by s.158 of the 1991 Act relating to the breaking-up of streets can be exercised.[46] Section 106 does not give the owner or occupier the right to enter or lay pipes on intervening land not owned by him and not forming part of a private street. He will have to negotiate for such rights in the form of easements or wayleaves. A sewerage undertaker making the communication is subject to the same limitation, for in the context of s.107 it has no greater rights than a private individual.[47]

Where the owner or occupier decides to execute the work of communication himself, he must, before commencing the work, give reasonable notice[48] to any person directed by the undertaker to superintend the execution of the work and afford him all reasonable facilities for superintending the carrying out of the work.[49]

Where the sewerage undertaker has given notice to the effect that **9–009**
it intends to execute the work of making the communication, it has "all such rights in respect of the making of the communication as the person desiring it to be made would have".[50] Before starting the work it is entitled to ask for payment of such sum, not exceeding the undertaker's estimate of all the cost of the work, as the undertaker may require to be paid to it, or for reasonable security to be given for payment of the cost of the work.[51] Where any advance payment

---

43 Or within 14 days of the determination of any question by the WSRA. The time limit is to be strictly applied, for the same reasons as those applicable to the 21-day limit in s.106(4): *Barratt Homes Ltd v Dwr Cymru Cyfyngedig (Welsh Water)* [2009] UKSC 13, above, n.8.

44 This notice must be in writing and duly served (1991 Act ss.216 and 219(1)). See also *Epping Forest DC v Essex Rendering* [1983] 1 W.L.R. 158.

45 1991 Act s.107, as amended by the Competition and Service (Utilities) Act 1992 s.35(9) and the Water Act 2003 s.36(2).

46 1991 Act s.108(2), (3).

47 See *Wood v Ealing Tenants Ltd* [1907] 2 K.B. 390.

48 This notice must be in writing and duly served: 1991 Act ss.216 and 219(1).

49 1991 Act s.108(1).

50 ss.107(3)(a). This would include, e.g. the right to enter on private land without payment of compensation, but only where that right is vested in the person in whose place they are acting: see *Wood v Ealing Tenants Ltd* [1907] 2 K.B. 390, decided under the earlier legislation. The powers of s.171 of the 1991 Act would not apply to such a case. If the private owner has no right to cause his drain to run through land belonging to some other person but lying between the premises to be drained and the public sewer (or public lateral drain), the communication cannot be made. A similar position obtains if the sewerage undertaker acts by agreement under s.160 of the Act.

51 1991 Act s.107(3)(b). Having given such notice, it seems that it could be compelled by a mandatory order to do the work.

exceeds the expenses reasonably incurred[52] in the execution of the work, the sewerage undertaker must repay the excess, and if its expenses[53] are not covered by any payment, it may recover the balance from the person for whom the work was done.[54] Any dispute between a sewerage undertaker and any other person as to the reasonableness of the estimate, any requirement of security or whether an excess is payable or expenses recoverable, or the amount of any such expenses, may be referred to the WSRA for determination under s.30A of the 1991 Act.[55]

(e) Offences

9–010 It is expressly made an offence to cause a drain or sewer to communicate with a public sewer (or public lateral drain[56]) without complying with the procedure of ss.106 or 108 of the 1991 Act, or before the expiration of 21 days after the receipt by the undertaker of the notice of proposals under s.106(4).[57] It is also an offence to proceed to make such a communication after a notice has been given to the effect that the authority intends to make the communication itself.[58]

(f) Rights, not duties

9–011 The power to communicate with a public sewer is a right, and not a duty. The sewerage undertaker (or the local authority) cannot, therefore, require the owner or occupier of premises to cause his drains to communicate with a public sewer, unless it can be said that "satisfactory provision has not been made for drainage" of the building, and that the only means of so providing would be by making such communication,[59] and in such an event action would have to be taken by the local authority, not the sewerage undertaker. Thus, where

---

[52] A reasonable sum by way of establishment expenses may be included: Local Government Act 1974 s.36.

[53] i.e. its reasonable expenses, plus establishment expenses.

[54] 1991 Act s.107(4). The means of recovery will be as a simple contract debt under s.293 of the 1936 Act, or by simple action in the local County Court or the High Court.

[55] 1991 Act s.107(4A), inserted by the Competition and Service (Utilities) Act 1992 s.35(9).

[56] See the 1991 Act s.106(1A), above, p.217.

[57] s.109(1). If a person fails to serve proper notice as required by the section, he will not be able to plead the section as a defence in nuisance proceedings brought as a consequence of the connection of his drains to the sewer: *Graham v Wroughton* [1901] 2 Ch. 451.

[58] 1991 Act s.107(2).

[59] See Building Act 1984 s.59.

premises are drained to a cesspit, which is in good order and adequate for the purpose, neither the authority nor the undertaker can, except by offering to pay the cost thereof,[60] require the cesspit to be abolished and main drainage substituted therefor. The local authority would also not be entitled to refuse to cleanse a cesspool or empty a privy, as a means of putting pressure on the owner of the premises to cause them to be communicated with the public sewer.[61]

THE DRAINAGE OF NEW BUILDINGS

The Building Act 1984 gives an effective means of control over the type of drainage proposed for a new building, but as this is exercised by the local authority (and *not* the sewerage undertaker) through the medium of the Building Regulations 2000,[62] it is first important to appreciate the types of work to which, and the circumstances in which, this control is applicable. **9–012**

(a) When the control is effective

In the first place, the control over the drainage of new buildings herein discussed depends on the terms of the Regulations, which apply only with respect to the design and construction of buildings,[63] and alterations and extensions of buildings, and also to the provision of services, fittings or equipment in or in connection with buildings.[64] Control in practice is most effective where plans are required to be submitted before the work is commenced, but these have to be submitted only where the Building Regulations so provide.[65] Where **9–013**

---

[60] See s.113 of the 1991 Act.

[61] Under s.45(5)(a) of the Environmental Protection Act 1990, above, pp.165–166.

[62] SI 2000/2531, as amended. See, generally, *Cross on Local Government Law*, 9th edn (London: Sweet & Maxwell,), paras 19–31–19–52.

[63] s.121 of the Building Act 1984 provides that "building" for the purposes of Pt I of the 1984 Act and any other enactment relating to building regulations "means any permanent or temporary building, and, unless the context otherwise requires, it includes any other structure or erection of whatever kind or nature (whether permanent or temporary)". "Structure or erection" includes a "vehicle, vessel, hovercraft, aircraft or other movable object of any kind in such circumstances as may be prescribed" by building regulations. Note that this definition does not apply to powers under Pt 3 of the 1984 Act (ss.59–90).

[64] Building Act 1984 s.1 and Sch.1.

[65] Building Act 1984 Sch.1 para.2; Building Regulations 2000 (SI 2000/2531) reg.12(2) (building notice or full plans to be submitted in specified cases where work is to be supervised by the local authority); Building Act 1984 s.47 (initial notice to be given jointly by person intending to carry out work and approved inspector where work is to be supervised by the latter).

a building is totally exempt from this control,[66] this section also is inoperative.

(b) Drainage provisions

9–014 When plans are received by the local authority, they must be considered, and if they contravene the provisions of the Building Regulations the authority must reject the plans, and give notice of such rejection to the building owner.[67] If such notice of rejection is not served within the prescribed period,[68] the plans cannot subsequently be rejected. Failure to serve notice of rejection does not of itself legalise any contravening work, but merely destroys the right of the authority to require the building owner to remove the contravening work.[69] Similarly, approval of work which contravenes the Building Regulations does not legalise such work, but the authority again loses its powers to order removal.[70]

The authority has no discretion, as has a local planning authority acting under the Town and Country Planning Act 1990, whether to pass or reject plans; if the Regulations or the Act are contravened, the plans must be rejected; however, if the provisions of the Regulations would be unreasonable in relation to a particular case, they may be dispensed with or relaxed by direction made by the Secretary of State or the local authority.[71]

---

[66] Building Act 1984 s.4(1), as amended by the Education Act 1996 Sch.37 para.59, the School Standards and Framework Act 1998 Sch.31, and the Transport Act 2000 (Consequential Amendments) Order 2001 (SI 2001/4050) art.7(a), exempting specified educational buildings and the buildings of statutory undertakers. Section 4 is to be repealed by the Sustainable and Secure Buildings Act 2004 s.11(2), from a day to be appointed.

[67] Building Act 1984 s.16. The notice must be in writing, and duly signed and served, in accordance with ss.92–94; Shaw's Form BR7 is appropriate. As to the grounds on which an "initial notice" (by which a person intending to carry out work and an approved inspector propose that the work be supervised by the latter) must be rejected, see the 1984 Act s.47(2) and the Building (Approved Inspectors, etc.) Regulations 2000 (SI 2000/2532) reg.8(3) and Sch.3, as amended by SI 2001/3336 reg.8. These include, in the case of an erection or extension of a building, where it is necessary for compliance with the regulations for a proposed drain or private sewer to discharge into an existing sewer, but the notice does not describe such an arrangement.

[68] Five weeks, or such extended period (not more than two months from the deposit of the plans) as may be agreed: Building Act 1984 s.16(12).

[69] Building Act 1984 s.36(5).

[70] In either case, the authority may still prosecute for an offence against the Regulations. It may also take proceedings for an injunction in the High Court, but in the circumstances the court may order the authority to pay compensation to the building owner: Building Act 1984 s.36(6).

[71] Building Act 1984 s.8.

(i) Satisfactory provision

Formerly, the Building Act 1984 itself required plans of a building or an extension to a building to be rejected unless they showed that satisfactory provision was to be made for its drainage.[72] This provision was repealed by the Building (Amendment) Regulations 2001,[73] and requirements concerning drainage are now set out in the Building Regulations 2000.[74] Part H of the Regulations deals with Drainage and Waste Disposal.[75] Requirement H1(1) provides that: **9–015**

> "An adequate system of drainage shall be provided to carry foul water[76] from appliances within the building to one of the following, listed in order of priority:
>
> (a) a public sewer or; where that is not reasonably practicable,
> (b) a private sewer communicating with a public sewer; or, where that is not reasonably practicable,
> (c) either a septic tank which has an appropriate form of secondary treatment or another wastewater treatment system; or, where that is not reasonably practicable,
> (d) a cesspool."

However this "does not apply to the diversion of water which has been used for personal washing or for the washing of clothes, linen or other articles to collection systems for reuse."

Requirement H2 deals with wastewater treatment systems and cesspools and H3,[77] rainwater drainage. Requirement H4 deals with building over sewers.[78] The erection or extension of a building or work involving the underpinning of a building must be carried out in a way that is not detrimental to the building or building extension or to the continued maintenance of the drain, sewer or disposal

---

[72] Building Act 1984 s.21(1).

[73] SI 2001/3335 reg.3(1), as from April 1, 2002.

[74] SI 2000/2531, as amended by SI 2001/3335 reg.2(12) Sch.

[75] See also DTLR, *Building Regulations 2000 Drainage and Waste Disposal Approved Document H* (2002 edn).

[76] In Part H "foul water" means "waste water which comprises or includes (a) waste from a sanitary convenience, bidet or appliance used for washing receptacles for foul waste; or (b) water which has been used for food preparation, cooking or washing": Part H1(2).

[77] As amended by SI 2003/2692 reg.2(6).

[78] Replacing provisions in s.18 of the Building Act 1984, repealed by SI 2001/3335 reg.3(1). Where para.H4 applies, the person must deposit full plans, including particulars of the precautions to be taken to secure compliance, and the local authority must consult the sewerage undertaker: 2000 Regulations regs 12(4A), 14(3)(aa) and 14A, inserted by SI 2001/3335 reg.2(7), (9) and (10).

main[79]; this requirement applies only to work carried out (a) over a drain, sewer or disposal main which is shown on any map of sewers,[80] or (b) on any site or in such a manner as may result in interference with the use of, or obstruction of the access of any person to, any drain, sewer or disposal main which is shown on any map of sewers.

Requirement H5 provides that any system for discharging water to a sewer which is provided pursuant to Requirement H3 is to be separate from that provided for the conveyance of foul water from the building. This applies only to a system provided in connection with the erection or extension of a building where it is reasonably practicable for the system to discharge directly or indirectly to a sewer for the separate conveyance of surface water which is shown on the map of sewers or under construction by the sewerage undertaker or by some other person (where the sewer is the subject of an agreement to make a declaration of vesting pursuant to s.104 of the Water Industry Act 1991).

9–016 Requirement H6 deals with solid waste storage.

These requirements only apply in respect of the drainage of the particular building and the authority cannot reject the plans because the sewerage system into which the drains (otherwise satisfactory) are to discharge, is unsatisfactory.[81]

Section 21(4) of the 1984 Act[82] provides that where plans of a building or of an extension of a building are, in accordance with the Building Regulations, deposited with a local authority, the authority, or on appeal a Magistrates' Court, may require a proposed drain to connect with a sewer[83] where:

> "(a) that sewer is within one hundred feet[84] of the site of the building or, in the case of an extension, the site either of the

---

[79] i.e. any pipe, tunnel or conduit used for the conveyance of effluent to or from a sewage disposal works, which is not a public sewer: H4(2).

[80] i.e. any records kept by a sewerage undertaker under the Water Industry Act 1991 s.199: H4(3).

[81] *Chesterton RDC v Ralph Thompson Ltd* [1947] K.B. 300; "I think, therefore, the court of quarter sessions were right in coming to the conclusion that the only matter they had to consider was the suitability of the particular drain which does connect with the sewer, and they are not concerned with what happens to the drainage of the houses once it passes into the sewer, or whether the sewer itself is satisfactory": per Lord Goddard C.J. at p.306. This concerned the forerunner of the Building Act 1984 s.21(1).

[82] As amended by the Building (Amendment) Regulations 2001 (SI 2001/3335) reg.3(3).

[83] Not necessarily a public sewer.

[84] The measurements must be taken "in a straight line on a horizontal plane": Interpretation Act 1978 s.8. The hundred feet is to be measured, not from the curtilege, but the site of the building drained: *Meyrick v Pembroke Corp* (1912) 76 J.P. 365.

extension or of the original building, and is at a level that makes it reasonably practicable to construct a drain to communicate with it, and, if it is not a public sewer, is a sewer that the person constructing the drain is entitled to use[85]; *and*

(b) the intervening land is land through which that person is entitled to construct a drain."

Any question arising under s.21(4) between a local authority and the person by whom, or on whose behalf, plans are deposited as to whether a proposed drain shall be required to connect with a sewer may, on the application of that person, be determined by a Magistrates' Court.[86] **9–017**

On the other hand, if the authority requires a connection to be made to a sewer which is not within the distance of one hundred feet above-mentioned, the authority must then undertake to "bear so much of the expenses reasonably incurred in constructing, and in maintaining and repairing, the drain as may be attributable to the fact that the distance of the sewer exceeds" that distance.[87] Such a requirement and undertaking are not matters of routine administration, and therefore they must be embodied in a formal resolution of the council if they are to be effective.[88] If any question arises as to the amount of a payment to a person under s.21(5), the question may on his application be determined by a Magistrates' Court, or he may require it to be referred to arbitration.[89]

(ii) Combined drains

The above provision, like its predecessor in the 1875 Act,[90] enables the authority to insist on a separate drain being provided for each building (or each separate premises), and to reject plans providing for drainage in combination, at least where there is an existing sewer available. This is not provided for in as many words in s.21(4), but it seems to follow from the wording of s.22(1),[91] and the authority is, under s.21(4), **9–018**

---

[85] In the case of a private sewer, the person draining thereto must have a right, acquired by grant or prescription, to drain thereto. Because a particular sewer is a public sewer, it does not follow that a particular person must have a right to drain into it, if he can only get access thereto through private land, and this point is therefore covered by the ensuing words of the section: see Building Act 1984 s.21(4).

[86] 1984 Act s.21(3), as amended by SI 2001/3335 reg.3(2).

[87] Building Act 1984 s.21(5).

[88] *Princes Investments Ltd v Frimley and Camberley UDC* [1962] 1 Q.B. 681.

[89] 1984 Act s.21(6).

[90] i.e. s.25 of the 1875 Act: see *Woodford UDC v Stark* (1902) 66 J.P. 536.

[91] "Where a local authority might under the last preceding section require each of two or more buildings to be drained separately into an existing sewer . . ."

apparently entitled only to insist on the drain being made to "connect with a sewer" (which, it is submitted, must mean "connect directly").[92]

Whenever separate drainage could be insisted upon for each of two or more buildings, to be made to communicate with an existing sewer,[93] the authority may as an alternative require the buildings to be drained in combination into the existing sewer, by means of a private sewer (which under the Public Health Acts Amendment Act 1890 s.19, would have been described as a "single private drain"), to be constructed by the owners to the directions of the authority, or (at the option of the authority), by the authority on behalf of the owners.[94]

This power may be exercised subject to the following:

(1) It must appear to the authority that the buildings in question may be drained more economically or advantageously in combination.

(2) Combined drainage cannot be insisted upon, except by agreement with the owners of the buildings concerned, in respect of "any building for the drainage of which plans have been previously passed by the authority".

(3) Combined drainage cannot be insisted upon otherwise than "when the drains of the buildings are first laid".

(4) The proportions in which the expenses of constructing, maintaining and repairing the communicating private sewer are to be borne by the owners concerned, must be fixed by the authority. The authority must give notice of its decision on such a matter to each owner affected,[95] and any owner aggrieved may appeal to the local Magistrates' Court.[96]

(5) Any sewer constructed by the local authority under this provision is not to be deemed to have become a public sewer as a consequence of such construction.[97]

---

[92] Provisions in s.21(4) enabling the local authority alternatively to require a drain to discharge into a cesspool or some other place were repealed by SI 2001/3335 reg.3(3).

[93] If the sewer was constructed before 1937, this must be a public sewer. If it is a private sewer, there must be an easement or some other right to connect to it, as the authority's requirement cannot here override private rights: see e.g. *Wood v Ealing Tenants Ltd* [1907] 2 K.B. 390.

[94] Building Act 1984 s.22(1).

[95] The notice must be in writing, signed by the authorised officer of the authority, and duly served, in accordance with ss.92 to 94 of the 1984 Act. The requirement of writing is mandatory, see *Epping Forest DC v Essex Rendering* [1983] 1 W.L.R. 158.

[96] 1984 Act s.22(4).

[97] 1984 Act s.22(6), and compare s.179(1) of the 1991 Act, Ch.2.

It has been said[98] that it was understood that the practicality of enforcing this has proved to be extremely bureaucratic and time-consuming for local authorities and that there is no evidence that the power has been exercised in practice.

(iii) Appeals

Provision is made by ss.21(3), 21(4), 21(6) and 22(4) of the 1984 Act for a person aggrieved by a decision of the local authority under the provisions hereinbefore discussed to appeal to the Magistrates' Court. Appeal in each such case will be by way of complaint for an order,[99] and the normal procedure of the Magistrates' Courts Act 1980 will then apply. From the decision of the magistrates, either party will be able to appeal to the Crown Court, under s.41 of the Building Act 1984. Alternatively, either party may appeal to the Queen's Bench Divisional Court on a case stated on a point of law.[100] **9–019**

(c) Enforcement of control

This control, effected through the Building Regulations 2000, can be enforced by the following means: **9–020**

(i) *Criminal penalty*. The execution of work without submission of plans, where such are required, the execution of work otherwise than in accordance with the deposited plans, and the execution of work which contravenes the Building Regulations, are made offences by s.35 of the 1984 Act.[101] On conviction by the Magistrates' Court a fine may be imposed, not exceeding level 5 on the standard scale, including a fine not exceeding £50 for each day on which the default continues after conviction. Criminal proceedings may be taken irrespective of the local authority's rights to serve a s.36 notice.

---

[98] DEFRA, Welsh Assembly Government, "Review of Existing Private Sewers and Drains in England and Wales", Consultation Paper, July 2003, para.3.10.

[99] 1984 Act s.103(1); proceedings must be commenced within 21 days: s.103(2).

[100] Magistrates' Courts Act 1980, s.111; and below, Ch.11, p.281.

[101] An information relating to an offence under s.35 may be tried by a Magistrates' Court if laid at any time within (a) two years beginning with the day on which the offence was committed or (b) six months beginning with the date on which evidence sufficient to justify the proceedings comes to the knowledge of the person commencing the proceedings: 1984 Act s.35A, inserted by the Climate Change and Sustainable Energy Act 2006 s.13(1), and amended by the Housing and Regeneration Act 2008 s.317.

(ii) *Removal or alteration of offending work*. If any work to which Building Regulations are applicable contravenes any of those Regulations, the local authority, without prejudice to their right to take proceedings for a fine, may by notice[102] require the owner (a) to pull down or remove the work, or (b) if he so elects, to effect such alterations as may be necessary to make it comply with the Regulations.[103] A broader power to serve a notice exists, in relation to the express powers or duties under Part 1 of the 1984 Act to reject plans, for the removal of work executed without plans having been deposited, notwithstanding the rejection of plans or otherwise than in accordance with the authority's requirements[104] subject to which it passed plans. The specific provisions applicable to building over sewers (s.18) and the provision of drainage (s.21(1), (2)) have, however, been repealed.[105]

The recipient may, within certain time limits,[106] notify[107] the authority of his intention to obtain a written report[108] concerning the work to which the s.36 notice relates. If having considered the report the authority decides to withdraw the notice it may reimburse any expenses reasonably incurred by the recipient as a result of the notice being served, in particular the cost of the report. On the other hand, if no report is submitted, or the local authority does not withdraw its notice, if the owner fails to comply with a s.36 notice within 28 days,[109]

---

[102] A notice under s.36(1) or (2) (called a "Section 36 notice"—s.36(4)) must be in writing, signed by the authorised officer of the authority, and duly served (1984 Act ss.92–95). Shaw's Forms BR21 and BR22 are appropriate. The requirement as to writing is mandatory: *Epping Forest DC v Essex Rendering*, above.

[103] 1984 Act s.36(1). A Notice may validly be served on a person carrying out works who has not made an application for building regulation approval: *Parlett v Kerrier DC, The Independent*, October 6, 1997.

[104] These must be requirements which the authority might have made under s.16 as a "condition of passing plans". Strictly speaking, there is no provision made in s.16 for "conditional approvals", and s.36(2), here referred to, must be read as contemplating a rejection of the plans, coupled with an intimation to the effect that, if certain amendments are made in the plans, they would be passed under the terms of the section. The burden of showing that the work does not comply with the Regulations is on the authority. Thereafter the appellant against the notice must show he has nonetheless complied with them: *Rickards v Kerrier DC* (1987) 151 J.P. 625.

[105] 1984 Act s.36(2).

[106] 28 days, or such longer period allowed by the magistrates under s.36(3).

[107] See n.102 above.

[108] ". . . from a suitably qualified person . . .": s.37(1)(a).

[109] Or such longer period as the Magistrates' Court may on his application allow, s.36(3); for the procedure see s.103.

the authority may itself act in default,[110] and recover its expenses reasonably incurred[111] from him.[112] No notice may be issued under this section after the expiration of 12 months from the completion of the work in question, or if the plans had been passed by the authority, or not rejected within the "prescribed period".[113] There is a right of appeal to a Magistrates' Court under s.40 within 28 days from the giving of a s.36 notice. If the court is satisfied that, although the authority was entitled to give the notice, the purposes of s.36 have been substantially achieved, it may direct the authority to withdraw the notice. Pending final determination, or withdrawal of the appeal, the notice will have no effect. Under s.41 either party may appeal to the Crown Court against the Magistrates' Court decision. Alternatively, on a point of law either party may appeal to the Queen's Bench Division of the High Court by way of case stated.

(iii) A claim may be made for an injunction for the alteration or removal of any work which offends against the Building Regulations. This action may be brought in the High Court, at the suit of the Attorney-General (on the relation of an interested person), or of a person aggrieved. In any such case, the court on granting the injunction may, where the plans had been passed by the local authority, or notice of rejection of plans had not been given within the "prescribed period",[114] order the local authority to pay compensation to the owner of the work.[115]

---

[110] A decision may lawfully be taken to enforce a notice after a substantial lapse of time provided the owner is given a further opportunity to make representations: *R. v Lewisham LBC, ex p. Bello* (unreported, July 27, 2000; lapse of 12 years); see also *R. (on the application of Bello) v Lewisham LBC* [2002] EWHC 1332 (Admin) (decision to proceed now held not to be *Wednesbury* unreasonable).

[111] A reasonable sum by way of establishment expenses may be included: Local Government Act 1974 s.36.

[112] Building Act 1984 s.36(3). The authority's expenses hereunder will be recoverable as a simple contract debt in the local County Court, or the High Court. The expenses will also be a charge on the property, being recoverable from the owner thereof, and should be registered in the local land charges register (see 1984 Act s.107(1), and Ch.11, below, pp.278–279).

[113] Five weeks or such extended period as may be agreed: 1984 Act s.16(12).

[114] Or such longer period as the Magistrates' Court may on his application allow, s.36(3); for the procedure see s.103.

[115] 1984 Act s.36(6). If the court proposes to make an order against the local authority, it must first make the authority a party to the proceedings, if it is not already a party.

(d) Planning control and the drainage of new buildings[116]

9–021 The capacity of existing infrastructure (including sewers) and the need for additional facilities should be taken into account in the preparation of all development plans.[117] In determining whether or not planning permission should be granted for a new development, the inadequacy of the arrangements for sewerage is capable of being a material planning consideration.[118] According to the circumstances, the council may be entitled to refuse permission on the ground that the development would be premature as appropriate sewerage arrangements are not in place or sufficiently advanced; the developer cannot simply rely on the duty of the sewerage undertaker to provide a public sewer where requisitioned under s.98 of the Water Industry Act 1991.[119] Alternatively, the planning authority may grant a *Grampian*[120] condition preventing occupation of the premises in question until adequate sewerage arrangements are in operation,[121] or

---

[116] See J. Bates, *Water and Drainage Law* (London: Sweet & Maxwell, 2010) paras 9.93, 9.94.

[117] Planning Policy Statement 12: Local Spatial Planning, paras 4.8–4.12. Local authorities should undertake timely, effective and conclusive discussions with key infrastructure providers when preparing a core strategy: para.4.10.

[118] Planning Policy, para.6.15; *George Wimpey & Co Ltd v Secretary of State for the Environment* (1978) 250 E.G. 241; *Parkin v Secretary of State for the Environment* [1993] J.P.L. 141 (risk of nuisance from smells from private sewerage system in built-up area); *W.E. Black Ltd v Secretary of State for the Environment* [1997] J.P.L. 37 (risk of flooding); cf. *Ynys Mon BC v Secretary of State for Wales* [1993] J.P.L. 225 (inspector entitled to conclude that the addition of the discharge of six small houses on a proposed development to the discharge of untreated sewage to coastal wasters was not sufficient to justify refusal of planning permission or sewerage grounds).

[119] *George Wimpey*, in respect of s.16 of the Water Act 1973, the forerunner of the 1991 Act s.98 (see pp.82–87). Forbes J. also noted that the duty under s.16 only arose once the private sewer was built, and that itself would require planning permission; *Ynys Mon BC v Secretary of State for the Environment* [1993] J.P.L. 225 (planning authority entitled to raise objections on sewerage grounds notwithstanding the statutory right of connection).

[120] See *Grampian Regional Council v Aberdeen CDC* (1984) 47 P. & C.R. 43.

[121] See *W.E. Black Ltd v Secretary of State for the Environment* [1997] J.P.L. 37 (inspector entitled to impose condition requiring the provision of surface water attenuation/storage works before dwellings were occupied; this was not inconsistent with the objectives of the Water Industry Act 1991, but assisted them by mitigating further stress on the water utilities system). The mere fact that a *Grampian* condition appears to have no reasonable prospects of fulfilment does not mean that planning permission must necessarily be refused as a matter of law: *British Railways Board v Secretary of State for the Environment* [1993] 3 P.L.R. 125, H.L. The Secretary of State is entitled to have a policy against the use of *Grampian* conditions that have no reasonable prospects of fulfilment, but this must not be applied so as to fetter the discretion of an inspector on an appeal: *Morritt v Secretary of State for the Environment, Transport and the Regions* [2000] J.P.L. 371.

require the provision of appropriate arrangements through an agreement under s.106 of the Town and Country Planning Act 1990.[122]

Schedule 3 to the Flood and Water Management Act 2010[123] introduces new provisions in respect of sustainable drainage systems (SUDS). These "mimic natural drainage that would occur on a greenfield site" and typically includes infiltration systems, swales (open, green drains that slow down surface water movement), ponds and wetlands. They reduce "the impacts of flooding by slowing the flow and reducing the volume of water draining from a site."[124] The use of SUDs has been encouraged,[125] but the take up was not regarded as having increased sufficiently as there was no organisation with a duty to adopt and maintain them and developers had an automatic right under ss.106 and 115 of the Water Industry Act 1991 to connect surface water to public surface water sewers and so had no need to change to new drainage methods.[126] Both of these matters are addressed in the 2010 Act.[127]

"Sustainable drainage" means managing rainwater (including snow and other precipitation) with the aim of: (a) reducing damage from flooding; (b) improving water quality; (c) protecting and improving the environment; (d) protecting health and safety; and (e) ensuring the stability and durability of drainage systems.[128] "Drainage system" means a structure[129] designed to receive rainwater except a public sewer,[130] or a natural watercourse.[131] Each part of a drainage system partly in England and partly in Wales is treated as a separate system (except that decisions in relation to one part may be made having regard to the existence and effect of the other).[132]

The Secretary of State (for England) and the Welsh Ministers (for **9–022**
Wales) must, after consultation, publish national standards for the

---

[122] *R. v Canterbury City Council, ex p. Springimage Ltd* [1994] J.P.L. 427.
[123] In force from days to be appointed.
[124] DEFRA, "Flood and Water Management Bill: Impact Assessment—Local Flood Risk Management and the increased use of Sustainable Drainage systems" (October 2, 2009), p.5.
[125] Planning Policy Statement 25, Annex F.
[126] DEFRA, "Impact Assessment", p.5. Systems could be adopted by virtue of agreements under s.106 of the Town and Country Planning Act 1990: see generally *http://www.ciria.com/suds/ [Accessed August 4, 2010]* (website of the Construction Industry Research and Information Association).
[127] See pp.127–130, 217–219.
[128] Sch.3 para.2.
[129] This includes a reference to: (a) any part of an existing or proposed structure; and (b) any feature or aspect of a design that is intended to receive or facilitate the receipt of rainwater: Sch.3 para.1(2).
[130] As defined in s.219(1) of the Water Industry Act 1991: Sch.3 para.1(3).
[131] Sch.3 para.1(1). "Natural watercourse" means a river or stream: Sch.3 para.1(4).
[132] Sch.3 para.3.

implementation of sustainable drainage. These must address the way in which drainage systems are designed, constructed, maintained and operate, and may permit or require approving bodies[133] to form judgments by reference to specified criteria and require approving bodies to have regard to guidance to be issued by them.[134]

Construction work which has drainage implications may not be commenced unless a drainage system for the work has been approved by the approving body.[135] "Construction work" means anything done by way of, in connection with or in preparation for the creation of a building or other structure,[136] and such work has "drainage implications" if the building or structure will affect the ability of land to absorb rainwater. The Secretary of State or Welsh Ministers may by order provide that a specified class of work is to be or not to be treated as construction work; provide for work to be or not to be treated as having drainage implications in specified circumstances; or provide exceptions to para.7(1).[137] If the construction work does not require planning permission, there must be a free-standing application for approval; if it does, the application may be free-standing, or combined with an application for planning permission. In the latter case, the planning authority must consult the approving body (if different) in determining the application for planning permission and inform it of its determination, and when informing the applicant of the determination of the application for planning permission it must also inform the applicant of the approving body's determination of the application for approval.[138]

On considering an application for approval, the approving body must: (a) grant it, if satisfied that the drainage system if constructed as proposed will comply with national standards for sustainable drainage; or (b) refuse it, if not satisfied.[139]

9–023 An approval may be subject to conditions; in particular, a condition may:

---

[133] i.e. a unitary authority or the county council in a two-tier area, being the council for the area in which the drainage system is, or is to be constructed, unless another body is appointed by the Secretary of State or Welsh Ministers as approving body for drainage systems in all areas or in one or more specified areas and for all or specified purposes: Sch.3 para.6.

[134] Sch.3 paras 4 and 5.

[135] Sch.3 para.7(1). This does not apply to work requiring development consent under s.31 of the Planning Act 2008 (nationally significant infrastructure projects): Sch.3 para.7(3).

[136] For the avoidance of doubt, anything that covers land (such as a patio or other surface) is a structure for the purposes, para.7(2)(a): Sch.3 para.7(5).

[137] Sch.3 para.7(4).

[138] Sch.3 paras 8–10.

[139] Sch.3 para.11(1).

(a) relate to the construction of the drainage system (which may involve modification of the proposal for construction);

(b) provide that approval takes effect only if and when the applicant provides a non-performance bond[140];

(c) relate to inspection; or

(d) require the payment of fees chargeable[141] by reference to work undertaken in connection with approval.[142]

Before determining an application the approving body must consult:

(a) any sewerage undertaker with whose public sewer the drainage system is proposed to communicate;

(b) the Environment Agency, if the drainage system directly or indirectly involves the discharge of water into a watercourse;

(c) the relevant highway authority for a road which the approving body thinks may be affected;

(d) British Waterways, if the approving body thinks that the drainage system may directly or indirectly involve the discharge of water into or under a waterway managed by them;

(e) an internal drainage board, if the approving body thinks that the drainage system may directly or indirectly involve the discharge of water into an ordinary watercourse[143] within the board's district.[144]

As soon as is reasonably practicable after determining an application for approval, the approving body must notify the applicant or, in the case of a combined application, the planning authority, and (b) any person consulted under para.11(3).[145]

A non-performance bond is a bond of a kind and to a value speci- **9–024**
fied in a condition imposed on the grant of an application for approval. Its effect must be that the value of the bond is payable to the approving body if it certifies that the drainage system has been

[140] under para.12.
[141] under para.13.
[142] Sch.3 para.11(2).
[143] Within the meaning of s.72 of the Land Drainage Act 1991.
[144] Sch.3 para.11(3).
[145] Sch.3 para.11(4). The Secretary of State or Welsh Ministers may make regulations: Sch.3 para.11(5).

constructed in a manner that is not in accordance with the approved proposals, or is unlikely to be completed. Before giving such a certificate the approving body must consult the applicant for approval ("the developer"). Where it gives a certificate, it must notify the developer, and may undertake any work necessary to ensure that the drainage system is completed in such a manner as to make it likely to operate in compliance with national standards for sustainable drainage. The sums received under the bond may be applied to the expenses of that work, and any excess is to be paid to the developer. In requiring a non-performance bond an approving body must specify a value which does not exceed the best estimate of the maximum likely cost of work required to ensure that the drainage system accords with the approved proposals.[146]

The Secretary of State or Welsh Ministers may issue guidance about what amounts may be required by way of non-performance bonds, to which approving bodies must have regard[147]; must by regulations provide for fees for applications for approval[148]; must by order provide for the enforcement of the requirement for approval in para.7(1)[149]; and may issue guidance about the process of seeking and obtaining approval to which approving bodies must have regard.[150]

Section 21 of the Building Act 1984[151] does not apply to works in connection with which approval is required in accordance with this Schedule.[152]

THE IMPROVEMENT OF EXISTING DRAINS

9–025 Apart altogether from the question of nuisances and "unsatisfactory" drains, considered hereafter,[153] the sewerage undertaker or the local authority may take certain action to secure the improvement of existing private drains—at their expense. Further, where a private individual proposes himself to alter an existing drainage system, the local authority can exercise control over such work.

[146] Sch.3 para.12(1)–(5).
[147] Sch.3 para.12(6).
[148] Sch.3 para.13.
[149] Sch.3 para.14.
[150] Sch.3 para.15.
[151] See above, pp.226–227.
[152] Sch.3 para.26.
[153] Below, pp.239–247.

(a) Water Industry Act 1991 s.113: power to alter drains

Under this section, a sewerage undertaker may close any existing drain or sewer[154] which communicates with a public sewer (or public lateral drain)[155] or a cesspool,[156] and fill up any such cesspool, and do any work necessary for these purposes. Such works are carried out at the expense of the undertaker. This power is exercisable only in the following circumstances: **9–026**

(i) The drain or sewer in question, though sufficient for the effectual drainage of the premises,[157] must either be "not adapted to the general sewerage system of the area" or, in the opinion of the undertaker, "otherwise objectionable".

(ii) Before exercising the power to close the existing drain or sewer, the undertaker must first provide in a position "equally convenient to the owner of the premises, a drain or sewer which (a) is equally effectual for the drainage of the premises; and (b) communicates with a public sewer" (or public lateral drain).[158]

(iii) Notice[159] of the undertaker's proposals must be given to the owner of the premises in question and, if he is aggrieved as regards either the position or the sufficiency[160] of the drain or sewer proposed to be provided by the undertaker, he may refer the matter to the WSRA under s.30A of the 1991 Act.[161]

(b) 1984 Act s.61: notice of drain repairs, etc.

This section prohibits the repair, reconstruction or alteration of the course of any underground[162] drain that communicates with a **9–027**

---

[154] The expression is here clearly intended to refer to private sewers only; the alteration, closure, etc. of public sewers (or public lateral drains) could be effected under s.116 of the 1991 Act.

[155] See the 1991 Act s.106(1A), above, p.217.

[156] See definition in s.113(7).

[157] If the drainage is not so sufficient, action could normally be taken under s.59 of the 1984 Act.

[158] Substituted drainage communicating immediately with a cesspool does not, therefore, comply with the section.

[159] Such notice must be in writing and duly served (1991 Act ss.216 and 219(1)); Shaw's Form PH60 is appropriate.

[160] But not on other grounds.

[161] 1991 Act s.113, as amended by the Competition and Service (Utilities) Act 1992 s.35(1). As to the WSRA's powers under s.30A, see above, p.31.

[162] Note the limitation of the operation of the section.

sewer,[163] cesspool or other receptacle for drainage, without giving to the local authority[164] at least 24 hours' notice[165] of an intention to do so. This prohibition does not apply to the following:

(i) a case of emergency; but in any such case, the prohibition applies to the covering over of the drain or sewer in question;

(ii) so much of any drain or sewer constructed by, or belonging to, a railway company as runs under, across or along their railway;

(iii) so much of any drain or sewer constructed by, or belonging to, dock undertakers, as is situated in or on land of the undertakers that is held or used by them for the purposes of their undertaking.

(c) 1984 Act ss.62 and 81: controls over disconnecting of drains

9–028 Where the use of a drain is being discontinued, the local authority may require it to be disconnected and sealed at such points as they may reasonably specify.[166] Disputes as to the reasonableness of such specifications may be determined by the Magistrates' Court.[167] In particular no person can be required to perform work on land in respect of which he has no right so to do.[168] Knowingly to fail to comply with a local authority requirement and failing to give a minimum of 48 hours' notice to the local authority before such compliance are offences punishable by a fine.[169]

The local authority may serve a notice[170] requiring persons engaged in the demolition of a building to disconnect and seal any sewer or drain in or under the building, at such points as it may reasonably require and/or to remove such a conduit and seal any connecting sewer or drain.[171] At least 48 hours' notice of compliance of such a requirement must be given and default is an offence punishable by a fine. Work may not be required beyond the demolition site where the person engaged in the demolition lacks the appropriate rights. In event of non-compliance the local authority may perform

---

[163] Not necessarily a public sewer; but even a private sewer must itself drain into a public sewer or a receptacle for drainage.
[164] *Not* the sewerage undertaker in this case.
[165] This must be in writing and duly served (see 1984 Act ss.92–94).
[166] 1984 Act s.62.
[167] 1984 Act s.62(2).
[168] 1984 Act s.62(3).
[169] 1984 Act s.62(4), (5).
[170] In writing and duly served, ss.92–94.
[171] 1984 Act ss.81, 82(1)(e), (f).

the works and recover the expenses of doing so.[172] Where a local authority has power to serve a notice in case of demolition works under s.81, the disconnection powers under s.61 are inapplicable.[173]

UNSATISFACTORY DRAINS

The Public Health Acts 1936 and 1961, and the Building Act 1984 vest several distinct powers in local authorities which enable them to deal with drains or private sewers that are unsatisfactory in one respect or another. These powers overlap to some extent, but it seems that the authority has a discretion in selecting which procedure to follow. The most specific of these powers is s.60 of the Building Act 1984, dealing with the condition of certain pipes and appurtenances to drains. Section 59 deals with cases where satisfactory provision has not been made for the drainage of a building, and the nuisance clauses of the 1936 Act, which are not confined in their operation to buildings, provide a residuary control whereby nuisances in drains may be abated. There is also a summary power given by s.17 of the 1961 Act to remedy stopped up drains, which is of great use in practice. In addition, a local authority may act as contractor, on the application of the owner or occupier of premises, to cleanse or repair drains, water-closets, sinks or gullies.[174] **9–029**

(a) Ventilation, etc. of drains

If it appears to the local authority that on any premises there is a contravention of any requirements contained in s.60 of the Building Act 1984,[175] it may by notice[176] require the owner or the occupier of the premises to execute such work as may be necessary to remedy the matter; in default of compliance therewith, the local authority may do the work itself, and recover the expenses reasonably incurred[177] by it from the person in default.[178] **9–030**

---

[172] 1984 Act ss.82(6) and 99.

[173] See 1984 Act s.62(6).

[174] 1961 Act s.22.

[175] As amended by the Water Act 1989 Sch.8 para.7, Sch.27 Pt I.

[176] This notice must be in writing, signed by the authorised officer of the authority, and duly served (see 1984 Act ss.92–94). Shaw's Form PH15 is appropriate.

[177] A reasonable sum by way of establishment expenses may be added to these: Local Government Act 1974 s.36.

[178] 1984 Act s.60(4), (5). The expenses will be recoverable as a simple contract debt in the County Court or the High Court (1984 Act s.107). If the owner of the premises is the party charged, it seems that the expenses will be a charge on the premises (1984 Act ss.107(1) and 129) and should, therefore, be registered in the local land charges register. See also Ch.11, below, pp.278–279.

The requirements specified in the section are as follows:

(i) no pipe for conveying rain water from a roof shall be used for the purpose of conveying the soil or drainage from any sanitary convenience;

(ii) the soil pipe from every water-closet[179] shall be properly ventilated;

(iii) no pipe for conveying surface water[180] from any premises shall be permitted to act as a ventilating shaft to any drain or sewer carrying foul water.[181]

(b) Satisfactory provision for drainage

9–031 Section 59 of the 1984 Act is a more general section, enabling the local authority to require (inter alia) satisfactory provision to be made for the drainage of an existing building. The control is exercised in a manner similar to that applicable to s.60 of the Act, in that the authority must serve a notice,[182] and may then act itself in default of compliance, and recover its expenses in so acting from the party in default. Only the owner[183] of the premises may be required to make satisfactory provision for drainage, but either the owner or the occupier[184] may be required to take the other action referred to in s.60. It should also be noted that the section applies only to buildings,[185] and not to all types of premises.[186]

Action may be taken by the local authority under the section whenever the authority considers that in the case of a building:

---

[179] Defined in s.126, and see below, Ch.10, p.258.
[180] This expression includes "water from roofs": 1984 Act s.126.
[181] This expression is not defined in the Act.
[182] Shaw's Form PN23D is appropriate. In the case of a break in a private sewer rendering it prejudicial to health, the notice may be served only on the owners of premises above the break: *Swansea City Council v Jenkins* (1994) 158 J.P. 952.
[183] As defined by s.126 of the 1984 Act: Ch.11, below, pp.285–286.
[184] The local authority has a discretion in selecting the appropriate party, but it must take into consideration the rights and duties as between the owner and the occupier, where appropriate: *Croydon Corp v Thomas* [1947] K.B. 386.
[185] See above, p.223.
[186] As defined by s.126 of the 1984 Act (which include buildings, lands, easements and hereditaments of any tenure).

"(a) satisfactory provision[187] has not been, and ought to be, made for drainage[188];

(b) a cesspool,[189] private sewer, drain, soil pipe, rain water pipe, spout, sink or other necessary appliance provided for the building, is insufficient or, in the case of a private sewer or drain communicating directly or indirectly with a public sewer, is so defective as to admit subsoil water;

(c) a cesspool or other such work or appliance as aforesaid provided for the building is in such a condition as to be prejudicial to health[190] or a nuisance[191]; or

(d) a cesspool, private sewer or drain formerly used for the drainage of the building, but no longer used for it, is prejudicial to health or a nuisance."

Paragraphs (a) and (b) of this subsection cannot be invoked in respect of any building which belongs to a statutory undertaker[192] or the Civil Aviation Authority or a person who holds a licence under Ch.1 of Pt 1 of the Transport Act 2000 (air traffic services) and which is held or used by them for purposes of their undertaking, other than houses,[193] or buildings used as offices or showrooms which do not form part of a railway station[194] or in the case of the Civil Aviation Authority not being on an aerodrome which it owns.[195]

---

[187] This expression is not expressly defined in the section, except that it is provided in s.59(3) that subss.(4), (5) and (6) of s.21 shall apply to the present section. If the drains are sufficient, the authority cannot use the present section to secure an improvement therein at the expense of the owner of the premises. If the sewerage undertaker decides to alter a private system of drainage, it may do so under s.113 of the 1991 Act, or if it wishes to alter its own sewerage system it may do so under s.116, but in either case any consequential alterations to private drains or sewers will have to be executed at the expense of the undertaker: see *St Martin's-in-the-Field Vestry v Ward* [1897] 1 Q.B. 40.

[188] The words "as defined in section 21(2) above" were repealed by the Building (Amendment) Regulations 2001 (SI 2001/3335) reg.3(4)(a) from April 1, 2002. This provided that " 'drainage' includes the conveyance, by means of a sink and any other necessary appliance, of refuse water and the conveyance of rain-water from roofs." The definition was then inserted in s.36 as subs.(5) by reg.3(4)(b), and numbered as subs.(6) by SI 2002/440 reg.4.

[189] See definition in s.126 of the 1984 Act, and below, p.258.

[190] i.e. "injurious, or likely to cause injury, to health": 1984 Act s.126.

[191] Below, pp.243–247.

[192] See definition in s.126 of the 1984 Act: these include sewerage undertakers under the 1991 Act, as operating an "other public undertaking".

[193] i.e. "a dwelling-house, whether a private dwelling-house or not": 1984 Act s.126.

[194] It seems that a house which forms part of a railway station is outside this special exemption, and subject to the control afforded by the section.

[195] 1984 Act s.59(4), (5), as amended by s.83(9) Sch.6 of the Airports Act 1986 and the Transport Act 2000 (Consequential Amendments) Order 2001 (SI 2001/4050) Sch. para.7. Subs.(4) and (5) are to be repealed, from a day to be appointed, by the Sustainable and Secure Buildings Act 2004 s.5(b), 11(2), Sch.

9–032 From a day to be appointed, s.59(1)(c) also applies to sustainable drainage systems,[196] and for that purpose it does not matter whether the drainage system, or any part of it, is adopted under Sch.3,[197] and a reference to a local authority is to be treated as a reference to the relevant approving body.[198]

The recipient of a notice may appeal to a Magistrates' Court on specified grounds.[199] The sewerage undertaker is entitled to be heard as an interested party on such an appeal that raises the defence that the sewer in question is in fact a public sewer.[200]

(c) Power to repair and unblock drains

9–033 Section 17(1) of the Public Health Act 1961[201] provides that where it appears to a local authority that a drain or private sewer[202] is not sufficiently maintained and kept in good repair and can be sufficiently repaired at a cost not exceeding £250, the authority may, after giving not less than seven days' notice to the person or persons concerned, cause the drain or sewer to be repaired; the authority may thus take the remedial action itself, without having to follow the more dilatory procedure of s.59 of the Building Act 1984, under which it must first serve a notice and wait for the person on whom the notice is served to default. By s.17(3) the local authority may give notice[203] requiring the owner or occupier of premises whereon it seems that a drain or sewer is blocked up to remedy the situation within 48 hours. If the notice is not complied with, the local authority may carry out the remedial work. For valid service of such a notice it is sufficient that it appears to the local authority that a drain upon the premises is blocked, even if it later transpires that the blockage is not in fact on those premises.[204] In *Rotherham BC v Dodds*[205] the Court of Appeal indicated that in such cases the court might properly use its power under what is now s.17(6) to relieve in whole or part any financial

---

[196] As defined by regulations under the Flood and Water management Act 2010 Sch.3 para.17(5): see pp.127–130, 233–236.
[197] See pp.233–236.
[198] 2010 Act Sch.3 para.26. For the definition of "approving body", see p.234.
[199] 1984 Act s.102. See below, pp.280–281.
[200] *R. v Preston Magistrates' Court, ex p. North West Water Ltd* [2000] E.H.L.R. 390.
[201] In this Part of the 1961 Act all the definitions of Pt 2 of the 1936 Act apply: 1961 Act s.1(1). Section 17 was substituted by the Local Government (Miscellaneous Provisions) Act 1982 s.27(1), and amended by the Building Act 1984 Sch.6, para.8.
[202] Or water-closet, waste pipe or soil pipe.
[203] See Shaw's Form PN75.
[204] *Rotherham BC v Dodds* [1986] 1 W.L.R. 1367.
[205] *Rotherham BC v Dodds*

liability arising from remedial action. Where powers under s.17(1) are exercised, expenses of the authority incurred under the section are recoverable from the person concerned,[206] to a maximum of £250. Where powers under s.17(3) are exercised, expenses are recoverable from the person on whom the notice was served; these are not subject to the £250 limit. The expenses may be apportioned. If they are not in excess of £10, the authority may remit and not attempt to recover them. In proceedings for recovery of expenses, the court must inquire whether the drain or sewer was in fact not sufficiently maintained and kept in good repair; and if the court considers that the authority was not justified in so concluding, the authority will not be able to recover the expenses.

A notice under s.17(3) may be served only upon the owner or occupier of the premises at which the blockage occurs. Under s.35 of the Local Government (Miscellaneous Provisions) Act 1976,[207] the owner or occupier of premises *served* by a *private sewer* may by notice[208] be required to remove the blockage. Such work may be performed by the local authority in default which may then recover its reasonable expenses from the persons served by the sewer.[209]

(d) The nuisance clauses

A detailed discussion of the provisions of Pt 3 of the Environmental Protection Act 1990 dealing with statutory nuisances (ss.79 to 82 inclusive) would be out of place in the present work,[210] but it should be appreciated that action may be taken under these provisions in a proper case, to secure the abatement of a nuisance in a private sewer or drain, or a cesspool or any other appliance used in connection with a private drainage system and, in certain circumstances, in respect of a public sewer or sewage works vested in the sewerage undertaker.[211] **9–034**

Statutory nuisances may exist as a consequence of a variety of causes. Those of importance for present purposes include "any premises[212] in

---

206 i.e. in relation to a water-closet, waste pipe or soil pipe, the owner or occupier of the premises on which it is situated, and, in relation to a drain or private sewer, any person owning any premises drained by means of it and also, in the case of a sewer, the owner of the sewer: s.17(2).

207 As amended by s.102(2) and Sch.7 of the Local Government Act 1985.

208 See s.44 of the 1976 Act ("notice" means "notice in writing"). Shaw's Form ML30 is appropriate.

209 s.35(2), (3). See Shaw's Form ML30A.

210 See *Cross on Local Government Law*, 9th edn (London: Sweet & Maxwell) paras 19–66–19–81.

211 See below.

212 This expression is defined by s.79(7) of the 1991 Act to include "land".

such a state as to be prejudicial to health or a nuisance"[213]; "fumes or gas emitted from premises so as to be prejudicial to health or a nuisance"[214]; "any dust, steam, smell or other effuvia arising on industrial, trade or business premises and being prejudicial to health or a nuisance"[215]; and "any accumulation or deposit which is prejudicial to health or a nuisance"[216]; and any insects emanating from relevant industrial, trade or business premises[217] and being prejudicial to health or a nuisance.[218]

It was held in respect of the forerunners to the first of these classes (now the 1990 Act s.79(1)(a))[219] that the term "premises" did not include a public sewer or sewerage works vested in the local authority or sewerage undertaker.[220] It cannot have been Parliament's intention that the "most difficult and thankless task" to improve sewerage arrangements imposed on local sanitary boards by the 1875 Act was to be made subject to the procedure in respect of statutory nuisances, under which the justices would have been entitled to substitute their view for that of the local board as to what steps should be taken. The relevant class of statutory nuisance was confined to cases where the premises themselves were "decayed, dilapidated, dirty; or out of order."[221] This limitation to the scope of the statutory nuisance procedure has been held to remain in effect in respect of the head of

---

213 1990 Act s.79(1)(a).

214 1990 Act s.79(1)(c).

215 1990 Act s.79(1)(d). By s.79(7), " 'industrial, trade or business premises' means premises used for any industrial, trade or business purposes or premises not so used on which matter is burnt in connection with any industrial, trade or business process, and premises are used for industrial purposes where they are used for the purposes of any treatment or process as well as where they are used for the purposes of manufacturing."

216 1990 Act s.79(1)(e).

217 i.e. premises that are industrial, trade or business premises as defined in subs.(7), excluding agricultural land of various descriptions, land included in an SSSI, and land covered by, and the waters of, any river or watercourse, that is neither a sewer nor a drain, or any lake or pond ("sewer," "drain" and "lake or pond" as defined in the Water Resources Act 1991): s.79(7C), (7D), inserted by the Clean Neighbourhoods and Environment Act 2005 s.101(5).

218 s.79(1)(fa), inserted by the 2005 Act s.101(2). This does not apply to insects that are wild animals included in Sch.5 to the Wildlife and Countryside Act 1981 (protected animals) unless they are included in respect of s.9(5) of that Act only: s.79(5A), inserted by the 2005 Act s.101(3). See "Insect nuisance associated with sewage treatment works" (July 2006, DEFRA website).

219 Public Health Act 1875 s.91.1; Public Health Act 1936 s.92(1)(a).

220 *R. v Parlby* (1889) 22 Q.B.D. 520; *Fulham Vestry v London CC* [1897] 2 Q.B. 76. *Parlby* concerned a complaint by one local authority that sewerage works located in its area by the local sanitary board for an adjacent area were a statutory nuisance.

221 See Wills J. in *Parlby* at p.525. This interpretation was endorsed in *Birmingham City Council v Oakley* [2001] 1 All E.R. 385, per Lord Slym at 390, 392 and Lord Clyde at 398–399.

nuisance now found in s.79(1)(a).[222] There was a presumption of construction, not displaced, that the word "premises" here had the same meaning as under the previous legislation. However, the limitation has been held not to apply in respect of the head of nuisance found in s.79(1)(d), which had no exact counterpart in the 1875 and 1936 legislation.[223] The definition of statutory nuisances had been entirely re-cast by the 1990 Act. While the terms of what was now s.79(1)(a) were identical to its predecessors and the *Parlby* interpretation remained applicable, the same was not true of s.79(1)(d), even though that meant that the term "premises" would have a different meaning under the two provisions. The policy arguments behind *Parlby* did not apply in 2003 as they did in 1889 so as to require the same approach to be adopted to s.79(1)(d); the sewerage undertaker would be entitled to rely on the defence of best practicable means under s.80(9). The court held, accordingly, that proceedings could in principle be taken under s.79(1)(d) in respect of the smell arising from sewage treatment works vested in a sewerage undertaker.[224] It is submitted that proceedings in respect of public sewers or sewerage works might also be taken under s.79(1)(c) which also had no exact counterpart in the previous legislation.

"Prejudicial to health" and "nuisance" are phrases that have been **9–035** subject to much litigation. Only the former is defined in s.79(7) of the 1990 Act as meaning "injurious, or likely to cause injury, to health". If this can be established, it is not necessary to establish a nuisance as well.[225] It is now clear that "nuisance" in this context is to be given its ordinary common law meaning as either a *public* nuisance (to a class of Her Majesty's subjects as such) or a *private* nuisance. The latter involves two properties: the defendant's, where the cause arises, and the plaintiff's, which suffers the nuisance, inconvenience, etc.; no statutory nuisance exists where premises are in such a state as to interfere only with the personal comfort of the occupiers.[226] Where a statutory nuisance exists by virtue of premises being prejudicial to health or a nuisance it is irrelevant that the premises are empty.[227]

---

[222] *East Riding of Yorkshire Council v Yorkshire Water Services Ltd* [2000] Env. L.R. 7 (public sewer cannot be "premises" for the purposes of s.79(1)(a)); followed by the Divisional Court in *London Borough of Hounslow v Thames Water Utilities Ltd* [2003] EWHC 1197 (Admin).

[223] *London Borough of Hounslow v Thames Water Utilities Ltd*

[224] Guidance has subsequently been provided in DEFRA, "Code of Practice on Odour Nuisance from Sewage Treatment Works" (2006, DEFRA website).

[225] *Betts v Penge UDC* [1942] 2 K.B. 154, read with *National Coal Board v Thorne* [1976] 1 W.L.R. 543.

[226] *Betts v Penge UDC.*

[227] *Coventry City Council v Doyle* [1981] 1 W.L.R. 1325.

Where a statutory nuisance is alleged to exist, and the authority is so satisfied, it is its duty to serve an abatement notice[228] on the "person responsible for the nuisance", which means the person "to whose act, default, or sufferance the nuisance is attributable".[229]

The notice may impose all or any of the following requirements:

"(a) requiring the abatement of the nuisance or prohibiting or restricting its occurrence or recurrence;

(b) requiring the execution of such works, and the taking of such other steps, as may be necessary for any of those purposes."

9–036 It must also specify the time or times within which the requirements of the notice are to be complied with.[230] Non-compliance without reasonable excuse is an offence;[231] whether or not it institutes a prosecution, the local authority may itself take action to abate the nuisance,[232] and recover expenses.[233] If the authority is of the opinion that a prosecution would afford an inadequate remedy, it may take proceedings in the High Court.[234] A person served with a notice may appeal to a Magistrates' Court.[235] Under s.82 of the 1990 Act, any "person aggrieved"[236] by the existence of a statutory nuisance may make a complaint to a Magistrates' Court, and a similar procedure and penalties apply as in the case of a local authority but without the prior need to serve an abatement notice or its equivalent.

It will be observed that this procedure is advantageous to the local authority, in that a decision as to the legality of the proceedings is

---

[228] As to service of notices under the 1990 Act, see s.160. Shaw's Form EPA30 is appropriate.

[229] 1990 Act ss.79(7), 80(2). If the nuisance arises from a defect of a structural character, the notice must instead be served on the owner of the premises (i.e. the premises which are prejudicial to health, even where the structural defect is on other premises: *Pollway Nominees v Havering LBC* (1989) 21 H.L.R. 462, in respect of the Public Health Act 1936); if the person responsible cannot be found or the nuisance has not yet occurred, it must instead be served on the owner or occupier of the premises.

[230] 1990 Act s.80(1).

[231] 1990 Act s.80(4)–(10). It is a defence to prove that the best practicable means were used to prevent, or counteract the effects of, the nuisance: s.79(7), subject to limits set out in s.79(8).

[232] 1990 Act s.81(3).

[233] 1990 Act s.81(4).

[234] 1990 Act s.81(5), (6).

[235] 1990 Act s.80(3) and the Statutory Nuisance (Appeals) Regulations 1990 1995 (SI 1995/2644), as amended by (for England) SI 2006/771 reg.2(2) and (for Wales) SI 2007/117 reg.2(2).

[236] See Ch.11, below, p.281. It has been held that the occupier of a single flat could not be a "person aggrieved" in relation to the whole block where the statutory nuisance of which he complained related only to his own flat: *Birmingham City Council v McMahon* (1987) 86 L.G.R. 63.

obtained from the court before the authority has acted in default and expended money on a private individual's premises. On the other hand, where proceedings are taken under s.59 of the Building Act 1984, default action will have to be taken first, and the legality of the authority's proceedings will be tested normally only after money has been expended, and in proceedings taken to recover such moneys from the party charged. Action under s.59 will, however, normally be more expeditious than nuisance proceedings.

(e) Improper construction or repair

If a water-closet, drain or soil pipe is so constructed or repaired as to be prejudicial to health[237] or a nuisance,[238] the person who undertook or executed the construction or repair will be liable to prosecution for an offence, unless he can show the prejudice to health or nuisance could not have been avoided by the exercise of reasonable care.[239] **9–037**

LOAN OF CONVENIENCES

In any case where work is being carried out at premises by a local authority or by the owner or occupier in pursuance of a requirement under s.59 of the 1984 Act,[240] the local authority may supply on loan any temporary sanitary conveniences required in substitution for any water-closet or other sanitary convenience disconnected as a consequence of the work.[241] Such a loan may be made only at the request of the occupier of the premises; the request need not be made in writing. The conveniences may be used free of charge for the first seven days, but the authority is entitled to make a charge for supplying, removing and cleansing any conveniences lent for more than seven days. If the works are necessary because of some defect in a public sewer, no charge at all may be made under the section. **9–038**

THE DRAINAGE OF TRADE PREMISES

The drainage of trade premises is regulated by Ch.3 of Pt 4 of the Water Industry Act 1991, which applies in particular to the discharge **9–039**

---

[237] See 1984 Act s.126.
[238] Above, p.245.
[239] 1984 Act s.63.
[240] Above, pp.240–242.
[241] 1984 Act s.67, as amended by the Water Act 1989 Sch.27 Pt 1.

of trade effluent into public sewers (or public lateral drains).[242] There is a power, not as yet exercised, to apply Ch.3 to other effluents.[243] It is now the duty of every sewerage undertaker, the Director and the Secretary of State in exercising their functions under this Chapter with respect to any discharge of "industrial waste water"[244] to secure that the specified requirements[245] are met in respect of that discharge.[246]

These requirements are that collecting systems and treatment plants for industrial waste water shall be subject to such pre-treatment as is required to protect the health of staff, ensure that the systems, plant and associated equipment are not damaged, ensure that the operation of the plant and the treatment of sludge are not impeded, that discharges do not affect the environment or prevent receiving waters from complying with other EC Directives and ensure that sludge can be disposed of safely in an environmentally acceptable manner. This duty is enforceable under s.18 of the 1991 Act.[247]

(a) Definitions

9–040 Trade effluent is defined in s.141(1) of the 1991 Act as meaning, subject to s.139,[248] "any liquid, either with or without particles of matter in suspension in the liquid, which is wholly or in part produced in the course of any trade or industry carried on at trade premises" and, in relation to any trade premises, means "any such

---

[242] See generally, guidelines issued by Water UK, "Trade effluent discharged to the sewer. Guidelines for control and charging" (2008); and "Guidelines for issue of trade effluent consents. Procedure used by water and sewerage companies" (2008) (see *http://www.water.org.uk [Accessed August 4, 2010]*). The discharge of trade effluent direct into "streams" is regulated by the Water Resources Act 1991, and now the Environmental Permitting Regulations 2010, discussed above, pp.167–202. The discharge of such effluent direct into the sea is in part regulated by the 1991 Act, but at common law the person discharging any matter into the sea will be responsible for any nuisance thereby caused: *Hobart v Southend-on-Sea Corp* (1906) 75 L.J.K.B. 305.

[243] 1991 Act s.139. A new s.139 is to be substituted by the Water Act 2003 s.88(1). This will provide a more flexible power for the Secretary of State to provide by order, in relation to discharge into public sewers, that a liquid or other matter of a specified description shall be treated as if it were trade effluent; or that the discharge restrictions (i.e. restrictions under s.106(2)(a), (b) or s.111(1)(a), (b)) shall not apply to such a liquid or other matter and that the liquid shall be deemed not to be trade effluent; and this is so whether or not the liquid or other matter would otherwise constituted "trade effluent" under the legislation. References to a "liquid" are to a liquid either with or without particles of matter in suspension in the liquid.

[244] For the definition, see above, p.45.

[245] SI 1994/2841 Sch.4.

[246] Urban Waste Water Treatment (England and Wales) Regulations 1994 (SI 1994/2841) reg.7(1).

[247] reg.7(7).

[248] Amendment inserted by the Water Act 2003 s.88(4).

liquid which is so produced in the course of any trade or industry carried on at those premises" but does not include "domestic sewage". "Domestic sewage" is not defined under the 1991 Act, and it is presumably intended to be understood in much the same sense as water supplied for "domestic purposes" in the Waterworks Clauses Act 1847.[249] It seems that neither the character of the effluent nor the nature of the premises producing the effluent is decisive. The purpose of the activity producing the effluent would be more significant.[250]

To understand the expression "trade effluent" it is also necessary to appreciate the definition of "trade premises". By the same section of the 1991 Act it is provided that "'trade premises' means . . . any premises used or intended to be used for carrying on any trade or industry", but it does not define "trade" or "industry", and these words must therefore be given their ordinary dictionary meanings. However, any land or premises used or intended for use (in whole or part and whether or not for profit) for agricultural or horticultural purposes or for fish farming, or for scientific research or experiment, are deemed to be premises used for trade or industry.

(b) The discharge of trade effluent

Section 118 of the 1991 Act provides that the occupier of any trade **9–041**
premises may discharge into the sewerage undertaker's public sewers (or public lateral drains)[251] any trade effluent proceeding from those premises, with the sewerage undertaker's consent, which may be "deemed" or express. If, in the case of trade premises, any trade effluent is discharged without such consent or an authorisation derived from an agreement under s.129 of the 1991 Act,[252] the occupier of the premises is guilty of an offence.[253]

---

[249] "If the purpose is one for which, according to the ordinary habits of domestic life, people require water in their houses, the purpose is a domestic purpose": per Atkinson J. in *Willesden Corp and Municipal Mutual Insurance Ltd's Arbitration, Re* [1944] 2 All E.R. 600, at p.602.

[250] See *Thames Water Authority v Blue and White Laundrettes Ltd* [1980] 1 W.L.R. 700.

[251] See the 1991 Act s.106(1A), above, p.217.

[252] See below, pp.255–256. Where a person prosecuted under s.118(5) relies by way of defence on the existence of a s.129 agreement (or earlier equivalent), an evidential burden lies on him to raise the issue that there is such an agreement; it is then for the prosecution to establish to the criminal standard that the discharge fell outside the terms of that agreement: *United Utilities Water plc v Moss Rose Piggeries Ltd* [2006] EWHC 2169 (Admin).

[253] 1991 Act s.118(5). Compliance with consents in respect of industrial discharges is less satisfactory than for discharges from sewerage undertakers' sewage works; between 1990 and 1992, only about two-thirds of industrial discharges fully complied: see NRA, *Discharge Consents and Compliance: the NRA's Approach to Control of Discharges to Water* (HMSO, 1994), pp.52–53.

(i) "Deemed consent"

9–042 Trade effluent may not now be discharged without consent, even if the discharge is made pursuant to an agreement made prior to, and still subsisting, at the time of the passing of the Public Health (Drainage of Trade Premises) Act 1937. The exemptions formerly provided for by s.4 of the 1937 Act were all withdrawn as a result of repeals of s.4(4) by the Water Act 1973[254] and of s.4(1), (2) and (3) by s.43 of the Control of Pollution Act 1974. Agreements previously safeguarded by s.7(4) of the 1937 Act were not thereafter exempt from the need to obtain consent to a discharge. However, in cases formerly covered by such exemptions, the owner of premises concerned could obtain a "deemed consent" by serving a notice on the water authority under s.43(2) of the 1974 Act; but this deemed consent may then be cancelled and an actual consent may be substituted therefor.[255]

(ii) Discharge with express consent

9–043 Normally the consent of the sewerage undertaker must be obtained under the 1991 Act to the discharge of trade effluent from trade premises into public sewers (or public lateral drains).[256] The application must be by notice[257] served on the undertaker by the owner or occupier of the premises, stating the nature or composition of the trade effluent; the steps proposed to be taken, in relation to the discharge or by way of subjecting any substance likely to affect the description of matter discharged to treatment or any other processes, for minimising the polluting effects of the discharge on any controlled waters and the impact of the discharge on sewerage services; the maximum quantity it is proposed to discharge in any one day; and the highest rate at which it is proposed to discharge the trade effluent.[258]

The undertaker may either give consent unconditionally, or subject to such conditions as it may think fit with respect to any of the following matters:

---

254 Sch.8 para.44.

255 1991 Act s.140 and Sch.8, and see the Control of Pollution (Discharges into Sewers) Regulations 1976 (SI 1976/958), as modified by the Water Act 1989 Sch.8 paras 1, 5(1), (2). "Deemed consents" having effect under the Water Act 1989 in relation to any sewerage undertaker have effect as a "deemed consent" for the purposes of Ch.3 of Pt 4 of the 1991 Act: Sch.8 para.2(1). "Actual consents" under Sch.8 are treated similarly to express consents (see below).

256 See the 1991 Act s.106(1A), above, p.217.

257 In writing: s.219(1) (definition of "notice").

258 1991 Act s.119, as amended by the Water Act 2003 s.89(1), adding the requirements to specify steps for minimising pollution and the impact of discharges on sewerage services.

(a) the sewer or sewers (or any altered drain or sewer[259]) into which the effluent may be discharged, the nature and composition of the effluent, the steps to be taken for minimising the polluting effects of the discharge on any controlled waters and the impact of the discharge on sewerage services, the maximum quantity that may be discharged on any one day, and the highest permissible rate of discharge.[260]

Conditions may also be attached with respect to:

(b) the period or periods of the day during which the trade effluent may be discharged from the trade premises into the sewer;

(c) the exclusion from the trade effluent of all condensing water;

(d) the elimination or diminution of any specified constituent of the trade effluent, before it enters the sewer, where the sewerage undertaker is satisfied that the constituent would, either alone or in combination with any other matter with which it is likely to come into contact while passing through any sewers:

   (i) injure or obstruct those sewers, or make specially difficult or expensive the treatment or disposal of the sewage from those sewers, or
   (ii) (where the trade effluent is to be, or is, discharged into a sewer having an outfall into any harbour or tidal water or into a sewer which connects directly or indirectly with a sewer or sewage disposal works having such an outfall) cause or tend to cause injury or obstruction to the navigation on, or the use of, the said harbour or tidal water;

(e) the temperature of the trade effluent at the time when it is discharged into the sewer, and acidity or alkalinity at that time;

(f) the payment by the occupier of the trade premises to the sewerage undertaker of charges for the reception of the trade effluent into the sewer, and for the disposal thereof, regard being had to the nature and composition and to the volume and rate of discharge of the trade effluent so discharged, to any additional expense incurred or likely to be incurred by a sewerage undertaker in connection with the reception or

---

259 1991 Act s.113(6), subject to regulations.
260 1991 Act s.121(1), as amended by the Water Act 2003 s.89(2), adding the reference to steps for minimising the effect of pollution and the impact on sewerage services.

disposal of the trade effluent, and to any revenue likely to be derived by a sewerage authority from the trade effluent;

(g) the provision and maintenance of such an inspection chamber or manhole as will enable a person readily to take at any time samples of what is passing into the sewer from the trade premises;

(h) the provision, testing and maintenance of such meters as may be required to measure the volume and rate of discharge of any trade effluent being discharged from the trade premises into the sewer;

(i) the provision, testing and maintenance of apparatus for determining the nature and composition of any trade effluent being discharged from the premises into the sewer;

(j) the keeping of records of the volume, rate of discharge, nature and composition of any trade effluent being discharged, including the keeping of records of readings of meters and other recording apparatus provided in compliance with a consent condition;

(k) the making of returns and giving of other information to the sewerage undertaker concerning the volume, etc. of trade effluent discharged.[261]

9–044 These powers, it will be noted, are wide but conditions may not be imposed outside these provisions. However, nothing in the powers to impose conditions is to be construed as restricting the power of a sewerage undertaker to impose such conditions as are necessary to comply with its duty under reg.7(1) of the Urban Waste Water Treatment (England and Wales) Regulations 1994.[262]

As mentioned above, a discharge without consent or a contravention of a condition is an offence.[263] If a consent is granted on the basis of permitting the discharge of specifically named substances, the discharge of substances not named, other than in a background concentration, constitutes the offence.[264]

---

[261] 1991 Act s.121(2).
[262] SI 1994/2841 reg.7(2). See above, p.248.
[263] 1991 Act ss.118(5), 121(5).
[264] Ruling of Judge Crowther Q.C. in *R. v Rechem International Ltd* (Newport Crown Court, September 10, 1993), discussed in S. Tromans and M. Grant, *Encyclopedia of Environmental Law* (London: Sweet & Maxwell, 2010), para.D23-094/1.

An appeal against a refusal of consent lies to the WSRA, which has wide powers to refuse or grant consent subject to such conditions as it thinks fit.[265]

The sewerage undertaker may give a direction varying the conditions of a consent to the discharge of trade effluent into a public sewer (or public lateral drain).[266] This may not be done within two years of the date of the consent or a previous direction without the agreement of the owner and occupier of the trade premises in question[267]; however, a variation may be made within the time limit if the undertaker considers it necessary to do so to provide proper protection for persons likely to be affected by the relevant discharges.[268] In the latter event, compensation is payable unless the undertaker is of the opinion that there has been an unforeseeable change of circumstances since the two-year period in question and otherwise than in consequence of consent given after the beginning of that period.[269] The Secretary of State may make regulations as to the payment of compensation.[270] The owner or occupier may appeal against the direction to the WSRA,[271] which may annul the direction and substitute another which is more or less favourable to the appellant. An appeal also lies to the Director on the ground that compensation should be paid in consequence of the direction.[272] **9–045**

Nothing shall, however, restrict the power of a sewerage undertaker or the Secretary of State to vary a consent in pursuance of the duty under reg.7 of the Urban Waste Water Treatment (England and Wales) Regulations 1994,[273] or render it or him liable to pay compensation.[274]

Consents must be reviewed and if necessary modified at regular intervals.[275]

---

[265] 1991 Act s.122, as amended by the Water Act 2003 s.36(3). The WSRA may state a case for the High Court: s.137. See OFWAT Information Note No.21, *Trade Effluent Appeals* (May 1993, Revised September 2001).

[266] 1991 Act s.124(1), (7). As to public lateral drains, see the 1991 Act s.106(1A), above, p.217. Notice must be given of the direction which must include information as to rights of appeal and state the date the decision is to take effect: s.124(5), (6).

[267] 1991 Act s.124(2).

[268] 1991 Act s.125(1).

[269] 1991 Act s.125(2). "Circumstances" includes the information available as to the discharges to which the consent in question relates or as to the interaction of those discharges with other discharges or matter: s.125(4). The undertaker must give reasons for its opinion: s.125(3).

[270] 1991 Act s.125(5).

[271] 1991 Act s.126(1)–(4). The WSRA on an appeal under s.126(1) may state a case for the opinion of the High Court: s.137.

[272] 1991 Act s.126(5), (6).

[273] SI 1994/2841. See above, p.248.

[274] SI 1994/2841 reg.7(6).

[275] SI 1994/2841 reg.7(4).

(c) Special category effluent

9–046 Special arrangements apply to trade effluents in which there are prescribed substances or prescribed concentrations thereof which derive from a prescribed process or one involving the use of substances in quantity exceeding prescribed amounts ("special category effluent"[276]). These arrangements implement both the government's own policy of seeking to minimise inputs to water of certain of the most dangerous substances, identified in the "Red List" published in 1988,[277] and the framework EC Directive on Pollution Caused by Certain Dangerous Substances Discharged into the Aquatic Environment of the Community[278] and daughter directives. The relevant regulations are the Trade Effluents (Prescribed Processes and Substances) Regulations 1989[279] and 1992.[280]

Under these provisions it is the duty of a sewerage undertaker to refer an application for consent with respect to discharges of any special category effluent to the Environment Agency for determination of the issue of whether the proposed discharge should be prohibited or made subject to conditions.[281] Such a reference must be made within two months of the day after service of the notice[282] and the references must be in writing.[283] A copy of a reference made under the section must be served upon the applicant by the undertaker.[284] Similar references must be made by the WSRA where, upon an appeal under

---

276 Defined in s.138 of the 1991 Act, as amended by as amended by SI 2000/1973 Sch.10 Pt 1 para.8 and SI 2007/3538 Sch.21 Pt 1 para.20, and to be amended by the Pollution Prevention and Control Act 1999 Sch.3 and the Water Act 2003 s.88(3).

277 *Inputs of Dangerous Substances to Water: Proposals for a Unified System of Control—The Government's Consultative Proposals for Tighter Controls over the Most Dangerous Substances Entering the Aquatic Environment* (DoE, 1988).

278 Dir.76/464.

279 SI 1989/1156, as amended by SI 1990/1629, listing 24 prescribed substances (List I substances under the Directive) and five prescribed processes, mostly involving asbestos or chloroform. The provisions as to prescribed substances apply when they are present in trade effluent in a concentration greater than the "background concentration". This term means such concentration as would, but for anything done on the premises in question, be present in the effluent discharged from those premises, and this includes such concentrations as are present in water supplied to or abstracted for use in the premises, and in precipitation onto the site within which the premises are situated: SI 1989/1156 reg.2.

280 SI 1992/339, prescribing further processes.

281 1991 Act s.120(1), as amended by the Environment Act 1995 Sch.22 para.105. No reference need be made if the undertaker refuses consent within two months: s.120(3). The Agency has power to require information to be supplied for the purpose of the discharge of its functions in relation to special category effluent: 1991 Act s.135A, inserted by the 1995 Act Sch.22 para.113.

282 1991 Act s.120(2).

283 1991 Act s.120(5).

284 1991 Act s.120(6).

s.122 of the 1991 Act, relevant matters appear to it to arise.[285] In any such case the period of two months for the purposes of s.122(2) will not begin to run until the beginning of the day after notice of the Agency's determination upon the matter is served upon the sewerage undertaker.[286] Existing consents to the discharge of special category effluent into a sewerage undertaker's public sewer (or public lateral drain[287]) are also subject to review by the Agency.[288] The detailed mechanisms of review are set out in ss.132 and 133 of the 1991 Act.[289]

Non-compliance with the duties of a sewerage undertaker under s.120 is an offence.[290]

Trade effluent is not, however, "special category effluent" if it is **9–047** produced, or to be produced, in any process which is a prescribed process designated for central control under Pt 1 of the Environmental Protection Act 1990,[291] as from the "determination date" for that process.[292] These processes were regulated by the Environment Agency under the system of Integrated Pollution Control, and these provisions avoided duplication of the control regimes. A similar exclusion now applies in respect of trade effluent produced, or to be produced, by operating any installation or plant or otherwise carrying on any activity which requires a permit under the Environmental Permitting (England and Wales) Regulations 2010,[293] from the determination date for that installation, plant or activity.[294]

(d) Agreements under the 1991 Act

In addition to the provisions above discussed, the Act of 1991 enables **9–048** sewerage undertakers to enter into agreements with the owner or the

---

[285] 1991 Act s.123(2), (3).

[286] 1991 Act s.123(1), as amended by the 1995 Act Sch.22 para.106.

[287] See the 1991 Act s.106(1A), above, p.217.

[288] 1991 Act s.127, as amended by the Environment Act 1995 Sch.22 para.107.

[289] Compensation may be payable by the Agency in respect of determinations made for the protection of public health or of flora and fauna dependent on an aquatic environment: s.134, as amended by the 1995 Act Sch.22 para.112.

[290] 1991 Act s.120(9), inserted by the Environment Act 1995 Sch.22 para.105(4).

[291] 1991 Act s.138(2). See the Environmental Protection (Prescribed Processes and Substances) Regulations 1991 (SI 1991/472), as amended; above, p.184. Subss.(2)–(4) are to be repealed by the Pollution Prevention and Control Act 1999 s.6(2) Sch.3, from a day to be appointed.

[292] i.e. the date on which authorisation is granted or refused by the Environment Agency or, in the case of an appeal against refusal, the refusal is affirmed: 1991 Act s.138(3).

[293] SI 2010/675.

[294] 1991 Act s.138(1A), (1B), inserted by SI 2000/1973 reg.39 Sch.10 para.8, and amended by SI 2007/3538 Sch.21 Pt 1 para.20 and SI 2010/675 Sch.26 Pt 1 para.7.

occupier of trade premises for the reception and disposal of any trade effluent produced on those premises.[295] Such an agreement may authorise such a discharge as, apart from the agreement, would require a consent under Ch.3.[296] There is no express provision in the legislation for the termination of agreements, although this may be covered by the terms of the agreement.[297] It is submitted that such a power should be implied, given the possible risks to the environment that might arise from an agreement that cannot be terminated. As such termination would be likely to interfere with that party's property rights as protected by the ECHR First Protocol Art.1, it is likely that compensation would have to be paid. If the agreement is to relate to special category effluents, it must be referred to the Environment Agency; and existing agreements involving such effluents are subject to review.[298] Nothing in any agreement between an undertaker (or its predecessor) and an owner or occupier of trade premises is to be treated as a consent or authorisation unless the terms are such as will secure compliance with the requirements of Sch.4 to the Urban Waste Water Treatment (England and Wales) Regulations 1994.[299] Authorisations given by virtue of these agreements must be reviewed and if necessary modified at regular intervals.[300] An undertaker may vary any s.129 agreement which provides for the discharge of industrial waste water to an urban waste water treatment plant without first entering a public sewer, and any such agreement is not enforceable to the extent that it permits the discharge of industrial waste water where the requirements of Sch.4 are not met.[301]

---

[295] See s.129 of the 1991 Act (formerly s.7 of the Public Health (Drainage of Trade Premises) Act 1937). For a precedent for such an agreement, see (1961) 25 Conv. N.S. 38 and 662.

[296] See ss.118(5) and 129(3) of the 1991 Act. Such agreements "authorise" the discharge without technically constituting a "consent" under Ch.3: see Recommendation No.2 of the Law Commission's "Report on the Consolidation of Legislation Relating to Water" (Cm. 1483, April 1991).

[297] See *United Utilities Water plc v Moss Rose Piggeries Ltd* [2006] EWHC 2169 (Admin) (Divisional Court held that, assuming there was power to end an agreement on reasonable notice, the trial judge had been entitled to conclude that three months' notice to end an agreement in respect of a large pig farm was not reasonable).

[298] 1991 Act ss.130, 131, as amended by the Environment Act 1995 Sch.22 paras 108, 109. See ss.132, 133, as amended by the Environment Act 1995 paras 110, 111, as to the procedure for review.

[299] SI 1994/2841 reg.7(3). As to Sch.4, see above, p.248.

[300] SI 1994/2841 reg.7(4).

[301] SI 1994/2841 reg.7(5).

(e) Other matters

Provisions are included requiring the undertaker to maintain a trade effluent register of consents and directions under Ch.3, agreements under s.129 and notices served under s.132,[302] and enabling the undertaker to obtain certain information,[303] and to take samples of trade effluents.[304] The 1991 Act provides that "nothing in this Chapter shall affect any right with respect to water in a river stream or watercourse, or authorise any infringement of such a right . . . ."[305] **9–049**

302 1991 Act s.196.

303 1991 Act s.204. Restrictions on the disclosure of information obtained under s.204 (and other provisions of the 1991 Act) are imposed by s.206, as amended.

304 1991 Act s.121(3)–(6).

305 1991 Act s.141(4), referring to Ch.3.

Chapter 10

SANITARY CONVENIENCES

INTRODUCTORY

10–001 Statutory provisions regulating the installation, maintenance, etc. of sanitary conveniences are to be found in several Acts of Parliament, of which the most important is the Act of 1936, while certain specific classes of buildings are affected in this respect by other statutes. These provisions are enforceable by the local authority, not the sewerage undertaker. In the first place, it is important to appreciate the specialised meanings of particular words, as used by Parliament in both the 1936 Act and the 1984 Act. These definitions apply, to the most part, only for the purposes of Pt 2 of the 1936 Act whereas they apply generally to the 1984 Act.[1]

By s.90(1) of the 1936 Act and s.126 of the 1984 Act, the words listed below have the meanings respectively assigned to them:

> " 'cesspool' includes a settlement tank or other tank for the reception or disposal of foul matter from buildings;
>
> 'closet' includes privy;
>
> 'earth-closet' means a closet having a moveable receptacle[2] for the reception of faecal matter and its deodorisation by the use of earth, ashes or chemicals,[3] or by other methods;
>
> 'sanitary convenience' means closet or urinal;
>
> 'water-closet' means a closet which has a separate fixed receptacle connected to a drainage system and separate provision for flushing from a supply of clean water[4] either by the operation of mechanism or by automatic action."

The question sometimes arises in practice whether "closet" in these definitions is intended to refer only to the sanitary apparatus itself, or whether it includes the room, shed or outhouse in which the apparatus is housed. This is a question to be determined according to the

---

[1] The Building Act provisions derive from the 1936 Act.

[2] An earth-closet having a fixed receptacle will, therefore, be a mere privy for the purposes of the statute.

[3] The usual type of chemical closet is therefore an "earth-closet".

[4] A slop closet is thus not a "water-closet".

context in which the term is used; thus, in the phrase "sufficient closet accommodation",[5] a reference to the apparatus alone is presumably intended, but in the reference to closets which are "prejudicial to health or a nuisance",[6] it seems that the shed, etc. in which the apparatus is housed is to be included in the term "closet".[7]

In several places in the pages which follow, we shall have occasion to refer to a requirement of the Acts of 1936 and 1984 to the effect that a building must have a sewer "available". Section 125(2)(b) of the 1984 Act provides that there shall not be deemed to be a sewer available, *unless*: **10–002**

> "(i) there is within 100 feet of the site[8] of the building or proposed building, and at a level that makes it reasonably practicable to construct a drain or communicate with it, a public sewer or other sewer that the owner of the building or proposed building is, or will be, entitled to use, *and*
>
> (ii) the intervening land is land through which he is entitled to construct a drain."

Subsection (3) provides that:

> "The limit of 100 feet does not apply, for the purposes of subsection (2) above, if the local authority undertakes to bear so much of the expenses reasonably incurred in—
>
> (a) constructing, and maintaining and repairing, a drain to communicate with a sewer, or
>
> (b) laying, and maintaining and repairing, a pipe for the purpose of obtaining a supply of water,

as the case may be, as is attributable to the fact that the distance of the sewer, or of the point from which a supply of water can be laid on, exceeds 100 feet."

---

[5] See 1984 Act s.64(1)(a)(b).

[6] See 1984 Act s.64(1)(c) and 1936 Act s.45(1).

[7] It is submitted that the primary meaning of "closet", which is not displaced by any of the statutory definitions set out above, is that of a small room or retiring chamber, and that the word should be used or understood in the more specialised sense as referring to the sanitary apparatus only where the context clearly shows that such was the intention of the legislature.

[8] See Ch.9, above, pp.226–227.

SANITARY ACCOMMODATION FOR NEW BUILDINGS

10–003 The requirements applicable in respect of the provision of satisfactory sanitary accommodation in new buildings are now found in Part G of the Building Regulations 2000.[9] Requirement G1 is that:

"(1) Adequate and suitable sanitary conveniences must be provided in rooms provided to accommodate them or in bathrooms.

(2) Adequate hand washing facilities must be provided in

(a) rooms containing sanitary conveniences; or

(b) rooms or spaces adjacent to rooms containing sanitary conveniences.

(3) Any room obtaining a sanitary convenience, a bidet, or any facility for washing hands provided in accordance with paragraph (2)(b), must be separated from any kitchen or any area where food is prepared."

SANITARY ACCOMMODATION FOR EXISTING BUILDINGS

(a) Buildings other than special[10] buildings

(i) Section 64 of the 1984 Act

10–004 Under this section, if it appears to the local authority:

"(a) that a building[11] is without sufficient[12] closet accommodation; or

(b) that a part of a building, being a part that is occupied as a separate dwelling,[13] is without sufficient closet accommodation; or

(c) that any closets provided for or in connection with a building are in such a state as to be prejudicial to health[14] or a nuisance[15]

---

[9] SI 2000/2531 Pt G, as substituted by SI 2009/1219 Sch. Formerly, requirements as to closets were set out in the Building Act 1984 s.26, but this was repealed by the Building Regulations 1985 (SI 1985/1065) reg.18.

[10] See para.(b), below, as to the sense in which the term "special buildings" is here used, as referring to shops, factories, workshops and workplaces, etc.

[11] Other than a factory, workplace or shop: s.64(6).

[12] This term is not defined.

[13] It would seem that "separate" in this context means distinct as a dwelling, not necessarily separated physically or partitioned off; see further *Woodfall on Landlord and Tenant* (London: Sweet & Maxwell, looseleaf edition,), para.23.014.

[14] i.e. "injurious, or likely to cause injury, to health": 1936 Act s.343(1).

[15] As to the significance of this expression, see above, p.245.

and cannot without reconstruction be put into a satisfactory condition,"

the authority is under a duty to serve a notice[16] on the owner of the building requiring him to provide such closets, additional closets or substituted closets as may be necessary, the closets in any such case to be either earth-closets or water-closets. In the special case of a building consisting of several dwellings, the owner of the building may appeal to a court on the ground that he has a cause of action in respect of the occupation of part of the building as a separate dwelling and that the need for the works to be executed would not arise but for that occupation.[17]

The local authority cannot, under this section, require the abolition of a privy, unless it is either insufficient, prejudicial to health or a nuisance, etc., and a water-closet cannot be required to be provided (except in substitution for an existing water-closet), unless a sufficient water supply and sewer are available.[18] It also seems that the authority cannot require a particular type of water-closet (or earth-closet) to be provided, if that proposed falls within the statutory definition.[19]

It will also be noted that this section can only be used in respect of nuisances, where the closet in question cannot be rendered satisfactory without reconstruction; if the closet[20] is capable of repair, the powers of s.45 of the 1936 Act (discussed below) should be used. It may be important, therefore, in a particular case to decide whether a closet is or is not capable of repair. Unfortunately, there is no rule of thumb or standard to be applied in answering such a question. In the law of landlord and tenant, repair has been said to include the replacement of parts, but not the renewal of the whole. At the same time new work which is an exact replacement of the old is none the less capable of being "reconstruction", as distinct from repair.[21]

---

[16] The notice must be in writing, signed by the authorised officer of the authority, and duly served (see ss.92–94 of the 1984 Act and *Epping Forest DC v Essex Rendering* [1983] 1 W.L.R. 158 in which it was held by the House of Lords that the requirement of writing is mandatory). Shaw's Form PH67 is appropriate.

[17] 1984 Act s.64(4).

[18] See definition of this expression in s.125(2) of the 1984 Act.

[19] See *Robinson v Sunderland Corp* (1898) 78 L.T. 19.

[20] The term here probably includes the shed, etc. in which the sanitary apparatus is housed: see above, p.259.

[21] See, e.g. *Agar v Noakes* (1905) 93 L.T. 605, a case on the meaning of "reconstruction", as used in a local authority's building byelaws.

10–005 Section 64(1)(b) covers the case of houses occupied as two or more dwellings; in a case where a building is in "multiple occupation" it may be found necessary to use the powers of Part 2 of the Housing Act 2004 in order that existing conveniences, etc. may be required to be maintained in a proper condition.[22]

If the notice of the authority is not complied with, the authority may itself execute the work required, and recover its reasonable expenses[23] thereby incurred from the owner of the premises.[24]

(ii) Repair of defective closets

10–006 It is provided by s.45 of the 1936 Act that, if it appears to the local authority that any closets provided for or in connection with a building[25] are in such a state as to be prejudicial to health or a nuisance,[26] but they can without reconstruction[27] be put into a satisfactory condition, the authority must[28] serve a notice[29] on the owner or the occupier[30] of the building, requiring him to take such steps[31] or execute such works as may be necessary.

Insofar as the notice requires work to be executed, in any case of default in compliance therewith, the authority may itself execute the work required and recover its reasonable expenses[32] thereby incurred, from the person in default.[33] Insofar as the notice requires steps other than the execution of works to be undertaken, any person required to take such steps is liable to a fine in the event of non-compliance with the terms of the notice.[34]

---

[22] And see Management of Houses in Multiple Occupation (England) Regulations 2006 (SI 2006/372) and the Management of Houses in Multiple Occupation (Wales) Regulations 2006 (SI 2006/1713 (W.175)).

[23] A reasonable sum by way of establishment expenses may be included in this sum: Local Government Act 1974 s.36.

[24] 1984 Act ss.64(3), 99 and 107.

[25] Other than a shop, factory, workshop, or workplace: s.45(4).

[26] See above, p.245.

[27] See the discussion of this expression in para.(i), above.

[28] The authority is under a duty to take such action.

[29] The notice must be in writing, signed by the authorised officer of the authority, and duly served (see ss.283 to 285 of the 1936 Act and *Epping Forest DC v Essex Rendering* [1983] 1 W.L.R. 158 in which the House of Lords held the requirement of writing to be mandatory). Shaw's Form PN20 is appropriate.

[30] The authority must select the person responsible as between the owner and the occupier: see *Croydon Corp v Thomas* [1947] K.B. 386, decided under s.75 (dustbins).

[31] "By cleansing the closets or otherwise".

[32] See n.23 above.

[33] 1936 Act ss.45(2) and 290, and below, Ch.11, pp.272–275.

[34] 1936 Act s.45(3). In any such proceedings the defendant is entitled to question the reasonableness of the requirements of the local authority, or its decision to serve the notice on him and not the owner, or the occupier (as the case may be).

(b) Special buildings

(i) Houses

The extent to which a particular house may be defective in the matter of sanitary conveniences is a matter to be taken into consideration in the application of Part I of the Housing Act 2004, under which local authorities have enforcement power in respect of hazards[35] that exist on residential premises. **10–007**

(ii) Workplaces

By s.65 of the 1984 Act, every building used as a "workplace"[36] must be provided with sufficient and satisfactory accommodation in the way of sanitary conveniences,[37] and provision must also be made (where necessary) for persons of each sex.[38] In the event of the local authority being satisfied that this requirement is not being complied with in respect to a particular building, it must by notice[39] require the owner or the occupier of the building "to make such alterations in the existing conveniences, and to provide such additional conveniences, as may be necessary". **10–008**

If the notice of the authority is not complied with, the authority may itself execute the work required, and recover its reasonable expenses[40] thereby incurred from the person in default.[41]

---

[35] There is a hazard of a prescribed description for the purposes of the Act where a risk of harm is associated with the occurrence of any of a number of matters and circumstances listed in Sch.1 to the Housing Health and Safety Rating System (England) Regulations 2005 (SI 2005/3208), in or at the building or HMO (house in multiple occupation). Paragraph 17 concerns personal hygiene, sanitation and drainage and refers to: "An inadequate provision of (a) facilities for maintaining good personal hygiene; (b) sanitation and drainage." Paragraph 19 refers to: "Falls associated with toilets, baths, showers or other washing facilities." See also ODPM, "Housing Health and Safety Rating System Operating Guidance" (February 2006), esp. pp.116–122.

[36] This expression is defined in s.126 of the 1984 Act. It "does not include a factory but otherwise it includes any place in which persons are employed otherwise than in domestic service". It will be noticed that the present section applies only to such workplaces as are buildings (and not being shops: s.65(4)), and that the reference to factories and workshops in the original section was deleted by the Factories Act 1937, but see now s.175 of the Factories Act 1961. In *Bennet v Harding* [1900] 2 Q.B. 397, a stable yard for London cabbies was held to be a workplace within the meaning of the predecessor of the present section.

[37] This term includes urinals: see definition, above, p.258.

[38] Regard must be had to the number of persons employed in, or in attendance at, the building.

[39] The notice must be in writing, signed by the authorised officer of the authority and duly served (see ss.92–94 of the 1984 Act, and *Epping Forest DC v Essex Rendering* [1983] 1 W.L.R. 158 in which the House of Lords decided that the requirement as to writing is mandatory). Shaw's Form PH46 is appropriate.

[40] See n.23.

[41] See 1984 Act ss.65(3), 99 and 107, and below, Ch.11, pp.277–279.

Provision as to sanitary accommodation in workplaces[42] is also contained in the Workplace (Health, Safety and Welfare) Regulations 1992,[43] which implement the EC Workplace Directive[44] and aspects of the EC Temporary Workers Directive.[45] These regulations came fully into effect on January 1, 1996. However, as from January 1993, they applied to all new workplaces,[46] and on the completion of the modification, extension or conversion of an existing workplace.

10–009 The term "workplace" means:

> "any premises or part of premises which are not domestic premises and are made available to any person as a place of work, and includes
>
> (a) any place within the premises to which such person has access while at work; and
> (b) any room, lobby, corridor, staircase, road or other place used as a means of access to or egress from that place of work or where facilities are provided for use in connection with the place of work other than a public road."[47]

The regulations apply to every workplace except (inter alia) those in or on a ship, or where the only activity being undertaken is construction work[48] or those located below ground at a mine.[49] Every employer must ensure that every workplace, modification, extension or conversion which is under his control and where any of his employees works complies with the regulations.[50] Furthermore, every person who has, to any extent, control of a workplace, etc. in connection with the carrying on by him of a trade, business or other undertaking (whether for profit or not) must ensure that it complies with any requirement which relates to matters within his control.[51] Finally,

---

[42] Not just workplaces in buildings.
[43] SI 1992/3004. See Health and Safety Commission, *Workplace Health, Safety and Welfare. Approved Code of Practice and Guidance* (L.24), 2nd edn (1996).
[44] 89/654.
[45] 91/383.
[46] i.e. a "workplace used for the first time as a workplace after December 31st, 1992": SI 1992/3004 reg.2(1).
[47] SI 1992/3004 reg.2(1).
[48] Within the meaning of the Construction (Design and Management) Regulations 2007 (SI 2007/320), and in which the only activity being undertaken is construction work, save that specified regulations are applied. "Construction work" is defined in SI 1992/3004 reg.2(1).
[49] SI 1992/3004 reg.3, as amended by SI 1995/2036 Sch.3, and SI 2007/320 reg.5.
[50] SI 1992/3004 reg.4(1).
[51] SI 1992/3004 reg.4(2), (3). This is not to impose any requirement upon a self-employed person in respect of his or a partner's work: reg.4(4).

every person who is deemed to be the occupier of a factory by virtue of s.175(5) of the Factories Act 1961 must ensure that the premises comply with the regulations.[52]

The regulations cover a series of matters, including ventilation, temperature, lighting and cleanliness. Specific provision is made by reg.20 for sanitary conveniences.[53] Thus "suitable and sufficient" sanitary conveniences shall be "provided at readily accessible places". Without prejudice to the generality of this provision, conveniences are not suitable unless:

> "(a) the rooms containing them are adequately ventilated and lit;
> (b) they and the rooms containing them are kept in a clean and orderly condition; and
>
> (c) separate rooms containing conveniences are provided for men and women except where and so far as each convenience is in a separate room the door of which is capable of being secured from inside."

As regards a workplace which is not a new or modified, etc. work- **10–010**
place, there is sufficient compliance if it was subject to the provisions of the Factories Act 1961 and now complies with Pt II of Sch.1 to the Regulations. This provides that in workplaces where females work, there shall be at least one water closet for use by females only for every 25 females, and an analogous requirement for males.[54]

These regulations are enforceable under the Health and Safety at Work etc. Act 1974.[55] Contravention of the regulations is an offence.[56] Inspectors appointed by the enforcing authority have powers of entry and to serve improvement and prohibition notices.[57]

Similar requirements are imposed in respect of construction sites by the Construction (Design and Management) Regulations 2007.[58]

---

[52] SI 1992/3004 reg.4(5). s.175 sets out an extended definition of "factory"; in general, a "factory" means premises where persons are employed in manual labour.

[53] reg.20 does not apply to aircraft, locomotives, or rolling stock or vehicles, and only applies so far as is reasonably practicable to temporary work sites and to land forming part of an agricultural undertaking away from the undertaking's main buildings: reg.3(2)–(4).

[54] In calculating the numbers, any number not divisible by 25 without fraction or remainder shall be treated as the next number higher that is a multiple of 25.

[55] As "Health and safety regulations" under s.15 of the 1974 Act, they are "relevant statutory provisions" as defined in s.53(1) and so enforceable in accordance with s.18.

[56] 1974 Act s.33, as amended; and see further ss.34–42.

[57] 1974 Act ss.19–26.

[58] SI 2007/320 regs 4(1)(b), 13(7) and 22(1)(c), and Sch.2.

(iii) Food premises

10–011 Premises of the type discussed in this paragraph may also be workplaces, in which case they will be subject to the provisions discussed in the previous paragraph; otherwise, if they do not fall within the scope of the 1992 Regulations and they form part of a building, they will be subject to the normal provisions of s.64 of the 1984 Act and s.45 of the 1936 Act. Apart from these, there are also requirements imposed to safeguard food hygiene.

A provision specific to food premises is found in Regulation 852/2004 of the Parliament and the Council on the hygiene of foodstuffs, which provides[59] that an adequate number of flush lavatories are to be available and connected to an effective drainage system; that lavatories are not to open directly into rooms in which food is handled; and that sanitary conveniences are to have adequate natural or mechanical ventilation. In the case of movable and/or temporary premises, and premises used primarily as a private dwelling house but where foods are regularly prepared for placing on the market, where necessary, appropriate facilities are to be available to maintain adequate personal hygiene (including hygiene sanitary arrangements).[60] These requirements are enforceable by the Food Standards Agency or the food authority[61] in whose area the food business operator carries out his operations.[62]

(iv) Places of entertainment

10–012 Section 20 of the Local Government (Miscellaneous Provisions) Act 1976, replacing s.89 of the 1936 Act, enables a local authority[63] to require the owner or occupier of a "relevant place" to provide sanitary appliances[64] as may be specified by the authority, to maintain and

---

[59] Annex II Ch.1 (General requirements for food premises) paras 3 and 7.

[60] Annex II Ch.3 para.2(a).

[61] i.e. London borough and district councils, county councils which are unitary authorities, the Common Council of the City of London, and, from April 1, 1996, county and county borough councils in Wales: 1990 Act s.5, as amended.

[62] Food Hygiene (England) Regulations 2006 (SI 2006/14) reg.5(1); and Food Hygiene (Wales) Regulations (SI 2006/31 (W.5)) reg.5(1).

[63] Other than a county council in England and the GLC. "Local authority" is defined in s.44(1).

[64] This means water-closets, other closets, urinals and washbasins: s.20(9). A notice may specify the number and location of the appliances and whether they are to be provided for continuing or occasional use (an occasional notice); in respect of notices requiring continuing rather than occasional provision there is a right of appeal to the County Court under s.21 of the 1976 Act. Under subs.(10) a duty is imposed to bear in mind, so far as is practicable and reasonable, the needs of disabled persons; the notice must alert the owner or occupier to the relevant regulations and codes of practice; subss.(11)–(13) inserted by the Disabled Persons Act 1981 s.4. See Shaw's Form ML34.

clean them to the reasonable satisfaction of the authority, and to make them available for public use, free of charge (if so required). A "relevant place" for this purpose means a betting office, or any place (including a building) normally used for public entertainment, exhibitions, or sporting events, or for the sale of food or drink to members of the public, or any place occasionally used for any of those purposes. It is an offence to fail to comply with the specifications contained in a notice served by the authority under this section unless there is a reasonable excuse for the non-compliance. It is a defence to prove that the alleged offence is in respect of an unreasonable requirement in an occasional notice, or that it would have been fairer to serve such a notice on some other person whose name and address was supplied by the defendant.

(v) Licensing Act 2003

The Licensing Act 2003 transferred responsibility for liquor licensing **10–013** from the justices to local authorities and replaced previous arrangements for the licensing of public entertainments and late-night refreshment houses. It applies to "licensable activities", which include the sale by retail of alcohol, the supply of alcohol to a club member and the provision of regulated entertainment[65] or late-night refreshment.[66] There is a wide power[67] to include conditions, consistent with the operating schedule submitted by the applicant.[68] There is no reason why conditions should not be imposed in relation to the provision of sanitary conveniences, and in practice local authorities have attached such conditions.

THE REPLACEMENT OF EXISTING CLOSETS

Under s.66 of the 1984 Act, provided the building has a sufficient water **10–014** supply and sewer available,[69] the local authority may[70] by notice[71]

---

[65] As defined in Sch.1. It includes the provision of entertainment for members of the public, including a play, film, indoor sporting event, live or recorded music, or dance. There are a number of specified exemptions.

[66] 2003 Act s.1(1), (3)–(7).

[67] 2003 Act s.18.

[68] Under 2003 Act s.17. This includes a statement of the relevant licensable activities.

[69] See definition in s.125 of the 1984 Act, p.259.

[70] The power is optional, not a mandatory duty similar to those imposed by s.44 of the 1936 Act and s.64 of the 1984 Act. The authority should not issue a notice automatically because of a blanket policy but exercise its discretion in each case: see *Wood v Widnes Corp* [1898] 1 Q.B. 463.

[71] The notice must be in writing, signed by the authorised officer of the authority, and duly served (see ss.99–102 of the 1984 Act). Shaw's Form PH11A is appropriate. The form of notice must state the effect of subs.(3): see s.66(2).

require the owner of a building to substitute a water-closet[72] for a closet[73] of any other type. Alternatively, the notice may require the owner to permit the local authority to execute the works of replacement.

This power may be exercised even where the closets are not insufficient in number or prejudicial to health or a nuisance.[74] If the owner executes the work himself he is entitled to recover from the local authority one-half of any expenses he reasonably incurs. Similarly, where the authority itself executes the work, it may recover from the owner an amount not exceeding one-half of its reasonable expenses incurred in doing the work.[75]

Insofar as the expenses of the authority are recoverable, they will be recoverable as a civil debt, and will be a charge on the property[76] but, on any appeal under s.102 of the 1984 Act, the necessity of the works cannot be called into question.[77]

SUPPLEMENTARY PROVISIONS

10–015 Sections 48 to 52 (inclusive) of the Act of 1936 contain a variety of supplementary provisions designed to promote the main controls over the conditions of sanitary equipment already discussed in this chapter.

(a) Overflowing and leaking cesspools[78]

10–016 If the contents of any cesspool[79] soak away or overflow, the local authority may require[80] the person responsible[81] to execute such works

---

[72] In any such case action should be taken under s.45 of the 1936 Act, above.
[73] ". . . provided for, or in connection with, the building"; and see definition in s.126, above, p.258.
[74] above, p.245.
[75] See s.66(3). Similarly, where the owner of a building, on his own initiative and without receiving any notice from the local authority, proposes to provide a water-closet for the building in substitution for a closet of some other type, the authority may (if it thinks fit) agree to bear half his expenses incurred in such replacement (see s.66(4)). In this case there need not be a water supply and sewer "available".
[76] s.66(5) and s.107, and see below, Ch.11, pp.277–279.
[77] s.66(5)(a).
[78] 1936 Act s.50, as amended by the Water Act 1973 Sch.8 para.40, and the Water Act 1989 Sch.8 para.2(8), Sch.27 Pt I.
[79] See definition in s.90(1), above, p.258.
[80] By notice: this must be in writing, signed by the authorised officer of the authority, and duly served (see ss.283–285 of the 1936 Act). Shaw's Form PN23 is appropriate.
[81] ". . . the person by whose act, default or sufferance the soakage or overflow occurred or continued . . ."

or take such steps[82] as may be necessary for preventing the soakage or overflow.[83]

Insofar as the notice requires work to be executed, in any case of default, the authority may execute the work, and recover its reasonable expenses[84] from the person in default.[85] However, in so far as the notice requires other steps to be taken, any person who defaults is liable to a fine.[86]

(b) Offences

The following matters are offences under this part of the 1936 Act: **10–017**

(i) The occupation, or the permitting of occupation, of a room, in contravention of s.49(1), after seven days' notice[87] from the local authority prohibiting such occupation.
This section provides that a "room which or any part of which, is immediately over a closet,[88] other than a water-closet or earth-closet, or immediately over a cesspool, midden or ashpit,[89] shall not be occupied as a living room, sleeping room or workroom."

(ii) Failing to cause the flushing apparatus of a water-closet[90] to be kept supplied with water sufficient for flushing or, where necessary, to be properly protected against frost or, in the case of an earth-closet,[91] failing to cause it to be kept supplied with dry earth or other suitable deodorising material.[92]

The only person who may be charged with an offence under this provision is the occupier of the building[93] in, or in connection with, which the closet in question is provided.

---

[82] By periodically emptying the cesspool or otherwise.
[83] The subsection does not, however, apply to the effluent from a properly constructed tank for the reception and treatment of sewage, if the effluent is of such a character, and is so carried away and disposed of, as not to be prejudicial to health or a nuisance.
[84] A reasonable sum by way of establishment expenses may be added to this figure: see Local Government Act 1974 s.36.
[85] See ss.50(2) and 290, and below, Ch.11, pp.277–279.
[86] See s.50(3), as amended by the Criminal Justice Act 1982 s.46.
[87] This notice must be in writing, signed by the authorised officer of the authority, and duly served (see ss.283–285 of the 1936 Act).
[88] See definition in s.90(1), above, p.258.
[89] These expressions are not defined in the Act.
[90] See definition in s.90(1), above, p.258.
[91] See definition in s.90(1), above, p.258.
[92] s.51, as amended by the Criminal Justice Act 1982 s.46.
[93] The section applies to all types of buildings: shops, factories, etc. not being excluded.

Sometimes the facts of a particular case may fall within both this section and s.45, but it is suggested that in such a case the machinery of this section should be used.

(iii) Where a sanitary convenience is used in common by the members of two or more families,[94] there may be an offence[95] if:

(a) "any person injures or improperly fouls the convenience, or anything used in connection therewith, or wilfully or by negligence causes an obstruction in the drain[96] therefrom"[97]; *or*

(b) "the convenience, or the approach thereto, is, for want of proper cleansing or attention, in such a condition as to be insanitary"; in any such case such of the persons having the use thereof in common as are in default or, in the absence of satisfactory proof as to which of them is in default, each of them, will be liable.[98]

It seems that action can be taken against any person who acts contrary to the terms of paragraph (a) even if he or she is not a member of the two or more families using the convenience.

(c) Power to examine drains, etc.

10–018 Section 48 of the 1936 Act[99] gives the local authority power to examine the condition of a sanitary convenience, drain, private sewer or cesspool.[100] For this purpose the authority may apply a test[101] and, if it deems it necessary, open the ground. However, this power does not extend to a drain or private sewer connecting with a public

---

[94] This term is not defined in the Act, but for the purposes of the Rent Acts has been widely construed as a popular rather than a technical term; it does not mean the same as household; nor is it restricted to cases of a *familial nexus* in a strict legal sense though it requires a de facto *familial nexus* recognisable as such by the ordinary man (see, e.g. *Price v Gould* (1930) 143 L.T. 333, *Brock v Wollams* [1949] 2 All E.R. 715, and *Carega Properties S.A. v Sharrat* [1979] 1 W.L.R. 928).

[95] 1936 Act s.52, as amended by the Criminal Justice Act 1982 s.46.

[96] Obstruction of a sewer is not, apparently, within this offence.

[97] The fine in respect of such an offence may not exceed level 1 on the standard scale (1936 Act s.52, as amended by the Criminal Justice Act 1982).

[98] Again the fine may not exceed level 1 on the standard scale, but there is a further fine not exceeding 25p for each day on which the offence continues after conviction: 1936 Act s.52, as amended by the Criminal Justice Act 1982.

[99] As amended by the Water Consolidation (Consequential Provisions) Act 1991 Sch.1 para.2(1), Sch.3 Pt I.

[100] See definition in s.90(1), above, p.258.

[101] Other than a test by water under pressure.

sewer.[102] A local authority may delegate this function (as in the case of other functions) to one of its officers.[103]

The power may be exercised only in the following circumstances[104]:

(i) the sanitary convenience, drain, private sewer or cesspool is in such a condition as to be prejudicial to health or a nuisance; *or*

(ii) a drain or private sewer communicating indirectly with a public sewer is so defective as to admit subsoil water.

The power will be enforceable by use of the right of entry given by s.287 of the Act.[105] However, once on the land the authority must be careful to act within the powers of the section or within the terms of any agreement with the landowner or other interested person.

If the convenience or drain, etc. is found on examination to be in a proper condition, the authority must, as soon as possible, reinstate any ground which has been opened and make good any damage done by it[106]; there is no provision made in the section enabling it to recover its expenses in so doing. Even if the convenience or drain, etc. is found not to be in a proper condition, the expenses incurred in the examination, etc. cannot be recovered.

A power in similar terms is conferred on sewerage undertakers in respect of drains and private sewers connecting with public sewers (or public lateral drains[107]), by s.114 of the Water Industry Act 1991.

---

[102] 1991 Act Sch.1 para.2(1).
[103] s.101 of the Local Government Act 1972.
[104] And where the authority, or possibly a local authority officer acting under delegated powers, considers there are reasonable grounds for believing these circumstances exist.
[105] See Ch.11, below, pp.275–276.
[106] 1936 Act s.48(2).
[107] See the 1991 Act s.106(1A), above, p.217.

Chapter 11

PROCEDURES

INTRODUCTORY

11–001 Whilst it is not the object of this book to provide a commentary on all the many statutory provisions relevant to sewerage services, or to take the place, so far as public health legislation is concerned, of the standard works on the procedure in Magistrates' Courts,[1] it is considered desirable that a brief summary should be included of those procedural provisions which are common to the preceding chapters, and to which reference has been made in the footnotes and the text.

In general, separate procedural regimes apply to (a) local authorities, exercising powers under the Public Health Acts 1936 and 1961 and the Building Act 1984; and (b) sewerage undertakers exercising powers under the Water Industry Act 1991. However, some provisions of the 1936 Act are expressly applied under the 1991 Act.

STATUTORY NOTICES

(a) Under the Public Health Act 1936[2] and the Building Act 1984[3]

11–002 Where the local authority is required to give a notice to a person under the 1936 or 1984 Acts, this must be in writing,[4] and it must be signed by an officer of the authority who has been duly authorised (either generally or specifically) by the authority.[5] A local authority may arrange for any of its functions to be discharged by a

---

[1] Such, for example, as *Stone's Justices' Manual*, to which reference should be made in any case of difficulty.

[2] The relevant provisions of the 1936 Act also apply for the purposes of the 1961 Act.

[3] The rules as to the form of, and persons to be served with, abatement notices under the statutory nuisance provisions of Pt 3 of the Environmental Protection Act 1990 are found within those sections: see above, pp.243–247. As to the methods of service, see the 1990 Act s.160.

[4] See s.283(1) of the 1936 Act and s.92 of the 1984 Act. "Writing" includes other modes of representing or reproducing words in a visible form: Interpretation Act 1978 s.5 Sch.1.

[5] See the 1936 Act s.284(1), and definition in s.343(1) and the 1984 Act s.93. A printed signature is sufficient (s.284(2) and s.93(3)), and so is a rubber stamp, provided it is affixed by an authorised officer: *Goodman v J. Eban Ltd* [1954] 1 Q.B. 550, and *Plymouth City Corp v Hurrell* [1968] 1 Q.B. 455.

committee, a sub-committee, one of its officers, or by another local authority.[6]

(i) Person to be served

It is the duty of the authority to select the appropriate person on whom the notice is to be served. If the wrong person is served, he will be entitled to appeal as a "person aggrieved",[7] and the court may quash the notice.[8] Information as to the ownership, etc. of property may be obtained by serving a requisition for information,[9] and it is made an offence for any person on whom such a requisition may be served[10] either to fail to give such information, or knowingly to make a misstatement in respect thereof.[11] **11–003**

(ii) Methods of service

The methods of service of notices are prescribed by s.285 of the 1936 Act and the similarly although not identically worded s.94 of the 1984 Act,[12] and one or other of the methods there stated must be followed strictly (unless actual service can be proved to have been effected by some other means); however, subject to compliance with the terms of the relevant section,[13] it seems that the authority is not bound to adopt any particular one of these possible methods of service in any specific instance.[14] The methods prescribed in these sections apply equally to a summons, as they do to other "documents" served under the relevant Act.[15] **11–004**

---

[6] Local Government Act 1972 s.101, but this does not authorise delegation to a *single* member of the authority.

[7] See s.290(3)(e), (f) of the 1936 Act and s.102(e), (f) of the 1984 Act.

[8] *Croydon Corp v Thomas* [1947] K.B. 386. As to the meaning of "owner", see the 1936 Act s.343(1) and the 1984 Act s.126(1), and below, pp.285–287.

[9] Shaw's Form ML33 or ML33A is useful for this purpose.

[10] Only the occupier of premises, or any person who either directly or indirectly receives rent in respect of the premises, may be asked to supply the required information, and the only information obtainable by this method is "the nature of his [the informant's] interest therein [the premises] and the name and address of any other person known to him as having an interest therein, whether as freeholder, mortgagee, lessee or otherwise".

[11] See Local Government (Miscellaneous Provisions) Act 1976 s.16(2).

[12] As to the references in s.94 of the 1984 Act to service by post, see s.7 of the Interpretation Act 1978. Specified documents under the 1984 Act may be served electronically: 1984 Act s.94A, inserted by the Building (Electronic Communications) Order 2008 (SI 2008/2334).

[13] For example, if the notice is to be affixed "to some conspicuous part of the premises", there must be no person there to whom it can be delivered.

[14] See *Woodford UDC v Henwood* (1899) 64 J.P. 148.

[15] See, e.g. *R. v Braithwaite* [1918] 2 K.B. 319.

(iii) Form of notice

11–005 Apart from the requirement that the notice must be in writing and duly signed,[16] the notice need not follow any particular form, as the Secretary of State has not used his power to prescribe the forms to be used for these purposes.[17] Nevertheless, the notice should follow as nearly as practicable the wording of the appropriate section, and the notice may be quashed by the court if it is satisfied that there has been some "informality, defect or error in, or in connection with, the notice",[18] unless it is also satisfied that such error, etc. was not a material one.[19] It is also important, where the notice is one requiring the execution of works, that the time within which the works are required to be completed, should be reasonable,[20] and the nature of the works required should be clearly stated.[21] Where there is a right to appeal against the notice this must be stated on the notice.[22]

(b) Under the Water Industry Act 1991

11–006 By s.219(1) of the Water Industry Act 1991, the term "notice" in the Act means "notice in writing". The Secretary of State may prescribe the forms of any notice or other documents to be used for the purposes of the "relevant sewerage provisions".[23] Sewerage undertakers are not given powers requiring the execution of works and so there are no general provisions corresponding to s.290 of the Public Health Act 1936.[24] There is also no express provision governing the authentication of documents corresponding to s.284 of the 1936 Act. Service of documents under the 1991 Act is governed by s.216, which, in accordance with a recommendation of the Law Commission,[25] applies to all the provisions in the water legislation consolidation.

Any document required or authorised by the 1991 Act to be served on any person may be served:

---

[16] See above, p.272.
[17] See s.283(2) of the 1936 Act; s.93(2) of the 1984 Act.
[18] s.290(3)(b) of the 1936 Act; s.102(1), (5) of the 1984 Act.
[19] s.290(4) of the 1936 Act; s.102(2) of the 1984 Act.
[20] s.290(3)(d).
[21] s.290(2) of the 1936 Act; s.99(1) of the 1984 Act. *Perry v Garner* [1953] 1 Q.B. 335.
[22] s.66(2) of the 1984 Act requires the purport of that section also to be set out. On the general principle, see s.300(3), and *Rayner v Stepney Corp* [1911] 2 Ch. 312, also *Nalder v Ilford Corp* [1951] 1 K.B. 822.
[23] 1991 Act s.214. This power has not been exercised.
[24] above, pp.272–274.
[25] "Report on the Consolidation of the Legislation relating to Water", Cm. 1483, 1991, Recommendation No.14.

"(a) by delivering it to him or by leaving it at his proper address or by sending it by post to him at that address; or

(b) if the person is a body corporate, by serving it in accordance with paragraph (a) above on the secretary or clerk of that body; or

(c) if the person is a partnership, by serving it in accordance with paragraph (a) above on a partner or a person having the control of management of the partnership business."

For the purposes of this section, and s.7 of the Interpretation Act 1978 (which relates to the service of documents by post) in its application to this section, the proper address of any person on whom a document is to be served is his last known address. However, in the case of (b) and (c) above, it is, respectively, the address of the registered or principal office of the body corporate or the principal office of the partnership.[26] A person may specify another address as the proper address. Where any document is to be served on the owner, or a lessee or on the occupier of any premises, then if that person's name and address cannot be ascertained after reasonable enquiry or, in the case of service on the occupier, if the premises appear to be or are unoccupied, the document may be served either by leaving it in the hands of a person who is or appears to be resident or employed on the land, or by leaving it conspicuously affixed to some building or object on the land.

POWERS OF ENTRY

(a) Under the Public Health Act 1936 and the Building Act 1984

A local authority may authorise in writing any of its officers[27] to exercise the power of entry on premises given by s.287 of the 1936 Act and ss.95 and 96 of the 1984 Act. 24 hours' notice[28]—at least—must be given of the intention to exercise this power, and it may be exercised only at reasonable hours. The power is exercisable only for the purposes listed in the section,[29] and the officer exercising the power must, **11–007**

[26] The principal office in the UK of a company registered or a partnership carrying on business outside the UK.

[27] See definition of "authorised officer" in s.343(1), which in an amended form is found in s.126 of the 1984 Act. See also s.127 of the 1984 Act.

[28] Except in the case of a factory or workplace: s.287(1), proviso. The notice must be in writing, signed and duly served: Shaw's Forms PH70A (for the 1936 Act) or PH70 (for the 1984 Act) are appropriate.

[29] See s.287(1) of the 1936 Act; s.95(1) of the 1984 Act; see, in particular, the power to enter "for the purpose of the performance by the council of their functions under this Act", or any byelaws made under the 1936 Act.

if required, produce a duly authenticated document showing his authority.

If the authorised officer is obstructed in endeavouring to exercise this power of entry, he may not use force, but must (if necessary) apply for a warrant to a justice of the peace and, if this warrant is issued, force, but only the minimum necessary, may then be used.[30]

11–008 (b) By sewerage undertakers

A sewerage undertaker may under the Water Industry Act 1991 authorise a person in writing to enter premises for a number of purposes:

(a) to carry out any survey or tests to determine whether it is appropriate and practicable for the undertaker to exercise any "relevant works power",[31] or how any such power should be exercised, or to exercise any such power[32];

(b) to ascertain whether there is or has been, on or in connection with the premises, any contravention of the "relevant sewerage provisions"[33] which it is the undertaker's function to enforce; or to ascertain whether circumstances exist which would authorise or require the undertaker to take any action or carry out any works under the relevant sewerage provisions; or to take action or carry out works authorised by or under the relevant sewerage provisions to be taken or carried out by the undertaker; or "generally for the purpose of carrying out the undertaker's functions under the relevant sewerage provisions"[34];

(c) to carry out surveys, tests, works or inspections in relation to metering, where the conditions in s.162(1)[35] are satisfied.[36]

---

[30] See s.287(2); he must be able to show that the statutory procedure has been strictly observed: *Stroud v Bradbury* [1952] 2 All E.R. 76. It is an offence wilfully to obstruct an officer in the exercising of his powers: 1936 Act s.288; 1984 Act s.112.

[31] i.e. any powers conferred by ss.158 (power to lay pipes in streets), 159 (power to lay pipes in other land), 161 (power to deal with foul water and pollution), 163 (water undertaker's power to fit stopcocks) and 165 (discharge for works purposes by water undertakers).

[32] 1991 Act s.168.

[33] i.e. (a) Chs 2 and 3 of Pt 4 (except ss.98 to 101 and 110 and so much of Ch.3 as provides for regulations under s.138 or has effect by virtue of any such regulations); (b) ss.160, 171, 172(4), 178, 184, 189, 196 and 204 and Sch.12 para.4; and (c) the other provisions of the Act so far as they have effect for the purposes of (a) and (b): s.219(1).

[34] 1991 Act s.171(1). There is an associated power to take samples of trade effluent: s.171(3), to be extended to any other liquid or substance by an amendment effected by the Water Act 2003 s.88(5), and amended by the 2003 Act s.96(6).

[35] above, p.138.

[36] 1991 Act s.172.

The impersonation of persons entitled to entry is an offence.[37] The detailed provisions regulating the rights of entry under (b) above are set out in Sch.6, Pt I; those regulating rights of entry under (a) and (c) are found in Sch.6, Pt II. Generally speaking, under Pt I, 24 hours' notice of intended entry to any premises which are not business premises must be given to the occupier; a warrant to enter, if need be by force, may be obtained from a JP in defined circumstances (e.g. if entry is refused or if the case is one of urgency); obstruction of persons exercising a right of entry is an offence. Under Pt II, no entry can be made except in an emergency, or at a reasonable time and after the required notice[38] of intended entry has been given to the occupier; and there are similar provisions governing warrants and offences of obstruction.

THE ENFORCEMENT OF STATUTORY NOTICES

In most cases, notices served under the Public Health Act 1936 and **11–009** the Building Act 1984 are enforceable by the authority, which is empowered to act itself in default of compliance with the terms of the notice by the person on whom the notice is served; in a few cases,[39] the notice is enforceable only by means of proceedings taken against the person in default.[40]

(a) Recovery of expenses

Where the local authority is authorised by either of the Acts of 1936[41] **11–010** or 1984 to execute works in default of compliance with the terms of a statutory notice, it is provided[42] that the authority may recover the expenses from the party in default.[43] These expenses must, however, have been reasonably incurred, and the work executed must not exceed that specified in the statutory notice. The expenses actually incurred may, however, be increased by a reasonable sum by way of establishment expenses.[44]

---

37 1991 Act s.173.
38 Seven days' notice, in respect of sewerage undertakers.
39 e.g. ss.49, 51 and 52 of the 1936 Act.
40 See below, pp.279–280.
41 Or the Public Health Act 1961.
42 This applies to notices served under ss.45 and 50 of the 1936 Act and ss.59, 60, 64 and 65 of the 1984 Act (and other provisions with which this book is not concerned).
43 See 1936 Act s.290(6); 1984 Act s.99(2)(a). The liability of a mere agent or trustee is limited to the total amount of money he has in his hands on behalf of his principal: s.294 of the 1936 Act; s.110 of the 1984 Act.
44 Local Government Act 1974 s.36.

The expenses are recoverable by serving a demand,[45] and interest on the sum demanded (at such reasonable rate as the authority may determine) will run as from the date of the demand.[46] The authority may also declare any sum so due to them to be repayable by instalments (with interest), over a period not exceeding 30 years.[47]

Any sum which a local authority is entitled to recover under either Act may be recovered as a simple contract debt in any court of competent jurisdiction.[48] The ordinary six years' time limit for actions in contract applies,[49] the period running from the date of demand. There is no time limit within which the demand must be served, and it seems that there is no reason why a fresh demand should not be served at any time; certainly this is so where there has been a change of owner.[50]

11–011 In cases where the person responsible for the payment of the authority's expenses is the owner of the premises, those expenses become a charge on the property,[51] and the authority has all the powers and remedies given by s.121 of the Law of Property Act 1925 (including a power of sale) for the enforcement of such charge.[52] The charge should be registered in the local land charges register[53] but, if the same is not so registered, or if a charge is not disclosed on an official certificate of the result of search, the charge will still be enforceable against a purchaser of the land affected. Any person who can prove he has suffered loss in consequence will be able to claim compensation from the registration authority.[54] In any case the local authority could always

---

[45] This must be in writing, signed by the authorised officer of the authority, and duly served, in accordance with ss.283–285 of the 1936 Act; ss.92–94 of the 1984 Act.
[46] 1936 Act s.291(1), (3); 1984 Act s.107(1), (3).
[47] 1936 Act s.291(2); 1984 Act s.108.
[48] 1936 Act s.293; 1984 Act s.107(4). This means "as though it were a simple contract debt" and it does not matter whether the debt would otherwise be so characterised: per Lord Evershed M.R. in *Great Yarmouth Corp v Gibson* [1956] 1 Q.B. 573, 577. The County Court has jurisdiction to determine the reasonableness of the expenses incurred: *Agodzo v Bristol City Council* [1999] 1 W.L.R. 1971; here, the expenses had been made a charge on the property, the property had been repossessed and the expenses paid to the council by the mortgagees, and A was now seeking a declaration that the expenses were unreasonable in anticipation of proceedings against him by the mortgagees.
[49] Limitation Act 1980 s.5.
[50] *Dennerley v Prestwich UDC* [1930] 1 K.B. 334.
[51] 1936 Act s.291(1); 1984 Act s.107(1).
[52] 1936 Act s.291(4); 1984 Act s.107(2). The charge must be enforced within 12 years (Limitation Act 1980 s.20) of the date when the works were completed (see *Hornsey Local Board v Monarch Investment Building Society* (1889) 24 Q.B.D. 1).
[53] Maintained under the Local Land Charges Act 1975 (as amended). This charge should be registered in Pt II of the register (see the Local Land Charges Rules 1977 (SI 1977/985), as amended).
[54] Local Land Charges Act 1975 s.10.

demand payment of the expenses from the "owner for the time being" of the premises.[55]

The remedies of taking proceedings (a) to enforce the charge and (b) to recover the expenses as a contract debt are concurrent.[56]

(b) Prosecutions

In addition to specific offences created in the various sections of any of the relevant Acts, the failure to comply with a statutory notice to which s.290 of the Public Health Act 1936 or s.99 and 102 of the Building Act 1984 applies, is itself made an offence,[57] and in addition to its right to execute works in default, the authority may prosecute for an offence under the section. **11–012**

All offences under these statutes may be prosecuted summarily,[58] but proceedings may be commenced only by the local authority concerned, or by a "party aggrieved"[59]; any other person who wishes to commence proceedings may do so only with the written consent of the Attorney-General.[60] Where a local authority is taking proceedings, it must be shown that the officer (or possibly, the member) who lays the information in its name has been authorised so to do either generally or specially.[61]

The maximum fine under s.290(6) of the 1936 Act and s.99(2) of the Building Act 1984 is at level 4 on the standard scale 4 (currently £2,500) with a further fine not exceeding £2 for each day on which the default continues after conviction. Where provision is made for the imposition of a daily penalty in respect of a continuing offence, the court may fix a reasonable period for compliance, after which the daily penalty is to come into effect.[62]

Prosecutions under the Water Industry Act 1991 in respect of sewerage offences[63] may not, without the written consent of the Attorney-General, be taken by any person other than a "party aggrieved",[64] a sewerage undertaker, or a body whose function it is to **11–013**

---

[55] See, e.g. s.291(2).

[56] *Sunderland Corp v Priestman* [1927] 2 Ch. 107.

[57] By s.290(6) of the 1936 Act and s.99 of the 1984 Act.

[58] 1936 Act s.296; 1984 Act ss.35, 61(3), 62(4)(5), 63(1), 68(2), 96(3), 112.

[59] 1936 Act s.298; 1984 Act s.113. For an illustration of the use of the term "party aggrieved" in this context, see e.g. *Sheffield Corp v Kitson* [1929] 2 K.B. 322.

[60] As to the proof of any such consent having been given, see s.26 of the Prosecution of Offences Act 1985.

[61] *Bob Keats Ltd v Farrant* [1951] 1 All E.R. 899.

[62] 1936 Act s.297; 1984 Act s.114.

[63] i.e. offences under the "relevant sewerage provisions": see above, p.276.

[64] See above n.59.

enforce the provisions in question.[65] Where a body corporate is guilty of an offence under the Water Industry Act 1991 or the Water Resources Act 1991, and the offence is proved to have been committed with the consent or connivance of, or to be attributable to any neglect on the part of, any director, manager, secretary or other similar officer of the body corporate or any person who was purporting to act in such a capacity, then he, as well as the body corporate, can be prosecuted for the offence.[66] Where the affairs of a body corporate are managed by its members, this applies in relation to the acts and defaults of a member in connection with his functions of management as if he were a director.[67] In the case of prosecutions under the "water pollution provisions"[68] of the Water Resources Act 1991, where the commission of an offence by any person is due to the act or default of some other person, the latter person may be prosecuted whether or not proceedings are taken against the former.[69]

APPEALS AND APPLICATIONS TO THE COURT

11–014 Various sections of the 1936 Act provide for a person aggrieved to appeal to the local Magistrates' Court against a notice or other requirement under the Act. In a number of cases where the 1936 Act empowers a local authority to serve a notice requiring action to be taken, it is also provided that the provisions of Pt 12 of the Act shall apply thereto,[70] and in that event a right of appeal is given by s.290, and a number of grounds of appeal are therein specified.[71] In some cases further special grounds of appeal are provided for in the particular section itself.[72] Also, in a number of cases,[73] the Act may provide for a particular matter or question to be determined, in case of dispute, by a Magistrates' Court. In any such case, the proceedings are

---

[65] Water Industry Act 1991 s.211.

[66] Water Industry Act 1991 s.210(1); Water Resources Act 1991 s.217(1).

[67] Water Industry Act 1991 ss.210(2), 217(2).

[68] i.e. the Water Resources Act 1991 Pt 3 (ss.82–104); ss.161–161D, 190, 202 and 203; Sch.25, para.4 and s.211 so far as it relates to byelaws made under para.4 and the Environment Act 1995 s.53(1), (2): s.221(1), as amended by the 1995 Act s.120(1), (3), Sch.22 para.177, Sch.24.

[69] s.217(3).

[70] For example, ss.45 and 50 of the 1936 Act.

[71] See also s.102 of the 1984 Act, in similar terms, which applies to notices served under the Act. The sewerage undertaker is entitled to be heard as an interested party on an appeal under s.102 against a s.59 notice (see pp.240–242) that raises the defence that the sewer in question is in fact a public sewer: *R. v Preston Magistrates' Court, ex p. North West Water Ltd* [2000] E.H.L.R. 390.

[72] For example, ss.64(4) and 66(5) of the 1984 Act.

[73] For example, s.62(2) of the 1984 Act.

commenced by means of a complaint for an order, and the provisions of the Magistrates' Courts Act 1980 will apply to such proceedings.[74] Once an appeal has been lodged against a notice, the local authority cannot withdraw the notice without the consent of the person(s) on whom it was served.[75]

In any case of an appeal, proceedings must be commenced within 21 days of the notice or determination, etc. appealed against,[76] but this time limit does not apply to an application to the court for it to determine a matter[77]; in the latter event the time limit of six months provided for in s.127 of the Magistrates' Courts Act 1980 will be applicable.[78]

Unless the case is one which the parties might have referred to arbitration as an alternative to a reference to the court,[79] there is a right of appeal to the Crown Court from the decision of the Magistrates' Court.[80] However, this right is given only to a "person aggrieved". A local authority may be a "person aggrieved" where a decision adverse to it is given in an area where it is required to perform public duties; it is not necessary that a legal burden has been placed on the authority by the adverse decision of the Magistrates' Court.[81] Alternatively, either party may ask the magistrates to state a case for the opinion of the High Court on a point of law[82] and, in the event of their refusing to do so, they may be ordered to state a case by a mandatory order. The Crown Court also may be asked to state a case but, in a non-criminal matter, a mandatory order will not lie against it in the event of refusal.[83]

Where proceedings are taken in the County Court (e.g. for recovery **11–015**
of the authority's expenses as a simple contract debt), an appeal lies to the High Court or the Court of Appeal.[84]

In any proceedings, a copy of a resolution of the local authority concerned or of the appointment of, or of an authority given to, any

---

[74] s.103(1)(b).

[75] *R. v Cannock Justices, ex p. Astbury* (1972) 70 L.G.R. 609.

[76] See, e.g. ss.45 and 50 of the 1936 Act incorporating s.290(3), and s.300(2) of that Act and e.g. s.103(2) of the 1984 Act. This is a fixed period which cannot be extended: *Stockton-on-Tees BC v Latif* [2009] EWHC 228 (Admin), [2009] L.L.R. 374.

[77] For example, 1984 Act s.103(2).

[78] *Nalder v Ilford Corp* [1951] 1 K.B. 822.

[79] See, e.g. s.21(6) of the 1984 Act; where the matter is determined by arbitration, the Arbitration Act 1996 will apply to the proceedings: see ss.94–98.

[80] s.301 of the 1936 Act, as amended by the Courts Act 1971 Sch.9 Pt I, and s.86 of the 1984 Act.

[81] *Cook v Southend BC* [1990] 2 Q.B. 1.

[82] Magistrates' Courts Act 1980 s.111.

[83] *R. v Somerset JJ., ex p. Ernest J. Cole & Partners Ltd* [1950] 1 K.B. 519.

[84] County Courts Act 1984 s.77, as amended; Access to Justice Act 1999 (Destination of Appeals) Order 2000 (SI 2000/1071), as amended.

officer of the authority, which is certified by the proper officer of the authority, is admissible in evidence.[85]

Powers to appear in legal proceedings (either as plaintiffs or defendants) are given to a local authority by the Local Government Act 1972, which also enable it to authorise one of its officers (or even one of its members) to conduct the proceedings on its behalf, even though he may not be of counsel or a solicitor.[86]

CLAIMS FOR COMPENSATION

11–016 Under s.278 of the 1936 Act, a local authority must pay "full compensation" to any person who has sustained damage by reason of the exercise by the authority of any of its powers under the 1936 Act or those provisions of the Act of 1961 incorporated therewith. This liability to pay compensation does not, however, apply in the following circumstances:

(a) Where the claimant himself has been in default.[87]

(b) In respect of action which the authority is under a duty to undertake, as distinct from a power. This is, however, to be construed strictly, and compensation is payable, for example, in respect of damage caused in the exercise of a power which is itself ancillary to a duty.

(c) No claim will lie unless the action in question would have given rise to liability had it not been for the statute.[88] Furthermore, if the power is exercised negligently then this will give rise to an action for damages and not a claim for compensation. Thus, where a sewer was laid through the claimant's land in a negligent manner, thereby causing special damage, it was held that he had an action against the authority responsible, and that his remedy did not lie under the statute.[89]

---

[85] Local Government (Miscellaneous Provisions) Act 1976 s.41.

[86] Local Government Act 1972 ss.222 and 223.

[87] s.278(1): see *Hobbs v Winchester Corp* [1910] 2 K.B. 471; *Place v Rawtenstall Corp* (1916) 86 L.J.K.B. 90.

[88] See, e.g. *Hall v Bristol Corp* (1867) L.R. 2 C.P. 322; *Lingké v Christchurch Corp* [1912] 3 K.B. 595, per Vaughan Williams L.J. at p.604 (obstruction of access caused by street works in laying a drain).

[89] *Brine v G.W. Rlwy Co* (1862) 2 B. & S. 402; *Clothier v Webster* (1862) 6 L.T. 461.

A claim under the section cannot be made in respect of damage to land other than that subject to the exercise of the statutory power.[90]

Any dispute as to the amount of compensation payable under this section is to be determined by arbitration,[91] unless the claim does not exceed £50, in which event the matter may, on the application of either party, be referred to the local Magistrates' Court.[92] Similar provision is made under the Building Act 1984,[93] and in respect of damage caused by a sewerage undertaker in the exercise of powers under the relevant sewerage provisions.[94] Rights to compensation may also arise under certain provisions of the Water Industry Act 1991.[95]

ARBITRATIONS

As a general rule, arbitrations, whether under the 1936 or the 1984 Act, will be conducted before a single arbitrator appointed by agreement between the parties or, in default of agreement, by the Secretary of State.[96] By contrast, claims in respect of the depreciation of a value of an interest in land as a result of the exercise of powers to carry out pipe-laying works, or other loss or damage, fall to be determined by the Lands Tribunal because the amount of the compensation for depreciation is to be determined in accordance with the principles contained in the Land Compensation Act 1961.

APPLICATIONS TO THE SECRETARY OF STATE: LOCAL AUTHORITIES

Under s.322(2) of the 1936 Act,[97] if the Secretary of State is satisfied that a local authority has failed to discharge its functions under the

---

[90] *Horton v Colwyn Bay and Colwyn DC* [1908] 1 K.B. 327 (no claim for depreciation to claimant's land caused by pumping station and sewage reservoir on other land, notwithstanding that it formed part of a system that included sewers that passed over the claimant's land).

[91] As prescribed by s.303, below.

[92] s.278(2).

[93] s.106.

[94] Water Industry Act 1991 Sch.12 para.4, as amended by the Competition and Service (Utilities) Act 1992 Sch.2 paras 30, 31. As to the "relevant sewerage provisions", see above, p.276.

[95] See pp.93–95, 98–100, 123, above.

[96] 1936 Act, s.303; 1984 Act, s.111; any such arbitration will be subject to the Arbitration Act 1996 (Pt 1, with adaptations and exclusions specified in ss.95–98).

[97] As amended by the Local Government (Miscellaneous Provisions) Act 1976, ss.27(3)(5)(7), 81(1), Sch. 2 and by the Public Health (Control of Disease) Act 1984, s.78 and Sch. 3. There is no longer express provision for any person to complain to the Minister about the default or for him to hold a local inquiry before exercising his default powers.

Act in any case where it ought to have done so,[98] the Secretary of State may make an order declaring the authority to be in default, and directing it to discharge its functions.[99] If, within the specified time limit, the authority fails to comply with the Secretary of State's order, he may enforce the order by way of a mandatory order or otherwise, or he may instead make an order transferring the functions to himself.[100]

ENFORCEMENT AND SPECIAL ADMINISTRATION ORDERS UNDER THE 1991 ACT

These are considered in Ch.1.[101]

OTHER PROCEEDINGS

In addition to proceedings provided for under relevant statutes, a private individual may have other forms of redress against a local authority or sewerage undertaker arising out of the exercise by them of their statutory functions. These may be summarised as follows:

(a) Action for damages. This has already been discussed; the main point is that a sewerage undertaker in the exercise of sewerage functions must not create a nuisance.[102]

(b) Action by the Attorney-General at the relation of a private individual for a declaration and/or an injunction. This may be brought where the authority or undertaker is acting ultra vires; the remedy sought is discretionary. Where the claim is based on public nuisance, a private individual may be able to sue for an injunction without joining the Attorney-General as a party, in circumstances where it can be shown that the plaintiff has sustained special damage.[103]

---

[98] See e.g. s.45 of the 1936 Act, above, p.262.

[99] The same default powers apply to local authorities in respect of their functions under the Building Act 1984; 1984 Act, s.116: see Ch.9.

[100] 1936 Act, s.322(3); 1984 Act, s.116(2). Under the similarly worded predecessor to s.322 (s.299 of the 1875 Act) it was more usual to resort to *mandamus* than to the alternative of appointing a person to perform the duty: see *R. v Staines Local Board* (1893) 69 L.T. 714; and see *R. v Worcester Corporation* (1905) 69 J.P. 296.

[101] See pp.20–24.

[102] 1991 Act s.117(6). See pp.71–82, 113–114, 155–156, 206–210, above.

[103] See, e.g. *Cook v Bath Corp* (1868) L.R. 6 Eq. 177 (a highway case). Claims based on public nuisance (unlike private nuisance) may include damages for personal injuries: *Corby Group Litigation, Re* [2008] EWCA Civ 463, [2009] 4 All E.R. 44.

(c) Proceedings on a claim for judicial review[104] seeking a quashing order, a prohibiting order, an injunction or a declaration, where it can be shown the authority or undertaker has erred in law or has acted unfairly to the prejudice of the applicant, or a mandatory order to require it to perform a duty. Cases where these will lie in the present context are exceptional, but they may arise.

RECOVERY OF CHARGES UNDER THE 1991 ACT

Section 142 of the Water Industry Act 1991 confers power upon sewerage undertakers to demand and recover charges fixed pursuant to the Act for the performance of their functions. It is expressly stated by s.142(1)(a) that this power extends to the performance of trade effluent functions. **11–017**

THE MEANING OF "OWNER"

In many cases under the relevant statutory provisions, action falls to be taken by the local authority or sewerage undertaker against the "owner" of the premises concerned. It is, therefore, of importance to appreciate the meaning of this expression as used in the Acts of 1936, 1984 and 1991. **11–018**

By s.343(1) of the 1936 Act, "owner" is defined as meaning "the person for the time being receiving the rackrent of the premises in connection with which the word is used, whether on his own account or as agent or trustee[105] for any other person, or who would so receive the same if those premises were let at a rackrent". The corresponding similar provisions of the 1984 and 1991 Acts are, respectively, ss.126 and 219(1). "Rackrent" is defined in the s.343 to mean, in relation to any property, "a rent which is not less than two-thirds of the rent at which the property might reasonably be expected to let from year to year, free from all usual tenant's rates and taxes . . . and deducting therefrom the probable average annual cost of the repairs, insurance and other expenses (if any) necessary to maintain the same in a state to command such rent."[106]

---

[104] Under Pt 54 of the Civil Procedure Rules.

[105] The right to recover expenses incurred by an authority against such an "owner" is strictly limited: see n.43 on p.277.

[106] This is to be computed with reference to conditions at the commencement of the lease: *Borthwick-Norton v Collier* [1950] 2 K.B. 594. "Rackrent" is not defined in s.219(1) of the 1991 Act: see further Recommendation No.18 of the Law Commission's "Report on the Consolidation of the Legislation relating to Water" (Cm. 1483, 1991).

These definitions have been the subject of much case law, which it is not the province of this book to discuss[107]; but the commonest case causing difficulty is where the property is occupied by a tenant who holds from an intermediate lessor. As a general rule (says Lumley[108]) where there are intermediate lessors, and the rent received by each is the same, the person ultimately receiving the rent is the owner, but where a lessor receives from his lessee more rent than he pays, he is the owner within the definition.

11–019 A rent collector or a trustee acting on behalf of the owner in the true sense may be an "owner" within the definition, but the amount that may be recoverable from such an "owner" is limited to what he actually receives,[109] and a mere receiver who can do no more than pay money into the owner's bank account on his behalf, is not an owner within the definition.[110]

In those cases where the section empowers a notice to be served on the owner *or* the occupier[111] of named premises, the authority should exercise care in choosing the most appropriate person in the circumstances, in the light of the information available to it; if the person so chosen considers it would have been equitable for the other party to have been served, this may give him grounds for an appeal to the Magistrates' Court under s.290(3)(f) of the 1936 Act.

INFORMATION

11–020 The Secretary of State has general powers to require the provision of information relating to any matter connected with the carrying out by a company of its functions as a water or sewerage undertaker or which is material to the carrying out by the Secretary of State of any of his functions under the Water Industry Act 1991 and related legislation.[112] Where it appears to the Secretary of State or the Director General of Water Services that an undertaker may be contravening or have contravened any condition of its appointment or any statutory or other requirement enforceable under s.18 of the 1991 Act, he may, for

---

[107] See, e.g. *Lumley's Public Health*, 12th edn (London: Butterworth & Co, 1951), Vol.3, p.2875.
[108] Vol.3, p.2875, and cases there cited, especially *Cook v Montagu* (1872) L.R. 7 Q.B. 418, and *Walford v Hackney Board of Works* (1894) 43 W.R. 110.
[109] Section 294 of the 1936 Act. See also s.110 of the 1984 Act, and ss.107(5), 109(3) and 160(2) of the 1991 Act, applying (inter alia) s.294 of the 1936 Act.
[110] *Bottomley v Harrison* [1952] 1 All E.R. 369.
[111] As, for example, in certain cases under s.290(3)(f) of the 1936 Act; s.102(1)(f) of the 1984 Act.
[112] Water Industry Act 1991 s.202, as amended by the Water Act 2003 Sch.8 para.44.

any purpose connected with such of his powers under ss.18 to 26 of Ch.2 of Pt 2 as are exercisable in relation to that matter, serve a notice requiring the production of specified documents or information. Non-compliance with the notice without reasonable excuse, and intentionally altering, suppressing or destroying any document required to be produced, are offences.[113]

The owner or occupier of any land on or under which is situated any sewer, drain, pipe, channel or outlet used or intended to be used for discharging any trade effluent into a sewer of a sewerage undertaker must, when requested to do so by the undertaker, produce such plans as he possesses or is able without expense to obtain, allow copies of such plans to be made and furnish all such information as he can reasonably be expected to supply with respect to the sewer, etc. Non-compliance is an offence.[114] Where different services are supplied to the same premises by different undertakers, they must disclose meter readings to each other provided reasonable expenses are covered, the duty being enforceable under section 18 by the Secretary of State. Any dispute is to be referred to arbitration.[115] There are restrictions on the disclosure of business information obtained under the Act.[116] The provision of false information is an offence.[117] There are similar powers in respect of information required for the purposes of the Water Resources Act 1991.[118]

---

[113] Water Industry Act 1991 s.203, as amended by the 2003 Act Sch.8 para.45.

[114] Water Industry Act 1991 s.204.

[115] Water Industry Act 1991 s.205, as amended by the 2003 Act Sch.8 para.46.

[116] Water Industry Act 1991 s.206, as amended by the Competition Act 1998 Sch.10 para.13(9); the Pollution Prevention and Control Act 1999 Sch.2 para.7; SI 2001/3649 art.328; the Enterprise Act 2002 Sch.25 para.25(10); the Water Act 2003 s.36(2) Sch.7 para.27 and Sch.8 para.47; SI 2008/960 Sch.3; the Flood and Water Management Act 2010 Sch.2 para.50.

[117] Water Industry Act 1991 s.207, as amended by SI 2002/794 Sch.2.

[118] ss.197–206; s.201 as substituted by the Water Act 2003 s.70; s.203 as amended by the Water Act 2003 Sch.8 para.53 and SI 2007/3538 Sch.21 Pt 1 para.21; and s.204 as amended by Sch.7 para.28.

APPENDIX A

DIAGRAMS

1. The distinction between a sewer and a drain

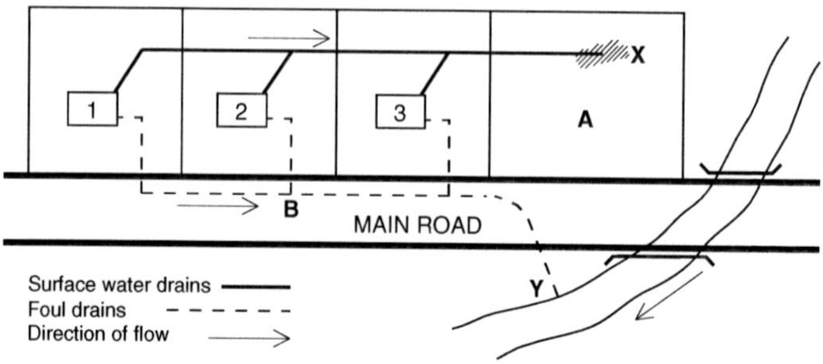

2. Public sewers: the effect of public ownership

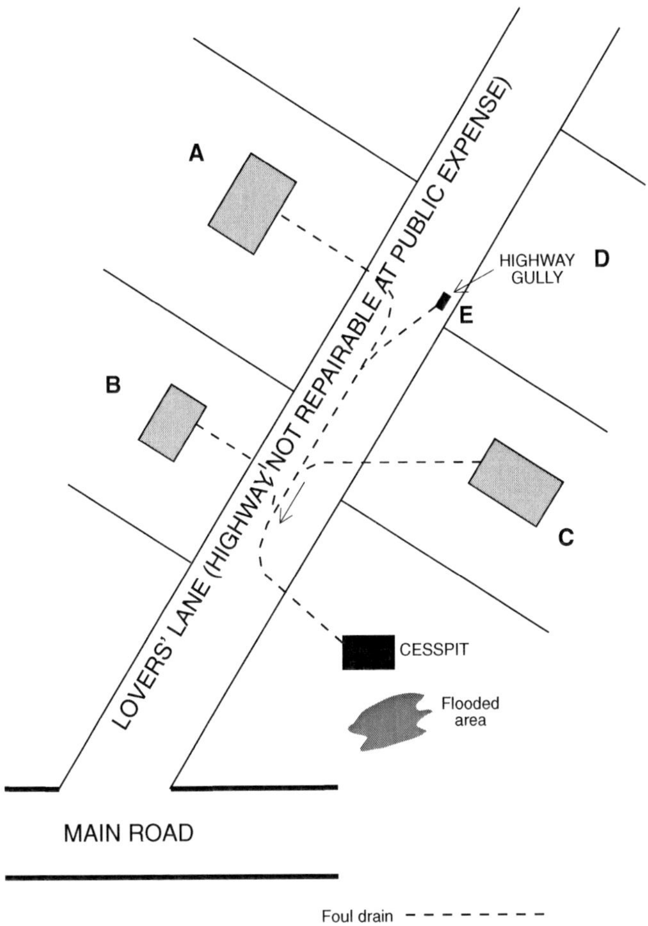

3. Adoption of sewers

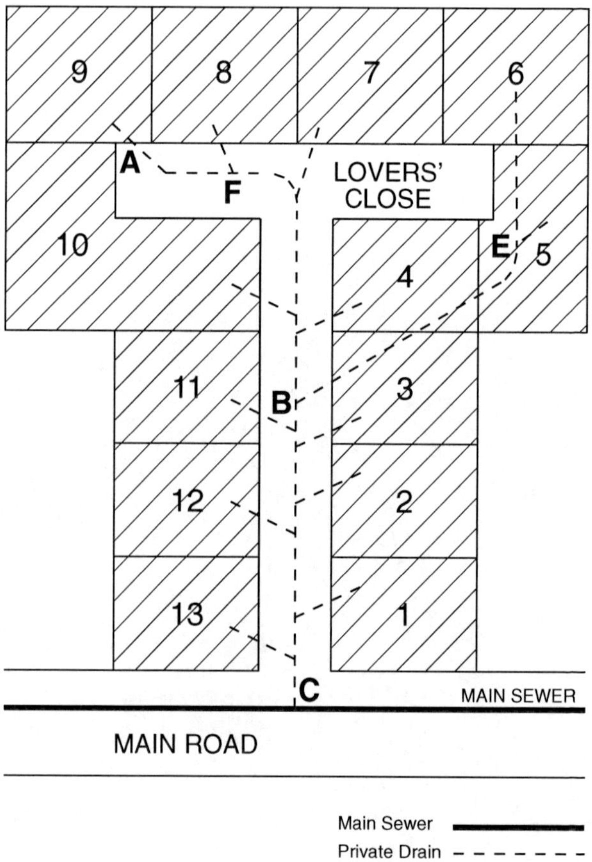

APPENDIX B

TYPICAL SEWER LAYOUTS

The following diagrams are taken from DEFRA, Welsh Assembly Government *Review of Existing Private Sewers and Drains in England and Wales. Consulation Paper* (July 2003), Annex C

1. Foul/storm/combined sewers

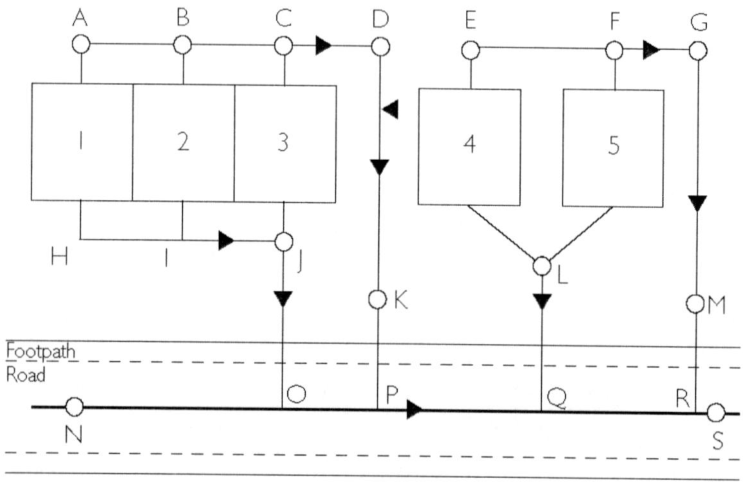

PIPELINE	STATUS	TYPICAL MAINTENANCE RESPONSIBILITIES	
		BUILT BEFORE 1937	BUILT AFTER 1937
AB and HI	Drain	House 1	House 1
BC and IJ	Sewer	Sewerage Undertaker	Houses 1 and 2
CDKP and JO	Sewer	Sewerage Undertaker	Houses 1, 2 and 3
EF	Drain	House 4	House 4
FGMR and LQ	Sewer	Sewerage Undertaker	Houses 4 and 5
NS	Sewer	Sewerage Undertaker	Sewerage Undertaker

2. Illustration of laterals

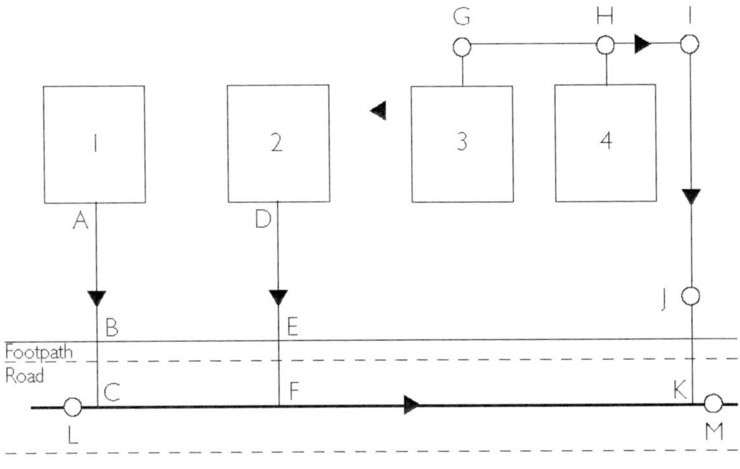

PIPELINE	STATUS	TYPICAL MAINTENANCE RESPONSIBILITIES	
		BUILT BEFORE 1937	BUILT AFTER 1937
ABC	Drain	House 1	House 1
DEF	Drain	House 2	House 2
BC	Lateral* (Drain)	House 1	House 1
EF	Lateral (Drain)	House 2	House 2
GH	Drain	House 3	House 3
HIJK	Sewer	Sewerage Undertaker	Houses 3 and 4
JK	Lateral (Sewer)	Sewerage Undertaker	Houses 3 and 4
LM	Sewer	Sewerage Undertaker	Sewerage Undertaker

**A lateral is the part of a drain or private sewer which is within public land (including roads) in order to connect into a public sewer.*

3. Septic tanks/treatment works

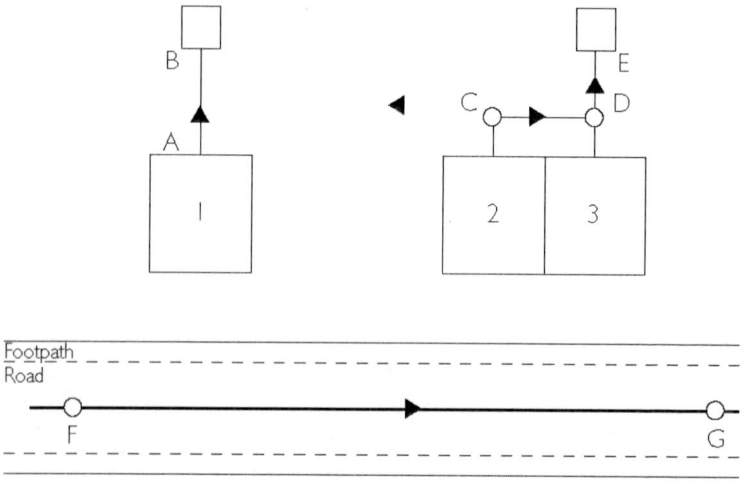

PIPELINE	STATUS	TYPICAL MAINTENANCE RESPONSIBILITIES	
		BUILT BEFORE 1937	BUILT AFTER 1937
AB	Drain	House 1	House 1
CD	Drain	House 2	House 2
DE	Sewer	Sewerage Undertaker	Houses 2 and 3
FG	Sewer	Sewerage Undertaker	Sewerage Undertaker

4. Cesspools

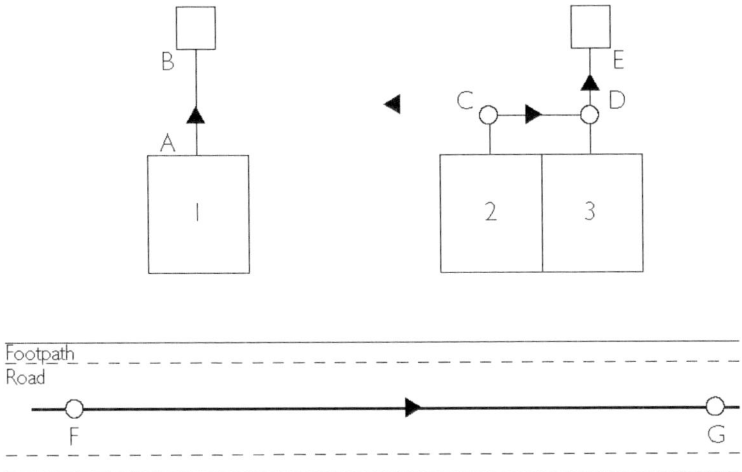

PIPELINE	STATUS	TYPICAL MAINTENANCE RESPONSIBILITIES	
		BUILT BEFORE 1937	BUILT AFTER 1937
AB	Drain	House 1	House 1
CD	Drain	House 2	House 2
DE	Drain	Houses 2 and 3	Houses 2 and 3
FG	Sewer	Sewerage Undertaker	Sewerage Undertaker

APPENDIX C

FUTURE ARRANGEMENTS OF NEW PROPERTIES

The following diagrams are taken from DEFRA, *Impact Assessment of Transfer of Private Sewers and Lateral Drains to Statutory Water and Sewerage Companies* (November 2008), Annex E

1. Example of existing arrangements

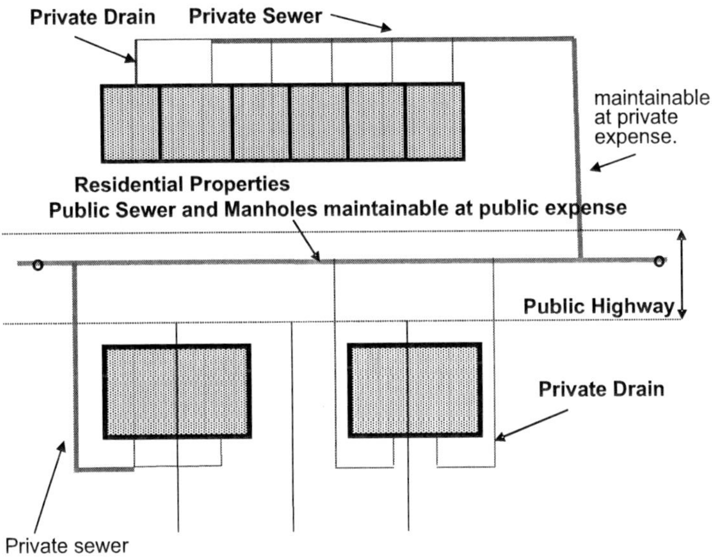

2. Example of future arrangements for new properties

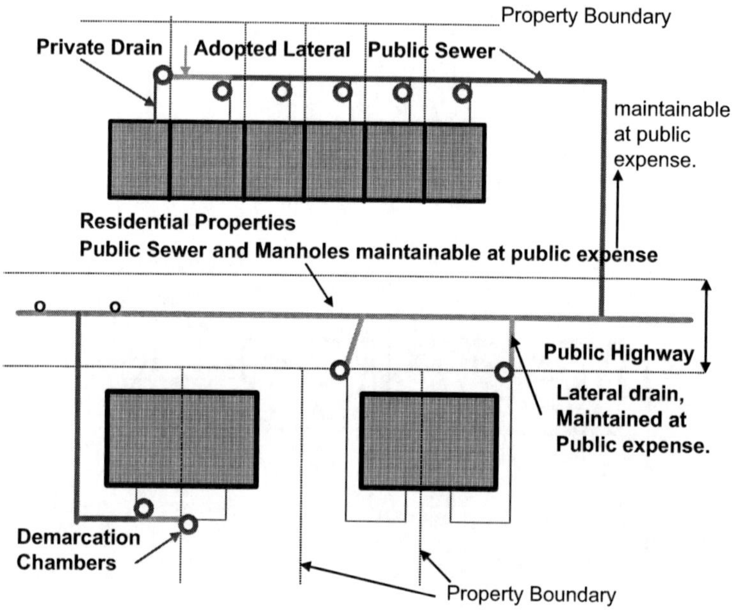

INDEX